THE

MOUNTAIN STATES

OF AMERICA

THE MOUNTAIN STATES

Author's Travels

A

NN.
Duluth
Lake Superior
Sault Ste. Marie
WIS.
polis St. Paul
MINN.
ux ls
ux ty
IOWA Madison
Chicago
Des Moines
ILL.
Springfield
coln MO.
Kansas City
a
St. Louis E. St. Louis
Cairo
sa
ARK.
Memphis
Little Rock
llas
LA.
Houston
New Orleans

L. Michigan MICH.
Lansing
Milwaukee
Gary
IND.
Indianapolis

L. Huron
Detroit
L. Erie
Cleveland
OHIO
Columbus
Cincinnati
KY.
Louisville Frankfort
W. VA.
Charleston

Nashville
Chattanooga
Huntsville
MISS. ALA.
Birmingham
Jackson Selma Montgomery

TENN. Knoxville

MAINE
Burlington VT. Montpelier Augusta
N.Y. Concord Portland
N.H.
Rochester Albany Boston
Buffalo MASS.
L. Ontario S. N.H. R.I.
H. P. CONN.
PA. Scranton N. New York
Pittsburgh T. N.J.
Harrisburg Philadelphia Atlantic City
W. Dover
MD. B. DEL.
Washington

VA.
Richmond Norfolk
A.- Annapolis
B.- Baltimore
W.- Wilmington
T.- Trenton
N.- Newark
NH.- New Haven
H.- Hartford
S.- Springfield
P.- Providence

N.C.
Charlotte Raleigh

S.C.
Columbia

Atlanta
GA. Charleston
Savannah Atlantic

Tallahassee FLA. Ocean
Gulf of Jacksonville
Mexico Cape Kennedy
Tampa
Miami

KAUAI
NIIHAU OAHU
Honolulu MOLOKAI
MAUI

Pacific HAWAII
Ocean HAWAII
Hilo

N

MILES
0 50 100 200

THE

MOUNTAIN

STATES

OF AMERICA

People, Politics, and Power

in the Eight Rocky Mountain States

NEAL R. PEIRCE

W · W · NORTON & COMPANY · INC ·
NEW YORK

FIRST EDITION

Library of Congress Cataloging in Publication Data

Peirce, Neal R
   The Mountain States of America.

   Bibliography: p.
   1. Rocky Mountain region.   I. Title.
F721.P45   1972   917.8'03'3   72–437
ISBN 0–393–05255–9

1 2 3 4 5 6 7 8 9 0

For my father
John Trevor Peirce

CONTENTS

FOREWORD

THIS IS A BOOK ABOUT THE Mountain West, part of a series covering the story of each major geographic region and all of the 50 states of America in our time. The objective is simply to let Americans (and foreigners too) know something of the profound diversity of peoples and life styles and geographic habitat and political behavior that make this the most fascinating nation on earth.

Only one project like this has been attempted before, and it inspired these books: John Gunther's *Inside U. S. A.*, researched during World War II and published in 1947. Gunther was the first man in U. S. history to visit each of the states and then to give a good and true account of the American condition as he found it. But his book is a quarter of a century old; it was written before the fantastic economic and population growth of the postwar era, growth that has transformed the face of this land and altered the life of its people and lifted us to heights of glory and depths of national despair beyond our wildest past dreams. Before he died, I consulted John Gunther about a new book. He recognized the need for such a work, and he gave me, as he put it, his "good luck signal."

But what was to be a single book became several, simply because I found America today too vast, too complex to fit into a single volume. A first book, *The Megastates of America*, treated America's 10 most heavily populated states. This volume, together with a companion book, *The Pacific States of America*, begins the exploration of people, politics, and power in the other 40. Succeeding books will view separately people, politics, and power in the Plains States. Deep South, Border South, Great Lakes, Mid-Atlantic, and New England States.

A word about method. Like Gunther, I traveled to each state of the Union. I talked with about 1,000 men and women—governors, Senators, Representatives, mayors, state and local officials, editors and reporters, business and labor leaders, public opinion analysts, clergymen, university presidents and professors, representatives of the Indian, black, and Spanish-speaking communities—and just plain people. Some of the people I talked with were famous, others obscure, almost all helpful.

I went by plane, then rented cars, made a personal inspection of almost every great city and most of the important geographic areas, and must have walked several hundred miles in the process too, insanely lugging a briefcase full of notes and tape recorder into the unlikeliest places. Usually I got names of suggested interviewees from my newspaper friends and other contacts in new states and cities and then sent letters ahead saying I would like to see the people. From the initial interviews, reference to still more interesting people invariably ensued. Rare were the interviews that didn't turn out to be fascinating in their own way; the best ones were dinner appointments, when the good talk might stretch into the late evening hours.

Altogether, the travel to 50 states took a year and a half, starting in 1969; then came more than two years of writing, all too often made up of 15-hour working days. The writing was complicated by the need to review hundreds of books and thousands of articles and newspaper clippings I had assembled over time. And then each manuscript, after it had been read and commented upon by experts on the state (often senior political reporters), had to be revised to include last-minute developments, and still once more given a final polish and updating in the galley stage.

Amid the confusion I tried to keep my eye on the enduring, vital question about each state and its great cities:

What sets it (the state or city) apart from the rest of America?

What is its essential character?

What kind of place is it to live in?

What does it look like, how clean or polluted is it, what are the interesting communities?

Who holds the power?

Which are the great corporations, unions, universities, and newspapers, and what role do they play in their state?

Which are the major ethnic groups, and what is their influence?

How did the politics evolve to where they are today, and what is the outlook for the 1970s?

How creatively have the governments and power structures served the *people?*

Who are the great leaders of today—and perhaps tomorrow?

A word of caution: many books about the present-day American condition are preoccupied with illustrating fundamental sickness in our society, while others are paeans of praise. These books are neither. They state many of the deep-seated problems, from perils to the environment to the abuse of power by selfish groups. But the account of the state civilizations also includes hundreds of instances of greatness, of noble and disinterested public service. I have viewed my primary job as descriptive, to show the multitudinous strands of life in our times, admitting their frequently contradictory directions, and tying them together analytically only where the evidence is clear. The ultimate "verdict" on the states and cities must rest with the reader himself.

For whom, then, is this chronicle of our times written? I mean the individual chapters to be of interest to people who live in the various states, to help them see their home area in a national context. I write for businessmen, students, and tourists planning to visit or move into a state, and who are interested in what makes it tick—the kind of things no guidebook will tell them. I write for politicians planning national campaigns, for academicians, for all those curious about the American condition as we enter the last decades of the 20th century.

From the start, I knew it was presumptuous for any one person to try to encompass such a broad canvass. But a unity of view, to make true comparisons between states, is essential. And since no one else had tried the task for a quarter of a century, I decided to try—keeping in mind the same goal Gunther set for *Inside U. S. A.*—a book whose "central spine and substance is an effort—in all diffidence—to show this most fabulous and least known of countries, the United States of America, to itself."

THE

MOUNTAIN STATES

OF AMERICA

THE
MOUNTAIN WEST

A REGIONAL VIEW

*Here in the Mountain West, space and nature shape us. Despite our
differences, we are made a hopeful people, as the mountain men and the
overland travelers and just yesterday's homesteaders were hopeful. As the
gold-seeker and the mining magnates and the cattle kings were hopeful.
Not always honest, mind you, not always capable or wise or successful, but
almost always hopeful and hence astride of life.*

—A. B. Guthrie, Jr.

*What is at the heart of the West? Where is the center from which
the shaping force and power radiate? The answer is simple if we would only
see and accept it. The heart of the West is a desert, unqualified and
absolute.*

—Walter Prescott Webb

THE EIGHT MOUNTAIN STATES, still boisterous juveniles among the 50, remain
our interior frontier, their ultimate destiny yet unknown. Several qualities
set them apart from the rest of the U. S. A.

Distance. Eastern and even West Coast scales of distance need readjust-
ment here. From the Canadian to the Mexican border, the Mountain West
stretches 1,260 miles, three times the distance from Boston to Washington.
From Colorado's eastern border to westernmost Nevada is 950 miles. Altogether, there are 863,524 square miles in this vast expanse of sagebrush and
mountain, 13 times as large as New England, five times as large as mighty California, the equivalent of the combined area of 13 European nations.

One can take issue with the eight-state grouping. The eastern reaches
of Montana, Wyoming, Colorado, and New Mexico are all part of the Great

Plains and about as unmountainous as any territory in the U. S. A. Arizona has many sun culture attributes in common with Southern California or Florida. Nevada is primarily a sin-and-fun appendage of California. Idaho lies within the Columbia River basin of the Northwest states.

But the similarities of the eight are all greater than their differences. The mighty Rocky Mountain ranges and the jagged line of the Continental Divide stretch through them from one international border to the other; only Nevada is outside the Rocky Mountain grouping, and it is mountainous enough. Nevada also has in the most extreme form the problem common to all eight:

Dryness. When the late Walter Prescott Webb wrote of the essential desert-like quality of the West in 1957, he aroused a hornet's nest of angry dissent; the Denver *Post*, for instance, carried an editorial with its message in its title: "Us Desert Rats Is Doing Okay." But subsequent water crises, forcing Arizona and Utah, for instance, to take irrigated farm land out of production in order to meet municipal needs, have only served to underscore what Webb said:

> The overriding influence that shapes the West is the desert. That is its one unifying force. It permeates the plains, climbs to all but the highest mountain peaks, dwells continually in the valleys. . . . The desert is the guest that came to dinner, never to go away. It has stripped the mountains of their vegetation, making them "rocky"; it has dried up the inland seas, leaving . . . Lake Bonneville a briny fragment in the Great Salt Lake. . . . For a million years a fire of low intensity has been burning, and it is still burning in the West. It is broader and more intense in the south, narrower and somewhat cooler in the north.

And then Webb printed a map to show the outlines of the desert, its limit of influence defined by the sharp cleavage of the 98th Meridian on the Great Plains (where annual rainfall goes below 20 inches), covering major chunks of the Pacific states but engulfing virtually 100 per cent of the eight mountain states.

Ten years later the distinguished Western analyst, Wallace Stenger, took only slight exception to Webb's definition: "I would prefer to call [the West] a series of deserts and semi-deserts separated by the snow fountains of high ranges, and with a rain fountain along its Pacific shores, but with Webb's insistence on aridity as a basic unity, I do not quarrel."

In the eight mountain states, the average annual precipitation is only 12 inches, barely escaping the true desert mark of 10 inches. Often there are droughts that last over many years. The Colorado River, coursing through much of America's most arid and water-starved territory, has ranged from record flood-year levels of 22 million acre-feet down to as little as 4 million acre-feet in a drought year. John Wesley Powell, the great conservationist, spoke well when he told the Montana Constitutional Convention in 1889 that "all the great values of this territory have ultimately to be measured to you in acre-feet." (For the uninitiated, we may note that an acre-foot of water is the amount it takes to cover an acre to the depth of one foot.) So the lean years follow the fat ones, and Westerners have known for a century that the economic salvation of their region is the storage of spring runoff from the high mountains for use during the long, hot, dry summers and beyond. The Bureau of Reclamation has been doing just that ever since it completed its large masonry dam on the Salt River in Arizona in 1911, a first step in making possible the farms and city of modern Phoenix in the Arizona desert. Two decades later came the mighty Hoover Dam in the precipitous gorge of the Colorado River's Black Canyon in Nevada. Hoover was the first of the great multipurpose dams, not only storing water for the people of Southern California and the great vegetable and fruit basket of the Imperial Valley but also providing flood control, massive electric power generation, and the spacious recreation area on the desert called Lake Mead. The 1940s also witnessed completion of Grand Coulee Dam on the Columbia in western Washington state, the first of many dams to tame and use to advantage the rush of water in that deepest and broadest of all Western rivers.

The frenetic pace of dam building continued and accelerated in the post-war years with similar projects in all the river basins of the West. Four great storage projects rose in the Upper Colorado River Basin—Glen Canyon (Lake Powell) in Utah and Arizona, Flaming Gorge in Utah and Wyoming, the Navajo in New Mexico and Colorado, and the Curecanti on the Gunni-

son River in Colorado. The construction of large-scale diversion projects went forward, piercing the walls of the Rockies to supply water to Denver and the Colorado Eastern Slope, and the Uintas to bring water to Salt Lake City and the Wasatch Front. Colorado won approval of the federally financed Frying-pan-Arkansas project to water its thirsty southeastern reaches; New Mexico got its San Juan-Chama Project to divert Colorado River water for irrigation in the Rio Grande River Basin and for municipal supplies for Albuquerque. Arizona received the $892 million Central Arizona Project to take Colorado River water over aqueducts to Phoenix and Tucson, saving its agriculture from almost certain destruction because of the dropping water table. In the Columbia River Basin, the massive John Day Dam was built in Oregon; along the Middle Snake on Idaho's western border rose three dams in Hells Canyon, built by the Idaho Power Company after years of controversy between private and public power interests. Montana got its Hungry Horse Dam on the Flathead River and the Yellowtail Dam on the Bighorn, largest and highest dams in the headwater tributaries of the Missouri River.

And so the list of great projects goes on and on, fostering new cities and desert-land agriculture, making mincemeat of the words a shortsighted Daniel Webster spoke in the Senate in 1852: "What do we want with this worthless area—this region of savages and wild beasts, of shifting sands and whirlwinds of dust, of cactus and prairie dogs? To what use could we ever hope to put these great deserts and these endless mountain ranges?"

The modern-day problems are different—not whether the West should be developed, but what to do once the great storage and hydroelectric sites are gone. Now they are nearly exhausted. Every acre-foot of the Colorado is spoken for by compacts between the states. The old public-versus-private disputes, red hot from the 1930s through the 1950s, have subsided. Now the private utilities and the public power agencies speak as one in trying to get at least one more dam built in Hells Canyon; their major adversaries are the conservationists who would stop further man-made intrusion in that wildest and deepest of all American river canyons. Already the dam builders have been defeated by conservationists in their effort to construct revenue-generating hydroelectric dams just above and below the Grand Canyon as part of the Central Arizona Project. Increasingly, the conservationists are fighting all new dam projects because of the way they deface the natural landscape and imperil the natural flora and fauna.

Many other basic questions are raised by continued federal funding for new dams, reservoirs, and aqueducts in the West. Do the nation's taxpayers have an obligation to finance increasingly ambitious water diversion projects to start new farms and cities on natural deserts like Arizona and Southern California? What is the logic of multimillion-dollar reclamation projects that create new farmland on which government-subsidized crops like cotton will be grown, and which force farmers elsewhere in the country out of work? Is there truth to the charge, raised by Ralph Nader's Center for the Study of Responsive Law and others, that the 70-year-old Bureau of Reclamation has really outlived its original purpose but continues to build dams and canals and aqueducts to "benefit politicians, bureaucrats and a few profiteering irrigators, but not the nation as a whole"? What of the abrogation of Indian water rights? And is "growth for growth's sake" necessarily good for these Western states, already the recipients of so much federal largesse?

Questions of interregional rivalry are also involved. The Pacific Northwest, for instance, knows that further Southwestern water development will require diversion of water from the Columbia River Basin—perhaps imperiling the full potential growth of Washington, Oregon, and Idaho. Northwestern Senators forced a 10-year moratorium in federal studies on transbasin diversion as their price for agreeing to the $1.3 billion Colorado River Basin Act in 1968, but the subject is sure to arise again with support of the vote-heavy Southwest. Already the Western States Water Council, a cooperative water planning organization of the 11 continental Western states, has issued a report listing seven major proposals to divert Northwestern water to the Colorado River Basin; there are also several plans to bring water down from Canada, or even Alaska, to replenish the water supplies of both the Mountain West and the Great Lakes.

Oasis Population. Although the mountain states account for 30 per cent of the land area of the continental U. S. A., their 8.3 million people, by the 1970 Census count, comprise a bare 4 percent of the population of the United States. (California alone has 2.4 times as many people.) For the most part, the shortgrass plains and mountains and canyonlands of the Mountain West are devoid of people. Wyoming has only 3.4 people per square mile, Montana 4.8, New Mexico 8.4, Colorado 21.3—compared to a national figure of 57.5.

The regional population has been growing, and at a rate faster than that of the United States as a whole. But the growth is very uneven. During the decade of the 1960s, Colorado grew 25.8 percent to 2,207,259 (more than a quarter of the regional total) and Arizona 36.1 percent to 1,772,482. Nevada led the nation with a 71.3 percent growth, to 488,738; in 1940, there were only 110,000 people in the state. Utah was up 18.9 percent to 1,059273. But New Mexico and Idaho added less than 7 percent and Montana only 2.9 percent. Wyoming gained less than 1 percent and ended up with 332,416 people, the smallest number of any of the 50 states except Alaska.

What is actually happening is that the number of people in most of the West's ranching and mining counties is declining, while the population increases in and especially around the cities where there is water—the oases of the West. Two well irrigated urban counties—the sun-industry-agriculture centers of Maricopa (Phoenix) and Pima (Tucson) now account for 75 percent of the entire population of Arizona. In Colorado, 57 percent of the people now live in the metropolitan region of Denver, self-proclaimed capital of the Rocky Mountain West; outside of Denver and other cities of the Rockies' well watered eastern front (Colorado Springs, Boulder, Pueblo), Colorado's population is extremely sparse. In Nevada, Clark County (Las Vegas) alone has 56 percent of the state's population; it rose 115 percent in population during the 1960s. The nearby Colorado River makes Las Vegas possible, but no one is fooled into thinking it would amount to much were it not for the gambling crowd from next-door California, where such pleasures are illegal. In Utah, 53 percent of the people live in and around Salt Lake City; outside of the other cities of the fertile, narrow Wasatch Front, the state has but a scattering of inhabitants. As with Las Vegas, there is a special but so different *raison d'être* for Salt Lake City: it is the Mormon's Jerusalem. New Mexico's oasis is the strip from Albuquerque north to Santa Fe in the Rio Grande Valley; while Albuquerque's population growth slowed down to 21 percent in the 1960s, the 30-year span since 1940 has seen it increase 587 percent. Federal atomic and space projects have been the spur for New Mexico's growth, but Tucson and particularly Santa Fe are a center of Hispanic culture and architecture.

The Mountain North, by contrast, has no cities that can even compare in population to Denver or Phoenix or the others we have spoken of. Eastern Montana and Wyoming in particular are high, dry places sharing the depopulation and lack of metropolitan centers typical of the nearby Dakotas and Nebraska. Idaho falls into a somewhat similar pattern, except that it has its moist northern panhandle and also the booming little city of Boise, which now has 74,990 people (metropolitan area 112,230) and promises to become the real capital of the Intermountain North, much as Denver is for the middle Rockies or Phoenix in the south.

Easterners and Southerners—Americans from east of the 98th Meridian —are accustomed to rural territory between their cities in which one farm follows neatly after the next. Not so in the Mountain West. In Wyoming, you can still drive for as many as 50 miles along a major highway without seeing a town or ranchouse or living thing (except plenty of antelope). The vast wilderness areas of central Idaho hold millions of acres where man's shadow has rarely if ever passed. Other extremely remote and isolated territories include the Strip Country north of the Grand Canyon in Arizona (where many excommunicated Mormon polygamists still hang out), or the land east of the Colorado and Green Rivers in Utah, scarcely bridged and touched by few roads. In the Arizonan and New Mexican deserts, a wrong turn in the back country and a vehicle breakdown can well spell death for a man. One could roam the gaunt, parched hills of Nevada for days without seeing a sign of human settlement.

The oasis cities of the West are quickly accumulating the archetypal ills of modern America: traffic jams and ugly arterial roads, polluted air, congestion, and urban decay. But the deserted spaces of desert and mountain, canyon and bluff, where the sagebrush or the pinon pine or saguaro cactus hold sway, are a world set apart. Some future advance of technology, perhaps desalinzation of the sea and economic ways to transport its water a thousand miles inland, may one day make them habitable. But now they stand lonely sentinel, reminders that America not long ago was uncharted wilderness. And they seem to say, as one man has written, "Take care. This is all there is left."

Water may be outshone as the most controversial aspect of Western policy in the 1970s and '80s by a development of immense regional and national import: massive-scale strip coal mining to provide fuel to meet the country's seemingly insatiable demand for electric power. Six Western states, according to a brilliant outlook article by Ben A. Franklin of the New York *Times,* "face a topographic and environmental upheaval." They are Arizona, Colorado, Montana, New Mexico, and Wyoming in the Mountain West, and neighboring North Dakota in the plains states. In 1970, for the first time in American history a Western mine—the Navajo strip mine of the Utah Construction and Mining Company near Farmington, New Mexico—became the country's largest single producer of coal. That single mine, on Navajo Reservation land, is only part of a series of gigantic coal mines and power-generating plants under construction or on the drawing boards for the Four Corners region, supplying electricity to New Mexico, Arizona, Nevada, and Southern California. In 1964, investor-owned public power companies formed an association known as WEST (Western Energy Supply Transmission Associates) which had grown to 24 member companies by 1971. Just one of the plants planned by WEST, on the Utah side of Lake Powell, will be the biggest coal-fired generating plant in the world, large enough to supply all of the energy needs of a city the size of New York. The sum capacity of power plants planned for the Colorado Plateau by 1985 will be 36 million kilowatts, three times the power of TVA. Belatedly, conservationists are up in arms about the fantastic burden of smoke and ash the plants spread across once-clear Western skies.

By 1971, nearly one million acres of public and Indian coal lands across the West had already been leased for strip coal mining by coal and petroleum companies. And the railroads, which were given sections of land as an encouragement to construction of track a century ago, found themselves owners of immense coal supplies. The Union Pacific alone has 10 to 12 billion tons under its land, for instance. According to estimates by the Bureau of Mines, 77 percent of the country's total of economically strippable coal (some 45 billion tons) lies beneath the 13 states west of the Mississippi. Some 25 billion tons are low-sulphur coal (which is less polluting to the environment); of that total, 21 billion tons are in Wyoming and Montana alone. The low-sulphur reserve of Wyoming is eight times as large as West Virginia's and Kentucky's put together.

While coal mining and electric power generation spread across the West in the 1970s, even more expansive plans are being laid for mines and plants of the 1980s which will be engaged in the process of extracting coal from the ground to turn it into natural gas in huge refinery-like plants. The strip-mining explosion for gasification, one government coal official told Ben Franklin, will make the excavation for electric power stations "look like a mere desert gulch." Coal gasification is seen as a way to replace the country's fast-depleting reserves of natural gas in wells, now expected to run out in about 15 years. Like coal mining for power generation, strip mining for coal for gasification will have a stunning effect on the Western landscape. But at least there will not be the polluting impact of on-site power generation.

Indians. A third of all American Indians live in the Mountain West, the bulk of them in Arizona, New Mexico, and Montana. As we will discover when we visit them in those states, their life continues, as it has ever since the white man usurped their territory, largely a thing apart. Federal "termination" programs for the reservations have been a crashing failure. Yet by the same token, more Indians are educated and more are living off the reservations than ever before. A rekindled pride in their own culture, crafts, and language is sweeping across the Indian lands, but at the same time there are excruciating problems as the Indian tries to accommodate to the white man's culture without imperiling what is peculiarly his.

The gambling psychosis, love of the outdoors and a reverence for nature, and the urge to withdraw. Is there a common character to the West? There is little reason to expect one. The people are arbitrarily divided into eight states that make little geographic sense and tend to promote disunity. As if that were not enough, they are separated by great walls of space (even though air travel and the interstate highways now make for more unity than ever before possible). Except for the deep-seated (and increasingly troubled) cultures of the Indians and Spanish-Americans, the Mountain West lacks depth in its history, the commonality of shared, slow development.

John Gunther could write a quarter of a century ago that "the West still carries the stigmata of the frontier civilization. . . . This is shirt-sleeve country, he-man country, where the beds are usually double and where you drink your beer straight from the bottle." Much of this remains, in overgrown mining camps like Butte, Montana, or among the dwindling numbers of cowboys on lonely ranches, or in the gambling saloon of a Nevada cow county. The prospector, the big rancher, the oil baron, the gambler, all still look for the pot of gold at the end of the rainbow. But there are many Westerners who share none of this: the retirees from Dubuque and Rochester and Milwaukee assembled at Sun City, Arizona; the new technocrats of the scientific-industrial complexes at Denver or Phoenix or Albuquerque; and yes, the rapidly multiplying Mormons of Utah, who always plowed their fields and worshipped their God in a special way and never shared in the plunder and gamble of the old West anyway.

Some common traits, though, can be seen. Almost all Westerners are addicted to the outdoors life, be it gawking at the scenic splendor of their region, skiing in Colorado, hunting in Wyoming, fishing in Idaho, rock counting in Arizona, or enjoying the sunshine and warmth of the Southwest. These are a people hell-bent for relaxation, whether it involves building a golf course on a gopher hill, carting their motorboats hundreds of miles to splash in Lake Mead or Lake Powell, or trudging with pack into remote wilderness areas. Overcoming obstacles seems to be part of the fun. And now Westerners' reverence for nature is fostering a new interest in conservation, a determination not to repeat the mistakes of the already violated eastern U. S. A.

The issue draws sportsmen, intellectuals, and many just plain citizens on one side; their natural adversaries become the mining, timber, and cattle interests, and increasingly, the dam builders. The federal government, because it owns so much of the West, often finds itself in the middle of their disputes.

Westerners enjoy the lack of crowds, the more amiable human relationships their environment makes possible. Many would like to keep out any more industry or development that would bring in more people. They share a self-satisfaction that they are so far distant from the crime-ridden and strife-torn centers of urban America—a kind of "there but for the grace of God live I" complex. Senator Mike Mansfield, as tolerant and urbane a man as the region has ever produced, often reminds his Montanan constituents how lucky they are to live where they do, not in crime-plagued Washington. The Mountain West has few Negroes, and apparently likes it that way; the blacks who do live there are no more euphoric about their lot than the even more disadvantaged Mexican-Americans. On the whole, the Mountain West takes little interest in its minorities. This should come as little surprise, because for many people the mountain states are withdrawal states, places in which to take refuge from the maddening times.

Fading colonialism. Montana's Governor Forrest Anderson has succinctly named five "human resource" problems which bedevil his and the other mountain states: (1) outmigration of working people; (2) a resulting small return on a heavy educational investment; (3) a burdensome per capita tax load resulting from sparse population and vast spaces, much of it owned by the federal government; (4) a colonial status that has been imposed by out-of-state financing of an almost purely extractive economy; and (5) the commercial disadvantage of distance from the market place.

The West's export of brains, youth, and talent is a relatively new problem, occasioned by the lure of high-paying jobs on the West Coast that started with World War II and has continued relatively unabated ever since. Generally, the problem is most serious in the northern Rocky Mountain states and less severe in those, like Colorado and Arizona, which have been able to attract substantial military payrolls and space-age industries on their own.

The other problems Anderson named, however, are as old as the civilized West and common to most of the mountain states. Since the first trappers and miners arrived, the West has been plundered of its natural resources. It has been a supplier of raw materials—furs, gold, silver, copper, oil and gas, uranium, lumber, wool, hides and grain—but rarely a processor of the materials; as a result the big factory payrolls have been back in the East or Midwest, and most of the great fortunes accumulated have been spent there too. Western wages (and thus per capita income) have lagged, and still do: as of 1970, the New Mexico per capita income was only 80 percent of the national average, Idaho's 83 percent, Arizona's 92 percent, Colorado's 97 percent; within the region, only Nevada, with its rather artificial gaming economy, was ahead of the national income average. In 1970 prospective manufacturers were being lured to Albuquerque and Phoenix by assurances that the labor force, figuring both wages and productivity, would cost 20 to 50 percent less than in the nation's big cities.

Fiercely competitive in their struggle for economic existence in earlier years, the mountain states are showing a new and mature willingness to work together, symbolized by the formation in 1966 of the Federation of Rocky Mountain States with headquarters in Denver. No one can be sure of the ultimate results, but the federation has made a brave start in coordinating economic planning of the eight states with an initial "data bank" for regional planning, making risk capital available on a regional consortium basis for experimental industrial projects, mobilizing a science advisory council on technological development, promoting export sales, identifying new mineral and water resources, and encouraging weather modification programs. There are plans to start tourist promotion on a regional basis, and the federation has also initiated a broad cultural program to tie together the region's distant population centers with touring art exhibits and guest appearances throughout the eight-state area of such groups as the Denver, Phoenix, and Utah Symphonies and the Utah Civic Ballet (now known as Ballet West).

Transportation remains a bugaboo of the Western economy. By definition, it costs more to ship goods in and out of the immense Mountain West than within confined urban corridors, a situation exacerbated by discriminatory freight rates. Any Western businessman will be ready with tales of how it costs him more to get a shipment of goods from Chicago than it would a competitor in Seattle or Los Angeles. By the constant efforts of Western businessmen and politicians, discriminatory freight rates have been ameliorated in recent years, but the problem remains.

Manufacturing has been growing in the Mountain West, especially around Denver, Phoenix, Albuquerque, Tucson, and Salt Lake City. Factory payrolls are now four times as great, in dollar terms, as they were 20 years ago, and for the first time in history, manufacturing contributes more to the regional economy than either mining or agriculture. The trend is sure to continue as the big national corporations decide to escape to the open spaces, mostly for the cheap labor but also for inexpensive land, clean air and water, the friendly and helpful welcome they get, and easy access to Pacific Coast markets. Only 2 percent of U. S. aerospace is in the Mountain West, an area of obvious growth potential. In 1969–70, Albuquerque got new manufacturing plants for Levi Straus (clothing), the Friden Division of Singer Company (office machines), the Lenkurt subsidiary of General Telephone & Electronics (electronic gear), and Ampex (recording equipment). Notably, these are all *clean* industries with light-weight products to ship. The fact that the Mountain West lacks water closes out many types of heavy industries and, in the process, some of the worst industrial pollution. (There are, for instance, two steel mills in the region—at Pueblo, Colorado, and Provo, Utah.) In 1969 a howl of protest went up in New Mexico when a new paper and pulp mill was proposed; the local joke was that everyone was willing to get affluent but preferred to do without the effluent.

Outside ownership remains the rule in the Mountain West, even in booming Denver and Phoenix. Colorado has developed two or three conglomerate-type operations of uncertain future prospects, and until the departure of Howard Hughes, Las Vegas was the nerve center of his vast industrial, mining, and casino empire. Strangely enough, the strongest headquarters town of the whole region may be little Boise, home of great corporations like Boise Cascade, Morrison-Knudsen, and J. R. Simplot's potato and mining empire.

Outside of the startling new prospects for coal mining, the mountain states harbor substantial mineral wealth. Copper is big in Montana, Arizona, and Utah; Idaho is still the top silver-producer of the U. S. A; uranium has been discovered and mined from New Mexico to Wyoming; oil plays a major role in the economy of Wyoming, New Mexico, Colorado, and Montana. But the future promises a yield in basic energy that might dwarf the value of all the minerals yet produced in the West. Gigantic oil shale deposits underlying parts of Colorado, Utah, and Wyoming could meet the foreseeable energy needs of the nation for centuries.

Cattle and sheep raising remain vital Western industries, and the ranchers are still a breed unto themselves and mighty powers in states like Wyoming and Montana. Some 21 million cattle and sheep roam Western ranges or fatten in feed lots, two and a half times the human population of the region. But millions of the cattle are owned, not by Westerners, but by smart financiers in New York, Chicago, or Houston.

Finally, our review of the West's economy turns to the dynamic factor provided by tourism. National affluence and good roads have encouraged more people to see the Mountain West in the postwar years than in all its prior recorded history. Of the wonders they come to see, perhaps the greatest panoply of rawboned natural splendor in the world, we will have more to say in our individual state chapters. But if the states' own estimates are to be trusted, they draw more than 80 million tourists (many counted twice and more for the various states they have visited) and spend more than $3 billion a year. Total farm income and the value of minerals mined are both in the $4 billion range; only manufacturing, about $5 billion in annual value, now adds substantially more to the regional economy.

Federal dependence. The mountain states remain in large degree what they have always been: wards of the federal government. Washington actually owns almost half the entire land area of the Mountain West, ranging from 30 percent in Montana up to 86 percent in Nevada. When one adds up the billions the federal government spends in the West each year—on land and forestry management, water resources, aid to agriculture, military installations, and the whole array of present-day federal programs, it turns out that the West is getting a lot more in services than it pays back in taxes. The direct federal payroll is also formidable—$2.7 billion within the region in 1970, counting both civilian and military employment. Preeminently, Denver is the federal office center for the Rocky Mountain states.

Without the federal factor, the mountain states' economy might not be viable at all. I was jolted during an interview with a former high official of the Interior Department to hear him state baldly that the West has always been and remains a deficit area, not really self-supporting, a subsidized area living off the rest of the United States. Most water projects, he insisted, involve far more actual and hidden costs to Washington than it can ever hope to get back in hydroelectric and water supply revenues. The decision to promote the growth of the West, even at the cost of the taxpayers of the other regions, may well have been a wise one in the interests of long-term development of the U. S. A. But the decision was not primarily economic, but rather political—the result of adroit maneuvering by Western Senators and Representatives on Capitol Hill.

The House Interior Committee, for instance, is headed by Wayne Aspinall of Colorado's Western Slope. Aspinall has obtained authorization for so many federal dam and reservoir projects in Colorado that even his home-state boosters admit some of them are uneconomic and should never be built. Yet it is interesting to note that no federal water programs deliver subsidized water to cities east of the Mississippi. The only big hydroelectric projects in the East are in the Tennessee Valley, but it took a Westerner, George Norris, to think of the idea of TVA!

When suggestions are made to increase grazing fees on Western public lands to rates even vaguely comparable to what private range owners charge, the big cattle and sheep operators rise up in angry protest and get even some liberal Democratic Senators to intercede with the Interior Department to block fee boosts. (Columnist Jack Anderson notes caustically that the going rate to graze a cow and calf on public range land for a month is 44 cents— what it costs a city dweller to feed a dog for two days.) And when a Public Land Law Review Commission was created to examine long-term policies for the 775 million acres of land in the U. S. A. owned by the federal government, the man appointed to head it—Colorado's Aspinall—was a man regarded by his conservationist critics as an apologist of Western mining, timber and grazing interests. Nothing to offend those interests appeared in the final report, which even failed to recommend repeal of the still operative 1871 mining law which permits extractors to stake claims and start operations almost anywhere on public land, without even notifying the government and regardless of the danger to the environment. (The ecologically delicate White Cloud peaks of Idaho are imperiled by a proposed molybdenum mine, for instance, because of the 1871 law. Molybdenum is in surplus in the U. S. A., and most of what would be mined would be shipped to foreign markets. Many believe the time has come for the federal government to restrict exploration for minerals on its lands and to license only the extraction which is clearly in the present national interest.)

Perhaps the most innovative idea in the entire Aspinall report was that the U. S. Forest Service be transferred from the Department of Agriculture to the Department of the Interior. Interior, of course, is the great patron department of the West. Stewart Udall, the leading conservationist Secretary of the Interior of the postwar years, was an Arizona Congressman until President Kennedy appointed him in 1961. Under Udall, Interior became less of a champion of ever increasing water projects and stockmen's grazing rights and began to take much more interest in environmental protection and promotion of tourism for the West. Environmental concern mounted on Capital Hill, too, and it was a Western Senator—Idaho's Frank Church—who led the floor fight for the landmark Wilderness Act of 1964.

The prime irony of Western politics is that this totally dependent region is the same one which produces so many rugged, independent frontiersmen who are ready to denounce the federal government for its every transgression. The ultimate example of this is Barry Goldwater of Arizona, crusader against socialized government and the man who toyed with the idea of selling the TVA. But Goldwater is equally dedicated to construction of the fantastically expensive Central Arizona Project.

Goldwater is not alone among Western Senators in fighting for his home state interests, no matter what his personal philosophy may be. But conservative Republican Senators have been something of a luxury in an era when the Democrats held Congress under almost uninterrupted control. The man who really brought home the bacon for Arizona was the durable Carl Hayden, chairman of the Senate Appropriations Committee until his retirement at age 93 after more than half a century on Capitol Hill. Two other Democrats, from neighboring New Mexico—Dennis Chavez and Clinton P. Anderson— used their Senate power to literally transform their state from a sleepy tourist-winter sun spot to a center of nuclear and space age research and development.

Many of the northern mountain states, normally Republican in their voting habits, have made it a point to keep one or even two Democrats in the U. S. Senate to protect their federal flank. Thus right-wing Wyoming returns Gale McGee, conservative Idaho reelects Frank Church, supposedly self-sufficient Utah returns Frank Moss, and Montana, traditionally a pawn in the hands of the big interests, sends to Washington men like Mike Mansfield and Lee Metcalf. Some of these men have made a national mark far broader than parochial Western interests. But for the most part, it was the parochial interests that prompted the voters to send them to Washington in the first place. The mountain states' split personality in matters political was well illustrated in 1969–70, when the Republicans held six of the eight area governorships, 10 of the 17 seats in the U. S. House, but only seven of the 16 U. S. Senate seats.

Aside from Barry Goldwater, the West has not for years sent an outstanding Republican Senator to Washington—a figure able to make impact comparable to Democrats Hayden, Anderson, Chavez, Church, Mansfield, or even Pat McCarran of Nevada. The last Republican of extraordinary stature was Eugene Millikin of Colorado, who retired in 1956.

Home-state Rocky Mountain politics tend to be an intensely personal affair, in which candidates are personally known to a large portion of the electorate. This doubtless saves the necks of a lot of politicians bucking prevailing political tides. And it may be a fading phenomenon, for in Arizona and Colorado, the two most heavily populated mountain states and both turning increasingly Republican, there are Republican governors and all-Republican Senate delegations. In most mountain states, however, split tickets are still the order of the day, a continuation of the independent Western streak that goes back as much as half a century ago, when Montana elected the first woman Congressman and Wyoming the first woman governor.

The region's people, despite the distances which impair communications, are active politically; of the eight states, for instance, five consistently turn out a substantially greater percentage of their vote than the national average. (The exceptions are New Mexico, Arizona, and Nevada.) This is also big initiative and referendum country—a politician is not to be trusted too far. Political nominations are by primary in all these states, but four—Colorado, Idaho, Utah, and New Mexico—are among the comparatively few in the U. S. A. that have seen fit to experiment with preprimary conventions that weed out some of the hopeless also-rans of politics.

After the 1960 election, when all but two of the area's states (New Mexico and Nevada) went for Nixon and the John Birch Society began to crop up like the ubiquitous mountain sagebrush, many thought the mountain states were ready to plunge down the right-wing road. It all sounded so logical for a people known for their independence, their distaste for the heavy hand of government (assuming it carries no subsidy), their scorn for the teeming cities and love of firearms. Barry Goldwater's strategists laid their national political plans on the assumption. It didn't work; Goldwater carried only his native Arizona and came close in only one other mountain state, Idaho. In 1968, however, Nixon carried 53.4 percent of the 2.9 million Presidential ballots cast in the region, a plurality in all eight states. (Humphrey got 37.9 percent, Wallace 8.7 per cent). At this writing, the Mountain West must be considered some of the staunchest Republican territory anywhere in Presidential politics. As long as the national Democrats seem associated with big cities and minorities and turbulent politics, the situation is likely to continue. But on their home turf, most Westerners are likely to keep on voting for the man, not the party.

COLORADO

LIFE BESIDE SHINING MOUNTAINS

ACROSS THE CENTRAL THIRD of North America, for more than 1,000 miles, the prairie rolls westward, shifting from the moisture of the Mississippi River Valley to the aridity of the high plains. And then, with swiftness and drama, the levelness ends. Looming before him, the traveler sees the great face of the American Rockies, the snowcapped spine of a continent. The Midwest has ended, the mountains have begun.

"The Shining Mountains," a now-forgotten pioneer at the head of a wagon train was said to have called them. In the words of the Denver *Post's* Bill Hosokawa,* they

dominate the Colorado scene as no mountains dominate any state. The Rockies are the source of much of Colorado's wealth. They are the magnet that attracted a substantial part of the population, the spine that splits it economically, the barrier that blocked development and the resource that spurred it. Without the water stored through the winter in alpine snowlands, the plains that make up half of Colorado would be little more than desert.

Traveling through the mountain West a quarter of a century ago, John Gunther paid, like the rest of us, obeisance to the scenery of Colorado. "Little

* In the Colorado chapter of *Rockies and Plains* (Litchfield, Conn.: Fodor Shell Travel Guides U. S. A., 1967).

in the world," Gunther wrote, "can compare. The vistas stretch the eyes, en-
lighten the heart, and make the spirit humble." But then he assessed the life
led there and entitled his chapter "—But Scenery Is Not Enough." Colorado,
Gunther said, "is conservative politically, economically, financially." He
pointed out that the state was 39th among the members of the Union in its
aid to education, in its rural health services and the like. "Colorado has, in
fact, an almost Olympian inertness. It has ridden for year after year on its
prestige, its reputation." Much more so than other Western states, Gunther
noted, Colorado had a large proportion of citizens born within its borders.

It is no longer so. Since 1945, the state's population has doubled to
2,207,259—a rate of growth almost twice as great as that of the nation as a
whole. First came thousands of servicemen who had trained during World
War II at Denver's Lowry Air Base, Fort Carson near Colorado Springs, or
Camp Hale for mountain troops near Leadville. Entranced by the scenery and
good air, they had vowed to return and did. And then, in an onrush that
reached monumental proportions in the 1950s, came hundreds of thousands
of new Coloradans to work in government offices and defense- and scientific-
related industries. Along the Eastern Front of the Rockies, a mini-megalopolis
began to take shape. Anchored by Denver and its exploding suburban counties at the center, it stretches through Boulder and on to Fort Collins and
toward Cheyenne in the north and through Colorado Springs to Pueblo in
the south. Fully 80 percent of Colorado's people now live along the Front. At
the same time, modern farming techniques have depopulated the eastern
plains; in the west, except for a number of boom-time ski centers, the population has dropped as well.

Colorado politics (to which we will return later in this chapter) still
show a strong streak of conservatism, but one could scarcely speak now of
Olympian inertness. On any scale of governmental performance, Colorado
now makes a quite respectable showing. Denver has cast off its ancient slug-
gishness and become a progressive, forward-looking capital for a vast intermountain region—and, in the process, has contracted a number of the urban
ills so well known to every other metropolis of the U. S. A.

Denver and Its Rocky Mountain Empire

A quarter of a century ago, George Sessions Perry wrote in the *Saturday
Evening Post* that Denver's role was to serve not only the state of Colorado,
but the entire Rocky Mountain region, "as doctor, lawyer, merchant, and (political) chief, as well as banker, butcher, teacher and supplier of transportation, markets, entertainment, culture, and shelter for the transient." The city
was far from that ideal when he wrote. The major transcontinental rail lines,
unwilling to scale the Rockies, ran north and south of it. Cheyenne, rather
than Denver, was the chief East-West air terminal of the Rocky Mountain
states. Denver's economy was basically stagnant, the gold and silver kings who

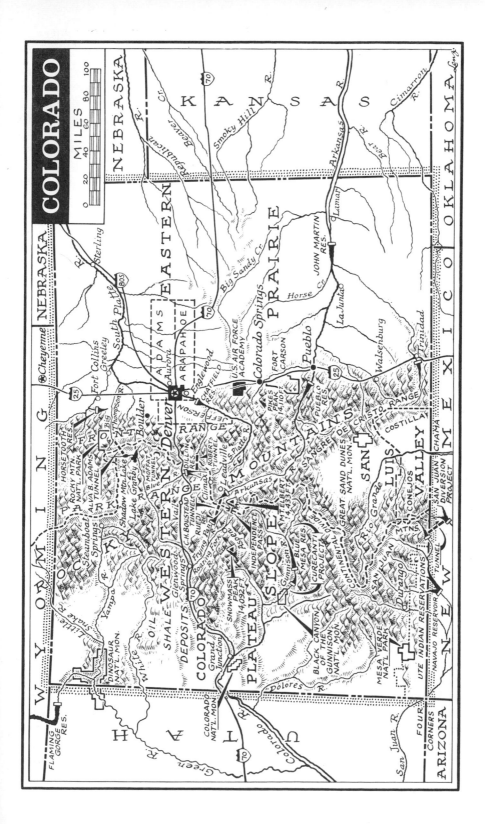

had first brought fame and fortune to Colorado were long since in their graves, the old wealth tied up in trust funds. Denver was packed with bond houses, its banks were sluggish in making risk capital available, and members of the ingrown power structure, in the words of one critic of the time, had "no rampage left in them."

Symbolic of the city's troubles was the isolationist Denver *Post*, which for years had fought foreigners, minorities, labor, and Democrats with a ferocity that made even the Chicago *Tribune* of those days pale in comparison. From 1911 to 1946, the paper had no editorial page; it maintained no Washington bureau, and, as Gunther observed, 'its front page looked like a confused and bloody railway accident."

In 1946, however, Helen Bonfils, daughter of the deceased cofounder, decided that the *Post* was hopelessly out of step with the returning war veterans. The search for a new publisher ended with the selection of Palmer Hoyt, successful editor and publisher of the Portland *Oregonian*. Soon Hoyt changed the paper beyond description. Where it had been isolationist, it became internationalist; where it had been closed to every new idea, it became a breeding ground of new approaches for the city and state. Hoyt's policy was strongly pro-civil rights and anti-extremist; the *Post*, in fact, was one of the first papers to fight Joe McCarthy and later the Birchers and Minutemen. The paper pressed for ever-greater school and university appropriations, for penal and mental health reforms, and for growth and progress in Denver. With Hoyt's backing, a vigorous young progressive, Quigg Newton, was elected mayor in 1947, defeating aging incumbent Ben Stapleton, who had bossed Denver in machine-like fashion since 1923.

When I interviewed Hoyt shortly before his retirement at the end of 1970, I discovered a genial, spunky gentleman in his early seventies, whose attitude toward the world seemed reflected in bright blue sports slacks and jacket and a vividly blue shirt—scarcely the image of the conservative newspaper. Hoyt could look back on more than two decades in which he and others whom he supported had literally transformed the face of the city and brought growths to the entire Front region. (Ironically, the *Post* became markedly more conservative as soon as Hoyt retired.)

It was Hoyt who gave open and behind-the-scenes backing to Texas financier Clint Murchison and developer William Zeckendorf. These two irrepressible gentlemen came to Denver in the late 1940s, cast a disdainful eye at the low, uneventful skyline of center city, and staged an urban renewal renaissance which makes Denver today one of the handsomest of American cities. The host of new buildings could not be built, however, until the new developers had won a titanic battle with Denver's old guard. Murchison left his mark with the new Denver Club and First National Bank Buildings, while Zeckendorf built a sparkling downtown center that includes an 880-room Hilton Hotel with a block-long lobby connected by an enclosed bridge over the street (a favorite Denver urban renewal device) to the May-D&F department store, Denver's largest. Center city includes the delightful old Brown Palace

Hotel, now with a handsome new annex in brown-red porcelain-enameled steel, and the Denver-United States National Bank Center, designed by I. M. Pei with a promenade, fountains, and trout pools that add a human dimension.

"Zeckendorf finally went broke, but it was great for Denver," one of Hoyt's associates told me. In fact, a momentum had been created which has continued right up to the present day. Numerous high office buildings have been constructed in the city's financial-headquarters district. And now lower downtown, Denver's old retail district heart, is being renewed; it includes a Federal Reserve Bank building in strong, masculine form akin to Boston's City Hall, and Larimer Square, an old city block that had degenerated into a skid row but was then restored by private investors into a delightful complex of shops, art galleries, and restaurants in a manner reminiscent of San Francisco's Ghiradelli Square. Not far distant is the new Denver Convention Center, dominated by a new exhibition hall of exhilarating interior spaciousness with an exterior sheathing of Core-Ten steel that started out rusty red but is promised to weather into a mellow patina. With these facilities, Denver has ambitions to become not only a regional but a national convention center, trading in on its central continental position and the Colorado mountain vacation potential for out-of-state visitors. In 1976, the city will be the site of the Winter Olympics.

Finally, note must be made of Denver's Civic Center, one of the noblest civic spaces in the country despite heavy automobile traffic and unplanned buildings on its borders. To the east, the center is dominated by the gray granite gold-domed State Capitol of 1890s vintage; to the west stands the exceptionally well designed City and County Building, constructed in the 1930s. The center has a colonnaded pavilion with reflecting pool, a Greek theater, and an inventive new $5.5 million Denver Art Museum. Through its central areas and vast parklands, Denver seems to retain a pleasant, clean feeling of Western spotlessness; the only really jarring notes are several thoroughfares radiating toward the suburbs, crowded with glaring neon signs, car lots, motels, and hamburger stands. In 1971, however, Denver took a long step toward ending the visible pollution of signs by enacting a stiff ordinance that decreed an end to all billboards within five years and ordered an immediate ban on all lighted signs that flash, crawl, or oscillate. The law was passed after a determined group of housewives, professionals, and businessmen put such pressure on the city council that it reversed its past position and voted against the powerful, well-heeled local sign industry.

Despite the city's strong growth pattern, Denver's pace of life is still slower, more relaxed, than that of most great American cities; a visitor from one of the coasts instantly appreciates the slower tempo. But all of that can be in serious jeopardy. Mass transit, for instance, is still no further than the talking stage, but it will be indispensable if Denver's future is not to be the auto-clogged Los Angeles of today. Automobiles pack the downtown streets, are increasing at an astronomical rate, and have gone far to darken and pollute the once-sparkling clean air of the 'Mile-High City." Some days, even the view of the nearby "shining mountains" is shrouded by smog.

Denver was able in the postwar years to solidify its position as the principal distribution point of the mountain states, and the local business community came awake and invested heavily. The very desirability of the Denver area as a place to live drew new population and in turn generated service industries and construction. Stapleton Airport became one of the continent's major air terminals and transfer points. Denver attracted more government offices than any city outside of Washington, including regional headquarters for virtually every important federal agency. The military pumped hundreds of millions of dollars into the Colorado economy through Lowry Field (the U. S. Air Force's major training installation), the Rocky Mountain Arsenal, the Air Force Academy and Fort Carson at Colorado Springs, and numerous other bases up and down the Front Range.

Finally, the Denver area began to take shape as the nation's most important scientific-technical center between Boston and California. The arrival in 1956 of the Martin Marietta Company to build Titan intercontinental ballistic missiles at Denver has been called the greatest event in the city's history since the arrival of the first railroad in 1867. Like most aerospace employers, Martin Marietta has had its ups and downs in Colorado, ranging from a high of 17,000 employees at one point to 7,000 in the late '60s and early '70s; gradually it shifted from military weaponry to space exploration equipment, including rocket boosters for NASA; in the late 1960s the firm got a $280 million project for Mars exploration and promised to remain the state's largest single employer for several more years.

The Martin Company's move to Colorado accelerated a trend toward light, electronic-type industries all along the Front Range. Many smaller service industries arose to service Martin at first, then other industrial plants. The University of Colorado at Boulder and Colorado State University went increasingly into scientific laboratory work in such fields as astrophysics, radiology, space, and forestry, often with major government contracts. Installations at Denver or along the Front Range now include the Denver Technological Center, the National Bureau of Standards, the National Center for Atmospheric Research, and companies like IBM, Beech Aircraft, Ampex, Sundstrand, Western Electric, and Ball Brothers (makers of the orbital sun observatory laboratory). Most of these industries are dependent to a high degree on government contracts, with corresponding (and unavoidable) fluctuations of employment depending on the contract flow from Washington. The state has only two really large "heavy" industries—Gates Rubber Company in Denver and the big steel mill in Pueblo. A new element was added in 1970, when Kodak began work on a major photo processing facility at the little town of Windsor, near Fort Collins on the northern end of the front Range. By that time, manufacturing already led the Colorado income picture with an annual output of more than $1.7 billion.

The day of the big, independent mineral baron in Colorado seems to have gone. A modern-day contender for the role was John McKandish King, whose initial investment of $1,500 in an Oklahoma oil-drilling venture led him, in little more than a decade, to a personal worth of no less than $480 million. King set up his King Resources in Denver in 1960 and got a beat on many of the big oil firms by using computers for geological surveys long before the practice became common in the industry. A big bear of a man— six feet, three inches, 230 pounds—King was described by *Time* as having "the hard blue eyes of a riverboat gambler." He reveled in the trappings of wealth, running his world-wide operations from a gigantic office atop one of the new Denver skyscrapers. At one point he owned nine airplanes, a condominium near Vail, a 400-acre ranch in Granby, Colorado, a house in Hawaii, a house in Palm Springs, California, and an apartment in New York. He possessed 3,000 pairs of solid gold cufflinks. Denver society at first rebuffed him, but not after he threw a 1962 party at which the guest of honor was none other than Dwight D. Eisenhower. King gave a reported $250,000 to Richard Nixon's 1968 Presidential campaign and was later made the President's representative, with the rank of ambassador, to the opening of Japan's Expo '70.

In 1970–71, everything turned sour for big John King. When creditors began to close in on Bernard Cornfeld's Investors Overseas Services, a Geneva-based mutual fund complex that had invested heavily in King's enterprises, King flew to Europe in an audacious (but failing) attempt to take over IOS. The incident prompted American creditors to look into King's own enterprises, and a number of questionable financial transactions were revealed, including an $8 million loan of dubious legality from the state of Ohio. King resigned as chairman of King Resources, and the Securities and Exchange Commission charged that he and two associates had improperly arranged loans from the company for their personal benefit. King began to transfer title to several of his houses to his wife and children in trust, saw his lavish ranch auctioned off at a foreclosure sale, and tottered on the brink of personal bankruptcy.

Another Denver conglomerate promoter who rose high and began to fall far is William M. White, only 28 when he created the Great Western United Corporation in 1968—a combination of Colorado Milling and Elevator Company, the Great Western Sugar Company (the nation's largest beet sugar producer), and eventually a California land development company, a string of franchised pizza parlors named Shakey's, a flour and pancake mix company, a Christmas tree company, a string of steak restaurants, and a lime quarry. This "creative marketing company," as White called it, even became a partner in oil exploration ventures. But the management was so amateurish that the conglomerate went deeply into debt, and by 1971 White was willing and anxious to sell off pieces to regain solvency.

For a quarter of a century, Denver had a voice that challenged not only the entrenched 17th Street business-financial leadership but also Palmer Hoyt, the big utilities, and every other force of the regular establishment. The voice belonged to Eugene Cervi, upstart son of a coal miner, whose *Cervi's Rocky Mountain Journal* delighted in exposing every chicanery it could detect among the vested interests. "What's good, thrilling, exciting about Colorado was produced by God—not the Denver Chamber of Commerce," Cervi told me once. "The mountains dwarf even men's ambitions and aspirations. There's less gut thinking here—the mountains dwarf you and make you feel small." As Cervi saw it, Colorado, together with its mountain neighbors, had become a "withdrawal state"—a refuge for the wealthy, fleeing from confrontation with every real problem of the modern world.

Cervi died of a heart attack in 1970, thus depriving Denver of its most spirited journalistic voice. But he is a hard man to forget, because his little weekly (10,600 circulation) lived up so well to being what he called it—"controversial, disagreeable, unfriendly to concentrated power." The paper did not write about youth protest or campus discord, but stuck to the territory where Cervi believed the action was: economics and politics. He was a constant critic of utility rates and what he called the "rigged" prices of the chain supermarkets; he was always for the little man, always against arbitrary power.* When he died, Tom Gavin, columnist for the Denver *Post*, could write that Cervi was often wrong, "but about seven times in 10 he was right—searingly, piercingly, abrasively right." *Cervi's Journal* continues under the editorship of his daughter, Cle, with the same aims as the founder, but his righteous fire and thunder could scarcely be bequeathed.

The *Post*, with a circulation of 260,000 weekdays and 350,000 on Sundays, is the leading paper of the Intermountain West, and incidentally has one of the largest "news holes" of major U. S. dailies. While the *Post* turns more conservative in the post-Hoyt era, the rival *Rocky Mountain News*, traditionally more frothy and light in the typical Scripps-Howard manner, is becoming both more thoroughgoing in its coverage and more liberal in its point of view. The best state and local television news coverage is provided by the Denver CBS outlet, KLZ-TV.

Denver Miscellanea: Government, Metro, Hispanos and Blacks

For all its material progress, Denver harbors a set of socioeconomic problems that will require new levels of skilled leadership if the city is to fulfill its potential as a national population center, not only growing in size but

---

* In an interview with author Neil Morgan in the early 1960s, Cervi said: "I believe in private property. I also believe in editors being in politics. If not, why are you in business? I say openly what others can't say. A lot of editors would like to be better men, but their economic survival is dependent on their supporting *other* big business. What is there but spirituality and politics? . . .

"I believe you've got to be constantly nagging and scolding, at the price of burdensome unpopularity. . . . [Denver is] hell bent for respectability. . . . The ranches are larger, fewer, and corporate interests are taking over. Colorado is growing sedate politically. Me, I'm the son-ofabitch who carried the hod around here 40 years ago, and I don't forget it."

livable for people. Inextricably bound up with local Denver problems are those of planning for the entire Front Range if it is to avoid becoming one characterless strip city in the shadow of the mountains. Regional zoning and mass transit plans are only in the talk stage. With 90 percent of the state's population living on the Front Range, the state government might well step in itself as a kind of metropolitan government for the region. But only the most tentative steps toward area-wide planning or government had been taken by the early 1970s; the Denver Regional Council of Governments, for instance, had acquired some powers but was still years away from the direct taxing and administrative powers necessary to draw the region together. The Colorado Environmental Commission suggested in 1971 that a population limit of 1.5 million be set for the four-county Denver metropolitan area, a quarter million more than the 1970 Census count of 1,227,529. The plan would be implemented in part by a green belt of parks and agricultural projects 35 miles wide around Denver and its satellite communities. The legislature failed to act on the proposal, however.

Any fast-growing region is likely to be one in which the vast bulk of decisions affecting the shape of the land and cities are made by self-interested private groups with little heed to the public interest. Denver's metropolitan growth has been no exception. In 1969, outgoing Denver Planning Director James Braman, Jr., cited selfish moves for zoning variances, or opposition to public improvements at the expense of the city's environment, as examples of what afflicted the city.

Unusual candor about the city's problems has also been shown by the Denver Chamber of Commerce, which in 1969 acknowledged that there was a pressing need for 15,000 low-income housing units to stem urban blight by 1975, an expenditure of $100 million for school construction by 1989, and huge outlays for effective flood control and storm drainage facilities to protect the city from the ravaging effect of flash floods in the wake of periodic torrential downpours. No one seemed to know just where the money for all these improvements might come from in a city with an archaic, stringent limitation on general obligation bonds—only 3 percent of the assessed value of the city.

An example of Denver's short-sighted policies was revealed in 1968 when its two-term mayor, Tom Currigan, abruptly resigned to take a job with Continental Airlines. Currigan's stated reason for leaving: that Denver voters on three separate occasions had refused charter revisions to increase the mayor's $14,000-a-year salary. The job at Continental, Currigan said, would "enable me to meet my family responsibilities." Ironically, the new exhibition hall at the convention center is named after Currigan, possibly the only case on record of a city naming one of its great public buildings for a mayor who quit in disgust.

As another kind of monument to Currigan, the voters subsequently agreed to a charter revision making the mayor's salary $27,500 a year. Denver has traditionally been regarded as a Democratic bastion in the state, but in

1970 it elected a Republican to Congress (after the old-line Democratic incumbent had been upset by a liberal, antiwar contender in the Democratic primary). And in 1971, Mayor Bill McNichols, a conservative Democrat, was narrowly reelected with Republican support in a technically nonpartisan election. Republicans gained control of the city council in the same election.

Underlying race tensions played a role in the Republican/conservative rise in Denver. Denver's population is about 9 percent Negro and 12 percent Mexican-American. The two groups share many of the same problems (miserable housing, decrepit schools) but have proven almost totally unable to work together, due in no small part to the seemingly irrational tactics of the disorganized and disjointed Hispanos. The latter are deeply split between a wealthy minority of those who try to, and often succeed at, "passing" in the Anglo world, and the more militant, separatist segments, led by a Chicano "liberation" leader, Rudolph ("Corky") Gonzales. Many Hispanos are below Negroes on the economic totem pole and deeply resent the fact. The medium income of the average Hispano family is below that of the average black family, and the average grade finished in school is the eighth or ninth—compared to the 11th or 12th for blacks. Nearly half of Denver's unemployed and child welfare recipients are Mexican-American. But geographically, the Hispanos have been less hemmed in than the Negroes. Despite advanced open-housing efforts in Denver, the great bulk of Negroes are concentrated in a clearly defined population belt reaching northeast from center city toward the airport on the east.

The Denver black belt shows few of the signs of decay in the familiar eastern ghetto, and there are in fact some very prosperous looking neighborhoods occupied totally by blacks. A local Negro leader told me this might be deceiving, since there may be multiple occupancy and fatherless families behind the neat façades. The well-kept appearance of the black areas has an historic root: starting first with Pullman porters and waiters, and later with an influx of teachers and government workers, the Negro came to Denver in the hope of a less abrasive environment than the South. Essentially middle class in their views, the Negroes struggled hard to get ownership of their own homes and then kept their lawns neatly manicured in the best traditions of middle America. Only in recent years has there been a lower economic black influx, largely from Texas, followed by some angry militance among younger blacks and a small Black Panther chapter.

With Denver's traditionally relaxed black-white relations, the city became one of the leading centers in the U. S. for blacks to "pass over" into the white community; today those blacks are finding they have a tough row to hoe, since there may be a ceiling on their promotions when someone knows they are Negro. They are also getting increased heat from other blacks who criticize them for "selling out to whitey." Denver also has a substantial group of black-white marriages; many of these form their own social set while others are active in promoting an integrated social set with black couples, white couples, and intermarrieds together. Reportedly, the intermarriages at the middle and upper income levels hold together better than those among poorer people.

Over many years, the black community felt it could work within the system and get its fair share of power in Denver. In 1956, George L. Brown of Denver became the first Negro elected to any state senate west of the Mississippi; though there were less than 2,500 Negroes registered in the city at that time, he received a vote of 109,935.* (His opponent received 109,922, making the winning margin only 13 votes!) "We've got the best legal front of any state in the country to bar discrimination," Brown told me in an interview. A law prohibiting discrimination in public accommodations was passed back in 1895, and Brown himself sponsored successful fair-employment-practices legislation in 1957 and a fair-housing law (one of the strongest in the country when it was approved in 1959). In Colorado, Brown said, blacks have a higher achievement level and income level than in any other state.

Denver's image of racial moderation began to fade rapidly in the late 1960s over the issue of school integration. Despite a growing minority population, the public schools were still 65 percent white to 15 percent Negro and 20 percent Hispano. With what looked like general community support, including the Chamber of Commerce and the locally dominant Democratic party, an integration plan requiring busing of about 3,500 of the city's 96,000 students was approved by the school board. Both blacks and whites would be bussed, and every school would be predominantly white. But critics said the changes were against the will of the "silent majority," and in a 1969 school board election, two conservative Republicans who campaigned against "forced busing" were elected. The balance of power was shifted on the school board, which promptly rescinded the integration plan; later, after court action carried all the way to the Supreme Court, the busing plan was reinstated. But irreparable harm might have been done to Denver race relations; as Brown put it, "whitey had rejected us, and the black community was not only up tight but up together." After integration went into effect, fighting broke out between blacks and whites at two high schools. And on a winter night of February 1970, dynamite explosions destroyed 23 of the school buses, parked in a lot; three young white men were seen fleeing from the scene. A series of ugly bombings ensued, including a firebomb tossed into the home of one of the newly elected conservative school board members. Three days later, a blast destroyed the front porch of a local Negro who filed a school integration suit. Bombings followed in other Colorado cities as well as Denver, many with ugly racial overtones—all this in the state thought foremost in the Union on assurance of human rights.

Yet the same spring as the bombings, Denver's East High inaugurated a highly successful, integrated experiment in which 93 students, ranging from

---

* The vote figures are so high because Denver then elected its state senators county-wide; since the mid-1960s, election has been by districts, instead, in effect guaranteeing blacks and Mexican-Americans more seats in the legislature.

middle-class whites on their way to college to ghetto boys and girls who were virtual dropouts, were taken out of class and put in a special life experience program for the last half of their senior year. Together, they visited construction sites, gave a helping hand to the city sanitary department in trash collection, went to ballet class, and shared such real life experiences as shooting dangerous river rapids and living for several days with isolated Indian families on the Navajo Reservation in Arizona. Out of the experience emerged a group tightly knit together, aware of the need for discipline in dangerous situations (such as shooting rapids), and, one would think, immensely matured and able to relate to people as people, across sex and race lines.

Suburbia and the Close-in Cities: Boulder and Colorado Springs

Denver had 415,786 people in 1950 and 514,678 in 1970, a modest population growth that has now been slowed to a trickle except through annexations. The story of the surrounding suburban counties is altogether different. Jefferson County, most of its people squeezed in between Denver and the mountains, grew by 318 percent to 233,031 in the same two decades. Within its borders are a big federal regional office center; most of its people are middle income and most vote Republican. Arapahoe County, to the south of Denver, had 162,142 people by 1970, an increase of 211 percent since 1950; this is big country club territory, mostly upper income, and gold plate Republican. Finally, the suburban ring includes Adams County to the north, the home of more low to middle income people—craftsmen, factory and foundry workers. In 1970, Adams had 185,789 people, up 361 percent since 1950. Once strongly Democratic, Adams is now gaining in wealth and drifting slowly in a conservative—i.e., Republican—direction. At least populationwise, the suburbs are now the tail that can wag the Denver dog; since they are Republican, and the city Democratic, the trend is there for all to see. But the Republicanism has its limits; in 1964, for instance, all three suburban counties went for Johnson over Goldwater, and in other isolated races they have given statewide Democratic candidates their margin of victory.

The new Denver suburbanites, drawn by scientific-type jobs and the climate, tend to be an extremely well educated lot. But their education is in engineering and other technical fields, not education of a humanistic sort; one would look in vain here for much social sensitivity. Many of these people grew up in conservative plains states like Iowa, Missouri, Kansas, and Nebraska. The new Denver suburbs may not be as conservative as Orange County, California (to name an extreme example), but they unquestionably lean in that direction, presenting a clear example of the suburban psychosis, modern U. S. A.: keep the cities, the turmoil, all the problems away from us.

Two of America's handsomest little cities—Boulder (pop. 66,870) and Colorado Springs (135,060)—lie north and south of Denver on the Front

Range. Boulder, home of the University of Colorado's attractive pink sandstone campus, has high mountains rising in its back yard and is said to be the only town in the country which owns a glacier (used in part for a water supply). It is also one of the world's windiest cities; during a 1969 snowstorm, the gauge registered 135 miles an hour. Much of the intellectual power in Colorado is closely connected to the university, and Boulder has done an excellent job in supplying the state with managerial and professional manpower. Some of the conflicts between the university, the regents, and the legislature, especially over the issue of academic freedom, have been little classics, but the university appears to have emerged strengthened and vital.*

Not surprisingly, the university emerged as a center of liberal "peace" politics in the 1960s. In the field of natural sciences, the university now excels where it was once mediocre. Its scientific preeminence has attracted to Boulder such installations as the National Bureau of Standards Laboratories and the new National Center for Atmospheric Research, the latter housed in an I. M. Pei-designed monastery-like structure high on a piñon-dotted mesa south of the city. Industries—all "clean"—include IBM and Beech Aircraft. Boulder is also a major center for the performing arts in Colorado and offers close-in skiing in the wintertime. Alarmed about heroin use in the city, people of all life styles there united in 1970 in an effort to push the pushers out of town. And, looking apprehensively to their future, Boulder's voters in 1971 approved a study of the feasibility of limiting the city's population. At the same time, a young, "hip" majority was elected to the city council.

Colorado Springs has long been a national tourist mecca, endowed with spectacular Pikes Peak, soaring abruptly to 14,110 feet beside the city, and the weird, colorful rock formations of the Garden of the Gods. Spencer Penrose's unique resort invention, the famous Broadmoor Hotel, is now more than half a century old and seems to be constantly expanding with new facilities ranging from year-round skating to a zoo on the slopes of Cheyenne Mountain. Penrose, a Philadelphia transplant who made his first fortune in silver and gold, would be pleased to see how the Broadmoor continues to profit—and to run Colorado Springs.

The greatest enricher of Colorado Springs today, however, is not tourism as much as the U. S. taxpayer, by way of the national defense budget. In 1946, a wartime air force base near the city was closed; the community leaders determined never to be in a position to lose a military base unnecessarily. An aggressive local group played the major role in getting Colorado Springs selected as the site for the new Air Force Academy, completed in 1958. Construction of the vast bombproof cave in Cheyenne Mountain where the North American Air Defense Command (NORAD) has its nerve center cost $143 million. And the largest military installation of the city, Fort Carson,

---

* An example of modern university conflict: Joe Coors, a brewer from Golden, Colorado, sits on the board of regents and tries to hold the university to more traditional ways; his efforts are aided immensely, of course, by the far-out tactics of some student dissenters. But in 1970, two liberal Democratic candidates for the board won election over two hard-line, conservative Republicans backed by Coors.

home of the Fifth U. S. Infantry Division, continues to pump money into the Colorado Springs economy.

The dramatic setting of the Air Force Academy, in the shadow of the rugged Rampart Range, is enhanced by the architecture of the multi-faith Cadet Chapel with its 17 aluminum-and-steel spires rising 150 feet above the valley floor. (Personally, I found the jagged spires unique but not beautiful; the architects did even better with the inside of the chapel and its combination of stained glass and clear windows that guide eye and spirit outside into the airman's infinite blue sky.) The remainder of the buildings at the base are clean-cut in glass and steel but low silhouetted; most of the installation (covering part of an 18,000-acre tract) reflects that seemingly inevitable sterility in military design. But the academy's popularity as a tourist attraction cannot be denied; more than a million visitors come each year. With time, the academy was living down the odoriferous reputation from the football scandal of its early years, but in 1972 a number of cadets were accused of academic cheating. The faculty, however, is said to be first rate.

Prepared for a Doomsday all hope will never come, the underground NORAD citadel has the capability to "button up" from the outside world and coordinate World War III for 30 days. The first warning of air attack on the U. S. or Canada would be flashed to this center from arctic radar, and the air defense battle directed from it. Ground was broken for the subterranean steel city of 11 structures, with a roof of granite some quarter mile thick, in 1961. Some five years, 1.1 million pounds of explosive, 470,000 cubic yards of excavated granite, 90,000 rock bolts, 42,000 cubic yards of concrete and 7,000 tons of steel later, the project was completed. Huge blast doors, each with a swing weight of 25 tons, open and then close behind the visitor to the strange buried complex of giant tunnels and three-story buildings—each on giant steel coil shock absorbers designed to minimize the effect of a nearby nuclear blast or an earthquake. Incoming air is filtered through a system of eight chemical, biological, and radiological filters to remove harmful germs or radioactive and chemical elements, and all communications to the outside are by microwave routes and coaxial cable hardened against nuclear blast effects.

Walking through this eerie, windowless, world—which was also scheduled to be missile command control center for the Safeguard ABM missile command—and glancing over the banks of computer controls and display screens in the command control post, I was overcome by a sense of total unreality. Those ghostly outlines of the continent on the electronic displays, one felt, had nothing to do with the real world of humans young and old, sad and happy, rich and poor, the world of field, forest, and plain, of farms, towns, cities where the existence we all know on earth takes place.

The major military presence in Colorado Springs abets conservatism, but long before the military arrived the town was a predictably Republican bastion. No small measure of right-wing extremism also raised its head in Colorado Springs, aided, abetted, and encouraged by the town's leading daily, the *Gazette-Telegraph*. The thinking of the late owner-publisher Raymond C. Hoiles, who died in 1970, was described by *Time* magazine as the "right of Herod. . . . He has attacked Herbert Hoover and the National Association of Manufacturers as too left-wing, called all taxes 'the theft of wages,' argued that fire departments, public libraries, highways and even armed forces ought to be maintained strictly through voluntary contributions." Other components of the conservative admixture in Colorado Springs have included such installations as the right-wing Freedom School and Rampart College at nearby Larkspur, supported, among others, by publisher Hoiles. The rival (and much more liberal) Colorado Springs *Free Press* was owned for many years by the International Typographical Union but was purchased in 1970 by Hank Greenspun, owner of the lively Las Vegas *Sun*.

A final note on the Front Range. At Fort Collins (43,337), north of Denver and Boulder, there is another facility behind great concrete walls. But it is quite different from NORAD. It is the National Seed Storage Laboratory, where specimens of thousands of seeds, including many varieties of vegetable, fruit, and plant now virtually extinct are kept dormant in vaults at a constant temperature of 35 degrees and relative humidity of 35 percent. The U. S. Agriculture Department maintains the seed collection as a source of genetic material for plant breeding. Some seeds can be preserved for as long as 100 years, ready to germinate and reintroduce special qualities for which they may be noted.

The Other Colorados: Eastern Prairie, the Depressed South

So far, we have viewed only the Colorado world of the Front Range. Within the perfect surveyor's dream that is Colorado, a perfect rectangle that measures some 400 miles from east to west and 300 from north to south, other civilizations prosper in vividly contrasting life styles. We will start on the eastern plains, move to the impoverished southern counties, and then across the divide into Western Slope lands.

The farm lands of eastern Colorado are part and parcel of the Great Plains climatic zone. Broken occasionally by sand hills and isolated buttes, much of it is as smooth and level as a tidal flat—which, in fact, it was in the distant past. Aridity is the overwhelming fact of life on these eastern Colorado plains; this is dry farming country of sparse rainfall, often afflicted by high winds, sometimes torn by an angry tornado. The brown, parched landscape is broken by the thin green ribbons of irrigated farmlands along the valleys of the South Platte River (angling northeasterly into Nebraska) and the Arkansas (southeasterly into Kansas).

Three times the land of eastern Colorado has almost been destroyed: first by the overgrazing of the early cattle syndicates; second by the exploiting wheat farmers at the time of World War I, who brought in steam tractors, tore up raw prairie, and sowed the seeds of the dustbowl of the 1930s; and finally when production was pushed to unnatural levels during World War II, to be followed by the drought of the early 1950s, actually more severe, albeit shorter, than that of the '30s. The last drought was not as economically disastrous, since the farmers were better equipped, technically, to deal with it. With increasing irrigation water diverted from the western slope of the Rockies, and especially through the tapping of the subsurface waters, many new lands are now available for sugar beets, corn, and other crops that could never subsist on the natural rainfall.* But the use of subsurface waters poses the threat of thoughtless exploitation once more; part of a dense aquifer of varying depths which runs from Canada to Mexico, the water table is dropping rapidly in many localities, with prognostications for its future accessibility running between 10 and 75 years, depending on the locality. When it becomes exhausted, and as increasing population along the Front demands more and more of the Rockies water, plains agriculture may again be in peril.

Colorado has been losing close to 1,000 farmers a year for most of the postwar era; smaller farms simply find their operations uneconomical and sell out to larger operations. Corporate farming has even had a toehold with a 10,000-acre operation run by Gates Rubber. The small farmers forced out of business often end up as workers in the golden industrial strip along the Front Range, their mechanical skills put to work in the new factories. Eastern Colorado also has substantial cattle grazing on its sand hills, though the great lands for cattle and sheep are in the western mountains with their greater moisture and grass cover. (Livestock production accounts for three-quarters of Colorado's $1.1 billion annual farm income, with cattle and calves nine times the dollar bulk of sheep.)

Anyone who thinks every farmer is a clod should meet Amer Lehman, the farmer from the tiny hamlet of Idalia, Colorado, near the Kansas line, whom I interviewed about eastern Colorado farming. Lehman's appearance —an angular, weathered face, crewcut grey hair—reflects the hard life on the land. But he attended a liberal arts college and spent several years working for the U. S. Department of Agriculture in Denver; his grasp of the great geophysical patterns of the plains and mountains, of the delicate balance between man and nature on the land, is as great as that of any man I have met. Apparently Lehman makes a solid success of farming the land his father first homesteaded, growing enough feed on several hundred acres of highly productive land to winter some 500 to 600 calves each year. He then turns some onto 4,000 acres of sandhill grazing land for the summer, sells others for feeders, and puts still others in feed lots (the cattle hotels), depending on market conditions and the grazing capacity of his land. To the novice, it

* A Colorado favorite for irrigating with subsurface waters is the "whirly bird," a kind of liquid pinwheel with watering arms, some quarter mile in length, rotating on wheels. The effect is like that of a giant, slow-motion garden sprinkler. A whirly bird uses much less water than flood irrigation and can cover 137 acres; each unit costs up to $18,000, however, an example of the heavy investment modern farmers must make. Seen from the air, the pattern left by the whirly birds is like that of great green lily pads set on the brown backdrop of unwatered fields.

all sounds like a highly complex operation, requiring immense knowledge and ability; in effect it is the sophisticated farmer, who also is willing to borrow enough money to get the most out of his resources, who is able to survive.

It was Lehman who pointed out to me that eastern Colorado is really a land of two cultures. North of the Arkansas River, it is virtually indistinguishable from Nebraska or western Kansas—strongly Republican, Protestant, a land of "Blue uniform families" from Civil War days. South of the Arkansas, one is in territory as southwestern as Arizona or New Mexico. Catholicism and Democratic sentiment are predominant, and much of the population is Latin. The county names—Las Animas, Costilla, Alamosa, Conejos—all testify to the special complexion.

The Spanish-American population is heavy on both the eastern and western sides of the mountains in Southern Colorado.* One of the most fascinating areas is the beautiful San Luis Valley, where Colorado's first permanent settlement was established in 1853. Set at 7,500 feet altitude and some 100 miles in length, the mountain-lined valley is naturally arid but heavily irrigated; the big crop is potatoes, followed by lettuce, cabbage, and carrots; there are many big farms akin to those in California's Central Valley. But if the agriculture is fairly unitary, the people are not. In Costilla County, the population is about three-quarters Hispano; many are descendants of the free Spanish settlers who followed the triumphal march of the Conquistadores, or of retainers of the *haciendados* who took control of various parts of the Southwest under the seal of the Spanish and Mexican governors at Santa Fe. Many people of Costilla County live today in deep poverty; their vote is unfailingly Democratic. The Hispanos also dominate in neighboring Conejos County, but there they vote Republican, for reasons said to be rooted in ancient ethnic rivalries. Oddly enough, the Democratic chairman of Conejos for many years has been a Polish Jew (he's said to be the only Jew in the county), while the Republican chairman is a Japanese Buddhist.

The San Luis Valley, steel-making Pueblo (97,453) and declining coal-mining towns like Walsenburg (4,329), Trinidad (9,901) are the best-known landmarks of the seriously depressed southern Colorado region which state and especially federal agencies have been trying to revive over the past several years. Many families live below the poverty level, and there are high rates of unemployment, illiteracy, infant deaths, and draft rejections. A Southern Colorado Economic Development Commission, operating with grants from the federal Economic Development Administration, has sponsored such projects as a tourist center at San Luis, hospitals, vocational training centers, and water, sewer, and irrigation systems. The development commission, with grass roots participation ranging from mayors and county commissioners to Spanish-speaking people, gets professional and technical aid from the "practical eggheads" at Southern Colorado State College. The project is considered

* The city of Pueblo, located in the south, is said to be the northern apex of a triangle of heavy Hispano population in the U.S.A., the other legs set at San Diego and San Antonio.

one of the more successful federally-aided recovery programs in the nation, but all admit it has a long way to go to create an economically viable base in a region of huge spaces, intense summer heat, and deprived, welfare-dependent people.

Southern Colorado is actually the southern anchor of the otherwise prosperous Front Range Corridor, where most of Colorado's growth is taking place. In much of southern Colorado, by contrast, population is actually declining. In 1970 the governor and local legislators moved quickly to condemn and then suppress a report to the state planning office which included such statements as these about southern Colorado:

In the region there are possibly two "Italian" organizations that may or may not be "Mafia."

There is relative stagnation of social, political, cultural, economic, intellectual, etc., atmosphere in the South Front Range area.

Gambling is prevalent—it has some local organizations and connections with out-of-region gambling interests.

There is much cynicism regarding the methods and objectives of the courts and law enforcement agencies and of their presumed connections with the Mafia or other powerful interests.

Other sources told me that the Mafia is particularly entrenched in Pueblo, where legend says $50 is the top price to get someone wiped out and the police have been reported to play both sides of the cops and robbers game. A purely blue-collar, lunch bucket town, Pueblo presents an overwhelmingly dreary face to the world, even though there is now real hope with a new Department of Transportation test site there and more adequate water supply through the Fryingpan-Arkansas project. But in the early 1950s the city's single greatest steel-producer, Colorado Fuel and Iron, had about 10,000 men on its payroll; now, with automation, the total is around 5,000. The once prosperous soft coal industry of the region is now reduced to a single operating mine near Trinidad which creates work for 800 men; at the heydey of coal production, 15,000 to 20,000 men were employed. For the remaining workers who have not moved away, life now consists of odd jobs or living on welfare; the towns of the region are uniformly run down, their streets still the old concrete slabs of the 1920s, many houses surrounded by weeds.

The labor history of this area is rife with tragedy. As the soft coal fields opened up, thousands of miners were imported from the Balkans and Mexico, many arriving literally in cattle cars. In 1913–14, the United Mine Workers sought recognition and some minimal rights for workers, but the Rockefeller-owned Colorado Fuel and Iron Company resisted stoutly. At Ludlow near Trinidad there was a clash between militia and striking coal miners in which 21 died, including women and children who were burned or suffocated to death in the miners' tents. Many more were killed or injured in another strike in 1927, and only then did the Mine Workers gain recognition. CF & I refused to recognize the Steelworkers until the time of World

War II. The Rockefellers eventually sold out in 1945, but in far-away West Virginia, young Jay D. Rockefeller is still politically embarrassed by the one-time barbarities of his great-grandfather's firm.

In modern Colorado, Pueblo is the center of labor political strength, with some 15,000 members spread out among Steelworkers, building trades-men, brewery, meatpacking, and machinists. The strong effort of the AFL–CIO is the major reason that southeastern Colorado sends a Democrat to Congress. But as union jobs decline, so does the comparable weight of this area—and thus organized labor—in statewide politics.

Western Slope: Mountains, Mines, and Skis

We come now to western Colorado and the chains of towering peaks along the Continental Divide, the ridgepole of a continent from which the waters flow north and west to the Pacific, east and south to the Gulf of Mexico. Coloradans are fond of quoting the startling height statistics: that of the Rocky Mountain summits which rise more than 14,000 feet, all are in Colorado; that of the 81 peaks of such altitude on the entire North American continent, Colorado has 54. By virtue of these lofty mountains, Colorado's average elevation is 6,800 feet—highest of any state of the Union.

This is the land of summer snow banks in high ranges, of mountain plateaus and icy Alpine lakes, of small emerald valleys with cascading streams where early autumns turn the delicate aspen to bright gold, of stands of pine and spruce, of passes 12,000 feet above the sea. Proceeding further west from the Divide, one comes on the semiarid uplands of the Colorado Plateau, where the western scourge of aridity again appears: here lushness of mountainscape gives way to the stark beauty of abrupt escarpments and deep gorges, preparing one for the desert-like stretches of neighboring Utah.

Western Slope culture is that of the Intermountain West: large cattle and sheep ranching operations (with much grazing on federal lands), ghost towns and remnants of old mining glory, the free and easy social attitudes, cowboy hats and secluded mountain towns. Tourism is the modern mother lode; millions come each year to see Rocky Mountain National Park and the cliff dwellings of prehistoric times at Mesa Verde National Park, to ski on the magnificent runs, to camp or spend some weeks at dude ranches, to fish, boat, or ride horseback, to golf, climb mountains, or hunt for upland birds and big game in the frosty autumn air.*

Skiing is without question the great tourist industry success story of Colorado's postwar years. In 1945 there were just two ski areas in the state with a total capital investment of some $50,000, the business largely restricted to weekends. Today Colorado has 29 ski areas with more than $40 million invested in lifts and mountain facilities, not to mention the millions spent

---

* Colorado's overall income from tourism has now reached $600 million a year.

for accommodations at major ski resort centers including Aspen, Vail, Breck-enridge, Snowmass, Crested Butte, and Mount Werner. Close to a million and half skiers visit Colorado's slopes each winter, the vast bulk necessarily from out of state. Only an exceedingly affluent nation could support such an industry; not only are there the substantial transportation costs in reaching Colorado ski areas from the population centers of the country, and in paying for accommodations, but skiing itself is an expensive sport; a skier must expect to spend somewhere between $300 and $600 for proper skis and clothing. Why does a vastly differentiated skiing public, ranging from college students to rich businessmen, shopkeepers to physicians, nurses to lawyers, make the investment? There are probably as many reasons as there are skiers, but it has been suggested that for many Americans, living under the pressures of an essentially artificial urban life, beset by a vague malaise about the lack of physical challenge in their everyday lives, skiing offers the totally unique and different. There is the exhilaration of exposure to nature in its pure white winter mantle, of sometimes being totally alone in a wilderness-like setting, of effortless speeds and a touch of the dangerous and the daring, and the special camaraderie of the skiing fraternity in a setting utterly cut off from the confines and terms of everyday life.

One of the most interesting ski developments is that of Vail, 110 miles west of Denver, where an entire Swiss Alpine village was created in the early 1960s out of what has been called by its founder, Peter W. Seibert, a "wasteland at the foot of a nameless mountain." Yet by the end of the decade, Vail was receiving some 350,000 skiers a season, had a total investment of $70 million and an annual budget of $650,000, and could boast 14 hotels and lodges, two dormitories, eight complexes of private homes, apartments, and condominium developments, 33 restaurants and bars, a bank, and numerous shops. It is a resort for all seasons.

Gold and silver mining, the industry that first opened the Western Slope to permanent settlement, has been in the doldrums for many years. This is not to say that the flow of valuable minerals from the high mountain country has ceased altogether; uranium, zinc, and lead are all mined in some locations, and at the Climax Mine, perched on a mountainside north of Leadville, there is a roaring $100-million-a-year business in molybdenum, a mineral vital to the hardening of steel. The single mine at Climax produces more than half of the wealth currently produced by metallic mineral mining in the state.

Colorado ranks 12th among the states in oil and gas production ($98 million value in 1970). But all the minerals ever extracted in the state pale in significance before the prospect of synthetic oil and gas production from the oil shale encased in the federally owned Piceance Creek Basin north of the Colorado River between Grand Junction and Rifle. Government geologists estimate that two *trillion* barrels of oil may one day be recovered from these deposits and others in nearby Utah and Wyoming; the total amount would be six times greater than all the proven reserves of crude petroleum on earth, enough to supply the oil needs of the United States for several centuries. The Colorado shale deposits, in thicknesses of up to 2,000 feet, account for about three-quarters of this total. Pilot plants have already demonstrated the feasibility of processing the shale to produce synthetic oil, though further technological advances are required before Kerogen (the crude oil equivalent that is heated, liquified, and extracted from the shale) can be processed at a price fully competitive with conventional crude oil.

The exploitation of this vast underground bonanza presents exciting possibilities, not only in satisfying the nation's energy requirements but in meeting environmental problems. Chris Welles, author of *The Elusive Bonanza* and a foremost authority on shale development, reports: *

Though resembling it physically, shale oil is *not* crude oil but a potential competitor of crude oil, just as synthetic fibers are competitors of natural fibers. Shale oil should not be thought of as a mere supplement to crude, to be produced only when it is "needed," but as a potential replacement. For many reasons, shale oil is a superior product. Disinterested estimates show production costs considerably lower than those involved in finding and developing additional domestic crude reserves, and while costs of crude are continually rising, shale costs, with improved technology and economies of scale, are likely to decline. Shale, according to recent studies, may also be an economical source of natural gas, the domestic supplies of which have been shrinking alarmingly. Substantial shale production could eliminate the country's eventual dependence on foreign imports. Unlike most crude, shale oil is very low in pollution-causing sulphur. And shale production would be free from many environmental hazards of crude, such as off-shore well ruptures, oceangoing tanker disasters, and despoilment of wilderness areas such as Alaska and the Arctic.

Shale would be recovered by strip mining and deep open-pit mines like those used in copper production. The natural landscape would be forever altered, but, as one Colorado oldtimer has put it, much of oil shale country is so bleak and remote that "a self-respecting jackrabbit wouldn't live there." After extraction, the residual ash could be used to fill in the open pits and nearby gullies and canyons and new grass cover begun on top of it. Balanced against the hazards of crude oil production and its sulphur content, Welles told me, the dangers to nature from shale production would not be a major environmental problem.

Yet there are problems in developing shale, 80 percent of which is on federally owned land, partially affected by old mining claims. Colorado is a water-scarce state, but great quantities of water would be required for shale processing, and the waters of the nearby Colorado River are earmarked by compacts to six basin states in addition to Colorado. The Interior Department, which controls the land, is leery of concluding any agreements with oil companies or other potential producers that could trigger charges of a public resource "give-away" or "Teapot Dome." Finally, there appears to be substantial foot-dragging on the part of the great American oil companies. They have purchased claims or sought long-term leases on vast amounts of shale land, but have invested little more than token amounts in research

* In an article entitled "Keeping Shale Under Wraps," *The Nation,* July 20, 1970.

leading toward production. (Atlantic Richfield appears to be an exception). The reason for the oil firms' reticence would seem to be that the industry fears a shattering reassessment of its monopolistic price structure, its tax depletion allowance and import quotas which inflate domestic oil prices. Nevertheless, Interior Secretary Rogers C. B. Morton announced in 1971 that the government would begin, in late 1972, offering leases on six 5,000-acre tracts of shale land in sealed competitive bids, looking forward to marketing on a limited basis by the late 1970s and full production by 1985. The government hopes to get a detailed inventory of how much shale is available and its quality, to assess the environmental impact of recovery operations, and to assess the value of other minerals that might be byproducts (including aluminum and "nahcolite," which can be used in the reduction of sulphur in smokestacks). If the remaining obstacles can be overcome, one expert in the field has said, cheap oil shale might make "Texas and Oklahoma start looking like another Appalachia."

The Western Slope has few cities worthy of the name—naturally enough, since the real action is in the great outdoors. The largest town is Grand Junction, but its 20,170 people account for less than 1 percent of Colorado's population. In the 1950s, Grand Junction was the hub of a heady uranium rush; then that industry declined and the town awaits a new boom, perhaps if uranium soars once more, or if commercial oil shale development starts nearby. As a shopping magnet for the Slope, Grand Junction has been losing ground rapidly to a "golden triangle" of the resort cities of Glenwood Springs, Aspen, and Vail. Durango (pop. 1933) in the southwest corner, once a wide-open frontier town, now lives off local trading and tourism; one of Colorado's most interesting tourist attractions is the narrow gauge train of the Rio Grande Railway, pulled to Silverton and back each day by an old cinder-belching steam engine.

For old western mining camp nostalgia, no Colorado town can compare with windblown, two-mile-high Leadville, which had a population of 30,000 in the late 19th century when it was one of the world's richest silver producers. Now there are only 4,314 people in Leadville, and while some of the ancient glory is preserved in places like the Hotel Vendome and the Tabor Opera House, a pervasive atmosphere of decay prevails along the down-at-the-heels main drag and the unpaved back streets. (I once stopped in Leadville for a haircut and found myself anchored in the chair for an hour as the old barber took the occasion to spin his yarns for what must have been a very infrequent customer.)

Leadville loves to tell the story of silver king H. A. W. Tabor, who built a fortune on a $17 grubstake but died almost penniless; his divorce from his first wife to marry beautiful Elizabeth McCourt (Baby) Doe in a glittering wedding attended by President Chester Arthur was a scandal that rocked Colorado and Washington, where he had gone to serve as an interim Senator. Tabor's last words to Baby Doe were: "Hang on to the Matchless—it will make millions again." So Baby Doe withdrew to the Matchless, the mine from which Tabor had once made as much as $100,000 a month (at the cost of many miners' lives). One can still visit the old shack at the mine, with cardboard and yellowed newspapers covering the walls, where she lived the life of a total recluse until she was found frozen to death in 1935, at the age of 80.

My favorite Leadville character, however, still lives; she is Helene Monberg, a Washington correspondent for a number of Western newspapers who is renowned for her salty language and willingness to tell Senators, Cabinet members, and anyone else who crosses her path just what she thinks of them. Her utter honesty and encyclopedic knowledge of the West have won her wide respect.

Has Success Spoiled Aspen?

Colorado's foremost ski resort—and a place famous for a lot of other things too—is Aspen, set among fast-rising mountain slopes in the valley of the Roaring Fork River across Independence Pass from Leadville. Unlike Vail, Aspen has a history. It began as a silver mining town, producing millions of dollars in silver-bearing ore and once a nugget weighing more than a ton. In its first heyday, Aspen was one of the major stops for theatrical companies on their tours from the East to San Francisco, and many of the fine old Victorian homes still stand. But in 1893, silver was demonitized and the Aspen boom ended; the town never became a ghost town, but it did go into a long decline.

Aspen's second birth was presaged by the arrival in 1945 of Walter Paepcke, chairman of the Container Corporation of America. Paepcke founded the Aspen Institute for Humanistic Studies, bringing men from American Business management to two-week conferences with moderators of national stature—men like Walter Reuther, John Dos Passos, and Clarence Randall. The high-level seminars touched such far-ranging subjects as Far Eastern Thought, Basic Assumptions, Man's Commitment and Decision Making, the Individual in Society, and Power and Responsibility. At their best, the seminars truly gave corporate leaders an opportunity to reexamine their basic beliefs and premises, to rediscover their humanism. In addition, music and art festivals, design conferences, and film festivals were all brought to Aspen, and a small artistic colony took shape.

Paepcke also took a lively interest in the development of Aspen as a ski resort, and from very modest beginnings in the 1940s skiing grew and grew in Aspen until today there are more miles of slope and trail (200) and more ski lifts (30) than anywhere else in the United States; several of the slopes are now of international renown. The combination of ski and culture made Aspen a favorite spot for some of America's leading families (the Kennedys most publicized among them) and industrial-government leaders (Robert S. McNamara, IBM's Thomas Watson, and others). Not a few of that peculiar postwar phenomenon, the ski bums, were also attracted. In the mid-1950s—early enough to make a difference—zoning was instituted to prevent the worst abuses in rapid development, and the town had the foresight to ban billboards on the approaches to town or large signs within. (Now there is even a Holiday Inn without that gaudy, flashing monstrosity of a sign that blights the rest of the American landscape.)

In the 1960s, the development of new facilities at Aspen began to accelerate at a breathtaking pace. Colorado's condominium law stimulated the building of many multistoried Swiss chalet-style apartment buildings. There was also the new Snowmass at Aspen, a superbly designed, self-contained ski village several miles from town which is not unlike Vail in its attempt to devise lodges, homes, and shops which blend in tastefully with the natural landscape. Opened in 1967, Snowmass at Aspen is intended by its aggressive promoters to be the nation's largest ski resort with close to $100 million invested in five self-contained villages and 250 miles of trails. But at the start of the 1970s, a slowdown in new developments became noticeable as a result of the national economic downturn, local opposition, and county zoning restraints.

I have had periodic contact with Aspen through my brother Everett, who decided in 1960 that he had had enough of Philadelphia suburban commuting and the treadmill with the family business. So he, his wife Freddie, and three children packed all their belongings in a trailer and headed West just as Horace Greeley had advised young men to do almost a century before. They started out camping on the banks of the Roaring Fork, then purchased a guest ranch not far from Aspen, and kept themselves busy in the winters by taking over the franchise for the restaurants at one of the ski runs. Everett would run the restaurant at the base, Freddie the restaurant at the top; her routine was to ride the lift up in the morning to start business and then, at the end of the day, to ski home!

Today such stories are much more frequent, as an increasing number of Americans leave their settled professional worlds behind them to strike out for a new place without guarantee of abode or livelihood. The inflow of new people into Aspen has made it, in a few short years, one of the most cosmopolitan places in the U. S. A. (especially heavy on young people searching an oasis of individualism). But there is still some of the spirit that writer Neil Morgan caught when he visited Aspen a decade ago, discovered my brother's family, and wrote of them in *Westward Tilt* as "a family who had all but abandoned themselves to nature, and who seemed among the happiest of people. . . . My last glimpse of them was as they skied off at the summit of the highest ski lift above Aspen into the dazzling, limitless blue and white of the Rockies."

Aspen in its early postwar years probably attracted as many free souls as any other small town of America; ironically, one hears that many of the early ski bums, now turned shopkeeper and affluent, are the most intolerant of the long-haired hippie generation that likes to lounge in their doorways. Aspen has changed in lots of other ways, too, and not necessarily for the better.

This I heard from none other than the mayor of the 1960s, physician Robert Barnard. Dr. Barnard is a transplanted Californian who has a love for sports car racing, collects antique automobiles (he has a magnificent old Pierce Arrow and 1928 Chrysler Imperial), lives in a stunning modern A-frame house with mountain view, enjoys flamboyant clothes (purple shirt and blue jeans the day I met him), and loves to tangle with the big interests. If for no other reason, Barnard should be remembered as the man who got Aspen's streets paved; this minimal task had been left undone until the 1960s, making the town, in Barnard's words, "the only place where you could be up to your knees in mud and still have dust blowing in your face."

Barnard's complaint list about Aspen is long. Twenty years ago, he said, it was a sleepy little town, extremely seasonal, with a winter ski season and brief summer tourist invasion. In the late 1950s, many new ski areas, including some miles out of town, began to appear. Now people need buses or must rent cars to get to the runs, and there are huge wintertime traffic jams. "The speculators and developers hit here around 1963," Barnard said, "building with total disregard for the need in the community or its capacities. They created a great burden on Aspen, a town with 2,400 permanent residents, for water, sewage, electricity, streets, even schools. Now we're struggling to get a new sewer system in; our system is built for 5,000, but we get up to 15,000, and as a result we've converted the Roaring Fork into a sewer." Barnard also complained that many condominiums had been built as tax shelters for people with big incomes from other sources, anxious to write off trips and the like. And many of the big ski operators, he said, were demonstrating utterly ruthless tactics to get things built quickly—and the way they wanted. Rapid development has forced the price of land and construction to soar, he said, and working people can scarcely afford to live in town; the city engineer, for example, has to drive 10 miles down the valley and live in a trailer court.

Along with its writers, artists, and profit-minded developers, Aspen still has a high quotient of ski bums, working on ski patrols, as instructors, or in restaurants, not a few to pay for drug habits. The housing shortage was forcing a lot of communal living among ski bums and hippies "on a coeducational basis." The town is said to be a great spot for marijuana smoking and some experimentation with stronger drugs. The editor of the local paper, when I asked him about this, gave me a blank look and said, "If you mean, is pot smoked here, the answer is it's just the same as in San Francisco, Denver, or New York." But the mayor reported that in 1968 a whole planeload of drugs was discovered by authorities on landing at the Aspen airstrip. "It boggles the mind," he said, but disagreed with the alarm of the local sheriff: "To listen to him, you'd think the whole place was going to pot." The mayor insisted that the local hippie population "are fairly unsightly looking rascals, but they cause little trouble. Some of the fat cats who object the most to having them are the same slum landlords who rent substandard type dormitories to them."

In the late 1960s, a group of relative newcomers to Aspen, mostly people in their thirties, became interested in shifting power away from the development-minded. To them, as to many long-time residents, it was clear that the very things that made Aspen unique and attractive—the beautiful mountain valley setting, the lack of crowding, pollution, or crime—were being destroyed by the surfeit of new population. One of the men most concerned by these developments, former Houston lawyer Joe Edwards, was almost elected mayor in 1969. A year later a colorful writer, Hunter S. Thompson, proclaimed himself the champion of "freak power" and ran with strong hippie support for the post of sheriff of Pitkin County (which includes Aspen). He lost rather decisively, but the resistance to unthinking development was certainly gaining ground.

As for the late Walter Paepcke's Institute, many felt in the late 1960s that it had lost its vitality, had become a device for company-paid vacations for businessmen. But Joseph E. Slater, president of the Salt Institute, took over its direction in 1970, and the focus seemed to be widening from executives alone to more participation of people from government, education, science, the arts, youth, and minorities. The chairman of the board of the Institute is now Robert O. Anderson of Roswell, New Mexico, one of America's wealthiest men and biggest landowners.

What does Aspen contribute to the rest of Colorado? From state leaders outside of Aspen, the general reply was that it helps to draw tourists to the state and pays a big tax bill.

Solving the Water Dilemma

"Water is blood in Colorado," John Gunther reported in *Inside U. S. A.* "Touch water, and you touch everything; about water the state is as sensitive as a carbuncle." The reasons for this state of affairs are deceptively simple. Eastward-scudding clouds collide with the Rockies and deposit most of their moisture west of the Continental Divide. While more than nine out of every ten Coloradans live on the eastern side of the Divide, 69 percent of the state's water yield is to the west. Add to this the fact that Colorado, notwithstanding its moist high mountains, shares the problem of aridity with the remainder of the Mountain West, and the dimensions of the problem which, at least until recent years, set East Slopers against West Slopers and Coloradans in general against their neighbors, become clear. Each group fights fiercely for its share of the rivers that rise in the Rockies, flowing toward each point of the compass. Chief among these are the Colorado, lifeline of the American southwest, and its tributary, the Gunnison; the Rio Grande, racing toward Texas; the Arkansas and South Platte, flowing toward a long course over the parched plains; the North Platte, descending northward into the lonely marches of Wyoming. Before they reach the sea, these rivers will have watered 19 states, with the great bulk of the flow going westward.

Eastern Colorado's water needs are multifold: for thirsty Denver, with its million-plus metropolitan population, for Colorado Springs, fond of lawns, pools, and golf courses, for Pueblo with its water-consuming steel mill, for irrigation of the plains. The Denver Water Board has long been extremely aggressive in obtaining the water it needs, tapping first every available drop in Eastern Slope streams and then, through the engineering wonder of trans-mountain diversion, from the Western Slope. The Moffat Tunnel, first built for a railway, has had its pilot bore lined and now carries water eastward under the Divide. The huge Dillon Reservoir, fed by the Blue River, has since the early 1960s sent an annual 150,000 acre-feet of water to Denver through a 23.3-mile tunnel bored deep under the mountains.

The $160 million Colorado-Big Thompson Project, completed in 1959 by the U. S. Bureau of Reclamation, includes a 13.1-mile tunnel under Rocky Mountain National Park as well as a vast man-made reservoir, Lake Granby, which is fed by the Colorado River. The project also includes electric power plants, canals, and massive pumps which raise the water 200 feet before it begins its long gravity-powered flow to the farmlands of north-eastern Colorado.

To the south, similar diversion plans supply Colorado Springs and the southern Denver suburbs, some of the water diverted from as far as 140 miles away in the high Rockies. After years of contention, Congress in 1962 authorized the $202 million Fryingpan-Arkansas Project to divert 70,000 acre-feet of water each year from the lovely Fryingpan River, which runs down to the Roaring Fork below Aspen to join the Colorado. The water will be transmitted under the Divide through a 5.3-mile tunnel to join the headwaters of the Arkansas. The object is to provide municipal water for Colorado Springs and Pueblo and supplemental irrigation water for 280,000 acres in the Arkansas Valley of Colorado. Approval of such expensive proj-ects requires proof of multiple benefits before the assent of Congress can be obtained; thus Fryingpan-Arkansas will also provide hydroelectric power, flood control, fish and wildlife, and recreational benefits. Jealous of their own water supply, Western Slopers were long adamant in opposition but were finally mollified by provision of a major storage dam and reservoir to assure a constant supply of water on their side of the Divide. The interstate com-plexity of such ventures is illustrated by the fact that Southern California, almost a thousand miles distant, was long opposed to Fryingpan-Arkansas for fear that the quality and amount of Colorado River water it receives might be impaired. But substantial Californian support was finally obtained; at that point, the opposition of Eastern Congressmen who challenged its economic feasibility was not enough to stop authorization and funding of the project.

The bitter East-West Slope conflicts which preceded approval of most of these projects now appear to have subsided, chiefly because every drop of water that flows seems to have been captured and earmarked for someone. But Sen. Gordon Allott told me he foresaw the possibility of accelerating conflict in the future as Eastern Slope demands for the limited water supply escalate with population growth.

Colorado has also been successful in getting Congress to approve a multiplicity of other dams, reservoirs, and hydroelectric projects. They are all designed to preserve for the state use of the water accorded it under the Colorado River Compact and the Upper Colorado River Compact, the latter assuring Colorado 51.75 percent of the water allocated to the Upper Basin. Among these have been the gigantic Curecanti, Smith Fork, and Animas La Plata Projects scattered along the Colorado and its tributaries throughout the western part of the state. Virtually all these projects provoked Eastern and Midwestern opposition on the grounds that the nation's taxpayers were being asked to fund multi-hundred-million dollar projects of dubious cost effectiveness. But the state's potent Congressional delegation, including House Interior Committee Chairman Wayne Aspinall, who represents the Western Slope, finally prevailed. An affluent America might be said to have seriously underinvested in programs to help its impoverished whites, blacks, Hispanos, and Indians, to safeguard the environment, restore the cities, and assure an adequate education and medical care for all. But no one could reasonably accuse it of selfishness in funding water and reclamation projects for the Western states.

Varieties of Environmental Crisis

Amazingly, the state famed for its clean, high air today faces serious environmental problems—not as grave, perhaps, as those on the coasts or along the Great Lakes, but enough to cause real concern. There are as many as 50 days a year when automobile and industrial pollution block the view from Denver to the Rockies, 15 miles away; yet it was not until 1966 that Colorado passed its first air pollution law. At Greeley, the largest cattle feedlot in the world produces a daily sewage burden greater than that of the entire Denver metropolitan area. A crash program has been required to clean up the South Platte River, flowing through Denver, which a few years ago was found contaminated from sewage and sugar beet mill waste. As real estate promoters sell off pieces of mountain slope land for vacation and retirement homes, septic systems begin to overflow and run downhill to contaminate ponds and streams, and access roads alter the natural flow of moisture. There is intense concern in the state about the complex of six huge coal-burning power plants under construction in the Four Corners area (where Colorado meets New Mexico, Utah and Arizona); already the first plant is casting a pall of smoke over great stretches of the landscape, together with noxious gases. The power being produced is not for consumption in Colorado at all, but rather for export over cross-country transmission lines to California and other distant points.

Some of Colorado's environmental problems are more esoteric and potentially a lot more dangerous. Consider these examples:

Deadly nerve gas is produced at the Army's Rocky Mountain Arsenal, a short distance from the Denver Airport. In 1962 the arsenal began to pump millions of gallons of noxious liquid wastes down a 12,000-foot shaft drilled into a supposedly insulated geological formation. As a result, great rock masses were shifted and Denver had its first earthquake in 80 years, followed by 750 more. The Rocky Mountain Arsenal also stored some 27,000 pounds of nerve gas and their containers from World War II onward; when the cannisters began to corrode in the late 1960s, the Army, in what must have been a fit of lunacy, first developed a scheme to transport the mess across the teeming cities of the Midwest and New Jersey and then dump it into the Atlantic Ocean. Finally the decision was made to destroy the gas by reportedly safe on-site chemical procedures. A plane crash into this plant could well cause the deaths of thousands of people.

The Rocky Flats nuclear warhead plant, operated by the Dow Chemical Company at a location between Boulder and Denver, is the only factory in the country equipped for the mass production of plutonium parts for nuclear weapons—specifically, the triggers for hydrogen bombs. The plutonium is both highly flammable and radioactive. On May 11, 1969, the most serious accident in the history of the American nuclear weapons program occurred here when several hundred pounds of plutonium accidently caught fire, spreading intense radiation throughout the building and causing damage of some $45 million. The Denver *Post* reported that there had been more than 200 smaller previous fires at Rocky Flats since the facility opened in 1953. The Atomic Energy Commission insists that the plant releases no hazardous radiation into the air; a local environmental group claims that soil samples from as far as 10 miles distant show traces of escaped plutonium oxide dust, which is known to be hazardous.

And so the list goes on and on: reports of high cancer deaths among uranium miners (which led to sharply lowered levels of permissible exposure); a proposal to build a permanent atomic graveyard for radioactive wastes in Colorado; allegations that a fine cloud of radioactive dust rises from uranium mill "tailings" piled high in Durango; charges by *Cervi's Journal* that workers at the Rocky Flats plant are sometimes afflicted with various forms of cancer and leukemia said to be associated with plutonium exposure. Late in the 1960s, the Atomic Energy Commission even picked Colorado as site for "Project Rulison," involving underground nuclear detonations designed to free natural gas from tightly compacted earth and rock formations. Up to 400 shots were originally planned at the Rulison, Colorado, gas fields, and some environmentalists charged that getting the gas to the surface would involve high radiation hazards. Significant earth tremors, including an earthquake recorded at 3.5 on the Richter scale, were reported within 50 miles of an original blast in 1969. Citizen groups for protection of Colorado's environment have asked why, with the vast new discoveries of new energy sources in recent years, potentially risky undertakings like Project Rulison need be started at all. The AEC, both originator and judge of projects atomic, seems likely to be put under greater and greater pressure during coming years to justify its projects, new and old—especially in states like Colorado, where the agency's presence is so great.

Colorado Politics and Politicians

On the surface, Colorado is one of the most competitive two-party states in the Union, given to constant oscillation in party trends and cycles of one party control after the other. Elections over the past few decades for federal and state offices suggest a near-even split between the parties. The partisan total may be misleading, however. The state's political character might best be described as clean (political patronage is severely restricted) and oriented to moderation and middle-of-the-roadism rather than any ideological extreme. Colorado lacks the rabid Republican conservatism of some mountain and plains states; at the same time, it never seems happy for too long with an avowedly liberal Democratic governor or Congressman. The most successful Democrats have been men like House Interior Committee Chairman Wayne Aspinall or the late "Big Ed" Johnson, U. S. Senator and governor for 24 years; Johnson, a champion vote getter, was generally said to be as much a Republican as a Democrat, though his registration was Democratic. The philosophy of Aspinall and Johnson, and many other successful Colorado politicians, has been to worry about special state and district needs first and let the ideological issues come second.

Colorado's most innovative and daring governor of the past generation was Stephen L. R. McNichols, a Democrat who served six years starting in 1957. On issues like mental health, McNichols instituted basic reforms and put the state on a modern course. But he spent too fast and taxed too heavily for the state's taste; in his last years in office, revenues actually outran needs, and the arrogant side of his personality paved the way for his downfall in the 1962 elections.

Republican John A. Love, the man who upset McNichols and in 1970 won his third four-year term as governor, is as good a representative of the modern-day Colorado political mood as one might find. A Colorado Springs attorney who rose from almost total political obscurity to win the governorship, Love campaigned on the conviction that Coloradans were "tired of overspending and overtaxation" but identified himself as a "pragmatic," Theodore Roosevelt-style Republican who would not "turn back the clock." The Denver *Post* described him as a man with "a pleasant personality and looks which please women without irritating men." * Within 16 days of taking office in 1963, Love was able to sign into law the personal income tax reduction he had promised; two years later, however, he was obliged to raise taxes to meet rising state budgets. A studious, earnest man, Love has given the state even-handed leadership, concentrating on economic development, sharply in-

* Love's startling victory was engineered by Gene Toole, a brilliant operative who rebuilt the Colorado GOP as state party chairman in the early 1960s, and another man of extraordinary political skills, Denver County Republican chairman Robert Lee.

creased state aid to education, local governmental reform, and environmental problems. To little avail, some Colorado Republicans have complained about Love's liberalism on national party issues; in 1964 he supported Pennsylvania's Governor William Scranton over Goldwater for the GOP Presidential nomination, and in 1968 he backed Governor Nelson Rockefeller. In 1969 Love won some measure of national prominence by his election as chairman of the National Governors' Conference.

A glimpse of Love's role comes from this predictably acerbic 1969 quote by the late Gene Cervi: "The greatest suburb of all is John A. Love—he's right out of the Broadmoor: affable, handsome, tall, stuffy, on the make without knowing what for. The only backbone he showed was when he bucked the local rightists for Rockefeller." Cervi, of course, was a little unfair; he failed to mention, for instance, that Love in 1967 signed a controversial bill giving Colorado what was then the most liberal abortion law in the nation. Love has made at least an honest effort to tighten and expand state laws to protect the environment, tangling with both industrial interests and the billboard lobby. And he has shown real concern about the helter-skelter suburban sprawl along the Front Range. But he has also been faulted for lack of follow-up, especially on his proposals—like statewide zoning—to protect the environment.* Increasingly, Love's role as a moderate (sometimes even liberal) Republican in Colorado is becoming a lonely one. Distraught about the lack of a strong moderate wing in their own party, several prominent liberal Republicans have defected to the Democrats in the last few years.

At least in comparison to its sister states, Colorado government today shows substantial sensitivity to the needs of its people. It ranks well above the national average in total taxation related to personal income; its per capita expenditures for education rank sixth in the country, welfare fifth, health and hospitals tenth.† Whether all this is done with proper efficiency is open to question, since Colorado is close to the highest among the states in the number of state and local employees as a percentage of the population. But the constitution has been amended in recent years to reduce the multiplicity of state agencies; now there are 18 departments, most of whose executives are appointed directly by the governor.

The base of Republican strength, according to Colorado political sci-

---

* At Love's urging, the legislature in 1970 passed a land-use act requiring each county to set up a planning group and write regulations to control the creation of subdivisions. An inventory of Colorado's resources (land, water, forests, minerals) has been drawn up by a commission appointed by Love. Ecologists, however, complain that enforcement of environmental controls is still too loose.

† Colorado has also developed one of the most progressive penal reform programs in the country. Teams of prisoners from the state penitentiary at Canon City were actually allowed to leave the prison, each team accompanied by a single unarmed guard, to tour the state telling citizen groups about the grim despair of normal life behind bars. The message, especially intended for young people: "I'm on the road to nowhere. Don't follow me." Many employers, impressed by the prisoners' sincerity and initiative, offered to help get jobs for inmates seeking parole. Penitentiary warden Wayne Patterson has also had the foresight to permit development of a "Black Cultural Development Society," devoted to promoting self-pride among black inmates of the prison. Prisoners have also been permitted to have their own experimental programs to combat alcoholism and drug addiction.

entist Rudolf Gomez, is in areas "rural, suburban, Anglo-Saxon, and agricultural"; the Democratic base is in counties "urban, industrialized, mining-rural, and ethnically variegated"—the latter referring particularly to areas with strong Hispano population. In recent years, some Hispanos have been experimenting with their own independent party, an ominous development for the Democrats. The Democrats, in fact, appear to have more than their share of problems. The only place where Colorado's population is increasing is in the very area where the Democrats are weakest, the Denver suburbs. (Not since 1964, for instance, have the suburbs sent a Democrat to Congress.) Population is stable or declining in the Democrats' traditional bastion of southern Colorado. And in Denver, middle-class-white-versus-Hispano-versus-black conflicts threaten to destroy the alliances that produced overwhelming Democratic majorities over long years.

Gordon A. Allott and Peter H. Dominick, the two conservative Republicans who presently represent Colorado in the U. S. Senate, are fairly symbolic of the old and new wings of their party. Allott, from the farming town of Lamar in southern Colorado, watches assiduously for Colorado's interests as ranking Republican on the Senate Interior Committee and member of the Appropriations Committee. He is also chairman of the Senate Republican Policy Committee. Allott's interests range from water to grazing fees to encouraging development of Colorado's scientific-intellectual depth. Helene Monberg describes him well as a "Martha-type of politician: industrious, conscientious, a nit-picker, the best long-haul politician of Colorado right now." But he is also not above grandstanding to the extreme right, as in 1970, when he condemned the President's Commission on Campus Unrest, headed by former Governor William Scranton of Pennsylvania, for making a whitewash of the New Left and "pouring kerosene on the flames" of campus unrest—before the commission had even issued its report.

Dominick, by contrast, is a Connecticut import to Colorado who made his political start as a House member representing the Denver suburbs for which he speaks so well. Despite occasional moderate votes, Dominick's record is overwhelmingly conservative, and some liberal Republicans were upset to see him elected chairman of the Republican Senate Campaign Committee in 1971. He is fond of taking emotional pot-shots at his liberal opponents; the issue in which he has taken the most interest over the years is a proposed tax credit for the costs of higher education—having the political effect, of course, of reducing the taxes of many suburbanite parents. A member of the Senate Armed Services Committee, Dominick was a floor leader for the Safeguard ABM system which would have its nerve center at Colorado Springs. (To quote Cervi again: "We send two of the biggest stuffed shirts in America to the U. S. Senate. Both are kept men of big money and big power—Dominick because he believes in it, Allott because he has to.")

The two Colorado Senate "greats" of modern times have been Democrat Edwin C. Johnson—"The Big Swede" to whom we referred earlier—and Republican Eugene D. Millikin. The two were in the Senate for 14 of the same years, working so closely together for Colorado interests that the relationship was once described as "practically incestuous." Johnson, a marvelously independent soul, declared on retirement that the Upper Colorado River Basin was "the most important thing I've worked for in my long public life"; in Colorado's long, tumultuous water history, he still ranks as a leading figure. Before World War II, Johnson was an isolationist; in 1954, his last year in the Senate, he made an uncannily accurate prediction of what would happen if the decision were made "to send American G.I.s into the mud and muck of Indochina" to relieve the then besieged French at Dienbienphu. "Committing American troops to a jungle war against the revolutionists fighting colonialism in Indochina," Johnson warned, "would be the most foolish venture in all American history." It would cost thousands of lives and billions of dollars in borrowed money, and would seriously weaken the American economy, he predicted. Several years later, with some justification, Johnson said: "That speech will stand the test of time."

Millikin, the perfect Establishment type, was an inveterate and skilled conservative who rose to be Senate Finance Committee chairman; old-time Coloradans remember him both for his splendid intellect and a kind of high barnyard humor. He left the Senate in 1956.

Wayne Aspinall has long been the most important House member from the state, fighting sturdily for its water interests as chairman of the House Interior Committee. Several major projects bear his imprimatur, and indeed might never have come to pass without his backing: the billion-dollar Upper Colorado River Storage Project, the Fryingpan-Arkansas Project, and the Colorado River Basin Project, the latter including five water resource projects in Colorado. In the battle between the conservationists and those who favor continued utilization of public lands, Aspinall has come down squarely in favor of the latter; this goes back to the battle of the early 1960s over the wilderness bill, when the conservationist camp attacked Aspinall so personally that he gravitated more than ever into the camp of the mining, timber, oil, and gas interests. But Aspinall has sponsored more park and outdoor recreation legislation ultimately enacted into law than virtually any other member of Congress.

Aspinall reached his 75th birthday in 1971; a likely future leader of Colorado Democrats is Congressman Frank Evans, 27 years Aspinall's junior. Evans, a moderate liberal, has represented the southeastern corner of the state, including Pueblo and Colorado Springs, since the mid 1960s, gaining stature and statewide regard.

The Legislature and the People's Will

Colorado's legislature is today apportioned, like every other in the nation, by a strict one-man, one-vote formula, the fruit of the Supreme Court's decisions during the 1960s. But Colorado requires special notice on this count, because it devised and was ready to implement, before the Supreme

Court finally stopped it, a carefully derived and popularly approved alternative formula. In no state was there a clearer case of the Supreme Court imposing a districting plan against the explicit wishes of the people.

Like every other state, Colorado had discriminated grossly against its urban areas in the apportionment of the legislature. After the 1960 Census, it was discovered that while Denver and its three suburban counties had almost half the state's population, they had only 11 of 35 seats in the state senate and 23 of 65 seats in the state house. The fruits of such urban underrepresentation had become apparent over the years—for example, gross discrimination against Denver in the apportionment of earmarked highway taxes, or allowing counties to tax railroads only on the basis of main line track, so that Denver, notwithstanding the millions of dollars of railway switching trackage, warehouses, stations and office buildings within its borders, could tax the lines only on a piece of main line track a fraction of the length of taxable track going through some huge cow counties.

Faced with the necessity of reapportioning in 1962, Coloradans were given a choice, on the election day ballot, between two entirely distinct apportionment formulas. One, the so-called "equal representation" amendment, provided that both the state senate and house would be carved up on the basis of population alone. The backers of this amendment were such groups as the Colorado League of Women Voters, the AFL-CIO State Council, and the Colorado Education Association.

A separate formula, the so-called modified federal plan, was submitted to the voters in the same election. Backed by such groups as the Colorado Farm Bureau, the Colorado Cattlemen's Association, and the Chamber of Commerce, it provided for one chamber (the house) to be divided strictly according to population. The other house (the senate) would be divided on a basis combining population with factors such as topography, economic interest, and customary political alignments.

Most Democrats tended to support the equal representation amendment, most Republicans the federal plan. But there was a major exception: former governor and Senator Ed Johnson, Colorado's elder statesman of the time, who led the battle for the federal plan despite his own Democratic background. Johnson pointed to the tradition of balanced representation between Colorado's distinct geographic regions, and their historic diversity.

Thus given a choice, the people made their will unmistakably clear. The equal representation amendment was decisively defeated, 149,982 in favor to 311,749 opposed. The federal plan, however, was approved, 305,700 to 172,725. "It is very unusual in annals of Colorado politics that any proposal or candidate receive a plurality in each and every county of this diverse state," Johnson said, pointing out that not a single county had voted against the federal plan, not even Denver.

In the face of that overwhelming mandate, the question was whether the courts would approve what the people had chosen. In a few months, a local three-judge federal court did indeed rule, 2–1, that the federal plan was constitutional. The court stressed the fact that Colorado had a liberal initiative process which would enable the people to change the apportionment plan later, if they so chose, and the overwhelming nature of the statewide approval of the federal plan. They determined that the plan provided for a balanced and reasonable treatment of the senate: Western Slope 13 percent of population, 45 percent of the land area, 20.5 percent of the senators; Great Plains (eastern) 8.1 percent of population, 26 percent of area, 12.8 percent of senators; south central region 3.8 percent of population, 14 percent of area, 7.7 percent of senators; and finally, Denver and the Front Range 75.1 percent of population, 14 percent of area, 59 percent of the senators. Upholding the voters' right to institute their own plan—one reversible by a one-man, one-vote referendum in any future election—the court noted: "The contention that the voters have discriminated against themselves appalls rather than convinces."

The U. S. Supreme Court, however, thought otherwise, and by its decision in the Colorado case erased any last vestige of state power or discretion in constituting their own legislatures. In legal briefs and oral argument before the court, the state did make the point that Colorado's case was essentially different from that of other states—there was no "rural stranglehold" to be broken, since every county of the state approved the federal plan. But the deeper issues of the nature of representation, of the interest of people to be represented in more viable units in a large and disparate state, were never examined. The Supreme Court, by a 6–3 decision, threw out the federal plan, noting: "An individual's constitutionally protected right to cast an equally weighted vote cannot be denied even by a vote of a majority of a state's electorate."

What has happened to Colorado under unadulterated one-man, one-vote? It has certainly not been a doomsday for rural interests, as some feared, even though some special tax concessions have begun to fade. Except for the house in 1965–66, the Republicans have controlled both chambers. Perhaps the general Republican trend would have caused this in any event. But while both chambers have been Republican, they have diverged in character. The senate, with longer terms and a higher percentage of veteran legislators (many with several decades of service), has been more conservative, less attuned to social demands from minorities and other dispossessed. Where rural conservatives used to control the senate, it is now the suburban conservatives who dominate, achieving a working majority by working with rural conservatives.

The house, interestingly, has gone a different course. Though Republican, it has attracted many more younger, more progressive members. Many of these are actually suburban Republicans.

It is hard to believe that the actual results in the legislature, in terms of the way government is conducted, which bills are passed and which fail, would have been substantially different if the federal plan had been allowed to stand. Perhaps one-man, one-vote is advantageous in a state like Colorado if only to make it clear that the legislature's perennial wrangles, roadblocks, and conflicts have deeper roots and causes than a simple issue of city versus country. An excellent example was offered in the 1969 session when Colorado's Mexican-Americans, taking a leaf from the book of the California grape strikers, staged angry demonstrations at the capital demanding a change from the old restrictive labor legislation that exempts farm workers from the right to organize, to collect unemployment compensation, or enjoy other benefits. Just as if the farmers still controlled things, the legislature refused to act. On the next to last day of its session, 14 angry marchers, including Mexican-Americans, two nuns, two priests, and several Anglos, pushed their way into the senate chamber and occupied the podium; a recess had to be called, and the marchers were removed by the police. And the legislature thereupon reacted angrily, dusting off several antiriot bills previously intended for legislative burial and passing them during its final night; one measure even said two people could be considered a mob with evil intent! The "New Lobby" which triggered all this activity promised to continue lustily into the 1970s, pressuring for changes not only in farm labor statutes but also in welfare, housing, consumer problems, race issues, and landlord-tenant relationships. The issues raised all seemed to go a lot deeper than lawyers' niceties about absolute mathematical equality in legislative districts.

Colorado's congressional districts, in fact, point out some of the oddities in a rigorously applied one-man, one-vote fomula. To satisfy the courts, the Colorado legislature in the 1960s felt obliged to take Wayne Aspinall's district, once a neat configuration of the unified, well-known Western Slope area, and to extend the district on its northern end down across the totally disparate plains region and clear to the Nebraska border! It would seem that the interests of all would be better served if the Western Slope could be left as a homogeneous district on its own, albeit slightly underpopulated, while the high plains counties could be appended to the district of a Congressman like Frank Evans, who already represents most of the plains territory of Colorado. The 1970 Census apportionment gave Colorado an additional congressional seat, which was assigned to the Denver suburban area.

The other changes in American society—more affluence, greater education—probably have far more to do with the essential changes in America's representative bodies than all the apportionment plans ever devised. As an example, Tom Gavin of the Denver *Post* asked a legislator of 34 years' standing, Senator Sam Taylor of Walsenburg, about the change in the Colorado legislature over the years. "The modern day legislator," Taylor said (in a reply I have heard echoed in many states), "is far better equipped to do his job than we were in the 1930s. He's much, much better informed. He works harder. He's a more serious-minded person, more concerned with the public welfare than we were when we first started out." Moreover, Taylor reported, there is much less hanky-panky and bizarre behavior among modern legislators. "I haven't seen any real high jinks since '49, when one of the house members was climbing around on the State House ledges," Taylor reported. "And it doesn't happen anymore, but once it wasn't unusual at all for a committee chairman to 'lose' a bill or two that he didn't want to see passed." Even the lobbyists, Taylor believed, "are not as rough as they were in the mid-'30s."

The lobbyists, of course, are still there, and still doing quite well at defending their interests, even if the techniques need to be a touch more refined these days. Some 200 lobbyists register with the legislature, representing every interest, according to one report, "from architecture to onions." The clout of the century-old Colorado Cattlemen's Association is still visible, even though ranching is comparatively less central to the state's economy. The big Denver financial interests are well represented, as are the oilmen, major manufacturers, billboard interests, the Colorado Education Association (long a major Colorado power), and the Colorado Municipal League. Colorado is one of the states where the League of Women Voters swings real political weight and is respected in the state capital. Several conservationist groups are active, but they have failed to coalesce into a single, unified group as their counterparts have done in a number of other states.

Organized labor enjoys moderate influence with the legislature, due in no small part to the skilled leadership of the state AFL-CIO Labor Council, headed by Herrick S. Roth. Labor in 1958 decisively defeated a ballot proposition to institute "right to work." Colorado has the highest percentage of workers organized of any mountain state, scattered from 3,000 at Gates Rubber and 2,000 at Samsonite, the luggage manufacturer, in Denver, to the steelworkers of Pueblo and miners on the Western Slope. Ironically, there is virtually no union organization yet in the great electronics plants that employ more than 40,000 people in Colorado, 22,000 in Denver alone. On occasion, the AFL-CIO has worked in close concert with the Colorado Farmers Union in pressing Colorado government in a more liberal direction; local Farmers Union influence is underscored by the presence of the organization's national headquarters in Denver.

Not surprisingly, the dominant influences at the legislature are still conservative. This state of affairs will continue to endure as long as Denver maintains its financial and headquarters boom, scientific industries continue their growth, and the world view of the cautious Denver suburbanites becomes more and more the world view of all Colorado.

WYOMING

THE LONESOME LAND

WYOMING IS BARREN UPLAND, scrub and sage, a giant mesa broken by out-thrusts of high, snowy peaks and low, grim buttes. It is a land of free-running antelope, cowboys and their ponies, of oil wells, sheep, and cattle. Governor and later Senator Milward Simpson called it "the land of high altitude and low multitude." The rainfall is sparse, the distances immense, and life has few frills; the Wyoming poet Wilson Clough wrote well of his people:

> Who pastures high will feed on slender fare,
> Austere and tough and brief.

For the tough life, of course, there are compensations. The Wyomingite loves his sparkling open spaces; vast terrain exhilarates rather than depresses him; the trappings of culture may be far distant, but beside the door there is always the rifle and the fishing pole, and there is a deer to be shot over the hill or a fast-running trout waiting the catch in a nearby stream. This is a uniquely masculine society, and always has been. Nowhere is the stranger greeted more warmly; nowhere, however, is he expected to conform more completely to the values of the state society. Dissent is not smiled on here.

Save for Alaska, there is perhaps no state on which man's imprint remains so light. One reason is that so few people live in Wyoming: 332,416 in 1970 (only 2,350 more than a decade before), scattered a meager three to the square mile, filling no town to more than 40,000 count, leaving stretches of 50 and even as many as 100 miles from one farmhouse to the next. Commercial air service is minimal, rail passenger service almost non-existent. Alaska is the only state with fewer people, but even it grows rapidly while Wyoming pauses, uneasily, wondering what its future may be.

The gods of nature favored Wyoming in selective locations, and stupendous those places are: the geysers of Yellowstone, the startling beauty of the Tetons, the grandeur of the Big Horn Mountains, a scattering of exquisite high valleys. Millions of tourists see the promise and come each year; a few thousand wealthy families make their homes beside these natural treasures.

Yet the fir- and spruce-bedecked mountains and their green valleys are but a small portion of Wyoming, and remote and northern at that; the scene that fills the eye, across the great reaches of this state, is the desolation captured in the words of Wilson Clough:

> . . . Looking sunward on leagues of gaunt, marginal land,
> With strange buttes rising, apart, far distant, mysterious,
> Against the glistening afternoon sky,
> Like great ship-bulks, forever stranded on a static sea. . . .

And so the question presses in: what is the role in America, and what is the future, for this wind-blown rectangle of space, 78 times the size of Rhode Island, this Wyoming that Gunther called "America high, naked, and exposed"? Few are the places where the soil is rich enough, even if irrigated, for crops. Grass there is, grass stretching as far as the eye can see, the grass that drew the buffalo, the Indian, and then the white man with his cattle. But that grass has its limits, too; there are but so many blades, and in the aridity each steer or sheep needs acres of his own. There are 10 times as many cattle and sheep as human beings on the Wyoming territory (and still, the state's livestock industry fails to rank among the 10 largest by state).

Then there is the treasure below the soil: vast deposits of oil, lodes of uranium and trona, and enough coal to heat the continent for generations if one ever chose to mine it. Gradually, more and more of these are opened to mining. But the age-old question remains: to whose profit? Wyoming has been America's classic colonial state, an exploited region from which wealthy interests take the riches of the soil and withdraw their profits to spend in gentler climes and distant cosmopolitan cities, leaving behind Wyoming with its scant capital and limited industrial resources. Not until the late 1960s could Wyoming bring itself to impose even a clear-cut severance tax on the natural resources being mined out of its land.

As for the making of goods, Wyoming's location is generally too distant, the costs of transportation too great; by 1970, manufacturing payrolls were below those of a generation before, ranking 50th among 50 states. And Wyoming's fiercely independent, nature-loving people are not so sure they want big factories anyway. To many Wyomingites, industry means polluting smoke-stacks, clogged freeways, city slums, and an alien black race in their midst.

Wyoming prefers its clean, uncluttered air, its simple towns, its monolithic white middle-class society. "We want to preserve the 'sweet values' of a modest population milieu," a leading newspaper editor told me. I asked him what those sweet values might be, and he defined them as "neighborly life, social cooperation, and human identity"—all threatened, my editor friend said, by the "strange byroads" into which he saw the greater American society veering: Freudian theory, behaviorism, John Deweyism. Wyoming would have none of this: a sanctuary it would be, an island of individual-istic frontier society, closing its frontier behind it.

Trails, Railroads, Indians, and the Ranch Wars

The feeling of emptiness one gets in Wyoming—the ache of vastness and of solitude—is not because it has no past. It is rather because the signs and monuments of the past are so meager and so few. The characters in its cavalcade—the Indians, the trappers, the miners, the scouts, the bull-whackers, the mule skinners, and the cowboys—left hardly a trace in their passing. They came, they did, and they went. The decaying logs of an old fur press, rotting sluice boxes, the stone abutments of a railroad trestle, a rusty beaver trap lying in the weeds along a river, a broken arrowhead kicked up in a field—these are the relics of Wyoming's history. Nearly everything else is scenery, emptiness, and the ever-enduring grass.
—Hamilton Basso in American Panorama

Until early in the past century, Wyoming was an uncharted wilderness, still the private hunting ground of the Crow, the Blackfeet, the Sioux, the Cheyennes. Trappers and scouts came early in the century, but the first real mark was laid by the transcontinental trails. The deep ruts of the old wagon trains can still be seen across the prairie today, so deep was the imprint on the baked soil of men and their families moving west on trails that bear the names of Oregon, Overland, Bozeman, Lander, and Lodgepole.

Before 1867, fewer than 1,000 people lived in the entire Wyoming Territory-to-be. Then came the great iron monster across the plains, the track-laying crews hammering out an epoch in rails and spikes. The historians record that on July 4, 1867, General Grenville Dodge selected a site on Crow Creek for the first Union Pacific terminal in the territory and named it Cheyenne after the Indians he had been chasing; a scant four months later, the town's population swelled from zero to 4,000, and there was a great celebration to welcome the tracks to the brawling, open frontier city. Cheyenne even had a newspaper which proclaimed: "This is the age of speed. The railroad works changes bewildering to contemplate."

The changes were indeed bewildering. With the railroad came burly Irish workingmen; they were supplied with food by one William Cody, an expert hunter, who killed some 5,000 buffalo for them in a year and a half and would be known forever after as "Buffalo Bill." With the railroad, the

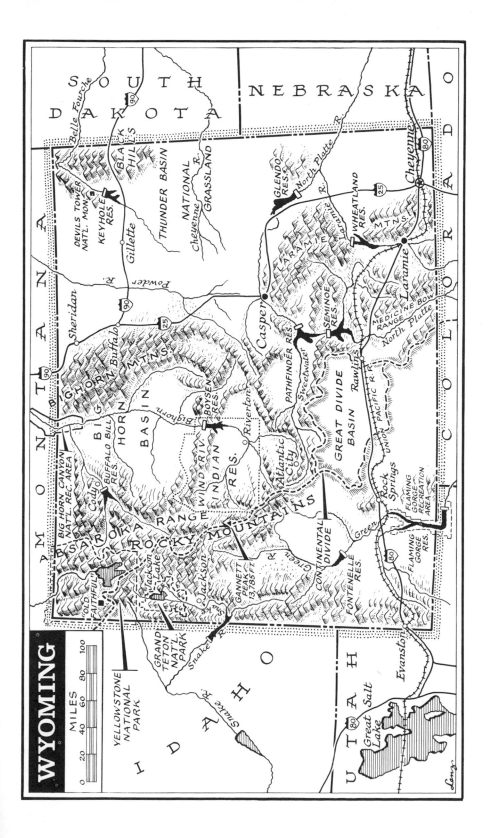

WYOMING

MILES

0 20 40 60 80 100

YELLOWSTONE
NATIONAL
PARK

buffalo became scarce, even shot from train windows. (The last wild buffalo disappeared from Wyoming's open plains in the late 1960s.) The railway construction towns must have been a sight to see; as one historian * describes the scene:

Tents were replaced overnight by tar-paper shacks, false-front stores, saloons, gambling dens, and houses daintily referred to as "dance halls." The streets of these rip-snorting towns were dust, echoing the cursing of men seeking solace from monotonous labor, the bawdy laughter of women after easy money, and too often the sharp crack of a gun ending a dispute.

The first decade of settlement brought irrevocable tragedy for the Indians. In return for Indian attacks on settler, wagon trains, and railroad crews, the United States Army wreaked cruel vengeance. Wyoming's settlers had little sympathy for the savages who had held their land. At a large public gathering in Cheyenne in October, 1876, the town's first mayor, H. M. Hook, offered this toast: "Here is to the city of Cheyenne: May she ever prosper, and the tribe of Indians after whom she is named be completely exterminated."

The climax of the Indian fighting came in the Battles of the Rosebud and the Little Big Horn, across the border in Montana, in 1876; in each engagement, the Indians acquitted themselves well and actually killed the bumbling General George Custer and 220 of his men in the second battle. But the great Indian chiefs—Crazy Horse, Sitting Bull, Gall, Rain-in-the-Face, Two Moon—lacked the supplies or weapons to defend against the marauding and revenging Army expeditions which followed. By 1880 the Sioux had taken their last scalp, and the unhappy Indians, driven onto reservations, had become the wards of the state and the excruciating problem of national conscience they remain today.

With the railroad came the cattle business. Wyoming was ideal livestock country with its rich short grass that cured into natural hay for winter grazing. Hundreds of miles to the south, in Texas, cattle were in excess. So the great cattle drives of hundreds of thousands of head a year began up the Texas Trail to Wyoming's open ranges and shipment by rail from the Union Pacific terminal at Cheyenne. John B. Kendrick, who would later become a U. S. Senator from Wyoming, recalled that as a cattle driver making his first trip in 1879, he traveled more than 400 miles from Forth Worth, Texas, to Running Water, Wyoming, without encountering a wire fence.

Appropriately, "don't fence me in" became the obsession of the new Wyoming cattle barons, who would stake out their right to a 160-acre homestead for ranch headquarters and a corral and then turn their cattle out to graze over thousands of acres of free (government-owned) range. Only the legendary brands would identify whose calf or steer was whose; thievery became such a problem that the Laramine County Stock Growers Association was founded for mutual self-protection and brand listing in 1873; it would grow into the Wyoming Stock Growers Association, the most powerful group

* Mae Urbanek in *Wyoming Wonderland* (Denver: Sage Books, 1964).

through most of the state's history and still potent today. Range justice for thieves, historians record, was swift and sure: a necktie party under the nearest tree.

More problematic for the ranchers was what to do with small homesteaders who put wire fences around their property, barring the way of cattle to water; desperately, the cattlemen tried to hold on to unfettered rights to the public domain which the U. S. Army had so conveniently seized for them from the Indians. Each year the range became a little less free. Yet the bloodiest battles would be with the sheepmen, who likewise chose to graze their flocks on public lands; disaster threatened for the cattlemen because, as Gunther colorfully records, "they saw, to their horror, the limitless rich grass of the open range disappear down the gullets of countless rams and lambs." The sheep, cattlemen claimed, also tore up grass roots and polluted water holes. As cattlemen, homesteaders, and sheepmen fought, anarchy reigned for years on the Wyoming plains; in 1892 there might have been a massacre in Johnson County if the U. S. Cavalry had not intervened in a battle between small ranchers and hired gunmen of the big ranchers, who had marked 40 men for death; as it was, only two died. A decade later, in the Big Horn Basin, masked cattlemen dynamited and clubbed 4,000 sheep to death and drove others over precipices; in 1909, two sheep owners and their herder were killed and more sheep clubbed to death. As historian Mae Urbanek concludes:

Determined to hold the range at any cost, cattlemen wrote a bloody chapter in Wyoming history. Eventually they were forced to yield and recognize the law. Some of them soon ran their own bands of sheep, grazing them to utilize the poorer land with its sagebrush and browse plants that cattle will not eat. . . . The plow of the homesteader buried the days of the open range.

In 1971 Wyoming was again astir with allegations that stockmen were taking the law into their own hands. Despite federal laws protecting bald eagles and golden eagles, dozens of the birds were found to have been killed by thallium sulphate, a poison used in predator control and fed in highly lethal quantities to antelope that were then used for bait. Stockgrowers believe eagles account for thousands of sheep deaths each year. Van Irvine, operator of one of Wyoming's largest ranches and then president of the Stock Growers Association, was arrested on 28 counts of violations of Wyoming fish and game laws. And there were reports of stockmen hiring helicopters to hunt down the federally protected eagles.

The ubiquitous Union Pacific did more than open up Wyoming for cattleman and homesteader; it also determined the geopolitical face of Wyoming for a century to come. A large strain of Wyomingites were born in Nebraska, coming in directly on the UP line; many others came from other Midwestern states served by the railroad. The cattle drives brought many Texans, who would never have come without the railhead at Cheyenne for their herds. Later, thousands of eastern and southern Europeans were imported; as Congressman Teno Roncalio, son of an immigrant miner, recalls: "The

Union Pacific brought people like my parents from Italy as cheap labor to work in the coal mines the railway needed to run its trains across southern Wyoming." Not surprisingly, the towns along the UP line became filled with the dispossessed, natural enemies of the stockmen and holders of privilege. Roncalio describes the people along the rail line:

The guy who immigrated from Greece or Austria or Italy or Germany some half century ago to work in the coal mines, all he wanted was to get his kids raised and to live the new American dream. He memorized the Constitution and raised his kids to respect the flag, but he was a Democrat, because he had to fight off the owners of the mines to get representation for unionism. He knew the Democratic party held the best future for himself and for his kids.

To the north, in the land of the big ranches, Republicanism more naturally prevailed, and still does today.

The railroad also determined where all Wyoming's major public institutions would be located. By decision of the legislature, Cheyenne got the capital since it was the nearest to Nebraska, the university went to nearby Laramie, the state penitentiary further west to Rawlins, a hospital for miners to Rock Springs, and finally, on the southwestern desert, Evanston got the insane asylum (now more genteelly called the Wyoming State Hospital)— all neatly astride the UP line.

Of course, it was not preordained that Wyoming must be a state. In fact, President Grant in 1872, in a discussion with the House Committee on Territories, said he favored abolishing the Wyoming Territory and dividing the land into four parts, to be given to Utah, Montana, Idaho, and Colorado. When wind of this reached Cheyenne, a great chorus of protest arose. Eventually the railroad brought enough people in—from 9,118 in 1870 to 20,789 in 1880 to 62,555 in 1890—for Wyoming to be able to win statehood in the latter year. Yet what is the result? Wyoming, one of the state's leading citizens told me exactly a century later,

is a state because it got what was left over—what the wheat farmers of Nebraska couldn't homestead, what the miners of Colorado didn't want, what the Mormons couldn't claim. So there was some plateau left over, and that became the square rectangle called Wyoming—the remnants of three territories, an accident in time and place.

Economy: Cattle, Oil, Troubled Prospects

From an economy that practically began and ended with livestock, Wyoming has altered its way of earning a living to the point where extraction of raw materials is the preeminent creator of wealth. Thousands, of course, still make their living from livestock, and there is no quicker way to make tempers flare in Wyoming (except by suggesting registration of firearms) than to propose that the federal government increase the grazing fees on the public land it leases to ranchers. But neither livestock nor farming can be called dynamic parts of the economy; in fact, individual Wyoming farmers' income actually declined some $4 million between 1948 and 1968, even while overall wages in the state were going up 150 percent. The farm and ranch products of neighboring Nebraska are more than eight times as great in value as Wyoming's, those of Colorado four times as great. Wyoming's livestock income ($211 million in 1969) ranks a puny 36th among the states (incredibly, behind even Maryland and Arizona).* Only in the number of sheep does Wyoming stand high (second to Texas), but mutton and wool have been in a great slough of demand ever since World War II. Thus we must now dismiss as an historical oddity John Gunther's report of Wyoming as being, of all American commonwealths, "the livestock state par excellence."

Oil has come in to fill the gap. The black mineral's presence has been obvious since the early days of the territory, when it was found oozing from the ground and was used by fur traders as an ointment for muscular pains or by travelers to grease the axles of their prairie schooners. The first commercial well was brought in in 1883. Since World War II, Wyoming has become a major oil-producing state, its production up fourfold from prewar years and ranked fifth among the states. The combined value of oil and gas production in the state in 1970 was $505 million. The greatest production has come in the territory east of Yellowstone Park and around Casper in center-state; in 1967, however, a huge find was made in the Powder River Basin in northeast Wyoming, sparking major new growth and reversing an ominous trend in which production had been outpacing the discovery of new reserves. (Wyoming has no proration laws.) Reminiscent of the old railroad town booms, the Powder River Basin town of Gillette quickly tripled in population to some 9,000, packed with mobile homes; the housing shortage was so severe that hotels rented out rooms to oil workers in shifts; suddenly the town faced a water crisis and had to ration people to a single shower a week. At the same moment in time, sadly, other towns in Wyoming were slowly dying.

Some Wyomingites shudder to think what might have happened to the state's economy if the postwar oil boom had not come to replace the relative decline in agriculture, the halving of railway employment, and the dramatic decline in coal production (the latter occasioned by closing down of the mines when the Union Pacific switched from steam to diesel engines). Oil and natural gas now account for about 95 per cent of Wyoming's mineral production and probably pay half of the state's entire tax burden; industry spokesmen claim that 14,000 jobs are created directly by oil and gas, or 20,000 if one counts service companies and other satellite industries. But many in Wyoming still chafe over the fact of out-of-state ownership; the largest single producer, for instance, is Pan American Petroleum Corporation, a subsidiary of Standard Oil of Indiana. A single act of the oil com-

---

* In crops, Wyoming's arid soil produces even less—some $38 million worth a year (largely sugar beets from irrigated land), thus ranking only 43rd among the 50 states. Almost pathetically, some Wyoming leaders like Senator and former Governor Clifford Hansen still talk of cloud seeding as a way to reverse the tables of aridity.

panies—such as their decision in 1964–65 to transfer 550 clerical and administrative employees from Casper to regional offices in Denver—can have frightening consequences for the Wyoming economy. These same oil companies now hold the leases not only on Wyoming's oil lands but on the great bulk of other energy resources—coal, oil shale, and uranium. On some future date, Wyoming's oil reserves (some fields now exploited 50 years) will be exhausted. The state has substitute energy sources: its share of the vast oil shale beds also in Colorado and Utah and, underlying vast stretches of its territory, the greatest reserves of soft coal in any state of the Union.* But strip mining of these resources endangers the landscape.

In far-away Oklahoma City, president D. A. McGee of the Kerr-McGee Oil Co. told me of his firm's hope for long-term profit out of its uranium mines in the Shirley Basin of central Wyoming; he considers Wyoming a key state to U. S. uranium development. The other major uranium producer of Wyoming is also from out of state—Utah Construction and Mining of San Francisco. Uranium has created its own boom town: Jeffrey City, a new mobile home settlement between Rawlins and Lander where a few years before the sole break in desert sagebrush had been the post office and filling station of Home on the Range. With demand for domestic power plants growing, uranium seems to have a bright future. Rapid exploratory drilling in 1969 pushed Wyoming to first place in uranium ore reserves, ahead of New Mexico. But mining of the yellowcake creates an immediate environmental problem: unsightly pits and dumps, and the danger of death for wildlife that drink water contaminated by leaching of abandoned low-grade uranium ores.

Wyoming has become the richest iron ore producer of the West, largely through pelletizing of low-grade ores. The big installations are run by Colorado Fuel and Iron Company for its steel mill at Pueblo and by U. S. Steel for its mill at Provo, Utah. Jobs for hundreds of Wyoming men are thus created, but as state historian T. A. Larson comments, "Wyoming ore [feeds] Colorado and Utah steel mills employing tens of thousands of men while Wyoming hopes of steel mills remain unrealized." Larson thus identifies what many see as the essential economic quandary of Wyoming: finding a way to require processing of raw materials within its borders, rather than simply shipping out the raw materials in the manner of any underdeveloped country.

Finally, our review of mining should mention the postwar boom in trona—chief source of sodium ash, a vital ingredient of glass, ceramics, and many other products. Along the Green River, not far from many of the abandoned coal mines, the trona industry now prospers, giving jobs to some 750 men, many of them old coal miners and their sons.

* For more than two decades, scientists at the University of Wyoming have been trying to devise an economical way to convert coal to liquid hydrocarbon fuels. This could turn out to be wasted effort in light of Alaskan oil strikes and the possibility of getting billions of barrels of oil, at less cost, from oil shale. The coal is likely to be used in vast quantities, however, for mine-mouth generation of power for long-distance transmission to Pacific Coast markets.

With these vast mineral resources, one feels it is not without reason that Wyomingites often say "the future of this state is in the ground." This is both Wyoming's promise and its problem. T. A. Larson points out, Wyoming's economic problems can be seen in classic balance of payment terms. In recent times the state has been exporting raw and semiprocessed goods ranging from crude oil and natural gas to cattle, sheep, wool, wheat, iron-ore pellets, and uranium yellowcake. In return it has been importing all kinds of manufactured goods, plus transportation, communications, meat, milk, fruits, and vegetables. Not surprisingly, the balance of payments on these obvious factors was severely weighted to cash outflow. What filled the gap? First of all, tourism—a money earner of some $150 million annually by the early 1970s. Secondly, the government—through reclamation, payments to local governments, and especially the big intercontinental ballistic missile system installation near Cheyenne. Thus the Wyoming economy has been able to share in some of the postwar prosperity but not enough to prevent static or declining populations or to prevent the per capita income, substantially ahead of the national average at the end of World War II, to slip substantially below by the mid 1960s.

What might Wyoming do to improve its situation? Some suggest that with increased irrigation, more crops can be produced, perhaps cattle pastures irrigated. But the most feasible reclamation projects in Wyoming have already been constructed; poor soil and high altitudes severely restrict agricultural growth potential, even if Wyoming does have millions of acre-feet of unexploited stream runoff. Another suggestion, long put forth, is that more raw materials be processed within the state. To date, the big oil companies and other powers have had enough financial and political clout to prevent any state legislation to force them in this direction. (Despite its huge deposits of natural gas, for instance, Wyoming has only one home-owned gas utility.) If more raw materials are to be processed within Wyoming, some local initiative, never before seen, will have to be forthcoming. Right now the state is totally lacking in home-controlled capital for major ventures; one big Denver bank, for instance, will have more assets than all of the banks of Wyoming put together.

Finally, there is the suggestion for attracting light industry, capable of exploiting the high educational level of Wyoming's people (12.1 years— second highest in the U. S.) and not requiring heavy transportation of materials to or from distant markets. State redevelopment authorities could name for me only two such plants (Control Data at Casper, Daytel at Riverton), employing only a few hundred people out of a state work force (excepting agriculture) that totaled 102,000. Except to fill low-paying electronic parts assembly jobs, it was difficult to see why such firms would pick isolated Wyoming, especially with the alternative of Colorado, with all its scientific, recreational, and metropolitan inducements, so close at hand.

Governing a Colonial State

From its infancy, and with scarcely a break until the 1960s, Wyoming government was prey to big financial interests: the Union Pacific Railway, the cattlemen, the oil companies. The objective of this feudalistic power nexus was simple: to keep taxes low by holding activities of government at a minimum, and to allow the least possible regulation of industry. Whenever higher taxes or controls on the oil industry were suggested, its spokesmen would utter dire threats about pulling up their stakes and leaving Wyoming; any legislator who dared defy big oil would know where his opponent's campaign money would come from in the next election.

Out-of-state interests had no interest in government services and neither, in fact, did the cattlemen, those self-sufficient barons of their own little worlds. Legislature sessions were restricted to 40 days every two years, about as much time as the cattlemen could afford in Cheyenne, and also short enough so that the lawmakers would have little time to concoct fancy new ways to raise and spend money. With a few exceptions, the Wyoming press was supine and abetted the exploitation. The issue of outside control also tended to be muted by the fact that many Wyomingites got their news from papers published outside the state, papers which took a minimal interest in Wyoming interests—the Denver *Post* circulating in southeastern Wyoming, the Salt Lake *Tribune* in the southwest, the Billings (Mont.) *Gazette* in the north. Even when television came, not one of the three Wyoming-based stations had a signal strong enough to cover all of the state's vast territory.

Some of the results of laissez-faire, special-interest government were all too clear. In 1947 Wyoming repealed the only law it had ever had to regulate lobbying. Until the late 1960s, there was no provision for referendum and initiative (a situation finally corrected in 1968). The state had no civil service system, a state of affairs which failed to create a rampant spoils system only because the pay for state government workers was so low anyway. The governor was denied most true executive powers, the real clout left in the hands of boards and commissions which the special interests apparently thought would be more prone to manipulation. And in 1971 the Citizens Conference on State Legislatures ranked Wyoming 49th among the states, ahead only of Alabama, on a scale of how well legislative bodies are equipped to do their jobs "in a functional, accountable, informed, independent, and representative manner." The continuing limitation of one 40-day legislative session each two years was noted as a chief defect.

"Right to work" was passed at a stormy 1963 session of the legislature during which the governor had the National Guard ready in reserve in case violence broke out. The 1963 legislature, in a burst of anti-federal sentiment, also voted resolutions to (1) oppose any further Social Security tax increases; (2) oppose creation or extension of wilderness areas in Wyoming; (3) ask a constitutional amendment barring federal courts from action on state legislative reapportionment matters; (4) ask for a 'Court of the Union" consisting of the 50 state chief justices, empowered to review Supreme Court decisions.

The ferocity of anti-federal sentiment in Wyoming is amazing to behold—especially when one remembers that Wyomingites are biting the hand of the federal government which owns half the land within Wyoming and pays half its state budget. In a talk with Charles Crowell, an attorney and dean of the lobbyists at the state legislature, I heard some edification:

If there's one thing that upsets Wyoming, it's the complete defensive we're on by reason of attempts by the federal government to encroach on what we regard as state jurisdiction. No matter where we turn, the feds are closing in on us!

On water, we formerly thought the states owned the water; now we find Uncle Sam may own it by virtue of federal lands ownership with riparian rights to waters that flow across them—a complete reversal of previous understandings.

In game and fish management, areas traditionally left to the states, now we find the Interior Department saying the feds own the fish and game on federal lands in Wyoming.

On ranchlands leasing from the Bureau of Land Management, owners of private property now have to open them to give anyone access to public lands they may be leasing.

On oil and gas leasing, on welfare, health, whatever, it's the same thing. Why, we even have a problem with highway stripes. We want to stripe our roads yellow, so we can see them better in snowy weather. But the Bureau of Public Roads says they'll cut off our funds unless we stripe them white.

Our interstate roads have the same frequency of access roads as New York. Driving north from Cheyenne, you pass exits to "Irma" and "Barber" and a lot of others indicating a turnoff to some community. Hell, it's one ranch house! We have as much use for those interchanges as flying a kite. Barber comes to town once a week, and he's the only one who uses the quarter-million-dollar highway exit we had to build.

But why, one may ask, do such petty grievances get Wyoming completely steamed up about Washington's bureaucratic ways? One answer may lie in the nature of politics in a small state like Wyoming. Since there are so few people, the candidates for office—even for governor and Congress— are expected to conduct intense town-to-town and door-to-door campaigns; a successful gubernatorial candidate may have shaken most of the hands in Wyoming. Since they know them, Wyomingites then feel free to turn to major officeholders to solve petty problems, especially in getting bothersome government regulations off their backs. Likewise, they think the federal government should oblige them by maintaining a low, noncontroversial silhouette like the Wyoming model. When it doesn't, they are annoyed and eventually frustrated and angry. Put another way, Wyoming has lived so long in dependency on Washington that a love-hate relationship in the familiar father-and-son mode develops.

A man said to be the perfect symbol of Wyoming politics was Milward Simpson, political leader in the '50s and '60s, who came up through the coal mines, earned his law degree, practiced in small towns, became an illustrious Wyoming booster, and turned in a performance as governor rated as one of the best in Wyoming history. In the words of historian Larson, Simpson was "outstandingly personable, energetic, forthright, and courageous." But Simpson had two political personalities. On one occasion he warned: "The little red schoolhouse is redder than you think." But he also served with distinction as president of the University of Wyoming board of trustees. As governor, Simpson loosened the purse strings some for expanded government services but did little to disturb the cattle-rail-oil power combine. Winding up his career in the U. S. Senate, he behaved—again in the words of historian Larson—"as if he counted that day lost when he could not issue a news release denouncing the administration."

The first governor of the postwar years to offer a really progressive platform was, amazingly, a former president of the Stock Growers Association—Clifford P. Hansen, a diminutive, friendly, modest man universally respected in his state. A Republican, like Simpson, Hansen decided during his first year as governor, in 1963, not to resist the legislature's right-wing binge of the year (discussed above), and he even signed the right-to-work bill into law with laudatory words. Two years later, however, Hansen struck out on his own with extraordinarily progressive recommendations: repeal of a 20-year-old law that had forbidden use of state funds to match federal grants for education, an enabling act for urban renewal, a minimum wage increase, enactment of a fair employment practices law, reapportionment of the state senate. "I took the position," Hansen explained to me some time later, "that it was not the function of the governor to veto federal programs, but to cooperate with the federal government." For Wyoming, it was heady stuff.

Even more fundamental change was to come. In 1966, an unassuming young pragmatist, Stan Hathaway, was elected governor, scoring first a highly significant primary victory over millionaire rancher-businessman M. Joseph Burke, who was considered more a spokesman of the older moneyed establishment. Hathaway turned out to be no status-quo governor. He recommended and won approval of a complete government reorganization, taking the autonomy and much of the power from the independent boards and commissions. He got through a long-overdue industrial health and safety law. He recommended and won approval of a law to insure restoring of the natural surface after strip mining activity. Consolidation of rural schools into efficient units was approved. And Hathaway signed into law, after a bitter fight among the legislators, a bill ferociously opposed by the Union Pacific because it would give trona mining interests underground access across sections of land the UP had held for a century. It was the UP's first great defeat, and, interestingly, the first infringement on the massive land grant the railway received for building its line across the empty prairie.

Finally, the 1969 legislature took an historic step forward by imposing a 1 percent severance tax on minerals taken from Wyoming's soil. For half a century, the oil industry had been fighting any such tax with every resource at its command. On two earlier occasions—1923 and 1949—a direct state tax on minerals had been proposed but narrowly defeated. The 1969 bill had to be considered a true watershed, a stinging rebuke for one of the most powerful lobbies ever organized in any American state.* "If the oil industry had been taxed properly in the past," Congressman Roncalio insists, "we'd be one of the wealthiest states today."

The severance tax, as passed, was a Hathaway recommendation—for him, a better alternative than the unpopular idea of an increased sales tax, or walking the political gangplank of an income tax (which Wyoming to date has avoided). In earlier years, Hathaway had actually been against a severance tax. A major share of the credit for the tax goes to the man Hathaway defeated for governor in 1966, Casper attorney Ernest Wilkerson. Refined, silver-haired, and a bit fastidious, Wilkerson was the most un-Wyominglike candidate one could imagine—which may account, in part, for his loss. But Wilkerson made modern history with his campaign slogan—"Wyoming's Wealth for Wyoming's People"—and by his call for a minerals severance tax he would set not at 1 percent, but 3 percent. (Wilkerson's suggestion: add 1.5 percent to the immediate state budget, put the other 1.5 percent into a trust fund for the future, for the day when Wyoming will have no further mineral resources. "I don't want us to become another West Virginia, that terribly exploited state," Wilkerson explained, pointing out that many mines there are exhausted while the mine owners "have taken all their money to New York and Pittsburgh and left those poor devils down there on their slag pile with nothing.")

With comparative tax charts, Wilkerson could show in his campaign that the average tax on a barrel of oil in Wyoming was 13 cents, in the four other leading oil states, 22 cents. He entered the governorship race, he told me later, not so much with the expectation of winning as in the hope he might start "a delayed Populist movement—to get the state thinking it should be run for the benefit of its people, not outside interests." The oil and rail interests, appreciating Wilkerson's contribution not a whit, threw heavy support to Hathaway.

With Wilkerson's defeat, many thought the severance tax dead, only to see Hathaway revive it in 1969. When legislative hearings were held on the proposal, a parade of mineral industry spokesmen came forward to protest that they could not afford a single additional penny on the dollar without

* Traditionally, Wyoming's public coffers have been enriched two ways by mining. First, local counties apply property taxes to all minerals extracted, including oil and gas; in the process, of course, some fortunate counties become extremely wealthy while others have a fraction of the tax base. Secondly, the state itself benefits from a share of royalties collected by the federal government on oil and gas extracted from federal lands. About 70 percent of Wyoming's oil and gas production is on such land; under a 1920 law, 12.5 percent of the royalties go to Washington; the state, in turn, gets 37.5 percent of the federal share. Around $14 million a year is conveyed to the Wyoming state treasury by this device—not insignificant in a state where the total budget is still around $200 million a year. Some Wyomingites have argued that the state should receive as much as 90 percent of the royalties collected, pointing to Alaska and offshore oil royalties as an example. Critics reply that the land was first the federal government's, and still is, and that the state is free—if it so chooses—to tax the 87.5 percent of the value of oil mined which the federal government does *not* collect.

losing their competitive advantage—a not very veiled threat that Wyoming would begin losing oil wells.

Only one man appeared in behalf of Governor Hathaway's bill—Ernest Wilkerson.

The irony of the situation was not lost on the Casper *Star-Tribune*, which fired an editorial shot heard round the state by endorsing the severance tax, commending Wilkerson, and condemning the "corporate interests, grown rich on Wyoming's wealth, trying to dodge a reasonable tax." Even the Cheyenne *State Tribune*, usually archconservative, felt obliged to tell the mineral companies that they'd "better lose this one" lest a "tougher and heavier levy" await them if they resisted completely.

There are probably few cases in American state politics where the losing candidate made such a mark on his state. If continued and expanded, the severance tax could one day be the device to give Wyoming's people a good life, free from the worst ravages of colonialism. Although their per capita income is behind the rest of the country, and falling behind more every year, Wyoming citizens still pay significantly more in direct personal state and local taxes than the national average. Building highways or gearing up an educational plant in a big but lightly populated state tends to cost significantly more, per capita, than in more compact and densely populated states, even for an equivalent level of actual service. Even though one hears many complaints within Wyoming that services for people are inadequate, expenditures per person rank high in the entire U. S. A.—second for education and highways, for instance, and third for health and hospitals.* Unless the dynamic sources of income generated within the state can be captured for the public coffers—in Wyoming's case, the income from oil, gas, uranium, and other minerals, the irreplaceable natural resources of the land—the people will be bled white. Thus the severance tax provides perhaps the only solution for a hard-pressed state.

Ernest Wilkerson, however, will not be around to see the long-term impact of the tax he advocated. With him and Wyoming, it was a case of brief incompatibility. In 1971 he closed his Casper law office, sold his home, and began graduate courses at New York University.

Politics, Politicians, and Women

Life on Wyoming's wind-swept plateaus, in a rigorous environment where distances between settlements are immense, where a man must be courageous and self-reliant if he hopes to survive, has fostered a fierce independence and individualism that survive to this day. Political bossism is

---

* The notable exception is Wyoming's expenditure for public welfare, which ranks only 43rd among the states, barely half the national average in actual dollars per capita. Apparently unappreciative of the cold-heartedness of his remarks, a Wyoming state official told me: "We're not a welfare state. When people lose a job here, we expect them to leave. They can come back when we have a job for them." Shades of Marie Antoinette!

unthinkable in such a setting, and while Wyoming usually votes Republican, it votes first and foremost for the man, not the party. Self-reliant people see no reason why others should not take care of themselves as well, with the result that over most of the state's history, both parties have offered conservative candidates for office.

The tough, direct men of the Wyoming Stock Growers Association have long been the dominant force of politics in the Cowboy State. In several legislatures of the late '50s and early '60s, they elected more than half the members of the state senate, an achievement all the more remarkable since their membership rolls were a meager 2,600. Reapportionment has diminished this control to substantial degree, so that today the legislature has as many lawyers or schoolteachers as ranchers. But the Stock Growers' influence lingers on, reinforced by the fact that one of their past presidents—Cliff Hansen—sits in the United States Senate. There Hansen fights to hold down grazing fees on public land, battles for oil import quotas,* and leads the fight against gun control legislation. ("Most people in Wyoming carry guns; it's a way of life," Hansen told me.)

Wyoming's Democrats seem to have fallen on lean years. Closing of the Union Pacific coal mines and eclipse of the big railroad payrolls took a heavy toll among the intensely loyal Democratic unionists. What's more, the Democrats seem to be blamed for the turmoil in the ghettos and on the campuses which television brings into every Wyoming home. Arriving in the mid-1950s, television broke down Wyoming's old insularity in which it had dealt with its own problems in the narrow confines of its own microcosm. Today one even hears that Wyoming faces a major narcotics problem because it's on a main East-West highway, with many drug-carrying hippies passing through and unloading drugs which show up at high schools, universities, and even factories.

The old brand of conservative Wyoming Democrat seems to be fading from the scene; there is, for instance, no modern counterpart to the late Tracy S. McCraken, longtime Democratic National Committeeman and a self-man man who eventually gained control of seven of Wyoming's 10 daily newspapers. A big, red-haired man whom many looked up to as "Mr. Wyoming," McCraken exerted substantial power behind the scenes in an era when Democratic candidates rarely strayed left of center. The last conservative Democratic governor, Jack Gage, sometimes called the "Will Rogers of the Mountains," was to the right even of Cliff Hansen, who defeated him in 1962. Gage blamed the Republican victory of that year on "liberalism among Democrats" and warned: "The people of Wyoming are conservative people."

One Wyoming Democrat, Senator Gale McGee, has been able to survive the Republican tides of recent years. A college professor by trade, McGee won his first Senate election in 1958 by an incredibly energetic campaign

---

* One reason it took Wyoming so long to put a severance tax on minerals was that many stockmen held oil and gas leases and feared diminution of their royalties.

that took him into every hamlet of Wyoming; he also demonstrated the best speaking skill of any politician in the state's history. Lyndon Johnson, then Senate Majority Leader, came to Wyoming and promised that McGee would go on the powerful Appropriations Committee if elected. Johnson later delivered on the promise, and McGee packs a wallop for Wyoming on all-important federal funding of local projects. He also sits on the Foreign Relations Committee and supported the Vietnam war with equal vigor under Presidents Johnson and Nixon, a hawklike stance not unpopular in Wyoming. Despite liberal votes on many social issues, McGee also protected his home flank by defending the oil industry's tax privileges. (The late Gene Cervi, the Denver editor, took a caustic view of McGee's performance: "McGee landed in Washington, sold his soul to LBJ, and LBJ clipped the coupons on McGee. McGee was the man who thought up the phrase, 'the arrogance of dissent.' He was right in attacking the Birchers, but he's no flaming liberal.")

McGee keeps his state fences in repair by frequent trips home and assiduous attention to constituents' requests. A still more basic reason for his success may be Wyoming's time-honored tradition of keeping a Senator of each party in Washington, thus protecting its flanks regardless of which party holds the Presidency. The state has had one Democratic Senator almost continuously since 1917; perhaps the greatest of these was Joseph C. O'Mahoney, an inveterate fighter for state interests who also won national respect as one of the Senate's more able members. Another was Lester C. Hunt, whom Gunther spoke of warmly in *Inside U.S.A.*; Hunt met a tragic end by his own hand in 1954. Wyoming has performed a balancing act in its Senate delegation ever since the earliest days, when it was said that the state had one Senator for cattle, one for sheep.

Except for the McGee phenomenon, Wyoming in each election seems to repeat a summary made of a typical election in the early 1960s: "A Republican state went Republican." For example, Congressman Teno Roncalio, whom we quoted earlier, wears his liberal heart on his sleeve and has a dynamism that would probably assure longevity in office in most states; for Wyoming, he is simply too far to the left to win except in strongly Democratic years. He won in 1970 with only 608 votes to spare. (Perhaps I am biased in Roncalio's favor. I interviewed him in Cheyenne in 1969, and in all my travels for these books, rushing from interview to interview across towns cold and hot, dusty and rain-drenched, forever learning the geography of a new city, Roncalio was the only man gracious enough to immediately offer to come to my hotel room to see me. As I learned from him, Gunther had operated that way when he hit Cheyenne a quarter of a century before. Not being Gunther, I went to Roncalio's office instead.)

With the Republicans in control of all state offices and the legislature, Wyoming politics today is really tripartite—Democrats, the ultraconservative Republicans, and moderate Republicans. Right-wing Republicanism remains a potent force, its chief bastion in the extreme northwestern part of Wyoming—the Great Horn Basin, Cody, Powell, Worland, and Thermopolis. The conservatives' chief spokesman has been Richard Jones, a state senator from Cody and veteran finance committee chairman whose absolute rule in the legislative halls was not broken until he was successfully challenged on the senate floor in 1969. Governor Hathaway and Senator Hansen are actually representatives of a more pragmatic, modern Republicanism (at least by Wyoming standards), a force which has been gaining steadily in power and influence over recent years. In earlier years, for instance, it would have been unthinkable for a Republican governor to suggest a minerals severance tax, as Hathaway did in 1969. The minority Democrats in the legislature delight in agitating and festering the splits among the Republicans, thus exercising influence beyond their own numbers. More normally, however, the real legislative fights are between the interests of the big lobbies. Chief among these are the Stock Growers Association, the Rocky Mountain Oil and Gas Association, the Farm Bureau Federation, the Wyoming Education Association, the Wyoming Association of Municipalities, the Union Pacific Railroad, and the Truckers Association.

Campaign financing is the Democrats' gut problem; they still have a diminishing base of support among working people in towns along the Union Pacific line, but organized labor is too fragile in Wyoming to offer significant financial help. The Republicans, by contrast, get heavy backing from the ranching and oil interests to which we have referred, as well as a relative newcomer called WYOPAC—the doctors' Wyoming Political Action Committee, a heavy investor in campaigns.

Lacking normal in-state campaign fund sources, the Democrats are obliged to depend for the lion's share of their financing on outside groups such as the national AFL-CIO COPE and the liberally oriented National Committee for an Effective Congress. A budget of $250,000 will buy a very respectable Senate campaign in Wyoming; officers of national groups acknowledge they rarely turn away the opportunity to elect a friendly Senator for such a low price (a mere fraction of the cost in a major state). In 1970, when McGee's Senate seat, the governorship, and the U. S. House seat were all at stake, the total campaign bill was between $424,000 and $714,000, depending on whose estimates one believed. The Senate race attracted the most money—McGee's expenditures between $150,000 (according to the Democrats) and $300,000 (according to the Republicans), and the campaign of the Republican contender, John Wold, between $150,000 and $250,000. Despite appearances by Vice President Agnew and other prominent out-of-state Republicans, McGee was reelected with 55.8 percent of the vote.

Heavy outside campaign financing may be yet another reflection of the way that out-of-state interests dominate Wyoming life. Even if true, this has not alienated the Wyoming voter: the state ranks among the very top in the nation in the percentage of its voting age citizens who actually turn out for elections.

One of Wyoming's nicknames is Equality State, and with some justification, since Wyoming led the nation in granting women the right to vote, first as a territory (in 1869) and subsequently as a state (on admission to the Union in 1890). Later Wyoming became the first state to elect a woman state legislator (in 1910) and the first state to elect a woman governor (Mrs. Nellie Tayloe Ross, in 1924). One of the first figures to really fight the Wyoming establishment in modern times was Velma Linford, an aggressive redhead from an old Star Valley Mormon family who was elected state superintendent of education in 1954 and 1958 and moved Wyoming past 38 other states in its school standards in eight years. (She fought, for instance, for federal aid for education when it was viewed locally as a great evil.) In 1970 one woman was speaker of the Wyoming house and another, Mrs. Thrya Thomson, was secretary of state (making her the highest ranking woman in American state government, since that office is next in line to the Wyoming governorship).

But Mrs. Thomson told me she had ruled out running for governor herself, and when one looks more closely, women's role in Wyoming is hardly an ideal one. Suzanne Hunsucker, a free-lance writer based in Riverton, notes in *The Nation:*

> Wyoming is a man's state—its men have stayed as rugged and forceful as the landscape, but most women have lost their pioneer drive. . . . Wyoming women are charming and hospitable, but basically uninvolved and unsympathetic with their national sisters who are pushing for a ticket to equality. . . .
>
> Males dominate the state's professions—for example, there are only eight women lawyers in the state total of almost 500. . . . Only 22 women have been elected to the state legislature in the past 100 years. The University of Wyoming graduates more than twice as many men as women, and [in spring 1970] 275 men and three women received doctorates. . . .
>
> In Wyoming, men desert wives and children for extended hunting, fishing, mountain climbing, and back packing trips. Rodeos and chariot races are man's domain; women are usually left to ogle in the dust next to the cold beer. . . .

According to the prevalent mythology in Wyoming, chief credit for the state's move to women's suffrage should go to Mrs. Esther Morris, a hardy pioneer woman who also became the first justice of the peace of her sex in America. Wyoming has gone so far as to send Mrs. Morris' statue to stand in Statuary Hall in the U. S. Capitol as Wyoming's most outstanding deceased citizen. The Morris myth has been effectively demolished, however, by the state's distinguished historian, T. A. Larson. He has shown that Mrs. Morris played no more than the most casual role in persuading the Territorial Legislature to take its historic step. The chief architect of the legislation was William H. Bright, a former Union Army major who came to South Pass City, Wyoming, to open a saloon and work as a miner in 1868; the next year he went to the legislature and personally led the fight for women's suffrage, a cause in which he had long been interested.

Why was Wyoming first? No major suffragette movement existed in the state. At the time, men outnumbered women six-to-one on this hard-drinking, heavy gambling frontier (and not a few of the ladies present were prostitutes). Thus the legislature had little to fear in giving women the vote, and it hoped to attract more to the territory; as the Cheyenne *Leader* reported at the time, "We now expect at once quite an immigration of ladies to Wyoming," adding that it was "nothing more or less than a shrewd advertising doge, a cunning device to obtain for Wyoming a widespread notoriety." Two years later, Susan B. Anthony came to Laramie and proclaimed: "Wyoming is the first place on God's green earth which could consistently claim to be the land of the free!" But the men of the territorial legislature, showing qualms over what they had wrought, voted a complete repeal of female suffrage; this dastardly act was thwarted only by a governor's veto, which was sustained by the slender margin of one vote. (The governor said he had been offered a $2,000 bribe to sign the repealer.) Esther Morris had a little trouble with her own saloon-keeper husband the same year, swearing out a warrant for his arrest on a charge of assault and battery.

Towns, Tourism, and the Great Parks

Boom and bust have been the order of the day for Wyoming's cities and towns since the days the railroad first came through. Today the two largest—Cheyenne (pop. 40,914) and Casper (39,361)—present dreary, low-slung skylines, their inner cores rotting as the action moves to suburban shopping centers. I found no sleepier capital in the U.S.A. than Cheyenne, a slow-moving town of squat brick buildings, saddle shops, cowboy hats, and that rarest of American things today—free parking places in every block. Take away the scattering of recent-model automobiles and the scene could as well be 1920. At one end of Capitol Street stands the quiet gold-domed State Capitol; at the other, its presence dominating the downtown area, the turreted pink and grey Union Pacific railway station, adorned by a handsome red, white, and blue UP shield that bespeaks an earlier glory.

Cheyenne in its early days was regarded, in the words of one Western writer, "as one of the roughest, toughest, six-shooting communities of the West—second perhaps only to Tombstone. . . . Liquor was cheap, pay was good, ammunition plentiful, and stakes were high." Today about the only real excitement comes with the legendary Frontier Days, the world's biggest, oldest, and best rodeo, a grand show of daring cowboys, bucking broncos, Indians in full regalia, picturesque cowgirls, and to top it all off, nighttime chuck wagon races. Despite the enormous size of their state, Wyomingites are willing to travel hundreds of miles over their lonely, speedy highways for a football or basketball game or a rodeo; anyone who hasn't made it to Cheyenne during the normal course of a year is likely to check in for Frontier Days. All of Wyoming is rodeo-happy, and each little town seems to have its own bronco show, a fair, or an illustrious event like Sheridan's All-American Indian Days, where Miss Indian America gets crowned each year.

For years, Cheyenne's economy has been based on the state and federal government offices, the Union Pacific, and Warren Air Force Base—the latter on the site of a fort built in 1867 to protect railroad workers from Indian attacks. With railroad employment in a long decline, the air base—which became the largest intercontinental ballistic missile base in the world—saved Cheyenne from becoming a semi-ghost town. Starting in the mid-1950s, construction of the Atlas missile complex sent employment up to 11,000 men. Then there was a bust, then the Minuteman came in with big payrolls again, and the town overbuilt in residential and business sites. Then the Minuteman bubble burst, and now Cheyenne is counting on another boom from the ABM—to be followed, predictably, by another bust.

Casper's booms and busts are based on oil, the business that made the town in the first place and sustains it as a sort of little Tulsa today. About 40 miles north of town are the famous Salt Creek wells, which sparked a great oil boom soon after World War I; next to Salt Creek is Teapot Dome, a name made infamous during the Harding administration. After Casper's boom of the '20s came deep depression in the '30s; then came wartime revival, then major hurt from the recessions of the '50s. Great alarms were sounded in the mid-'60s when big oil companies started pulling their office forces out. But the strong upturn from new discoveries in the late '60s started yet another boom, to last no one knew how long. Casper is enough of an office and equipment center for oil that it thrives even when the strikes are miles away, in much the same manner that Fairbanks in Alaska now prospers from distant North Slope strikes.

Casper shares another similarity with Fairbanks: wintertime "cabin fever," or a surfeit of alcoholism, sexual promiscuity, and violence that seems to be rooted in multiple factors, ranging from economic uncertainty and the common possession of guns to people's feeling of physical isolation. Cheyenne is 180 miles away and Denver, the closest metropolis, 300 miles distant. Snow often falls during nine months of the year, and the long, cold winters are punctuated by howling wind storms that shake people awake in their beds. And then there is the "Chinook," a warm, dry wind of early spring that blows in from the Laramie Mountains and sends temperatures soaring as much as 40 degrees in a matter of hours. Like Europe's *foehn* wind from the Alps, it is said to cause serious disorientation and contribute some to the amazing statistics on Casper that were assembled by the Los Angeles *Times'* David Shaw: homicide and divorce rates 60 percent above the statewide average, the highest suicide rate for any American city on which statistics can be reliably gathered, and exceptionally high degrees of mental health commitments, alcoholism cases, and juvenile delinquency.

Casper merits special note as the home city of KTWO-TV, respected as the most influential news medium in Wyoming. The station won the du Pont award for its broadcast editorials, all of which deal with state and local issues and are often more crusading and outspoken than the Wyoming newspapers. The station has fought the ultraconservatives, favored a severance tax on minerals, and backed school reorganization. Its general manager,

Jack Rosenthal, also takes special pride in the station's postcard poll of Wyoming voters in statewide elections—which through 1970 had correctly picked the winner in 12 contests. (The station sends its postal query cards to cross-sections of voters on registration lists in all counties of the state and uses sophisticated sort-out and weighting techniques to come up with re- markably accurate predictions.) I can recall no other small-state television station—and few in large states—which make an effort in public affairs com- parable to this station, operating from its windy hillside location outside remote Casper.

Laramie (pop. 23,143), outgrowth of a one-time tent city on the UP line, is of interest because it houses the land-grant University of Wyoming. It is recorded that in early years the legislature appropriated less for the university than it did for wolf and coyote bounties, but gradually an im- pressive physical plant and major state funding evolved. The state has no other four-year state college; since most Wyoming college students go to Laramie, a common bond and society is formed in each generation. The university is also Wyoming's music and art center, or at least as much of a cultural center as Wyoming could be expected to have. The isolated loca- tion does make it difficult to attract enough topnotch faculty; the winters at its 7,200-foot altitude, I heard, are long and miserable.

Negroes constitute less than 1 percent of Wyoming's population, but the university does have a number, especially on football scholarships. In 1969 a great imbroglio erupted when 14 black football players, wearing black armbands, walked into the office of football coach Lloyd Eaton and asked to discuss the racial policies of the Mormon Church. The team was sched- uled to play Brigham Young University the following weekend. Eaton, a stiff disciplinarian of the old school, told the players he had a rule against talking with demonstrating team players—and fired all 14 from the team, on the spot, without further discussion. Football fans all over Wyoming rushed to applaud Eaton's action before the full facts of the case had even been reported—suggesting, in the eyes of many observers, a deep racism and anti-intellectualism in the state. The arts and sciences faculty of the uni- versity passed a resolution calling the coach's precipitous action "unjust, un- constitutional and unwise, bringing the entire university into disrepute." But Senator Hansen was doubtless right when he said: "A lot of Wyoming people are proud of a coach willing to be that tough—having the courage to stand by his rules."

After Laramie, there is no Wyoming town with substantially more than 10,000 people. A booming tourist industry thrives in and around the towns close to Yellowstone, the Tetons, and the handsome, glacier-packed Big Horn Mountains of northern Wyoming. This is big dude ranch territory and has also attracted a number of rich out-of-staters who have purchased or built their own ranches—Robert Woodruff of Coca-Cola and H. L. Hunt near Cody, for instance, or millionaire Oliver Wallop at Sheridan (he once entertained Prince Philip at his ranch), and the Rockefellers in the Jackson

Hole area. After a long dispute with local cattlemen and other citizens, the Rockefellers in 1950 finally cleared a gift of a major tract of land to be part of Grand Teton National Park. (A former high Interior Department official reminded me that Wyoming interests, especially the stock growers, "fought tooth and nail against Grand Teton. They wanted to keep the land for grazing. Hell, an acre of tourists is more worthwhile than an acre of cows any day." It was an example, he said, "of how most people let themselves get led around by the nose, by the special interests who have control of newspapers and radio stations and make the big political contributions and screw the rest of a state whenever they can get away with it.") Jackson Hole, a vast, green, fertile valley bounded by mountains on all sides, has two magically beautiful lakes—Jackson and Jenny—some of the most luxuriant hay meadows of the West, and a prospering ski industry which promises to make it what local partisans call "Wyoming's answer to Sun Valley." The town of Jackson has developed into something of a shop-, bar- and motel-laden tourist trap, but it does recall the old West with the ancient board-walks around the city park. Lively summertime theater is one of the newer attractions. Nearby, the largest elk herd in the world winters; as many as 9,000 or 10,000 can be seen on a single feed ground.

A tasteful and valuable man-made addition to the natural beauty of northwest Wyoming has also evolved in recent years with construction of the Buffalo Bill Historical Center at Cody, the town Buffalo Bill himself founded. The center includes not only colorful memorabilia of Buffalo Bill, but the Plains Indian Museum and the magnificent Whitney Gallery of Western Art, donated by Cornelius Vanderbilt Whitney, Jr.

The Yellowstone and Grand Teton National Parks, of course, remain the crowning jewels of Wyoming. Though only eight miles separate their borders, they are totally different. Yellowstone, the first, greatest, and largest of the national parks (more than 2 million acres), offers more geysers than any other place on earth, brilliant pools and boiling springs and mud volcanoes, bear and elk and moose and other animal herds, and seemingly endless miles of handsome lakes and streams and waterfalls. The idea for this first national park (now one of 36), it will be recalled, was conceived one night in 1870 by explorers gathered around a campfire in the Yellowstone. A century later, the summertime traffic jams, especially at Old Faithful, can be fearsome, and close to 2.5 million people visit the park each year. Yellowstone is now becoming accessible in winter, too, by snowmobile travel. Only occasionally does nature strike back against this heavy use of its once remote treasure. In 1959, for instance, an earthquake in the Yellowstone vicinity killed 29 persons.

Grand Teton, just to the south, presents a mountain drama with few earthly equals: the glacier-packed, ragged peaks of the geologically youthful Tetons thrusting abruptly skyward from the floor of Jackson Hole. The attendance at this park has risen spectacularly in recent years as Californians, the heaviest travelers of the West, visit it both for its own sake and on their way to Yellowstone.

A Sportsman's Paradise

An outsider wondering what it is that draws and holds people in Wyoming's immense solitude does well to talk to a man like Charles Crowell, chairman of the state's Game and Fish Commission. As a boy, Crowell went to Wyoming from Pennsylvania, later returning East to attend Yale as an undergraduate and law school student. But he selected Wyoming for his adult years precisely because of the rugged outdoor life it offers. A grey-haired man with a ruddy complexion and rough-hewn features mildly reminiscent of George Romney, Crowell points out that within range of his Casper home and office he can be on antelope hunting grounds a mere two miles distant, hunting deer within five miles, or shooting geese or mallards in less than an hour's drive.

"For the big game hunter, Wyoming has opportunities second to none— moose, elk, antelope, deer, bighorn sheep, mountain goats, brown and grizzly bear" Crowell points out. The Game and Fish Commission—its activities totally supported by fishing and hunting licenses mostly paid for by out-of-staters—stocks the streams with fish like rainbow trout that grow an inch in a month, transplants elk from the Yellowstone area, where they are in surplus, to other parts of the state, has abetted a huge growth in the antelope and deer populations, and has even introduced wild turkeys to Wyoming. An absence of people makes Wyoming territory a perfect wildlife preserve.

Does Crowell miss the cosmopolitan amenities of the East? Only in part, he replies:

When I go to New York City there are two things I do. I go down to the Grand Central Oyster Bar. And then I go down to the lower level at Grand Central about 9 A.M. and see them getting off those commuter trains—getting punched with elbows and attaché cases and umbrellas. Then I'm convinced I made the right choice in coming to Wyoming.

I also like this romantic testimony to Wyoming, made several years ago by Dr. Lester C. Hunt, later governor and U. S. Senator:

The trapper, the explorer, the pony express rider, and the cowboy may have passed over these hills, but the sunsets against which the pioneers saw them silhouetted still flame over Wyoming in scarlet and gold. Times may change, but the fundamental character of Wyoming will never change. . . .

MONTANA

HIGH, WIDE, HANDSOME — AND REMOTE

FAR-FLUNG MONTANA, larger than all American states save Alaska, Texas, and California, once the private satrapy of the Anaconda Copper Mining Company, is packed with contrast and contradiction.

Eastern Montana is high plains country, mile after mile of level or gently rolling wheatfield and grazing land, covering fully three-fifths of the state, sharing a common culture with the neighboring Dakotas and Wyoming. This is the Montana of dryland farming and great cattle spreads, interspersed with occasional buttes and the gorges cut by the Missouri and Yellowstone Rivers. Close to the rivers, one finds spots of irrigation where a few cottonwood groves appear, and there are a few forested areas. Otherwise, the lonely expanse is broken only by an occasional grain elevator or water tower looming over a little town, or perhaps by an oil rig.

Western Montana is something else again. This is high Rocky Mountain and Continental Divide country, stretching from Glacier National Park at the Canadian border to Yellowstone on the Wyoming border. It is a terrain of snow-capped peaks and mountain streams, hillsides richly forested with fir and larch and pine, of mining gulches and cool lakes and green valleys. This western two-fifths of the state has some cattle, like the east, but everything else is different. Preeminently, this is mining, lumber, and tourist territory.

The weather is as different as the landscape. Eastern Montana lies on the unprotected Great Plains of Canada and America, where the ranchers and wheat farmers bake in summer heats that have soared to 117 degrees; then, in winter, they must steel themselves against fierce blizzards and sleet storms that have more than once killed thousands of head of cattle. On the day that Lewis and Clark first pushed into Montana in 1805, an inch of snow fell and covered the wild flowers of these plains, and Clark wrote in his journal of a "verry extraodernarey climate."

Western Montana, by contrast, is protected from the Arctic winds by its mountains, and while the snow cover is deep, the prevailing Pacific weather patterns make the winters milder and even permit cherry orchards in some counties. There are exceptions even to this, however; near Helena, in 1954, the temperature plunged to −70 degrees, coldest ever recorded in the continental U. S. A. West Yellowstone so often has the nation's coldest temperatures—in the range of −30 to −40 degrees—that the town fathers tried to get the Weather Bureau to drop it from the nationally broadcast reports.

Ugliness and beauty reach extremes in Montana too. The ugliness, man-made, can be seen in the gruesome slag heaps from the mines around "the richest hill on earth" at Butte, where the Anaconda Company rose to fame and fortune. But natural beauty abounds in these same western mountains. John Steinbeck, in *Travels with Charley*, wrote of Montana as "a great splash of grandeur. . . . The land is rich with grass and color, and the mountains are the kind I would create if mountains were ever put on my agenda. . . . Montana has a spell on me. It is grandeur and warmth. If Montana had a seacoast, or if I could live away from the sea, I would instantly move there and petition for admission. Of all the states it is my favorite and my love."

Montana is so vast and disjointed, its cities and towns separated by such gulfs of space, that it has traditionally been difficult to talk of any common Montanan culture. "Provincialism," one resident told me, "engulfs Montana." Communications are rather inadequate, and there is no single leading city. Montanans from the mountainous west talk of the eastern plains as if they were as far distant as the Florida Keys or Maine's rock-bound coast. Indeed, the northern border of the state sweeps along for 540 miles, touching three of Canada's gigantic provinces along the way, the same distance as Boston to Richmond or New York to Detroit. It used to be said that Butte was Butte and that was copper, and eastern Montana was wheat and cattle, and that never the twain shall meet.

Yet the isolation has never been as total as it appeared. For many decades, Montanans have thought nothing of driving hundreds of miles for a high-school football game or a social occasion, a job now made all the easier by the interstate highways. At least political Montana has long met at Helena each two years for the legislature. Historian K. Ross Toole of the University of Montana has written of Montanans' "strong sense of belonging," stemming from their common adversities with nature, since the very beginning of the state. Scotty Campbell, publisher of the *Montana Standard* at Butte, recalls that when he was on the *Stars and Stripes* in the Pacific during World War II, scores of Montana GIs would hit him for a loan because of the common state bond—and would invariably return the money later.

Yet even those strands of commonality were weak in comparison to what some Montanans hope and believe is developing in their state today. Montana has a history of rather brutal exploitation of its natural resources —the kill-and-run fur trade days, uncontrolled timber cuts, overgrazed sheep and beef eroding the land, the frenetic dig for copper at Butte. Until very recent times, few were the voices raised to question what was being done to nature. Yet since 1960, the shrug-of-the-shoulders apathy has disappeared. Montanans are desperately concerned about the natural environment. Conservationist groups, fighting every threat from uncontrolled mining to poisoned pulp mill air, have sprung up across the state. The newspapers are crusading. Montanans talk of their genuine feeling that they still have one of the few places in the country where the final decisions have yet to be made concerning water, natural resources, coal, and the entire environment. Suddenly, on this issue, the concerns of Billings, which is a wheat and oil town, seems to be pulled together with those of Missoula, a timber town, and with Bozeman, a farming recreation center. As Ross Toole explained it to me, "There's a subliminal kind of idea in the Montanan's mind, that what used to be our curse—the space and distance and freight rates and so forth—is somehow now going to turn to our blessing." Montanans have an idea, Toole believes, "that we have something of great value here—it's air, it's sky, it's mountains, it's prairies, it's space—we share this in common."

A decade ago, the burning issue in Montana was taxes; today it is the environment. Some want to see the state's resources quickly developed at any cost; others want economic development provided Montana's land and forests and air can be adequately protected in the process; still another camp consists of narrow-minded preservationists who want no development at all. Not a few Montanans would like to keep Montana untouched as their private fishing and hunting preserve; of these I heard it said that they "would like to put a wall around the state and grant three-day visas to visitors."

Montana has good reason to be in the blues about its economic condition. The flight of its young people to attractive out-of-state jobs accelerated in the 1960s, a decade in which Montana barely missed an absolute drop in population. (The Census in 1970 found 694,409 people in Montana, far below official expectations and only 2.9 percent ahead of 1960. Rural areas especially are declining in population, due to increased mechanization and the trend to larger and corporate farms. There was a population drop of 13.9 percent in 18 eastern Montana farm counties during the 1960s.) Compared to the rest of the U. S. A., Montanans' per capita income has been dropping precipitously: in 1950 it was 108 percent of the national figure; in 1960, 92 percent, and in 1970, 86 percent. Thus the anomalous, contradictory picture emerges of optimistic faith in the future combined with a deteriorating economic condition. Toole recalls that "Montana has been

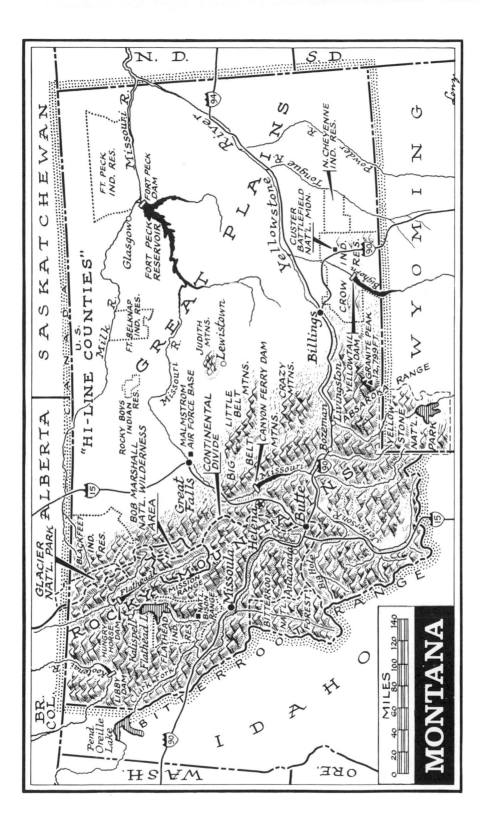

optimistic before, and then brought down crashingly." It could happen
again.

Our catalogue of Montana contradictions has a few more entries. The
state is one of don't-fence-me-in individualists, but it also has the lustiest labor union movement in the mountain states, centered in the mining town of
Butte. Whether justified or not, Montana has the reputation of being the
rowdiest, hardest drinking territory west of Chicago, but it also has one of
the lowest crime rates in the nation. The proportion of first and second
generation immigrants (especially Scandinavians and Germans) is the highest
in the intermountain region, but the number of rebel-stock Southerners from
Texas and Missouri is extremely high for a northern state. The Montana
Power Company is said to exercise inordinate influence, but the counter-
vailing forces of the rural electric cooperatives and the Farmers Union are
exceptionally strong for the Mountain West. And while Montana elects some
of the toughest, most conservative governors of the U. S. A.—men who
have refused to proclaim United Nations Days or to back public power
projects for their state—it sends to Congress some of the most liberal Senators, a tradition of many years' standing now carried on by Lee Metcalf,
arch-foe of the private power interests, and the prestigious Mike Mansfield,
an internationalist and fervent opponent of foreign military ventures, the
Vietnam war in particular.

"The Companies" and Lesser Powers

In one of the most colorful and controversial chapters of *Inside U. S. A.*,
John Gunther reported that the Anaconda Company had "a constrictorlike
grip on much that goes on, and Montana is nearest to a 'colony' of any
American state, Delaware alone possibly excepted." Actually, Anaconda was
already starting to relax its grip and to extricate itself from direct involvement in election campaigns by the time Gunther wrote (1946). But the
story he depicted, of one corporation's feudalistic control of every aspect of
a state, was true of what had existed well into the 1930s. Secretive and often
vindictive, Anaconda controlled almost all elections—dragging in the "ceme-
tery vote" where necessary. A common saying in the state was that Anaconda "has only lost one governorship since statehood." State legislators
were often vassals of the company, and Gunther could quote one Anaconda
lobbyist as saying, "Give me a case of Scotch, a case of gin, one blonde, and
one brunette, and I can take any liberal!" To top it all off, Anaconda owned
most of the newspapers of Montana, stifling public debate and providing
Montanans with a homogenized, sanitized view of their state and the world.
Dissent was so frowned on that letters to the editors were never printed.

The reasons for Anaconda's onetime deep involvement in Montana politics go back to the titanic "War of the Copper Kings" before the turn of
the century, a story vividly capsulized by Gunther:

First came William A. Clark, of Scots origin, and a savage, magnetic Irishman named Marcus Daly; at that time, in the 1880s, the Butte gulches were supposed to contain only gold and silver, which gave out, whereupon Daly struck deeper and found copper; Clark, one of the most tidily ruthless men who ever lived, busied himself bribing his way to the United States Senate, and Daly created Anaconda. . . . Then money from the East came in, partly from the Rockefellers, and a new corporation called Amalgamated was formed. Clark and Daly became bitter enemies. Wealth incalculable depended on conflicting mine sites. . . . Inevitably the murderous fight for copper involved everything else in Montana since, first, rival magnates sought to control the courts . . . and then the legislature. At the turn of the century a dashing young engineer, F. Augustus Heinze, of German blood, "hijacked" both Clark and Daly. He bought judges right and left, harangued vast crowds from the steps of the courthouse, howled against the absentee "kerosene interests" (Standard Oil), sued Amalgamated for 100 million dollars worth of claims, and left Montana in 1906 with a fortune estimated at 50 million dollars. Seldom has financial history known a more muscular and successful raid. . . . Meanwhile Daly died and Clark sold out his interests. The interrelations between these grotesque potentates is as complex as that of the Holy Roman emperors after Diocletian. Presently Amalgamated, which had swallowed up Anaconda, was in turn swallowed up by Anaconda which revived. Then an Irishman who had been a department store clerk, John D. Ryan, succeeded Daly, and ran Anaconda single-handed until his own death in 1933.

This bitter early history goes far toward explaining why Anaconda, once it had the upper hand in Montana, determined to keep the press and political system under its thumb. The Copper Kings had all used newspapers as pawns in their struggles for power, and Anaconda was not about to forget how Heinze had manipulated the press to whip up sentiment against the company. The "bought" legislatures of the early 20th century were but logical successors of their predecessors of the 1880s and 1890s. Politicians and businessmen were forced to bow their heads and acquiesce to the wishes of Anaconda, or they quickly found themselves frozen out of the system. A vital ally of Anaconda, frequently tied in by interlocking directorates, was the Montana Power Company. Often, the two were referred to as "the Twins" or simply as "the Company," a close union symbolized by their use of the same legal counsel.

The vital change in Montana began in the early 1930s when Ryan died and W. H. Hoover took over the presidency of Anaconda. Hoover was determined to curb the company's bludgeon-like activities and to adopt a more subtle approach. When some company officials pointed out to him that Anaconda's 24-hour-a-day "hospitality rooms" at Helena were making "tramps" out of some members of the legislature, Hoover decreed that the free booze be limited to three hours a day in a single room (a policy held until 1971, when Anaconda and Montana Power finally gave up their legislative "watering holes" altogether, finding them no longer effective with the new sophisticated legislator). A key figure in the company in the transitional years was Al Wilkinson, a skillful lobbyist who had started with Anaconda as a miner working underground in 1912. Wilkinson became public relations director for Anaconda in 1928, traveled the state extensively building up an unparalleled set of personal contacts, and maintained the legislative operation until 1953, when he went to Washington as the company's chief lobbyist for the final 13 years of his career. Wilkinson saw that the old blackjack and payoff-style lobbying was out of date, and he operated in a thoroughly professional way; several legislators with whom he dealt told me of their respect for him, based on his candor and honesty. Knowledgeable Montana sources consider Wilkinson a key figure in persuading Anaconda, starting in the early 1940s, to extricate itself from open involvement in political campaigns—an extreme break with its past custom; later Wilkinson was reported to have played a key role in getting the company to divest itself of its newspaper holdings. Apparently a counterforce to change for many years was Cornelius F. Kelley, a throwback to the old Irish days who had started out as Daly's office boy and later headed Anaconda for a period of time.

But forces more powerful than personalities were forcing Anaconda to change. Anaconda was becoming a massive corporation with worldwide holdings (especially in Chile); to remain the heavy-handed wielder of power and target of political opponents back home in Montana was obviously bad for its public image. The emergence of new economic forces—big oil and timber among them—also changed the economic complexion of Montana. Finally, Anaconda ceased to be the overwhelming consumer of Montana Power's electric output, and a feud actually broke out between the two behemoths. So the Twins stopped using the same legal counsel. Their political divorce was symbolized by the decision of Robert Corette, who had been an Anaconda lobbyist but failed to get a promotion he wanted with the company, to quit and go to work for the power company—headed by his brother, J. E. (Jack) Corette—instead.

Ownership of the newspapers also became more of an embarrassment than a help to Anaconda. By virtue of the papers' decisions on whether and how to cover controversial issues and events, the company found itself dragged into every public dispute in Montana; it was also under no little pressure to kill stories on officials in trouble with the police. So in 1959 the papers were sold to the Iowa-based Lee Syndicate, and for the first time in more than half a century, Montana had a legitimately free statewide press.

The copper giant of the West has not, of course, lost all interest in Montana elections or what happens in its state government. For many years in the postwar period copper from Chile completely outshone Anaconda's domestic production, but high-handed expropriation by the Chilean government is obliging Anaconda to turn to its second and original line of defense, North America. The hill at Butte is still Anaconda's major U. S. copper source, although the firm has large mines in Nevada and Arizona. In 1969, Anaconda and its subsidiaries did $1.4 billion worth of business, ranking 76th among U. S. industrial corporations. So, like any company of that magnitude, Anaconda and its executives necessarily play a strong home-state role. As always, Anaconda is quite nonpartisan about its preferences in candidates.

In the legislature, it watches carefully to prevent new taxes on minerals and to hold down unemployment compensation levels. In 1966, Anaconda's Helena representative Glen Carney was described by one state legislator as such "a skillful and agreeable lobbyist" that a lawmaker "is ashamed of his suspicion that the old dragon is still there, wearing angora mittens." Some of the young, "high-powered professional lobbyists" brought in during recent years may not be quite as effective. But one thing is sure: Anaconda's eye on Helena has never blinked.

The Montana Power Company is the most powerful political organization in modern Montana and seeks to wield much the same power—albeit more discreetly and quietly—that Anaconda did in days of yore. Consistently, it lobbies against cooperative power, against stiff air and water pollution control standards, to put its friends on the Montana Supreme Court, and to keep the absolute control of the rate-setting Montana Railroad and Public Service Commission which it has maintained since before World War I. In 1970 the Lee Newspapers disclosed that Governor Forrest Anderson, when he was attorney general, had received land at bargain prices from Montana Power; then John Kuglin of the Great Falls *Tribune* reported how the wife of a Supreme Court justice, Wesley Castle, had purchased 40 acres of valuable lakefront property from Montana Power at $25 an acre. Thereafter, Castle never disqualified himself from cases involving the company; he often wrote the majority opinion of the court, favoring the utility in every case.

Senator Lee Metcalf, an implacable enemy of Montana Power, speaks admiringly of its political methods:

> Montana Power has a man in every community. He will be the company's manager or whatever, one of the better paid men in town, one of the best educated and one of the most personable. He belongs to all the service clubs—if he's a Protestant, he's a Mason; if he's a Catholic, he's a Knight of Columbus. He may head the local United Fund Drive. Inevitably, he is a man of great respect and regard in his community. When election time comes, the Power Company will take no overt positions, but will operate *sub rosa*. Its local men will operate subtly, not talking outright as power company men. It's an insidious type of influence and very hard for an opponent to strike back.

Metcalf, of course, has made a career of striking back, and his book, *Overcharge,* is a classic modern attack on the electric utilities and their price structures. Montana Power, he asserts, is one of the big overchargers—among the top 10 U.S. power companies in rate of return, benefiting, among other things, from the purchase of cheap power from the Bonneville Power Administration and from the best Montana hydroelectric sites, which it picked up at an early date. Metcalf criticizes Montana Power for its program of institutional ads in Montana papers "when they really don't have to advertise anything—they have a complete market for the product they sell." The real purpose of the ads, Metcalf suggests, is to dominate the newspapers; he says there are records of country weeklies which have had their advertising withdrawn when they wrote editorials hostile to the company.

One source of Montana Power's influence is alleged to be its tie (through interlocking directorates) to the First Bank System of St. Paul, a chain which controls banks all across the Upper Midwest. Local bankers are said to use their influence with local legislators in the interest of Montana Power. Finally, the power company is a potent influence in the Montana State Chamber of Commerce, a reactionary outfit that spends its time fighting environmental bills and trying to get authorities to enforce Montana's open and notorious fornication statute as a device to drive hippies and other nonconformists out of the state.

In one respect, Montana Power differs from the old Anaconda pattern in that its political support goes almost exclusively to one party—the Republicans. In 1966, Montana Power worked to defeat Senator Metcalf—while Anaconda, on the other side, was reportedly pulling strings to effect Metcalf's reelection.

Jack Corette, chairman of the board of Montana Power, is widely regarded in his state as a brilliant businessman, ruthless and determined that what's good for Montana Power is good for Montana. But the power company's role, Professor Toole believes, is not as blatant as its enemies suggest. When monster corporations play the heavy role they have in Montana, the blame for everything wrong in society is likely to land on their back. Toole comments: "It used to be Anaconda, and now Montana Power replaces it. The power company is much less of an ogre, but it's still an ogre. I don't know what Montana would do without some kind of an ogre."

Easy to forget is that there are other skillful power brokers in Montana. The railroads, Northern Pacific and Great Northern, have been adept lobbyists ever since Northern Pacific's 1864 coup in getting Congress to give it free every other section of land along its Montana right of way, a land area of 23,000 square miles, more than three times as large as New Jersey. Truckers, liquor dealers, oil and timbermen, teachers, doctors, nurses, and assorted taxpayer and business groups all are potent forces in the state today. Still a force to be reckoned with are the stockmen, representing a clearly conservative force, and the Farmers Union, dominant above all other farm groups (as it is in North Dakota) and a distinctly liberal force. Allied with the Farmers Union are the public power cooperatives, both natural enemies of the power company and conservative "establishment." The electric coops showed their strength in 1971 by getting the legislature to pass "territorial integrity" legislation barring the investor-owned utilities from pirating their service areas.

The labor unions have 63,000 workers in Montana, representing more than a third of the work force, well above the national average. The principal groups, all known for their political clout, are the AFL-CIO, the independent Mine, Mill and Smelter Workers Union, and the Railroad Brotherhoods. They have been more successful in electing liberals to the congressional delegation than to the state legislature, where their strength is concentrated in a limited number of districts.

Montana newspapermen, it has been said, enjoy the free air daily because many can remember the not-distant time when the Anaconda Company owned eight dailies in the state, including those in all the larger cities save Great Falls. Up through the 1920s, Anaconda had used its papers to fight any opponent in vituperative style; in later years the company press was simply a monument to apathy and bad journalism. Any news hostile to Anaconda—for example, a proposed bill to label silicosis as an industrial accident—was simply not printed at all. Prof. Thomas Payne of the University of Montana has noted that "a variety of historical, exotic, or other wise irrelevant topics graced the editorial pages, constituting in all probability the blandest diet of editorial comment ever served to any group of American newspaper readers."

Since the 1950 sale, all the former Anaconda papers have improved vastly in quality; as the editor of one told me, "It's fun now." Some have even taken to crusading, especially the *Missoulian* on the environmental issue. The Lee chain leaves each paper free to formulate its own editorial policy, and their stands vary widely—the *Montana Standard* at Butte most Democratic, the *Missoulian* independent, the Billings *Gazette* generally Republican like its own eastern end of Montana, and the Helena *Independent-Record* most staunchly conservative and least changed from the old days. Sometimes the papers tangle on issues; for example, the Helena paper attacked the University of Montana at Missoula as a hotbed of drugs, only to get a hot retort from the *Missoulian*.

The vital competition, however, is between the Lee papers, which do cooperate on business affairs and share a common Helena bureau, and the Great Falls *Tribune*, which was the great holdout of independent journalism during the years of Anaconda domination. O. S. Warden, founder and longtime publisher of the *Tribune*, was a Democratic National Committeeman for Montana, and the paper has always had that politics. In 1965 the paper was sold to the Minneapolis Star-Tribune Company—an example of the extension of Twin Cities influence across the Upper Midwest. Under Cowles management, the old gray *Tribune* was soon brightened with more aggressive reporting. Many regard it as Montana's best newspaper. It may be faulted, however, for a bias in favor of Senator Mansfield which gets in the way of objectivity.

As in many states, the vast bulk of the weekly press is conservative and dull. An exception is the Pulitzer Prize-winning *Hungry Horse News*, published by Mel Ruder in Columbia Falls. In 1969 death came to the 30-year-old *People's Voice*, which had been organized by Lee Metcalf and others as a spokesman for labor and the cooperatives back in the days of the Anaconda press monopoly. For years, editor Harry L. Billings attacked every element of the establishment with gusto. But in the late 1960s, as Billings turned the *People's Voice* to strong attacks on the Vietnam war, he found support from organized labor and some Farmers Union groups falling away. Success was apparently spoiling the appetite for controversy of some of the paper's traditional supporters. Farm organizations were becoming preoccupied with grain marketings, heavy truck haulings, and oil production. Directors of the rural electric coops, some of them wealthy and conservative, showed little appreciation for the liberal coalition which brought the REA program to rural U. S. A. in the first place. Machinists and pipefitters earning their money from the huge Malmstrom Air Force Base had no desire to attack the military. So, in the words of Billings' wife Gretchen, "Ultimately [the *Voice*] was killed by its own founders who reached the day when they could no longer tolerate or accept the independence that served them so well so long ago when they were victims rather than defenders of the status quo."

Butte: The Ultimate Company Town

A. B. Guthrie, Jr., describes Butte, that company town to end all company towns, as "a place of sporty extravagance, a settlement on a scarred and ugly hill in a hairpin of the Continental Divide where nature deposited such a load of metals as no man can imagine and chance brought together a cast of brash and colorful characters." Gunther called Butte "the toughest, bawdiest town in America." No one who has ever seen it is likely to forget it—the city set on a bare slopeside slanting to the south, surrounded by gaunt mountains, the massive open-pit Berkeley Mine begun by Anaconda in 1955, skeleton-like frames of the deep mines, grimy mine shacks and slag piles unnumbered, an aging center district palely reflecting some past glory but now far beyond its point of no return, dilapidated buildings with boarded-up windows, weed-infested empty lots, old and unemployed men walking the streets. In 1970 it was possible to buy the biggest building on the choice corner of the old business district—the old Metal Bank Building —for its unpaid tax bill of $40,000.

The dingy face of Butte should not obscure its wealth. Since the first gold glimmered in a prospector's pan there in 1864, some 400 million pounds of ore worth $3.5 billion—chiefly copper but also zinc, lead, manganese, silver and gold—have been taken from this richest hill on earth. Yet the known ore reserves still in the hill are greater in value than all that has so far been extracted. Also, though small potatoes in comparison, Butte has a well known school of mines, the headquarters of Montana Power, stockyards, tourism (especially winter sports), and a touch of diversified industry centered in an industrial park on land donated by Anaconda.

The postwar years have seen a fundamental change in Anaconda's mining methods. Underground mining, the exclusive method of the first 90 years, has become largely uneconomic and now employs less than 600 men, working two deep mines of high-grade ore; today most of the 2,758 miles of underground shafts and tunnels, some as deep as 5,300 feet, are deserted. Instead, the lion's share of activity has shifted to the yawning Berkeley Pit, now 600 feet deep and scheduled to go down to 2,000. Some 500 million tons of material have already been removed from the pit in a constant blasting, loading, and moving operation; close at hand are a giant gyratory crusher and concentrator plant, and then Anaconda's private railway to take the ore 25 miles distant to the town of Anaconda, where the smelting operation takes place. With automation and the manpower economies of open pit operation, Anaconda has been able to cut its Butte payroll down to 2,700 from about double that amount in the mid-1950s—even while production remains high. Anaconda's concentration on its Montana facilities is expanding with the imminent expropriation of its Chilean properties (which as recently as 1969 accounted for two-thirds its world production). The output of the Berkeley Pit has been increased and $26 million invested (half of it for pollution control) at the company's smelter at Anaconda. But the state health department, to Anaconda's horror, has labeled the Anaconda smelter, which pumps 1,000 tons of sulphur dioxide into the air daily, Montana's worst polluter, and has insisted on a 90 percent emission reduction by 1973. The action would cost Anaconda an extra $24 million, and true to its old ways, the company tried to exert political pressure behind the scenes —in this case, to get its friends in the White House to force the federal Environmental Protection Administration to rescind its technical opinions on which the state agency had taken action. Responding to the pressure, the EPA did indeed weaken its prior opinion that Anaconda could install the new antipollution equipment "without significant effects on sales revenues." The state health department stuck with its original order for early compliance but found itself in conflict with Governor Forrest Anderson, who refused to approve the agency's plan, saying it would hurt Montana economically.

Despite Anaconda's new investments, the city of Butte is suffering. Its population decline, beginning in the 1950s, speeded up to a 15.5 percent net loss in the 1960s (the 1970 Census report was 23,368).* Anaconda has had its booms and busts in the past, but it is a sad picture these days in comparison to 1917, when 100,000 people lived in or around Butte, 20,000 of them miners digging ore out of the slopes and drifts that lie beneath practically every inch of Butte city. Now there is even talk that the whole city, as it now stands, may have to be demolished to make way for the Berkeley Pit as it advances steadily against the city's eastern flank. Butte would move to the "flats," a level valley area to its south. Already the pit has moved westward to gobble up some old neighborhoods like Sin Town or Dublin Gulch, and Anaconda has bought up property to within a block of the center of the city.

Butte has a long, stormy history of labor relations going back to the 1890s when the Butte Miners' Union succeeded in playing the Copper Kings off against each other to gain recognition and a closed shop, decades ahead of most other U. S. unions. There followed a few years early in this cen-

---

* The figure may be deceptively low, since Anaconda saw to it that Butte's city lines were drawn in a contorted way to leave Anaconda properties outside, and thus free of city taxation. Silver Bow County outside Butte has another 18,613 people.

tury when a local editor could call Butte "the strongest union town on earth." Then came great disputes over whether the union should join the avowedly anticapitalist Industrial Workers of the World (IWW). There was a conservative takeover of the Butte Miners' Union, followed by a successful left-wing counterrevolt in 1914, marked by rioting, gunfire, death, declaration of martial law, and establishment of an open shop which would prevail for two decades. In 1917 the death by suffocation of 164 Butte miners in an underground fire led to a bitter strike in which the IWW was accused of aiding the German enemy. Martial law was again declared, and one of the IWW organizers was dragged from his sickbed and hanged from a railroad trestle on the edge of town. In the same years, federal agencies found widespread cases of pneumonia, tuberculosis, and silicosis—called "miner's consumption"—stemming from unhealthy conditions and inadequate safety protections in Anaconda's mines; this led the company to spend several millions of dollars on safety devices. Underground work for years remained hot, dangerous work, a situation still not altogether corrected. (Writer John Kuglin tells me that the last time he was at the 3,600-foot level of the Steward Mine, it was 85 degrees with 100 percent humidity.) Not until 1934, and a four-month strike, could the Butte miners again obtain the closed shop which they still have today.

Discordant labor relations still afflict Butte. Soon after World War II, Anaconda decided to take a more constructive community role by building recreation facilities for miners, a hospital for the city, and the splendid Columbia Gardens recreation area on its outskirts. But the Butte miners remained leery of their old adversary. In 1967–68 they were part of a disastrous eight-and-a-half-month strike of copper workers across the West which netted them only 56 cents extra an hour, minus fringe benefits, stretched out over three years. For that, many Butte miners were personally bankrupted, more than 1,000 felt obliged to leave Butte for good, local unemployment hit 49 percent, local businesses collapsed, and the city was left in a financial shambles. And now Anaconda is thinking of starting a new pit in the Columbia Gardens area.

The passing of the era of the underground miner is making Butte less liberal and less the Democratic stronghold it was for so long. Most of the work force now consists of "hard hat" men—shovel operators, drivers of quarter-million-dollar trucks or operational engineers—who are basically conservative and go home and live in a three-room suburban house. Their similarity to the saloon-visiting, hard-rock, transient miners of yore is small indeed. History records that many of the first miners to arrive at Butte were Irish who came in with Marcus Daly when the potato famine hit their native country; at Butte they started spots like Dublin Gulch or Cabbage Patch. Butte ballots still abound with names like "Depot Dan" Harrington or "Red Neck" Kelley. The other ethnic strains have included English, Cornish, Italians, Finns, and Slavs, and in the last few years, a new domestic strain—the Appalachians. But miners now need to be so skilled and able that only a quarter of the Appalachians can make the grade. The average weekly earnings of miners is $137, but contract workers who work on a carload basis, using dynamite and their own power tools, can earn substantially more.

One of the flavorful historical signs written some years ago by Robert H. Fletcher of the Montana Highway Commission and scattered across Montana stands on a hill overlooking the city, proclaiming in part: "Butte . . . was a bold, unashamed, rootin', tootin', hell-roarin' camp in days gone by and still drinks her liquor straight." Some of the old flavor may be gone, but Butte still knows how to sin pretty well. In the late 1960s the town worthies were shocked by the revelations of former Butte madam Beverly Snodgrass about illicit activities going on under their very noses. (Mrs. Snodgrass told a lurid story of how a prominent Butte politician, whom she called "Dimple Knees," "was extremely attentive to me and took me out to the remote 'Flat' area south of Butte where we made deep, sexual love." Gradually he took over her prostitution business. Mrs. Snodgrass said she paid the Butte police department thousands of dollars in annual payoffs, and when she stopped, one of her houses was gutted by fire. In 1968, when all this came to light, the police chief denied there was any illegal gambling or prostitution in Butte. But Mayor Tom Powers confirmed the presence of gambling punch boards in town, telling John Kuglin of the Great Falls *Tribune*: "Butte is a depressed area. They help the economy." His Honor also said: "The people of Butte want prostitution.")

But I am sure oldtime (and now fading) Butte will never have another tribute comparable to this by a stranger who passed through one night in the late 1950s—Jack Kerouac of *On the Road* fame, in a posthumously published piece called "The Great Western Bus Ride" *:

I walked the sloping streets in super below-zero weather . . . and saw that everybody in Butte was drunk. It was Sunday night, I had hoped the saloons would stay open long enough for me to see them. They never even closed. In a great old-time saloon I had a giant beer. On the wall was a big electric signboard flashing gambling numbers. The bartender gave me the honor of selecting a number for him on the chance of beginner's luck. No soap. "Arrived here 22 years ago and stayed. Montanans drink too much, fight too much, love too much." What characters in there: old prospectors, gamblers, whores, miners, Indians, cowboys, tobacco-chewing businessmen! Groups of sullen Indians drank red rotgut in the john. Hundreds of men played cards in an atmosphere of smoke and spittoons. It was the end of my quest for an ideal bar. An old blackjack dealer tore my heart out, he reminded me so much of W. C. Fields and my father, fat, with a bulbous nose, great rugged pockmarked angelic face. . . . I also saw a 90-year-old man called Old John who coolly played cards till dawn with slitted eyes, and had been doing so since 1880 in Montana, . . . since the days of the winter cattle drive to Texas, and the days of Sitting Bull. . . . There were Greeks and Chinamen. The bus didn't leave Butte till dawn. I promised myself I'd come back. The bus roared down the slope and looking back I saw Butte on her fabled Gold Hill still lit like jewelry and sparkling on the mountainside in the blue northern dawn.

* Published in *Esquire*, March 1970.

Cities, Environment, and the University Scene

Butte is not Montana's largest city—far from it. Billings and Great Falls are both twice as large, Missoula is several thousand greater, and if present population trends continue, even little Helena will be larger within a few years.

Billings (61,581) is a bustling, modern plains city, which seems to relate more to Minneapolis-St. Paul than to the rest of Montana. It is big in livestock and an important regional trade and transportation center. The city also has oil refineries and a substantial number of federal government branch offices. The physical setting could not be more unlike Butte's, but Billings also has notorious open prostitution. It suffers from air pollution, which comes from the refineries, feedlots practically within the city limits, and from sulphur dioxide emissions of a Montana Power generation plant named after Jack Corette.

Great Falls (60,019) best combines the worlds of west and east in Montana. Set on a great bend of the Missouri, it is named for falls on the river where major hydroelectric facilities are located. A special tie to the west is the 512-foot smokestack of Anaconda's refining plant, wire and cable mill, a chief consumer of the hydroelectric power. But while the mountains can even be seen to the west, Great Falls is also a plains city, set in the midst of great fields of winter wheat, and a major livestock center. In a way, it has always been a good area for livestock; at the nearby falls, Lewis and Clark recorded seeing "not less than 10,000 buffalo within a circle of two miles." An essential economic fact of Great Falls is the Strategic Air Commands Malmstrom Air Force Base, the central command post for 200 nuclear-tipped Minutemen. The new Safeguard antiballistic missile site, some miles northwest of the city, is expected to generate a major construction boom through 1974.

Great Falls still pays reverence to its native son, Charles M. Russell, whose meticulously honest paintings of early Western life—the Indian, the cowboy, the open plains as they were—were and are classics in their genre. Congress was even persuaded to make Russell's home and the log cabin where he did his work into a National Historic Landmark. Great Falls has another kind of symbol, noted by virtually every writer who passes through: Hill 57, a sequestered, tumble-down Indian slum on the edge of town, where shacks are surrounded by abandoned automobile hulks, old furniture, and broken appliances. Anthony Ripley of the New York *Times* noted that the Indians here "seem themselves a tragedy of history—landless, without tribe or reservation, most living on white man's welfare in squatters' shacks. . . ."

Helena (22,730), among the most remote and lightly populated of state capitals, sits amid low mountains, looking out over the flat and almost treeless Prickly Pear Valley. It would not be the capital at all if it had not won an exceedingly close election in 1894 when Marcus Daly was intent on making his town of Anaconda the seat of government and W. A. Clark was equally intent on Helena. Helena won by less than 1,000 votes. (Anaconda today is one of the uglier cities of America, practically overwhelmed by the company's huge smelter smokestack. One wonders if it would have been the same if it had won the statehood election.)

Helena's whole life has been based on chance. Its Main Street runs along Last Chance Gulch, where a small group of Georgians discovered gold as their "last chance" in 1864. In 1891 the Helena *Journal* said the city was "the richest city on earth per capita" and described "the magnificient banking houses that line Main Street" as "superb specimens of the architects' and builders' skill." But today all that ornate Victorian architecture has lost its splendor, and Helena strikes the visitor chiefly as an especially poorly planned town. (Things are now perking up with a big downtown urban renewal project.) The valuable minerals gave out decades ago; now the town lives off smelting and refining plants in nearby East Helena (generating sulfur dioxide in alarming quantities), a cement plant, and, principally, the state government. Helena really comes to life when the state legislature convenes. Appropriately, the capitol building has a copper dome.

Missoula (29,497) is home of the University of Montana and a pleasant town tucked into the western Rockies which has faced only two really serious problems in recent years: urban sprawl along an ugly miles-long commercial strip, and highly odoriferous air pollution from the pulp and paper mill industry. The chief villain in the dirty air crisis was identified as the Hoerner Waldorf Corporation, which opened a paper and pulp mill in 1957 at a location several miles upwind of the city. The company promised that the plant would provide for the "virtual elimination of undesirable water and air pollution." But while the company's economic promises came true—by 1970 it had some 500 local men on its payroll—the smoke and skunklike stench from the mill, often settling into the valley for days on end in a weather inversion, propelled Missoula into an environmental controversy of remarkable intensity. Local housewives formed a group called GASP—"Gals Against Smog Pollution"—to fight the mill. Private pilots, protesting alleged flight hazards from Hoerner-Waldorf's smog, "picketed" the plant by flying overhead with antipollution slogans emblazoned on streamers.

All the while, the campaign against the mill's pollution was encouraged by the *Missoulian*, which had already made its mark as a conservation voice by campaigning against the pumping of raw sewage into the Clark Fork (a tributary of the Columbia), eventually securing approval of a big bond issue to clean up the river. The paper had also played a role in persuading Anaconda to install a $1 million boiler to utilize waste material (burning chips and wastage) at one of its pulp mills, thus eliminating the outpouring of black smoke from the old-style tepee burners. Few indeed were the local voices raised in support of the pulp and paper mills. One of them was Dale G. Moore, chairman of the board of KGVO-TV in Missoula (possibly Montana's most outstanding station in the public affairs field), who told me that pollution laws were threatening the lumber industry and that Missoula should be more considerate of a business generating 60 percent of its income. (The forest products industry hires a total of some 5,000 men in the Missoula area.) Referring especially to university activists on the pollution issue, Moore said "the intellectual community in Montana has assumed a position of more power . . . than the state can healthfully accommodate." Its spokesmen, he said, were placing too much emphasis on education and tourism at the expense of basic income-producing activities.

By 1970, the Hoerner-Waldorf problem seemed to be on its way to solution as the company announced it would go ahead, at a cost of $14 million, with a complete air clean-up program to include a huge low-emission recovery furnace, a new liquid concentrator, and an electrostatic precipitator reported to be 99.5 percent efficient in stopping release of particulate matter. Interestingly, the county government made the financing possible by floating tax exempt bonds under the Montana Industrial Development Act. The arrangement, approved by the state's supreme court, meant Hoerner-Waldorf would be able to get its $14 million at a cost as much as 2 percent below standard borrowing rates.

Gradually, the environment becomes an issue pulling rich and poor Montanans together. In western Montana, for instance, virtually everyone is outdoors oriented; on weekends the cities and towns will be almost deserted as the residents head to the mountains, lakes, and streams for fishing, water sports, or hunting. "The people may not have many worldly goods," *Missoulian* editor Edward Coyle commented, "but they'll have an old camper or an old boat to go fishing with." For the rich, there are scores of prosperous dude ranches and pack trips into the wilderness areas. Yet everywhere the pollution problem follows: waste disposal on campgrounds, rowdiness by heavy-drinking campers in National Forests, motorcycles brought into remote mountain areas. At Glacier National Park, the Park Service has sought to ban all motorboats on two of the largest lakes. The pristine streams of the park are being polluted by inadequate sanitary facilities provided by the Park Service.

A new and highly controversial environmental issue sprang to public view in 1969 when the *Missoulian* published a series of articles highly critical of excessive "clear cutting" of timber stands and despoliation of the land in the Bitterroot National Forest. In effect, the *Missoulian* was simply giving exposure to the long-held concerns of the former ranger of the Bitterroot Forest, Guy Brandborg. He complained that his former employer, the U. S. Forest Service, was violating both the letter and the spirit of federal legislation requiring that national forests be maintained for multiple uses—not only for timber but also for grazing lands, recreation, wildlife management, and to retain moisture in the earth:

It's forestry gone mad [Brandborg was quoted as saying]. A clear-cut should be maybe 30 or 40 acres at most. Some of the cuts on the Bitterroot approach 1,000 acres. They're wiping out animal habitats. They're scraping logging roads out of steep slopes where the gashes in the soil pour mud in the streams. They're destroying some of the forest's most beautiful campsites. They're no longer a multiple-use agency, they're sawlog foresters.

In the wake of the *Missoulian* series, separate investigations were started, one an in-house Forest Service undertaking, the other by a seven-man University of Montana faculty group headed by the dean of the university's school of forestry at Missoula, Arnold Bolle. Both investigations, in effect, vindicated the charges of misuse of the Bitterroot Forest; in fact, the Bitterroot episode provided a *cause célèbre* with which conservationists could mount a major, national attack on the Forest Service and its alleged coziness with the big lumbering interests. Chief Edward P. Cliff of the Forest Service, however, insists that the situation in the Bitterroot has been over-dramatized. A total of 244,150 acres of the forest, he points out, have already been set aside as wilderness, and of the 750,000 acres in the Montana portion of the Bitterroot, only 5,500 acres have been cut over annually in recent years. And less than half of that acreage was clear-cut.

Complementing the school of forestry at the University of Montana at Missoula are two facilities in the forefront of the fight against forest fires in the U. S.—the exceptionally fine Northern Forest Fire Laboratory, and the Smokejumpers center run by the Forest Service to teach parachutists the techniques of jumping into critical fire areas.

The university at Missoula is actually part of a six-part Montana University System with other branches at Bozeman, Butte, Dillon, Billings, and Havre. Sectional fights over funding of these branches often reach a fever pitch in the state, leaving the universities, whether they like it or not, deeply involved in politics. Missoula, which also has a well known school of journalism, enrolls about 8,000 students (up from a mere 2,000 in 1945). In 1970 it joined the ranks of striking and protesting campuses, much to the anger of the board of regents and state legislators.

Hope for the Indians?

Montana has 27,130 Indians living on seven reservations scattered to the compass points of its 94 million acres, the remnants of proud nomadic tribes who once held the Intermountain West as their own—Blackfeet and Crow, Flathead and Sioux and others. At the University of Montana one morning, I was able to spend several hours talking with a group of young Indians—ages 21 to 44—who were participating in a pilot project, financed through the national Office of Economic Opportunity and administered by the university, to provide them with career counseling, upgrade their basic skills, and instill new confidence in their own capabilities. As we have seen elsewhere in this book, the process of sensible acculturation of American Indians, preparing them to deal on relatively equal terms with the white man's world, is an excruciating and sometimes near-impossible one.

The program at Missoula is surely no panacea, but one does sense glimmers of hope—a group of Indians working cooperatively together, free (they tell the visitor) of bossy white management—prevocational training in woods, metals, electricity, forestry, wildlife conservation, or even data processing, so that a man can make a wise choice on his further development —half-day work experiences with stores and shops in Missoula—family life training in cooking, budget keeping, family planning, and even a self-generated Alcoholics Anonymous chapter. Sensitive to the cooperative nature of Indian life, the program is set up to enroll whole families and let them work together with the counselors at Missoula for 24 weeks to a year.

Just to hear the Indians tell their own stories evokes the image of their immense reservations, of the lonely spaces and dusty little towns, of grinding poverty and unemployment the likes of which no white town of the U. S. A. has seen since the Great Depression; the rekindled interest in ancestral crafts and dancing, tribal language and history, yet the cultural shock of television in what was once a self-contained and far more content world; the love-hate relationship with the Bureau of Indian Affairs.

Yet withal, the fierce pride remains. The New York *Times* had recently published a sympathetic story on the seeming hopelessness of the Blackfeet Indians, their young people suspended between two worlds but part of neither, the high suicide rates of the youth and the utter dependence on the federal government. The Blackfeet, I was quickly told, were upset that the article cast them in a bad light, not mentioning the "good things": that 30 percent of the Blackfeet high school seniors go on to college now, that the dust bowl is being relieved by more streets and sewers, that there is already light industry (a small saw mill, making of ship doors and prefabricated house parts). Harold Gray, assistant director of the university's Indian program, is himself a Blackfeet, his father a street maintenance man at Browning who never made it beyond the third grade but harped at his children to get an education; as a result Harold now has a degree in school administration, one brother works for IBM at Boulder, and a third will soon earn a master's degree at Northern Montana College at Havre.

Harold Gray's future, one feels, is quite assured. But what of those enrolled in the program? Will Herman White Grass, the intent young Blackfeet whom the Army made a guard for 13 months in Korea, realize his dream to go to drafting school at Denver and build a career as an engineering draftsman? Is there a chance that sometime logger Alex Woodcock from the Flathead Reservation can get the specialized forestry training he would like? Can Blackfeet Robert Monroe, a Vietnam veteran, get his high-school certificate and enter the university in social work so that he can spend his life "working with people"? What will become of a young Blackfeet and his new Sioux wife, she from a broken home, he with a record of two years at the Deer Lodge State Prison for taking a watch and wallet from a man? Will young Al Caplitt, a Crow Indian always drawn back home by the sun dances and rodeos he loves so much, make it into specialized heavy equipment training and shake off the drinking problems he had at a school in Oklahoma? What are the chances of Kenneth Brien and his wife, also Crow, to improve their lot so they can get their seven children through college? For Brien, a chunky, genial man who was in the Army for 13 years and then returned to work on the tribal police force, there is the goal of taking a criminology course at the University of California so that he can work effectively with Indian youngsters on crime prevention; as for Mrs. Brien, she would like to go into social work. These, too, are determined and somehow will succeed. But what of shy, taciturn Nancy Big Back, a Cheyenne, trying to get her high-school equivalency degree, thinking of beauty school in Billings, but anxious to live on her reservation?

The poignant, human stories go on and on, and could be duplicated hundreds of thousands of times across the U. S. A. But little of the pessimism that lies like a heavy blanket over so many Indian reservations today was to be felt in the room where we spoke. A springtime of hope was there that day. The little band of trainees is now off to the four winds, succeeding or failing in their dreams. The visitor knows he will never see them again but will think of them often.

The Colonial Economy

Montana is a storehouse of natural riches in timber, metals, oil, coal, water power, beef, and wheat. But the state is so remote from the mainstreams of American transportation and capital that it has always had to look to outsiders for the money to develop its resources. As a result, the stocks in its great enterprises—Anaconda Copper and Aluminum, Montana Power, the railroads, lumber companies, and oil firms—are largely held by out-of-staters. In 1970, for instance, Montanans held only 36 percent of the stock of the Montana Power Company. There is great fear in the state of a land development grab by large out-of-state corporations, including the Chrysler Corporation and Reforestation, Inc., of Spokane. Montanans were apprehensive that fishing streams and recreation areas once open to the public would become private preserves. Another great outside client, owning 30 percent of the land, is the federal government. Only a few "middle millionaires"—owners of timber spreads and some big corporate farms—have surfaced on Montanan soil, and the outlook is for continued dependence for decades to come.

In terms of payrolls, government exceeds all others in Montana—some 43,000 men and women working for the state and local governments, 11,000 for the federal, the combined total more than twice what it was 20 years ago. Federal spending is a mainstay of the state economy. In fiscal year 1969, for instance, Washington spent $644 million in Montana but got back only $343 million in taxes from the state. The biggest federal spender was the Department of Agriculture ($187 million), followed by Health, Education and Welfare ($162 million), Defense ($81 million), Transportation ($73 million) and Interior ($46 million). The federally financed multipurpose Fort Peck, Canyon Ferry, Yellowtail, Hungry Horse, and Libby Dams have stimulated substantial agricultural and industrial activity. Federal soil bank and price support payments inevitably make the difference between loss and profit for Montana wheat farmers. The closing of the Glasgow Air Force Base in the 1960s was a bitter blow to the state, but it still has Malmstrom and the outlook for massive outlays for the ABM program in the 1970s.

Agriculture outshines every other source of income in Montana except government. Annual farm receipts are more than half a billion dollars. North of Great Falls and along the "Hi-Line" of counties just below the Canadian border are the great wheat fields which have made Montana the country's third-ranking wheat producer, trailing only Kansas and North Dakota. But two-thirds of the farm income actually comes from livestock now. The state is 13th in cattle and fourth in sheep among the 50, most of the livestock grazed on the endless miles of rolling plains in southeastern Montana. The trend, as elsewhere, is toward ever greater farms with fewer and fewer operators. The rural farm population, 175,707 in 1940, dropped to 88,460 in 1970. In 1940, Montana had 41,823 farms with an average value of $8,-373; in 1969, there were 24,953 farms with an average value of $150,213. Average farm size is now over 2,500 acres. The consolidation of farms is seriously weakening the Farmers Union, traditionally strongest of all Montana farm groups and vital liberal force in state politics. Now the more militant National Farmers Organization is making a bid for power in the state.

While agriculture, concentrated in the eastern part of the state, makes more money for less people, lumbering has grown by leaps and bounds in the western mountains and created thousands of new jobs since World War II. Mainly as a result of this development, the value of manufactures—forest products along with metal and food processing—has gone over $300 million. The dollar total is only 44th among the states, but it is big money for Montana.

Employment in the mines has plunged from close to 10,000 at the end of World War II to about 2,700 today (almost all of it at Butte). Early in the 1950s, major oil discoveries were made in the Williston Basin in eastern Montana; with subsequent strikes in the 1960s, petroleum production rose to about $125 million a year. But the direct benefit to Montana was not especially great: only 2,000 men were employed in the oilfields, with another 1,000 in refining. By 1970, the value of oil and gas production had risen to $109 million a year. Other important payrolls for Montana are the railroads (about 6,800 men), construction (9,000), wholesale and retail trade (44,000), and services (28,900).

An area of great promise and possible threat to Montana is the developing program to strip-mine the vast fields of coal which underlie practically the entire eastern third of the state. Montanan fields are estimated to hold between 15 and 20 *billion* tons of strippable coal. Montana coal is interesting the big energy companies because of the growing national electric power demand and the fact that Montana's deposits are exceptionally low in sulphur that pollutes the air and sodium that coats burners. (Low sulphur coal is usually low in BTU value, however, so that more has to be burned for the same caloric return—and thus more air pollution.) According to Dr. S. L. Groff of the Montana Bureau of Mines and Geology, a chief booster of the state's coal industry, three stages of development can be foreseen—up to 1980, shipping Montana coal out to Midwest steam generation plants, plus construction of more generating plants in Montana itself; starting about 1980, construction of first coal conversion plants to produce gasoline and diesel fuel in Montana; and later Montana production of by-products from the conversion plants. Leaders like Senator Metcalf think the best way to haul the coal to distant markets is over high-tension lincs, with the power generation done directly at the mine sites. Existing power interties have shown that power can be transmitted over long distances with relatively low line loss, and with the power plants on the windy and lonely high plains, a lot less people would be getting emphysema from burning of the coal.

By the late 1960s, modest quantities of Montana coal were already being shipped to Midwestern power plants which ordered it for its low sulphur content. But the project's backers envisaged vast stretches of eastern Montana soon crawling with gargantuan mucking monsters that can remove huge quantities of overburden at a single pass and mine hundreds of tons of coal in a day. Some thorny problems are at hand, however. Under existing methods, strip miners bury the topsoil (which some botanists say would take 1,000 years to rebuild naturally); it would cost more to remove the topsoil separately and then restore it, a necessary procedure if the land is to be returned to wheat farming. (In 1971 the legislature went part of the way toward solving the problem by enacting a fairly tough coal strip-mining reclamation law.) Secondly, there is the threat of thermal pollution from coal-fired steam generation plants and the possibility that required new water storage would sacrifice many of Montana's free-flowing trout streams.* Third, there is the question of whether Montana's modest taxes on mining would provide adequate return for state government, or whether highly automated strip-mining procedures would generate a significant payroll for Montanans. The 1971 legislative session did enact a new tax on coal,

* To cool the power plants required for the year 2020, when the U. S. Bureau of Reclamation estimates Montana's generation capacity will be 21,745 megawatts, an annual diversion of 455,000 acre-feet from the Missouri River and 600,000 acre-feet from the Yellowstone River would be required, necessitating major new storage reservoirs. Montana Power's 180,000-kilowatt steam generation plant already opened at Billings, when it is fired up to full capacity, will heat the water it takes from the Yellowstone River 30 to 40 degrees before returning it to the river. Senators Metcalf and Mansfield have been trying to get Congress to appropriate $50 million over a five-year period for a pilot plant in Montana to generate power from coal by a new technique known as magnetohydrodynamics which involves burning coal at an extremely high temperature —actually turning it to gas. Air pollutants are easily removed and almost no cooling water is needed.

averaging 10 cents a ton. That same year, several new coal developments were underway and Montana Power announced it would spend $60 million to build a 350,000-kilowatt coal-fired power generating station at Colstrip, a prime strip-mining area 100 miles east of Billings.

"Big Sky" Tourist Country

Tourism is a growing Montana business (some $160 million a year), but still far behind its potential—the result of low investment in tourist facilities or promotion. Some 3.5 million tourists visit the state each year, generating over 20,000 jobs for Montanans, but all the other mountain and coastal states draw far more people and earn more money from them. Tourist attractions range from the two magnificent national parks (Glacier and Yellowstone) to ghost towns, trout fishing, dude ranching and big game hunting. An out-of-stater who wants to hunt for elk must buy a $150 license, which also entitles him to bag two deer, a black bear, and birds and fish to his heart's content.

Though Yellowstone National Park edges a few miles into Montana, it is really a Wyoming phenomenon, and a large portion of its 2.5 million annual visitors never make it into "Big Sky" country. Montana's real pride and joy is Glacier National Park—actually part of the Waterton-Glacier International Peace Park on the Canadian border. In 1929, remote Glacier had only 70,742 visitors, but four decades later, in 1969, it was seen by more than a million, ranking 16th among 33 national parks reporting. The park's alpine solitudes, the breathtaking (though often bumper-to-bumper) Going-to-the-Sun Road, the multitudes of glaciers and glacial lakes and cool green forests, remain one of the loveliest sights on the continent. Yet, as with so many of the national parks today, many tourists see it only from their automobiles, never taking the time to follow the thousands of miles of trails leading into its remote inner reaches.

South of Glacier lies the massive Bob Marshall Wilderness, some 950,000 acres of pure solitude where the mountain streams yield trout up to 23 inches in length and nine pounds in weight. Even Colorado fishermen fly up for weekend forays along the magnificent and uncrowded Montana streams. Mountainous western Montana also offers the visitor eight other wilderness areas and abundant state parks. At the National Bison Range, established in 1908 to save the then almost extinct lords of the plains, round-up time each October revives a page of American history as hundreds of the great shaggy beasts, their cloven hooves sounding like a running river, are driven coughing and snorting and butting into corrals for the annual sort-out. Ghost towns abound in the western hills, the most colorful of them all Virginia City where 10,000 people once lived and the territorial capital was housed. Thanks to a masterful restoration, Virginia City reveals more authentic details of the mining frontier than any other spot in the

West; it also can recall the days when vigilantes took things into their own hands after outlaws had murdered more than 200 residents (twice the town's present-day population). Eastern Montana has much less to offer the tourist, though there is the massive Fort Peck Reservoir, one of the world's largest, and the battlefield where General Custer made his ill-starred last stand.

With its limited hotel and motel development, Montana probably welcomes proportionately more of the house trailer-tent-camper-mobile home traveling set than any other Western state. Great Falls is the jumping-off point for the thousands of trailers headed north on the 5,100-mile journey along the Alcan Highway to Alaska. Sometimes they travel in great caravans, gathering in concentric circles at Great Falls like an Old West wagon train to get their marching orders for the northward trek. The hundreds of thousands of trailers crowding western highways in recent years are evidence of an affluent nomadism the likes of which the world has never seen. The problem for the mountain states is that the trailers clog the highways but leave few dollars behind.

One of Montana's problems has been that it has had no strong income-producing area like Idaho's Sun Valley or Colorado's Aspen and Vail. Now this is being changed by development of what promises to be Chet Huntley's $15 million "Big Sky of Montana" recreational complex next to the Spanish Peaks primitive area north of Yellowstone Park. The plan includes two villages with condominiums, hotels and restaurants, golf courses, stables, ski runs, and mountain trails; one is at the base of 11,166-foot Lone Mountain and the other a few miles distant at Sam S. Smeding's Lone Mountain Ranch. Huntley is intent on building his development out of Montana wood and stone and to prevent any touch of gaudiness. But environmentalists, including a conservative set of professors at Montana State University in nearby Bozeman, tried to block or at least delay the development, on the grounds that wildlife and the natural terrain would be imperiled. Huntley was also accused of being a front for Eastern money, since his personal financial stake in "Big Sky" is quite small. The Forest Service also blocked some of the necessary land exchanges. Fighting back, Huntley barnstormed the state in a small plane, telling local groups that "Big Sky" would mean $100 million for the state's economy and 400 permanent jobs. "Damn it," he was quoted as saying, "we can't build a fence around Montana. We're a depressed area." He argued that Big Sky's utility lines would be buried, roads limited, snowmobiles banned, and the sewer system would be the best in the state. (Somehow, it was hard to see a despoiler of the land in a man who could write a vivid account of his boyhood years in Montana, *The Generous Years,* capturing the homesteading life and such scenes as the crackling vibrance of the Montana winter and springtime when "the ground was a moving, writhing, stirring mass of movement and growth.")

Schizophrenic Politics

Montana's split personality in matters political goes back to the first years of statehood. The two traditions—which we might describe as the conservative-exploitive and the liberal-welfarist—are alive and thriving today. Practically without exception, Republicans are conservative; their base of power is firmly anchored among stockmen, businessmen, professionals, and oilmen, and they have not nominated a liberal for major office in decades. The Democrats fall automatically into the liberal-welfarist mode, depending as they do on organized labor in the western mining and lumber counties and the co-op and REA-minded wheat farmers of the "Hi-Line" eastern counties. Oil- and livestock-minded Billings is a major Republican center; the Democrats, on the other hand, can count on wheat-minded Great Falls, labor's stronghold in Butte, and university-oriented Missoula. The result of this split, until the last few years, was to make western Montana dependably Democratic, eastern Montana predictably Republican. Now this is changing: Republicanism weakening in eastern Montana as a result of rising liberalism in the Billings area, the Democratic vote faltering in western Montana as Butte's population decline continues and retired Republicans move into areas like the Bitterroot Valley. Up to 1968, eastern Montana had a Republican Congressman, western Montana a Democratic Congressman; now the roles are precisely reversed.

The conservative-exploitive tradition goes back to the days of the Copper Kings, when Daly and Clark and their cohorts expended vast sums of money to buy legislatures and courts and newspapers as tools in their fights for mining rights and seats in the U. S. Senate. Clark, who was once quoted as saying he never bought a man who wasn't for sale, spent $431,000 for the 47 legislative votes to send him to the U. S. Senate. He and Daly reportedly spent $3 million between them in the struggle over whether the state capital should go to Anaconda or Helena. The Montana constitution to this day prohibits many taxes on mining companies or livestock operations, simply because the miners and stockmen controlled the convention that wrote the constitution preceding Montana's entry into the Union in 1889.

Anaconda and Montana Power, having established their hegemony, did all they could to fight off regulatory legislation and all and any taxes that would impair their profits. Not until 1971 did the legislature approve the first minimum wage legislation of Montana history. Despite the growth of environmentalist sentiment, only weak air and water pollution laws had won passage by 1971. The state in that year took the first, halting steps toward statewide planning and land use. When it comes to appropriating money, Montana is extremely generous with road-building funds—its highway department is virtually a sacred cow. Only four American states spend more per capita on roads. But even counting the highway bill, Montana ranks

only ninth among the 13 western states in overall tax effort. Within the
region, only Nevada spends less per capita for education; even poor Wyoming, next door, lays out 56 percent more per capita for training its youth.
Montana's public welfare expenditures rank 38th among the 50 states, her
outlays for health and hospitals 45th. Before increases in 1969 and 1971,
benefits under the state's unemployment compensation laws ranked 50th
among the 50 states.

Montanans' preference for Republican rule at the state level is indisputable; six of the past eight governorship elections have been won by Republicans. If one counts in control of the two houses of the legislature in all
elections since 1940, the Republicans have won 26 of 40 contests. Divided
party control of the legislature has become commonplace, inevitably mini-
mizing innovative state programs. Such displeasure with the legislature is
present in Montana that many people would reduce its unwieldy size (55 senators and 104 representatives) or even make it unicameral. A constitutional
convention, meeting early in 1972, actually submitted a unicameral option to
a vote of the people. (Nebraska has had a unicameral, nonpartisan legislature
since the 1930s; Montana's, however, would retain party organization.)

Montana's legislature has been called consistently conservative, no matter which party controls, but Margaret Scherf, a mystery writer turned Montana politician, disputes those who say all legislatures are "dead and ripe
for burying." The snail's pace of bills, the trial and error and occasional
corruption, she wrote, are flaws one might call "the inevitable lice on the
hide of Democracy. Shall we butcher the beast to get rid of the lice?"
Moreover, she suggests, state legislation *is* more progressive than local thinking. A legislative session obliges a member to learn where his state stands
compared to the others in income, education, taxes, and economic growth,
and it "helps a state reconcile its thinking and its aims with national thinking and national aims," the writer suggests. She concludes:

> I should not like to see any state legislatures disappear, but in Montana where
> the sparse population is divided by miles and mountains, this is a forum, a battle-
> ground, a town meeting we must have. Its creaking machinery, its tedious debate,
> its insane rush at the end, may impede but do not cancel its primary function, which
> is to voice and deal with the stresses and the needs of the people of Montana. In
> our state, the legislature is very much alive.

The early 1970s have demonstrated unusual vigor in the legislature,
despite the very mediocre rank of 41st among the 50 states accorded it by
the Citizens Conference on State Legislatures. Accomplishments have included overhauling the state's fiscal structure, reorganizing the executive
branch, enacting a landmark territorial integrity law outlining the relationship
between investor-owned power companies and rural electric co-ops, passage
of the state's first minimum wage law and collective bargaining mechanisms
for teachers, and stronger pollution controls.

For most of the 1950s, Montana's chief executive was a genial Swedish
emigrant and self-made oilman and trucker, Republican J. Hugo Aronson,

affectionately called the "Galloping Swede" by his constituents. He did little to rock the boat at Helena and later became a lobbyist, announcing at one point, "Old governors don't just fade away, they become lobbyists." Then, in the 1960s, came the hard-core GOP conservatives: Donald G. Nutter, who was elected in 1960 but died in a wintry plane crash in 1962; and Tim M. Babcock, an ex-truck driver who happened to be Nutter's lieutenant governor and held the office for seven more years. Both made great political hay out of their enmity for the United Nations, federal dams, taxes, and government expenditures (though Babcock, ironically, made his fortune hauling cement when his trucking company got the contract for the Bureau of Reclamation's Yellowtail Dam). Despite his image, Nutter was a pragmatist and skilled administrator who might have ended up making fundamental changes if he had lived. Babcock, by contrast, was generally regarded as an incompetent administrator with a third-rate staff who simply let the state drift. Finally, Babcock came out for a sales tax, which proved his undoing in the 1968 election.

The liberal-welfarist strain in Montana history reads like that of an altogether different state. The chapter has its beginnings in the free silver-populist era just before the turn of the century, getting underway in earnest with passage of a wide variety of progressive laws between 1900 and World War I. These included bills to prohibit child labor, guarantee initiative and referendum and the direct primary, assure an eight-hour work day, guarantee workmen compensation for their injuries, and regulate grain grading and marketing for protection of the wheat farmers. But Montana did not go the third-party farmer-labor route of North Dakota and Minnesota, largely because of the personal role of one extraordinary politician, Senator Burton K. Wheeler. Like Borah of Idaho, Wheeler is now remembered chiefly for his fervid isolationism just before World War II. But in his earlier days, he was an agrarian progressive of the Norris-LaFollette-Borah stripe. Wheeler started in politics as a Democrat, went the independent route for a period of time as La Follette's Vice Presidential running mate in 1924, and then returned to the Democratic fold, bringing with him the state's powerful farmer-labor coalition.

Since then, Montana progressives, becoming champions of the New Deal's reclamation, farm aid, and labor laws, have all been Democrats. Their successes at Helena, where they have to buck "The Companies" and the stockmen, have been limited. But they have been spectacularly successful in winning seats in Congress. The dichotomy was explained several years ago by A. B. Guthrie, Jr., who commented that Anaconda and Montana Power "preferred Washington to the state capital as the abiding place of a dangerous man." Senator Lee Metcalf, an out-and-out liberal who makes no bones about it, explains the Montanans' political schizophrenia as "a real cynical sort of an approach—'We'll save our own taxes, but let's send those Senators back to Washington.'" In Washington, of course, "those Senators" can be expected to fight tooth-and-nail for federal dollars to enrich Montana. In the 45 elections for the U. S. Senate or House since 1940, Democrats have won 31 times. Yet the Montana Democratic party is a thin affair, not unlike its counterparts in the other mountain states. It depends heavily on organized labor; the salary of the party's state executive director, for instance, is split evenly between the AFL-CIO COPE and a single international union. The party is also heavily dependent on out-of-state financing in its crucial campaigns. As powerful a figure as any in Montana Democratic circles is said to be Washington attorney James Rowe, a prominent behind-the-scenes operative in the national party whose public relations and fund-raising talents make him an influence in this distant mountain state.

Forrest Anderson, the Democrat elected to the governorship in 1968, is a middle-of-the-roader not identified with the populist-liberalism of the party's men in Congress. His chief interests have been economic development and reorganization of the unwieldy state government; at his instigation a constitutional amendment to limit the number of state departments to 20 was placed on the 1970 ballot and approved by the people. But Anderson brought the anger of Montana's increasingly vocal conservationists down on himself by rebuking a fish and game director who was trying to include environmental controls in new industrial planning. Anderson also backed a disputed land easement for the Anaconda Company in Lewis and Clark County (site of a proposed new open-pit copper and molybdenum mine). Had Anderson decided to run for reelection in 1972, it would have been an interesting test of the environmental issue. But he decided, for reasons of health, to retire.

Montana in Washington

Montana has sent some exceptional men—and one woman—to Congress. The woman, Jeannette Rankin, was the first member of her sex ever to sit in Congress, and she must be considered the "original dove." Serving a term in 1917–18, she voted against United States entry into World War I; elected again for a single term in 1941–42, she was the only member of Congress to vote against the declaration of war in World War II. Miss Rankin was also an active leader for women's suffrage. When her 90th birthday came in 1970, the Montana delegation held a birthday party in her honor in Washington, and one Congressman told her, "You look at the record now. We're voting your way, Jeannette." A liberal professor from New Hampshire traveled down to Washington for the party, announcing. "I had to be here. Miss Rankin was 50 years ahead of her time. She has been a shining light to everyone who believes in peace and women's rights all these years."

Another still remembered Montanan is Senator Thomas J. Walsh, who led the investigation that unearthed the Teapot Dome scandal in the 1920s; Walsh was actually Wheeler's early mentor. The liberal tradition was carried on for a quarter of a century by Senator James E. Murray, a staunch friend of farm and labor groups and author of such measures as the proposed Missouri Valley Authority, the Small Business Administration Act, and the Full Employment Act of 1946, a keystone of postwar economic policy.

Senator Lee Metcalf, of whom we have spoken already, must be considered the true inheritor of the populist-progressive mantle. In the House for several years, Metcalf was a founder and leader of the liberal Democratic Study Group. But his straight-arrow aim on the nation's electric utilities, publicizing little known facts about utilities' planned rate increases, their net income per revenue dollar, and their sales promotion and advertising costs has been his major preoccupation—and possibly a reason that his own legislative scorecard is not more impressive. Congress has turned a cold shoulder, for instance, on Metcalf's proposed consumer-counsel bill to provide for federally funded consumer representation in utilities regulatory decisions. One extremely imaginative Metcalf bill, to make it possible for states to levy mineral severance taxes of up to five percent without fear of losing their competitive position to other states, was not even given a legislative hearing in the first two years after its introduction. The proposal, which would be a boon to financially hard-pressed states, would actually impose a 5 percent federal severance tax but then allow the mining companies to take a credit of up to that amount if the individual states imposed their own severance taxes. The states could be expected to institute or increase their severance taxes up to the 5 percent, since it would be immaterial to the mining companies whether they paid the tax to Washington or a state treasury.

Now comes the name of Senator Mike Mansfield, a tall, quiet, self-effacing Montanan who reluctantly took the mantle of leadership of the Senate Democrats in 1961 and within a decade had become one of the most influential leaders of his time. An Anaconda lobbyist—who ought to know—told me that Mansfield was "absolutely pure, a man who has never accepted money from a special interest group." The son of Irish immigrant parents in the Hell's Kitchen section of Manhattan, Mansfield was sent to Montana to live with relatives when he was three years old, went into World War I as a teenager, and for several years was a mucker in the Anaconda mine at Butte. But he worked his way up to engineer status, took courses at the Montana School of Mines and then Montana State University, eventutally became a professor of history specializing in the Far East and Latin America, and in 1942 ran for Congress and defeated none other than Jeannette Rankin.

Mansfield's progress in Congress has been as quiet as it has been spectacular. In the House, he became a close associate of the late Sam Rayburn and served on the Foreign Affairs Committee. In 1952 he defeated one-term Republican Senator Zales Ecton, who has been aptly described as a "dull, droning ultra conservative." Again Mansfield concentrated on foreign relations and became a modest right arm to Lyndon Johnson in the latter's heyday as the wheeler-dealer of Senate Democrats. According to some accounts, John Kennedy picked Johnson as his Vice Presidential running mate so that he could have the more cooperative Mansfield as his Senate floor leader.

Especially in his first years as Democratic Leader, Mansfield was criticized as being much too "gentle" a captain of his unruly troops. Mansfield's leadership style, Drew Pearson once wrote, was as different from LBJ's "as ginger ale is from a martini." Instead of the wheeling, dealing, arm-twisting Texan style, Mansfield insisted on treating all his fellow Senators as individuals. "Lyndon was an extrovert, I'm an introvert," Mansfield has said. "I sometimes wonder why I'm in politics. I just don't seem to have all the attitudes of backslapping that seem to be necessary. If I can't get what I want by cooperating and accommodating, then that's just too bad." The advantage of the Mansfield approach, of course, is that it enables him to work with ideologically diverse Senators—and even Republicans.

Long an opponent of the Vietnam war, Mansfield also has fought the Nixon Administration's ABM program; his political position in Montana has become so impregnable that he did not need to fear any repercussions at home from local interests anxious to have the multimillion-dollar federal investments from the missile sites near Great Falls. Mansfield quickly drew in his horns on the issue of gun control, however, when opposition mounted in the state to his support for firearms registration.

Mansfield's role as Senate Majority Leader may have reduced the number of bills with his name attached, but in 1970 he was credited with being the chief author and strategist of the voting-rights bill amendment to assure all young Americans the vote at 18. As usual, Mansfield suggested the credit should go to others. In his calm way, he seems perennially surprised about his own power and position. "I was lucky to get to be a Senator, lucky to get to be a Congressman in the first place," he said. "I was very, very lucky." Somehow this gentle, pipe-smoking man, so thoroughly accepted by his fellow Montanans, seems light-years away from the swashbuckling and unscrupulous Marcus Daly, in whose copper mine he got his first permanent job. Montana still bears many of the marks of the raw, frontier state it was when its development—or should we say its exploitation?—began a mere century ago. Mike Mansfield, internationalist and conservationist, man of reason and reflection, suggests a side to the state's personality no one would have thought to predict even a few years past.

IDAHO

DIVIDED IT STANDS

THINLY POPULATED IDAHO, distant and so little known to other Americans, is an oddly shaped piece of real estate wedged between six other states of the Intermountain West. Its 83,557 square miles leave it smaller in area than 12 other states, but it is still bigger than Maryland and Delaware and all of New England combined. As the crow flies, it is more than 500 miles from north to south, 300 miles across on the state's wide southern plain, but only 44 miles across the odd northwestern Idaho panhandle which stretches up to the Canadian border. This geographic extremism is the handiwork of congressional mapmakers who in 1863 created an Idaho Territory bigger than Texas but within five years had chopped away what is now Montana and Wyoming. In the words of my friend John Corlett, long-time political editor of the *Idaho Statesman*: "When the great planners in Washington finally got through breaking things up, they left us with a crazy patchwork of a state. . . . Geographically, Idaho is a state that should not have been."

Northern and southern Idaho are broken into two separate, isolated entities by the fiercely mountainous backlands of central Idaho, where the Salmon River Mountains brood over some of the most remote and impassable territory of the continental United States, including its largest wilderness area. Until 1927, if a governor of Idaho wanted to visit the northern reaches of his state, he had no alternative other than to pass through Montana or Washington to get there. A single highway, completed in 1927, is still the only land connection, and no north-south railway has ever been constructed. All of Idaho seems young and relatively untouched by coastal standards of "civilization." As late as 1919, Idaho historians recall, there were only five miles of paved road in the entire state.

Northern Idaho is the land of the forest gods, where the handsome stands of pine and fir and larch, of cedar, hemlock, and spruce, spread their cover over the mountainsides. Water is pure and abundant in the great rain forests and the rivers to which they give birth. The people make their living from lumbering and mining and the tourist trade; a few grow wheat. The political climate, born in the old mining camps, is much more liberal and more Democratic than the rest of Idaho. Morals are apparently a bit looser, too, for it is reported that the region harbors the only big houses of prostitution left in Idaho. Exquisite lakes help to make this prime tourist territory, and after the visitor has been exposed to the surfeit of sterile shorelines on the artificial lakes which the busy dam-makers have brought into being, the soft and natural tree-lined lakes of this region are balm for the eyes.

Northern Idaho slipped out of the Idaho mainstream about a century ago when the capital was literally stolen from Lewiston, the panhandle's leading city—the state seal and state records captured by horsemen and taken to Boise in the south. Now towns like Coeur d'Alene cater, summer and winter, to the vacation stream from Spokane, Washington. Economically, the panhandle is a part of Spokane's vaunted "Inland Empire." The Spokane papers are dominant, and Coeur d'Alene is on the verge of becoming part of the Spokane metropolitan area. In past years, there was even talk of uniting northern Idaho with eastern Washington and western Montana to form a new state to be called Columbia or Lincoln. Like many rationally sound but politically unsettling ideas, nothing ever came of it.

Southern Idaho is dominated by the arid prairie and sagebrush plains that run along each side of the Snake River, a 600-mile arc from the Snake's headwaters near Yellowstone National Park on the east to the Oregon border west of Boise. The Snake, major tributary of the still greater Columbia, is literally southern Idaho's lifeline. Virtually all the people of the region live close to its banks, and without it the area would be a desert, pure and simple—like the neighboring territory of northern Nevada, arid eastern Oregon, and the land stretching northward from Utah's Great Salt Lake. But with the Snake River, extensive irrigation has been made possible and thus the creation of splendid farmlands which grow, among other things, those famous Idaho potatoes.

Two distinct cultures flourish along the Snake Valley. To the east, constituting the southeast quadrant of the state, is land settled by the early Mormons, the first great irrigators of Idaho's soil. Almost two-thirds of the people of this region are still affiliated with the Church of Jesus Christ of Latter-day Saints. (Statewide, the Mormons are about 26 percent). Economically, the major southeastern cities—Pocatello and Idaho Falls—are relatively self-sufficient. But in matters spiritual and cultural, all eyes look to Salt Lake City; there is in fact no area of the U. S. outside of Utah itself where the Mormon imprint is so deep.

Southwestern Idaho, likewise sustained in large part by the irrigated farming along the valley of the Snake, contains the city of Boise, which, in turn, has the state capitol, Idaho's best climate, thriving light industry, and the income of a strong distribution center. Perhaps even more important for modern Idaho, Boise is headquarters city of some major national corporations—Boise Cascade, Ore-Ida, Morrison-Knudsen, J. R. Simplot. Thus in a state still predominantly agricultural, still close to its pioneer roots, an element of sophisticated finance and industry is introduced—and not the classic out-of-state exploiters of old, but home-grown capital-creating enterprises. Nowhere in the Intermountain West, not even Denver, is this much corporate control to be found. Boise glows with prosperity and hope. Once it was one among several Idaho cities of moderate population, but as a result of a startling population growth in the 1960s, Boise and its metropolitan area (112,230 people in 1970) are twice as large as any other Idaho settlement and in fact the state's only metropolitan area. Boise metro still has but a sixth of Idaho's population, but any significant city in this people-sparse state is a new thing. Helped along by the interstates and air travel, Boise will perhaps someday be the economic and cultural capital for all of Idaho, not just its political capital. Many think the rigid provincialism of old Idaho is fading. But it is probably still true, as reported in times past, that Idaho has three capitals—Boise, Spokane, and Salt Lake City.

In clear distinction from the liberal north, southern Idaho has been conservative through most of its political history. Tillers of the land are usually less likely to be radicals. The Mormons in the southeast, thrifty and reserved, brought an innate caution to politics. For reasons never well explained, Boise and other parts of the southwest have long harbored the most ultraconservative politics of Idaho. Since the south, in aggregate, has four to five times as many people as the north, Idaho has been a normally conservative and Republican state. But it has distinct liberal-radical strains in its character, to which we will return later.

The only geographic quadrant we have not mentioned is the northeast. Robert Smylie, Idaho's outstanding postwar governor, likes to say that the whole northeastern section of the state was bitten off and swallowed up by Montana.

Brief History: From Lewis and Clark
to Processed Potatoes

Idaho was the last of the American states to be seen by Europeans when Meriwether Lewis and William Clark crossed over the Continental Divide on a fair day of August, 1805, thus passing what is now the Mon-

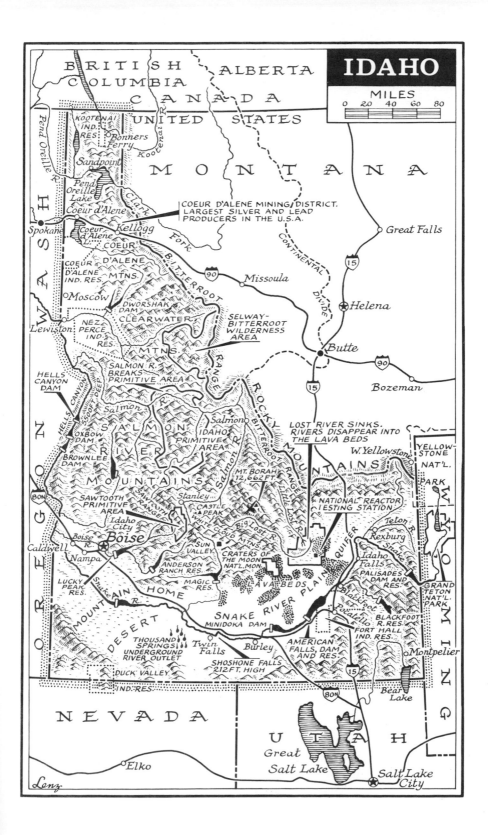

tana-Idaho border. Soon they would meet with Indians who had never before encountered a white man. Characteristically, the rough wilderness of central Idaho—especially the impassable canyons of the Salmon River, which the Indians call "the River of No Return"—obliged the party to go back to Montana and then traverse the panhandle at a more northerly point on their way to the Pacific.

Lewis' and Clark's reports of the wild, untamed country, and especially of fur-bearing animals—so many, they said, that they got in each other's way—was a signal for trappers to invade the territory, starting a vigorous, competitive trade that would reach its peak in the 1820s and '30s. Hundreds of trappers lost their lives from exposure or at the hands of the Indians, but in a single season some 80,000 beaver pelts were taken from the Snake River Valley. In the wake of the trappers came missionaries anxious to save the souls of the Indians, and along the valley of the Snake rolled thousands of covered wagons following the Oregon Trail from distant Independence, Missouri, to the Pacific Coast.

Idaho's first permanent settlement was made in 1860, by Mormons in the southeast who actually thought they were settling in Utah. The Saints' geometric little towns with communal irrigation projects would set one life style for Idaho; quite another began, also in 1860, with Captain E. D. Pierce's discovery of placer gold in the clearwater country of northern Idaho. A great gold rush began, unique up to that point in American history because the tide of emigration came from the West rather than the East. Across from Oregon, Washington, and California came the prospectors, by boats up the rivers and then foot, muleback, and pack train into the rugged mountains. Soon gold strikes were being made all over the north, and in 1862 in the Boise Basin as well. Silver ledges and gold-bearing quartz were discovered, and Idaho was on its way to becoming a principal mining state.

Territorial status came in 1863. The 1870s witnessed the Indian wars and now legendary struggle of the Nez Percé against confinement on a reservation; at the end of a 1,300-mile retreat into southern Idaho and across into Montana, their wise leader and master strategist, Chief Joseph, sick of the butchery, uttered his haunting words of surrender: "From where the sun now stands I will fight no more forever."

The 1870s brought, too, the great cattle grazing interests, and the 1880s the railroads. Editor Sam Day of the *Intermountain Observer* has written:

Following the old Oregon Trail which the wagons had carved across southern Idaho, the railroad worked its way from east to west, bringing much of Idaho its first permanent population influx. The railroad built Pocatello and Nampa, shared the location and destiny of scores of other towns, and brought habitation to much of the countryside in between.

Southern Idaho literally grew up alongside the railroad tracks. The railroad provided the first viable basis for livestock and agricultural industries which were to become the mainstay of the young state's economy, supplanting the booms and busts of the gold and silver mines which had given the region its initial character.

The era of the railroad—except for freight—came to an end almost a century later, in May, 1971, when the entry of the Union Pacific Railroad into the

Amtrak system deprived all of southern Idaho of its rail passenger service.

Even as the railroad gradually civilized late 19th-century Idaho, and the territory became a state in 1890, violence persisted in the wars of religion and valuable minerals. The state erupted with bitter and vengeful labor wars between unions and the silver mine owners of the Coeur d'Alene region, leading to dynamiting of mines, calling in of federal troops to restore order, and in 1906 the assassination of former governor Frank Steunenberg (who had called in the troops) by a bomb set to his garden gate by an ex-miner. The courtroom trial pitted Clarence E. Darrow for the defense against a youthful William E. Borah for the prosecution; both would make their reputations from the trial, Borah going on to win election six times as United States Senator from Idaho.

Idaho's early government set a moderately progressive course. The 1890 constitution, for example, established state control over water rights, provided for an eight-hour work day on all public works, prohibited child labor in the mines, and allowed the legislature to set up boards of arbitration to handle labor disputes. The document did, however, contain a controversial provision disenfranchising Mormons who practiced polygamy. Six years later women's suffrage was approved and, in the 1910 initiative and referendum, control of banking practices, regulation of lobbying, and workmen's compensation. But Idaho was a state torn by conflict in its early years. Not only was it wracked by the labor wars, assaults on the Mormons, and conflicts between Masonic Republicans and Irish Catholic Democrats, but the distinct geographic regions engaged in ferocious sectional rivalry. Modern Idahoans have had to make and keep a lot of truces in order to live together in peace.

Idaho had 712,567 people by the 1970 Census count, an increase of 6.8 percent over 1960. Almost half the counties actually lost population during the decade as young people continued their flight from the land; only a surge in places like Boise, Lewiston, and Pocatello prevented an overall loss. The historical charts show an Idaho population of 14,999 in 1870, of 88,548 when statehood came in 1890, 325,594 after the big irrigation and reclamation decade of 1900–10, and then slow but steady growth ever since. For three decades now, the population increase has lagged behind the national rate, and it seems almost certain that within a decade Idaho will be reduced to a single Representative in the U. S. House.

Almost $3 billion worth of minerals have been extracted from the hills and mountains of Idaho in the 11 decades since the gold rush began. But gold itself has long been overshadowed by less glamorous treasures—silver, lead, zinc, phosphates, and copper chief among them. Gold currently accounts for no more than 1 percent of the annual mining income of some $125 million. Idaho remains the state of states for silver, is second in lead and third in zinc. Practically all the valuable ores come from the Coeur d'Alene mining district in the north, a 5-by-30-mile forested strip packed with incredibly productive mines—the Sunshine, Galena, and Lucky Friday, which lead the U. S. in silver production, and the Bunker Hill and Sullivan, which have yielded 2.5 million tons of lead and more than 100 million ounces of silver. A wide variety of rarer metals, ranging from the nation's largest deposits of phosphate, discovered near Pocatello in southeastern Idaho, are being mined in great quantities. Despite the long decline of mining as a factor in the Idaho economy, the fact is that more than half the value of minerals extracted in the state has come since World War II.

Still, there are 30 states which earn more from mineral production than Idaho, and the payroll which Idaho's 3,300 miners take home is only 1.4 percent of the personal income earned in the state. Most of the wealth goes out of Idaho, and there is no severance tax to capture some for the state's own interests. (A minimal 1 percent severance tax, for instance, would have provided $30 million over the years—enough to have built a magnificent university campus.) Not a few ghost towns nostalgically recall the glory of the early mining days; one of the most remote and picturesque, Silver City, once had 4,000 inhabitants but just in the past decade lost its last resident, "Two Gun" Willie Hawes. The conservationists, it might be added, are just as happy to see mining, especially for gold, on the downturn. They point to a legacy of ugly weed-infested gold dredgings all over the state. And centuries may pass before the last slag heaps of the Coeur d'Alene region meld back into the natural landscape.

The commercial lumber industry has flourished in Idaho since the turn of the century, taking timber both from its own holdings and National Forest Service land. Haunted by the ghosts of lumber towns like Spirit Lake and Laclede, which ate their cake at one sitting and then expired, the present-day commercial loggers are almost all operating on a sustained yield basis with regular reforestation. Just as in the days of the early lumberjacks, one company, Potlatch Forests, Inc., still floats logs down the Clearwater River to its mill; the loggers, supervising the log flow, eat and sleep in floating bunkhouses. Idaho has both the nation's largest stand of white pine and the world's largest white pine sawmill at Lewiston. Among other varieties heavily timbered are Douglas fir, Englemann spruce, red cedar, western larch, lodgepole, and ponderosa pine, all at an annual value of some $200 million.

Agriculture overtook mining to become Idaho's leading industry in 1890, and has remained there ever since. Gross farm income exceeds $600 million a year. Potatoes, the product that made Idaho famous, are grown chiefly on irrigated land along the Snake River Valley, where the volcanic ash is especially hospitable to the crop; driving through in the summertime, one sees literally hundreds of miles of fields kept moist by the ever-present sprinklers. For most of this prosperity, the Bureau of Reclamation, with its many dams along the Snake and its tributaries, is to be thanked. Deep-well pumping also adds to the farm water supply.

At a rapid pace, the small potato farmer is being forced out of business by the difficult economics of his business and the power and efficiency of huge farm corporations which also dry or freeze the potatoes and then sell them all over the United States. By 1969, 5 percent of Idaho's farms accounted for almost half of the state's 14.4 million agricultural acreage. Corporations like Ore-Ida,* J. R. Simplot, French's, and American Potato have gigantic mechanized farms covering tens of thousands of acres on the irrigated desert lands, and are also the chief consumers of the potatoes produced by their smaller competitors. Enraged by the low prices they were receiving, many of the smaller farmers in the late 1960s joined the National Farmers Organization and staged some highly publicized potato burns to dramatize their plight. They failed, however, to force higher pay for their crop. The big corporations operate chiefly with migrant labor—mostly Texan Mexicans—and house them in cheaply built labor camps. Ore-Ida has imported large work crews from the Navajo Reservation in Arizona. But for native Idahoans, the processing plants have been a godsend, employing thousands.

The Idaho potato crop is first in the country and worth about $120 million a year, well ahead of Maine and California, the closest competitors. But one hears that the fine Idaho russet that long brought Idaho potato farmers premium prices may fade from the market, since the corporate processors insist that restaurants and housewives prefer dried or frozen potatoes instead. In processed form, it matters little if a potato was raised in Idaho or Maine or California; in fact, the big processors occasionally go outside of Idaho to buy their potatoes in order to hold down the prices they have to pay other Idaho farmers. Ore-Ida officials agree with a *Wall Street Journal* report that "the fresh potato will soon be as rare as the steam engine." The situation, one supposes, may not be unlike that in Florida, where most restaurants insist on serving frozen orange juice rather than the fresh pressings of the fruit that grows at their doorsteps.

Altogether, field crops account for just over half of Idaho farm income, including potatoes, sugar beets (second biggest crop in the U. S.), wheat, barley, beans, hay, and others. Another $250 million a year comes from livestock products. Some 850,000 sheep and 1.5 million cattle graze the plains of the south and the mountain valleys of central and northern Idaho. Like potatoes, the livestock industry is moving toward fewer and fewer owners. The Circle C Ranch at New Meadows is one of the largest in the United States. Much of the tending of sheep is done by immigrant Basque sheepherders on contract; their native land in northern Spain is not unlike parts of Idaho. Idaho's Basques form the largest colony from their region in North America. One of their number, a 1958 arrival named Claudio Abanzabalegui, expressed the directness and simplicity of his trade in these words quoted in a Time-Life regional book: "This is big country. I was lonesome at first. But I like my work. I herd sheep. They must graze and fatten and I must protect them from bears and cougar."

Less happy is the plight of the Mexican-American farm workers who do much of the harvesting of crops in Idaho. They complain of low wages, substandard living conditions, and serious joblessness in their ranks. Since

---

* Ore-Ida has been a subsidiary of the mammoth H. J. Heinz Food Company since 1965.

1970 they have been trying to organize as a branch of César Chávez's United Farm Workers Organizing Committee—a development that makes many of the growers, quite figuratively, see red.

Our farm review can be ended by noting that the Snake River Trout Farm near Buhl, largest in the nation, sells two million pounds of rainbow trout each year.

Depending on the yardstick one uses, Idaho appears better or worse-off than many of its Mountain North neighbors. The economy is basically extractive with many raw products shipped out of state; on the other hand, Idaho does have a $500 million-a-year manufacturing industry, based largely on processed foods (especially potatoes and sugar beets) and wood and paper products fabricated from the yield of its own forests. The state has two major federal installations: the U. S. Air Force Base at Mountain Home and the Nuclear Reactor Test Site on the desert near Idaho Falls, which employs nearly 1,000 engineers, chemists, and physicists. But the overall defense-generated civilian employment is only 0.5 percent of the work force, ranking 50th among the 50 states. Tourism brings in more than $200 million a year, one of the most dynamic elements in the economy of recent years. But tourism has probably reached only a fraction of its potential. Many of the great natural wonders of the state are either inaccessible or scarcely known to most Americans. There is only one national monument —the eerie Craters of the Moon, an area of twisted black volcanic rock and ash, bedecked in summer with beautiful wild flowers. But it is not a resort area to draw thousands. Fabled Sun Valley caters to a fairly narrow clientele. The excellent state park nucleus in northern Idaho still lacks a national reputation. To date, there is no national park, though the one now proposed in the Sawtooth Mountains could be the catalyst to make Idaho a much more visited state.

Idaho is badly in need of some new economic stimulus, including but going beyond the corporate headquarters complex at Boise. Per capita income presently ranks 37th among the 50 states, 17 percent below the national average, and personal income growth has advanced over the past decade at a rate slower than the national average. The population shows a bulge at the juvenile and oldster level, with a great outmigration of people in their productive 20s and 30s, many heading to California or the Northwest for better jobs. In a study issued in 1969, the suggestion was made by W. LaMar Bollinger, an economics professor at the College of Idaho at Caldwell, that Idaho has been in an economic tailspin since the day it was admitted to the Union in 1890. In rollicking territorial days, the mines were booming and the average Idahoan earned half again as much as the average American.

But [writes Bollinger] almost at her birth of statehood, the curtain came down on the age of abundance of the Gem State. . . . As the gold and silver veins diminished, these pioneer citizens found themselves isolated from metropolitan centers and banished from the American market by the Rocky Mountains on the east, the Cascade Mountains on the west, the barren Great Basin on the south, and an international boundary on the north.

The deserts in the southern part of the state were covered with sagebrush which could be conquered only by capital—intensive irrigation projects—and the forest in the northern panhandle suffered a distinct geographical disadvantage in competition for the American consumer.

As a land of economic opportunity, the economist suggested, Idaho peaked out about 50 years ago.

Boise: Beacon of the Intermountain West

Descending from the high arid desert country into a fertile and wooded valley in southwestern Idaho, French voyageurs were said to have exclaimed about "Les Bois" or "The Woods"—thus giving birth to the name of Boise, capital of Idaho since 1965. The physical setting, with a broad central artery running from the Mediterranean-style Union Pacific depot on benchland to the south to the high-domed Capitol to the north, is one of the most attractive in the West. Since World War II, this small city (74,990 people by 1970) has emerged as the most progressive and least insular city in the intermountain area north of Denver. With annexations, the city population actually increased 117 percent between 1960 and 1970.

What makes Boise grow? First there is the growth of state government, whose general fund has tripled in the past 20 years and doubled in the past decade. The Boise Valley is an increasingly prosperous farm area, and while the little towns wither, Boise becomes the marketing center for a huge region. It is also an important medical center, grows in importance as a cultural oasis, has attracted a mobile home manufacturing complex, is the site of thriving Boise State College, and provides a home for several major national corporations. These include Boise Cascade, which by 1969 had risen to be the 55th largest industrial corporation of the U.S. with $1.7 billion in sales; Morrison-Knudsen, the sixth largest construction-engineering firm in the country with a quarter billion dollars in annual sales (ranging from military construction in Vietnam to subway tunnels under San Francisco Bay); J. R. Simplot, a multimillion-dollar potato and mining empire; Ore-Ida, the big corporate farmers; and Albertson's, a big food store chain that ranks 43rd among American retailing firms. If I had to name a prototype city for the energetic, self-sufficient regional capital and headquarters town which the United States should encourage to meet its population growth problems, Boise would be the easy choice.

Much of the corporate growth is pure good luck; the city simply happened to be the home of several corporations which grew from little acorns into great oaks by dint of skillful management. But in the past few years a snowball effect has been in evidence, witnessed by the decision of a firm like Ore-Ida to join the other corporate leaders in town.

In years past, Boise and surrounding Ada County were regarded as a right-wing stronghold in Idaho, the conservatism based in older people and fundamentalist sects. The harshest application of laws against homosexuals in 20th century America took place in Boise in 1955, when a series of prosecutions and convictions shook the city to its roots—a gruesome story told a decade later by John Gerassi in *The Boys of Boise*.

Up to a decade ago, Boiseans still hesitated to enter into contracts with the federal government, and as late as 1967 the city elections were dominated by an organized attack on planning for urban renewal, the use of federal funds, and the alleged threat to personal liberty posed by a modern housing code. But by 1969 the right-wingers were routed and Boise was in the midst of an urban renewal plan of gargantuan proportions for a town its size, including 60 square blocks. The first parcel was to include a large mall-type shopping center in the middle of town, to be followed by parcels with apartment and business buildings. A major Capitol Mall building project was being pushed forward by the state government. The new building promised to overshadow a previous building boom which started in 1963 with a 12-story Bank of Idaho building and included a later $7 million federal building. By 1969 an estimated $50 million worth of construction was underway and plans were advancing for a city core redevelopment based on a downtown plan devised by Skidmore, Owings & Merrill of San Francisco. Perhaps the greatest impetus of all was the 1968 announcement of Boise Cascade that it would build, in the center of Boise, a new world headquarters building at a cost of $14 million; the announcement ended happily a decade of fingernail biting by Idaho officials who feared their biggest industrial enterprise would tear up its roots and move to a new headquarters on the West Coast. Soon after the Boise Cascade announcement, Morrisen-Knudsen revealed major new headquarters building plans for Boise as well.

An atmosphere of delightful low-pressure informality pervades Boise. Robert V. Hansberger, the skilled industrialist who made Boise Cascade into the great corporation it is today, finds time to drop by a visiting reporter's hotel and discuss his global business interests over breakfast. Potato king J. R. Simplot, said to be worth $200 million, quickly clears an entire morning to discuss his rags-to-riches story. In the big coastal cities, I have been obliged to fight through bevies of secretaries and wait hours to see men of far lesser import. (Only one, I might add, ever refused an interview entirely; he is a pompous New Orleans shipping magnate.)

Hansberger confesses that many people question why Boise Cascade chooses to remain "in a little Western cowtown." Practically, the telephone and air travel ease the isolation; rare is the arriving or departing flight at the Boise airport that does not carry a Boise Cascade executive. But the firm's main reason for remaining, Hansberger insists, is human: "We brought young people here, many from the East, and they put their roots down. For a company which emphasizes people, this is a good place to have your home and raise your children. Time has more value here—less of it is spent on freeways and traffic. And I can leave Boise and be elk hunting in an hour, or fishing for steelhead trout. People can go out and get their limit of ducks near Boise and be at work by 8:30—or they can leave work at 4:30 and be skiing in 40 minutes. There never was any question that we would stay here." The only real question, Hansberger insists, was whether to build the new world headquarters outside of town on some kind of campus or in center city. "We felt that if we were going to be a part of the community, we ought to put our roots right in the center of it. If our people were working in a peripheral campus setting, they'd be 'out of it' in terms of the city." Another factor was that Boise Cascade was consulting for the city of Boise on urban renewal plans to stem center-city rot, and would have been in an awkward position to desert downtown itself.

Boise Cascade also encourages its people to become involved in community affairs. Hansberger himself was the first head of the Idaho Arts and Humanities Commission. There is no shortage of culture in the city, he insists. The Joffrey Ballet has visited the city for several years. Boise has its own excellent small symphony orchestra begun in 1948, an art gallery with an excellent permanent collection of works from Idaho and all over the world, and a completely self-sustaining theatre building which houses a thriving community theatre. A national music week is held in the city each year, and the city is home for the unique Oinkari Basque Dancers. The variety and quality might not match New York or Los Angeles standards, but it is doubtful whether anyone in Boise feels that he is stranded in a cultural backwater.

Robert Vail Hansberger is at once an intellectual of no mean repute and a hard-headed business executive adept in the use of new tools of analysis and decision. A native of Minnesota, he graduated second in the celebrated class of 1947 at Harvard Business School—the man who graduated first became president of Litton Industries—and held a number of important corporate jobs before taking office in January, 1957, as president of what was then called the Boise Payette Lumber Company. The firm had been in business for 44 years, extracting a modest living from Idaho forests with annual sales of about $35 million. Within 12 years, chiefly through acquisitions of firms in allied fields, Boise Cascade had equaled or passed in revenues major competitors such as Georgia-Pacific, Weyerhauser, and International Paper. With assets of almost $2 billion, Boise Cascade had 40 executives who had earned more than $250,000 in stock options and several who were millionaires; Hansberger's personal holdings in the company were estimated by *Fortune* at $20 million in 1969.

The first mergers under Hansberger's leadership were with other lumber companies, whose vast land holdings created an asset against which Boise Cascade could borrow to get into one related field after another. There was terrific waste, Hansberger noted, in making round logs into square boards, so the company first acquired pulp and paper mills. This led to newsprint manufacture, boxes and envelopes, and eventually into office supplies and even a publishing firm (CRM Inc. of San Diego, publisher of *Psychology Today* and textbooks). Moreover, wood products are chief components of building materials like plywood and fiberboard, and before too many years the company was deep into prefabricated houses and other shelter industries like mobile homes, travel trailers, and campers. Since timber growing and house building both require land, the company moved into residential housing developments, eventually becoming the largest homebuilder in the United States, and then into recreation land development, golf courses and recreational lakes, ski resorts and hotel-resort complexes. Housing led naturally into urban renewal and urban redevelopment. Boise Cascade did not try to dominate any of the fields it moved into, but rather to achieve full integration from raw material to end product. By applying its formidable knowledge of finance, taxes, and mergers, it could increase the earnings of its component companies without falling into the slipshod ways of many conglomerates, which suddenly find themselves perplexed by the operational problems of acquired industries they scarcely understand.

No matter how sophisticated its management, however, Boise-Cascade could not be immune to a general economic recession which hit especially heavily in several of its areas of prime activity: home-building, heavy construction, and real estate. In 1969 the company's profit was $81 million, in 1970 only $36.6 million, and in 1971 it lost a staggering $85 million—about half of which was attributable to the company's write-off of its investment in the Burnett-Boise Corporation, a joint venture with Winston Burnett, the nation's largest black contracting firm.

The unexpectedly rapid rise of the environmental movement compounded Boise-Cascade's fiscal woes. Myriad objections, both justified and exaggerated, were raised about the potential impact of the company's recreational land developments on watersheds and the natural landscape. Boise-Cascade felt obliged to abandon several projects, including one in California and another in Vermont, and several were at dead standsill because of local objections. The most publicized case was that of Incline Village, a 9,000-acre development on the north shore of Lake Tahoe. Boise Cascade brought the land in 1968 and quickly began clearing it for housing units and ski runs. As the bulldozers tore away the ground cover, huge areas were laid bare and conservationists raised alarms about the possible flow of silt and algae-feeding nutrients into the lake itself. The company moved to take corrective steps, including quick reseeding of stripped land, but a California conservation group still gave it a mock award as "polluter of the year."

Hansberger acknowledges that "some of the concern over ecology is well founded. There hasn't been enough attention paid to the ecology issue in the past by some developers. And I think some of the units we acquired were in that category." The firm has cut down sharply on its recreational land acquisition and shifted gears to anticipate full and continuing management of such areas (instead of concentration on speculative land development alone). And rather than risk another blow to its image like the one it suffered at Lake Tahoe, Hansberger says, "We'll never go to a spot of natural beauty again." Commenting on that decision, *Time* noted that its ironic effect "would be to leave second-home development in the hands of the shoestring operators who created most of today's mess."

From breakfast with Hansberger, I went to the downtown Boise offices of the J. R. Simplot Company to interview the potato king himself. The contrast in personalities could not be more striking. Hansberger is the calm, highly public-spirited chief of a great public corporation, the product of America's most professional business training. Jack Simplot was an eighth-grade school dropout at Declo, Idaho, at the age of 14. He made his start in business that year feeding weaner pigs on a mash of cull potatoes and the meat from wild horses he went out on the range and shot himself. Simplot quartered the horses with an axe, skinned them, and then cooked them with the tubers in a home-made vat using sagebrush for fuel. Some 45 years and $200 million in personal wealth later, he is a hearty, jovial, down-to-earth Idaho farm boy still, compactly and powerfully built, bald and ruddy in complexion, with blue eyes quick to take the measure of any man. Few men in the food business have ever shown such an uncanny ability to see developing markets years in advance. *Fortune* describes Simplot as "one of the most successful, least conspicuous, big businessmen of his time." He is indisputably the richest man in Idaho, and probably the wealthiest individual of the mountain North.

The Simplot knack of making all things turn to gold has been with him, apparently without interruption, since his teenage days. From feeding pigs, he graduated to raising his own potatoes and then got into sorting the tubers for neighboring farmers with a new-fangled potato sorter he bought for $254. One thing led to another, and by 1940 he was shipping about 10,000 cars of potatoes and onions out of Idaho each year. Simplot still likes to call himself a "gol-durn potato farmer," and he has 4,000 acres of potatoes in Idaho alone and buys so many from other farmers for processing that they would fill 150,000 railroad cars each year.

In World War II, he got into the dried vegetable business and had plants all over the West dehydrating everything from potatoes to cabbage and parsnips. He became the biggest single shipper of dried potatoes to the armed forces. When he couldn't get lumber for boxes to send his dried vegetables overseas, he acquired a sawmill in Idaho and another in the Sierras. Today he has three sawmills that grind out 100 million board feet of lumber each year.

Another wartime problem for Simplot was getting fertilizer for the farmers who were supplying his big potato drying plant. So he got the government to lend him money for a million-dollar fertilizer plant at Pocatello. Then it turned out that phosphate rock was unavailable from earlier suppliers, so Simplot went to examine a reported outcropping near Pocatello. "I drove up there one day and scratched around with a scraper. Damned if I didn't latch onto the biggest phosphate deposit west of Florida." Now

Simplot has big fertilizer plants at Pocatello and in Canada, with annual sales in the neighborhood of $65 million. He has also branched out into other mining—iron, silica, clay, gypsum, lead, zinc, barium, uranium, copper, coal, gold, and rare earths—properties so vast that one geologist has estimated their worth at close to half a *billion* dollars.

After the war, Simplot had his scientists experiment with the freezing of potatoes. They scored a big breakthrough with french fries, and today Simplot has annual sales of some $100 million from his six potato processing plants (three in Idaho, two in Canada, one in Maine), gobbling up 16 million 100-pound bags of potatoes each year. No one else in the world has a comparable production. Already the biggest frozen potato supplier for the institutional market, Simplot talks exuberantly of prefreezing complete meals and then shipping them hundreds of miles for direct delivery to restaurants, which will heat them up to individual order, a process he says will avoid all the problems of uneven restaurant cooking skills and spillage of fresh produce en route.

Finally, it should be recorded that Simplot runs more cattle and sheep than anyone else in Idaho. This started when he was searching for a way to get rid of his potato plants' offal, or waste—the peelings, sprouts, and eyes cast off in processing. Offal mixed with alfalfa or barley and some chemical supplements, Simplot discovered, was not only nutritious for cattle but made it possible to fatten them at costs well below those of normal feedlots. So now Simplot owns more feedlots than anyone else in his state, accommodating some 150,000 steers each year. Wool production is also big, and Simplot's men fatten 50,000 lambs for market every 12 months.

With $275 million annual sales in the various parts of his personal conglomerate, Simplot might well have been expected to "go public" to solve his self-acknowledged problem—"to get enough dough to do what you'd like to do"—and to avoid the risk of his properties being broken up when he dies. Simplot will hear none of it: "Sure, I know I could be a hell of a lot bigger today if I'd gone public. . . . I just never liked to work for the other guy. What I own, I built. It's mine. . . . I make the decisions, and believe me, I enjoy makin' 'em."

Simplot expounds a sky's-the-limit free enterprise philosophy entirely appropriate to the self-made man:

If we will continue to operate this country on the free enterprise system and keep enough bait on the hook to keep people out hustling, building new products and gimmicks and new ideas—why, we can build a utopia for three times as many people as we have and every one of 'em can have two automobiles and five boats and two homes and whatever the hell you want. We have the products here, the raw materials, the know-how to do it. That's simple, and we're gunna do it.

But goddammit, everyone wants to get their foot in the trough and get somethin' for nothing, and it won't work. . . . Somehow we gotta keep them out hustling, keep 'em out digging. . . .

Not surprisingly, he is ultraconservative in his political views and has some true-blue right-wingers among his top men. Simplot's money, I heard, was a key element in electing Goldwaterite Don Samuelson to the governor-ship in 1966, and in 1968 was invested heavily in the failing attempt to oust Senator Frank Church. In his own shop, if reports around Boise are to be believed, Simplot indulges his obsession about avoiding taxes by spending great sums on counsel to reduce his tax. But the truth is that he has bene-fited enormously through government help in his enterprises, from assistance in finding markets to cheap loans to agricultural subsidies. A new Simplot processing plant in Colorado is financed with a 6 percent federal loan, sav-ing his company $195,000 off the commercial rate. A Simplot Plant at Presque Isle, Maine, near the famous Aroostook County potato fields, is made possible by a $1 million loan by the state-sponsored Maine Industrial Building Authority. In 1968–69, Simplot companies and subsidiaries in Idaho received $184,482 in federal farm subsidy payments. Smaller Idaho farmers associated with the National Farmers Organization become jealous of Sim-plot's favored position and his tough line on the potato prices he will pay them. Finally, not a little resentment is engendered by Simplot's statements that he will not clean up pollution from his various operations until the government forces him to do so. It all adds up, the *Intermountain Observer* reports, to a "slipping image" for "Idaho's all-American boy."

The Lesser Cityscape

After Boise, the cities of Idaho are few and lightly populated. Poca-tello (1970 population 40,036), in southeast Idaho, started in a boxcar at a Union Pacific yard and has a sprinkling of ethnic groups fairly rare in the Mountain West—Greeks, Italians, Mexicans, Japanese—whose fathers and grandfathers were hired in successive stages by the railway in its early fights with the unions. The biggest growth factor in recent-day Pocatello has been Idaho State University, but the city has its share of economic bad luck because two big phosphate plants are located just across the county line and thus fail to pay local taxes even though many miners' children are in the Pocatello schools.

Pocatello's most illustrious citizen is Perry Swisher, a liberal Republican who ran as an independent for governor in 1966 to protest both major parties' failure to nominate a backer of the badly needed and just-passed state sales tax. A man of exceptional intellect and sensitivity to Idaho's needs, Swisher spoke the most sensibly about state problems but was run-ning in the wrong year, with the wrong political credentials. In 1969 he led the ticket to win a seat on the Pocatello city council, adding a much-needed breath of fresh air in his city's government. He has also given great chunks of his time, both independently and in connection with a university-connected program, to work with the Indians on the nearby Fort Hall reservation. Swisher drove me one evening through part of the reservation, speaking with care and concern about the poverty in which the Indians still live, their difficulties in adapting their communal and cooperative way of life to acquisitive American society, and the cultural conflicts that lead to glue-sniffing and so many suicides among young Indians. "We lose the best ones to that, not the worst ones," Swisher believes. But he also thinks Indians may have as much to teach the white men, by their calm and cooperative view of life, as even the best white civilization can teach them.

Idaho's third largest city is wind-blown Idaho Falls (35,776), a strong Mormon town with an old LDS temple that my newspaper friends call "one of the squarest places in Idaho." The city is the center of Idaho's potato industry, and, because of its location near the Atomic Energy Commission's National Reactor Testing Station, benefits from federal employment. Some miles to the west in south central Idaho is Twin Falls (21,914), an agricultural center which in the past few years has renewed its downtown, started its own successful junior college, and attracted a major hosiery plant from the South. Former Governor Smylie believes Twin Falls has begun "to develop breakout velocity" as Boise did a decade before.

Hundreds of miles north of the Boise-Pocatello axis is the workingman's town of Lewiston, (26,068 people in 1970), which has high hopes of becoming a major grain and lumber shipping point when dams on the lower Snake and the Columbia make slackwater barge transportation possible from the Pacific coast. The city is set in a bowl at the confluence of the Clearwater and Snake Rivers; this is where the Snake, which drains all of Idaho, leaves the state, and consequently Lewiston has the lowest elevation (735 feet). There are few U. S. cities where air pollution has so influenced population patterns. A stinky pulp mill is on the upwind side of town, which has caused suburban (and recently annexed) Lewiston Orchards to prosper much more than the old city of Lewiston proper.

Gem State Power and Politics

Idaho presents a more democratic rivalry of forces than Wyoming, Utah, or old-time Montana. There are indeed the traditional establishment forces and special interests, representing private power, wealthier farmers and stockmen, the mining and forest industries, and the railroads. The Idaho Power Company, operating more quietly but just as determinedly as its counterpart in Montana, has shown such finesse as to get both Hansberger and Simplot on its board. Not a little power is also said to emanate from the county courthouses and the Mormon church. Nonetheless, the special interests rarely seem to exert total control. The cattlemen have not represented the monolithic force they are in Wyoming, and the Idaho Farm Bureau has been declining from a pinnacle of strength achieved about a decade ago. The mining interests are split between old-style lead and silver shaft mines in the north and the newer open-pit mines for phosphates in the south. As we noted, J. R. Simplot and his men are finding themselves increasingly challenged. Other corporate behemoths in Idaho, especially Boise Cascade, have traditionally been reluctant to take too immediate a role in state politics. With their national and international interests, it might be said that they have bigger fish to fry.

The "liberal" forces of Idaho are by no means cowed or perennially on the defensive, nor were they silenced by the virulent outbreak of John Birch Society activity, noted especially in Boise and Pocatello, during the 1960s. The Idaho Education Association has a well-organized lobby and wields substantial power. The AFL-CIO operates openly in politics with a moderately liberal orientation, although the preponderance of craft over industrial unions averts any strong turn to the left. (Only 18 percent of the nonfarm workers are unionized, but Idaho voters did reject right-to-work in a 1958 referendum, in contrast to several of their mountain state neighbors.) As we will note later, Idaho has an increasingly strong conservationist movement; perhaps the single most influential group is the Idaho Wildlife Federation, headed by Ernest Day. And the university communities (Moscow, Pocatello, and Boise) provide forums for liberal ideas.

Idaho lacks the conservative press dominance of many lightly populated states, with the result that the people have an opportunity to escape from rigid mental patterns far more rapidly than might otherwise be possible. The Lewiston *Morning Tribune* has been strong for social welfare and Democratic candidates for years, and opposed the Vietnam war in no uncertain language. The *Statesman* in Boise, the state's largest paper, used to have an archconservative image but has turned around 180 degrees to a quite progressive stance, largely as a result of its purchase by Federated Publications and the installation of a highly regarded liberal Republican, Eugene Dorsey, as publisher. And both Boise television stations budget substantially for news and in-depth shows, well over the average for stations their size.

The weekly *Intermountain Observer* published in Boise, wields a liberal influence that far exceeds the proportions of its meager 3,500 circulation. Nothing in Idaho—be it the state prisons, race relations, poverty programs, Indian or youth affairs, the big corporations, J. R. Simplot, the environment, problems of the aged, school budgets, or oppressive police tactics—is beyond the scope of the *Observer's* carefully researched and sharply pointed critiques. Editor Sam Day, a career newsman who took over in 1964, has been remarkably successful in attracting top-notch writers and important figures as columnists or writers, including Perry Swisher, former governor Robert Smylie (who proceeded to roast his less-than-competent successor, Don Samuelson, in a weekly column), Lewiston *Tribune* editorial page editor Bill Hall, Dwight William Jensen, and Alice Dieter. Only three or four weekly state opinion journals of comparable quality exist in the U. S. today—the *Maine Times, Texas Observer,* and *Argus* from Seattle among them. One wishes there were more, for they serve to crystallize public opinion and provide a journalism delightfully free of the business-oriented restraints of the normal daily press. One could say of all those I have mentioned what the *Columbia Journalism Review* said of the *Intermountain Observer*—that it "comforts the afflicted and afflicts the comfortable."

The cross-pressures of Idaho politics can leave an outsider thoroughly confused. Often the sectional rivalries of the "liberal" north versus the "conservative" south are crucial, and in the future it may well be the Boise area versus either the north or southeast. Especially in the past, conflicts of Mormon versus non-Mormon bubbled to the surface, and any analysis of the state should not ignore the strong injection of former Southerners. Finally, traditional vote analysis has proven elusive because Idaho has differed from most northern states in having a rural vote that is traditionally liberal and Democratic and a city vote that is conservative and Republican. One reason for the Democrats' strength in the countryside was the loyalty the party built among mountain and farm people through New Deal farm programs, reclamation, and Social Security—a loyalty now dissipating as the national Democrats orient themselves increasingly to the problems of the cities. Meanwhile, the little towns, filled with people living on low fixed incomes and hard pressed by inflation, see themselves cut off from the mainstream.

The issues preoccupying the Idaho voter today, according to its state politicians, range from taxes to crime in the streets (though Idaho has one of the lowest crime rates in the U. S.), from economic development to threatened pollution of rivers and streams. Idaho is a small state where partisan politics often takes a back seat to personal politics, a trend all the more apparent among voters under 40 who lack any strong ties to the established parties. But young voters are less of the population pool than in coastal states, leaving a combination of nonvoting juveniles and oldsters on fixed incomes that results in many conservatives winning office.

Robert Hansberger told me he found the Idaho character marked by a high degree of individualism, harking back to pioneer times and reflective of farmers' dislike of being pushed around. "The people are very friendly," he said, "but they also love to disagree and argue." There are enough Southerners, Hansberger said, for Negroes to experience real prejudice; he recalls that in 1968, following the assassination of Martin Luther King, Boise blacks requested permission for a Good Friday memorial parade, but the mayor unwisely refused permission. As a result, the city was an armed camp for a day. Sam Day of the *Observer* detects "a rationalization among those who remain in Idaho because they think it's God's chosen place. They're not willing to recognize problems where they exist." But the problems are there, he insists, pointing to discrimination suffered by Idaho's small black population, the plight of the Indians, and the sorry lot of the migrants living in decrepit labor camps on the edges of the towns.

Idaho can take credit for one of the highest U. S. participation records in elections—often over 80 percent of voting-age citizens in a Presidential election year. Perplexed by the problem of many candidates winning primary elections with small percentages of the vote in broad fields of contenders, the legislature has experimented with more varieties of direct primary and endorsing conventions than any other state. The last experiment, in effect from 1964 through 1970, let any candidate who received more than 20 percent of the vote at his state's party convention request a place on the primary ballot. But the 1971 legislature junked it, returning the state to a straight primary system.

Idaho has had a viable two-party system ever since statehood and has voted for the winning Presidential candidate in all but two elections of this century. Most legislatures have been Republican-controlled, but at least until World War II, the party control of governorships was about even. Then a long chain of Republican gubernatorial victories ensued, unbroken until Democrat Cecil Andrus won a four-year term in 1970. Part of the Republicans' luck was attributable to their attractive candidates, like Len Jordan (now a Senator) in 1950 and Robert Smylie in 1954 and two succeeding elections. Twice, Smylie was blessed with Democratic opponents, chosen by less than a majority of the party's voters in split primaries, who favored legalized gambling in Idaho—a device, some think, that would make Idaho into a new Nevada and attract all sorts of tourist dollars. Many regular Democrats refused to back the gambling candidates, and it takes little imagination to guess how the Mormon Church reacted to the idea. In 1966, the unhappy Democrats endured a divisive three-way primary only to have their candidate die in a September plane crash and many party members withhold support from Cecil Andrus, nominated that year as a last-minute substitute. A pro-gambling candidate filed as an independent in the general election, as did Perry Swisher, and the Republicans ended up winning by 10,842 votes.

Smylie's dozen years in the governorship came to an abrupt end in 1966 when he was defeated for renomination by Don Samuelson, then a right-wing state senator known chiefly for his fight against a sales tax. The Smylie story is a vivid illustration of the vicissitudes of state and national politics. During the first 10 of his 12 years in office, he showed unusual administrative skills and ran a steady ship, but he decreed no especially innovative new courses for the state. Then, in the final two years, he worked with progressive forces in the 1965 legislature to enact landmark legislation for Idaho, especially the sales tax which revolutionized the state tax structure and let the state assume a much larger share of local school taxes by increasing its budget 33 percent. (Perry Swisher, then a state senator, was the key legislative leader for the tax legislation.) At the same time, Smylie got through a far-reaching state park and recreation program, which included negotiating with the Harriman family of Union Pacific fame to will their family estate in eastern Idaho, called "the Railroad Ranch," to the state as a park. Smylie could also claim credit for the permanent building fund program set up for state government and a water resources board. Many consider him the best governor Idaho ever had.

But Smylie had always had his problems with right-wing Republicans, problems that boiled to the top in 1966. He had been less than enthusiastic about Goldwater's Presidential candidacy in 1964, and on election day plus one he became the first nationally known party figure to call for the resignation of Barry Goldwater's Dean Burch as Republican National Chairman. As chairman of the Republican Governors Association he tried to point the party from Goldwaterite extremism to a moderate course. The Idaho conservatives, led by an extremely able political operative, then Republican National Committeewoman Gwen Barnett,* never forgave him. When he decided to try for a fourth term as governor in 1966, they were waiting in ambush with cash and organization to back Samuelson. Praised for his record in the state press and nationally acknowledged as a Republican party leader, Smylie lapsed into overconfidence at home. Don Samuelson, sometimes tongue-tied in trying to argue points of law, knew how to campaign at the grass roots and charm the party workers. A big, square-jawed man with a crewcut, Samuelson exuded a right-off-the-range feeling. Rural Idaho took to him quickly, and in a great upset he defeated Smylie with 61 percent of the vote.

The right-wing tide that engulfed Smylie was no will-of-the-wisp. In 1964 Barry Goldwater lost Idaho by less than 2 percentage points, his highest share of the vote in any non-Southern state except his native Arizona. In 1970, the *Statesman's* John Corlett and other reporters noted continuing and deep right-wing penetration into Republican organization ranks.

As governor, Samuelson turned in a dismal performance both as an administrator and on the newly sensitive environmental issue. His hearty backing for the mining interests that wanted to start mining molybdenum in the exquisite White Clouds area (an issue to which we will return later) was a key factor in his 1970 defeat. Cecil Andrus, the young Democrat and experienced state senator who defeated him, made protection of the environment the central issue of his campaign. For once, the Democrats let up on their usual internecine battles, and the party won the governorship for the first time in 24 years. But the Republicans kept control of both houses of the legislature and both Idaho seats in the U. S. House.

A potent force pulling Idaho to the right is the imbalance in party organizations. The Republican is much tighter-knit and better financed. In the Boise area, now looming as a much greater force in statewide politics, the executives of firms like Morrison-Knudsen, Simplot, and Boise Cascade and their wives have become increasingly interested in politics. They were almost invariably on the Republican side until 1970, when many backed the Democrats because of the environmental issue. Organized labor helps to balance the score in its strongholds like Lewiston and Pocatello, but a Democratic Senate candidate may have to look outside Idaho for 50 percent or more of his campaign financing. State and local Democratic candidates, almost by definition, have to run on shoestring budgets.

* Mrs. Barnett, whom Smylie once called "the philosophic ideologue, field marshal, and guru" of the ultraconservative Idaho Republicans, maintained her control of the party machinery until 1971, when she divorced her husband and moved out of the state.

Notwithstanding the conservative pull, Idaho has a vigorous tradition of spunky liberal opposition to the established powers that goes back to the first years of statehood and the role of Progressive Republicans in the Grand Old Party in the 1910s and 1920s. The grand exemplar of this tradition was William E. Borah, liberal Republican who served Idaho in the U.S. Senate from 1907 to 1940, exhibiting a fearsome independence that prompted the conservatives to challenge him time after time. Regrettably, many now remember Borah only for his opposition to U.S. entry into the League of Nations and his isolationist stand just before World War II—he predicted the war would not occur just a few months before it broke out. But he was such a prominent progressive leader on domestic issues that some historians speak of a period of "Borah liberalism" in the Senate. In the 1920s, Borah was the only leading figure in either party to favor diplomatic recognition of the Soviet Union.

John Gunther reported that Borah "left no political family of any kind, no tradition or inheritance, no machine." The judgment may be questioned, however. One-term Senator Glen Taylor, who was Henry Wallace's running mate in 1948, was a liberal and noncomformist not soon to be forgotten. But Taylor was too much for Idaho Democrats, and they retired him in the 1950 primary; for those who wonder what ever became of him, it may be reported that he eventually moved to California and became a wig manufacturer.* Even closer to the Borah tradition is Democrat Frank Church, who went to the U.S. Senate in 1957 at the tender age of 32 after defeating Republican Senator Herman Welker, a vindictive right-winger who was a close ally of Wisconsin's Joseph McCarthy. Church went on the Senate Foreign Relations Committee and became one of the first Senators to oppose the Vietnam war. He remained a foremost "dove" for years, even though he was the first to admit that "the whole state tends to be hawkish —close to its pioneer roots." Church also dared to take a strong stand for conservation when it appeared his stand might cause his defeat at the hands of logging, mining, and grazing interests.

In a sense, Idaho voters have given Church the same independence in Washington they accorded Borah. Church, in turn, has peppered his liberalism with stands with which many liberals differ. In 1971 he reversed his previous stand against the Senate's filibuster rule, saying that unlimited debate was sometimes necessary because "whenever the big interests line up together . . . big government, big business, and big labor, they seem always to be able to control a majority, no matter how unprincipled or outrageous their legislative proposal might be." He has catered to home-state sentiment

---

* Revisionist historians suggest that Taylor may simply have been a man ahead of his time, driven from office for espousing views which are now widely held in the U.S. F. Ross Peterson, author of a new book, *Prophet Without Honor,* observes that Taylor was an outspoken advocate of the rights of minorities who played a vital role in Theodore G. Bilbo's unseating by the U.S. Senate, a bitter opponent of McCarthyism, a severe critic of the containment policy who saw mutual culpability of the U.S. and the Soviet Union in the Cold War and warned—years before President Eisenhower did so—of the danger of a military-industrial alliance that would encourage the Cold War and divert resources from solving domestic problems.

by opposing gun-control laws. And he has been assiduous in protecting Idaho interests on touchy issues like water.

The occasional election victories of Democrats like Church and Andrus make it possible to say that Idaho, despite all its conservative signs, is not a wholly Republican and right-leaning state today. And even the Republicans sent to Congress are not monolithically conservative. Senator Jordan, when he was governor in the early 1950s, was a parsimonious administrator who curbed expenditures for schools and welfare and left the mental hospitals in scandalous condition. But later, in the Senate, he compiled a strong civil rights record and acted with sensitivity on conservation issues. When Jordan announced his retirement (effective at the end of 1972), Perry Swisher wrote a warm review of his record, saying: "Len Jordan has never stopped learning." Swisher suggested that Jordan be invited to appear at Idaho universities to give present-day students, so given to moralistic and self-righteous judgments of others, a chance to communicate with a man seasoned in the area of self-knowledge and reconciliation of unlike people.

Another Republican of interest is Orval Hansen, a Congressman first elected in 1968 after several years of especially creative work in the state legislature. Hansen has somehow managed to keep cordial relations with the conservative wing of his party while sponsoring bills such as a program of massive federally financed services for disadvantaged children and the children of working mothers. But meanwhile, back in Idaho, the Republican-controlled legislature has refused to approve funding for state-supported kindergartens. The kind of Idaho Republican said to be most popular among the party rank and file is James McClure, first elected Congressman from the state's northern district in 1966, whose voting record is rated extremely favorably by groups like the ultraconservative Americans for Constitutional Action. McClure, for instance, was an early favorite over former Governor Smylie in the 1972 Republican primary race for Jordan's Senate seat.

A final note on Idaho government. It is exceptionally honest—the last major scandal occurred more than 20 years ago. The state ranks 13th in the U. S. A. in tax effort related to income and provides about average levels of state support for education, highways, health, and welfare. Because of the high per capita school-age population, however, the state ranks only 38th in the U. S. in actual dollars spent per pupil. The state has the lowest per capita state and local debt of any in the U. S. A., indicating cautious fiscal management but a failure to make capital investment in state facilities when they were really needed and before inflation bloated construction costs. Psychiatrists in other states told me they considered the psychiatric staffing at Idaho's state mental hospital exceedingly inadequate. Conditions at the Idaho State Penitentiary have evoked frequent criticism, and there have been well documented cases of brutality behind the prison walls.

In terms of organization, state government is desperately in need of consolidation of its innumerable boards, commissions, and agencies. Environmental protection is inadequately handled by the state health department, and the state is still a long way from unified control of its land and water use. Andrus has promised early action on these issues.

Fiscally, the great modern test of Idaho government was passage of the sales tax in 1965 under the leadership of Smylie and Swisher. Ironically, it was the last legislature before reapportionment, not the first after, that did this vital job of giving the state an adequate base for financing its schools. In a 1966 referendum, even while they were voting Samuelson in as governor, the people voted 61 percent in favor of retaining the new tax. Average educational levels achieved by Idahoans rank a very respectable eighth in the country, and a major job of school consolidation has been accomplished in recent years. But no university of exceptional quality exists in the state; the land grant University of Idaho campus at remote Moscow on the northern panhandle suffers from all the problems of trying to operate a respectable university in a backwoods setting.

Water: The Overriding Issue

Nature endowed Idaho, alone among the mountain states, with a magnificent water supply. The Snake River, unfamiliar to most Americans outside its own region but doubtless one of the greatest rivers of the continent, enters the state on the eastern border with 4 million acre-feet each year and departs many hundreds miles to the west with 38 million acre-feet. High on the panhandle are the Kootenai and Pend Oreille Rivers, carrying 27 million acre-feet between them. The wild, five-forked Salmon River at mid-state carries 7.5 million acre-feet. Altogether, the great river systems, fed by the rain and snow packs in the high mountains, provide 71.5 million acre-feet annually. By contrast, the Colorado River, the great lifeline of the American Southwest, has an average flow that ranges between 12 and 15 million acre-feet each year—a mere fifth of the water in Idaho's rivers.

Until the Bureau of Reclamation some 70 years ago began its extensive series of dams and big storage reservoirs along the river of the Snake, one could witness the anomaly of a deep, fast-flowing river moving through millions of acres of land where not much grew other than sagebrush and bunch grass, cactus and desert shrubs. The average natural rainfall in the Snake Valley is no more than 10 inches. But now 3.5 million acres of the valley are irrigated. The primary sources of moisture are the great river storage reservoirs behind federal dams. But there are also some 6,000 to 7,000 deep-well pumps, many going down 800 or 900 feet, tapping the great Snake Plain Aquifer in eastern Idaho. This mighty underground water flow, one of the greatest on the continent, is fed at least in part by the mysterious Big Lost and Little Lost Rivers, which disappear into coarse lava beds near the Craters of the Moon and are thought to reappear 150 miles westward where Thousand Springs leap out of the wall of the Snake River gorge. The aquifer discharges thousands of cubic feet of water per second. It seems in little danger of being exhausted, since its annual flow has increased markedly over the past half-century, apparently as a result of irrigation water seeping below plant root and into the underground supply.

Another three or four million acres of Snake Valley land could be irrigated, including the vast Mountain Home desert of southwestern Idaho, but the state will have to transfer water from its northern rivers (the Boise, Salmon, and others) to do that job. Idaho already has more land under irrigation than all other states save California and Texas, and adds 60,000 to 70,000 more acres per year. The Bureau of Reclamation continues to build dams along the Snake, even as the biggest it ever constructed there, the 1927 American Falls Dam, deterioriates and needs to be replaced.

Idaho's great fear, and consequently a preoccupation of its politics, is that California and other areas of the parched Southwest will try to tap the Snake River and other Idaho waterways by gigantic diversion schemes. One proposal would divert water from the Snake in Wyoming, channeling the water into the Green and then the Colorado River system. Another would create a trans-Nevada siphon from the Snake by means of an aqueduct starting near Twin Falls in south central Idaho. Californians claim the diversions would take but a fraction of the unutilized millions of acre-feet of water passing each year through Idaho and on to the Pacific Ocean. Idaho's heated response is that Snake River diversion would make (or recreate) a desert in southern Idaho and stunt the state's growth. A typical comment comes from John H. Merriam, chairman of the department of economics at Idaho State University:

Must California really have our water to survive? Of course not. California is sitting next to the world's largest supply of water, the Pacific Ocean. The technology is available to extract fresh water from the sea, but this is *expensive* water. What California wants is a federal project to deliver Idaho's water. This is *cheap* water.

Perry Swisher suggests that in the face of Californian advances on the water issue, "Idaho's best response is no response. Prolonged, the Californian barrage becomes a kind of advertisement for the economic development of this region: We have potable water and living room. Not that the Northwest isn't charitable: Our delegations can be counted on to vote for desalination projects on the coast." Among other things, Idaho thinks that water diverted south would be used chiefly for agriculture; some on submarginal land. "So why," goes the argument, "go to all the trouble to ship water south so that California can raise crops that could be raised right here in Idaho, like grain or hay or potatoes?"

At least until 1978, government planning for trans-basin diversion is frozen in its tracks and may not continue. A 10-year moratorium on such investigation was written into the 1968 Colorado River Act that included the Central Arizona Project, at the insistence of Senate Interior Committee Chairman Henry M. Jackson of Washington. Jackson's Northwestern neighbors, Senators Frank Church and Len B. Jordan, were his helpers in what must be considered a classic use of small-state power in the U.S. Senate. As Church looks back on the battle, he says:

We had far fewer people in the Northwest than the mighty array of people in the Southwest, including the political muscle of California. The only place Idaho had protection was in the Senate and more particularly the Senate Interior Committee, where fortunately Senator Jordan and I had senior positions. We could be very effective in that key Senate-House conference [on the final bill]. Jackson was a great leader, but the votes in conference are made up of live Senatorial bodies, and our seniority on that committee was critical.

All of this is keenly appreciated back in Idaho. Columnist Gene Shumate of the *Idaho Statesman* has pointed out that the Snake River is not a vested property of Idaho but a navigable river, an artery of interstate commerce, which Congress may do with as it likes. "So our future lies not in the courts. Our future lies in the hands of United States Senators like Church and Jordan—strong and selfish."

As it finishes its east-to-west course across Idaho, the Snake River turns northward for some 200 miles, forming the state border with Oregon and then Washington, before it veers westerly at Lewiston and plunges into Washington state for its union with the Columbia. Thus northern as well as southern Idaho has intense interest in the use of the river's waters. For years, many southern Idahoans have dreamed of irrigating the vast southwestern Idaho desert. In the mid-1960s, the Bureau of Reclamation put together a grandiose plan involving new dams on the Snake, Boise, and Payette Rivers, tunnels and irrigation pumping stations. The idea has little chance for congressional funding, however, and in 1970 the Idaho Water Resources Board and Idaho Power Company came up with a modified plan to build, with local funds, two new dams on the Snake, producing both power and irrigation potential for 125,000 acres of the Mountain Home Desert. Environmentalists complain that there would be considerable damage to fish and wildlife resources, including the largest known nesting concentrations of golden eagles and prairie falcons in the U. S. And northern Idaho is opposed to the scheme because it fears the diversion of water could imperil recreation and navigation projects in the Lewiston area.

Controversy about irrigating the desert is likely to stretch out over many years, but the more immediate crisis—itself two decades old—concerns the proposed power dams along the "middle Snake," the stretch of the river flowing northward along the Oregon border. Here it is that the icy waters of several mountain tributaries, including the Salmon, America's greatest wild river, join the Snake. And this is the location of Hells Canyon, deepest gorge on the North American continent, where the walls of basalt, greenstone, rhyolite, and andesite tower more than a mile above the river bed. Despite its depth—up to 7,900 feet—Hells Canyon is not the raw, narrow defile that the Grand Canyon of the Colorado is. Hells Canyon is heavily wooded and goes up in a series of benches so that one doesn't get the same feeling of being at the bottom of a mile-deep well. Nevertheless, the very wildness and remoteness of the country, with its abundance of wild animals, the rough, solid rock faces of the canyon, and its turbulent and dangerous waters, make it a water wilderness the conservationists prize—and would preserve, if they could, untouched.

But Hells Canyon is also one of the best hydroelectric sites in the country; in fact, the Snake is said to possess one-eighth of the nation's entire hydroelectric potential. Moreover, the middle Snake is literally the last remaining viable water storage site of major proportions in the United States. Thus the dam builders—the power companies interested in electric generation, and the Interior Department's Bureau of Reclamation concerned about water storage to prevent disastrous floods in the Columbia River Valley—have been casting covetous eyes on the middle Snake for many years. In the 1940s and early 1950s, a grand battle was fought between public and private power interests over the proposal of the Bureau of Reclamation for the second highest dam in the world, to be constructed at Hells Canyon. The Idaho Power Company favored instead five run-of-the-river dams, without storage capacity. The issue—popularized, perhaps, by the very romantic name of Hells Canyon—became one of the great resource controversies of the 1950s, ranking with Dixon-Yates and the tidelands oil controversy. Some said the high dam was a "socialist experiment" bound to undermine states' rights. Irrigators along the Snake worried that there would not be enough river flow both to fill up the dam's huge reservoir and to water their fields. But the Interior Department, as long as the Truman Administration stayed in office, fought hard for a single dam with major storage capacity to provide flood control and irrigation for the lower Snake and the Columbia. Then the Eisenhower Administration came in, the private power company modified its request to include just three dams (one with important storage capacity), and with the approval of the Federal Power Commission, the three private dams could and did go ahead, reaching completion in 1968.*

Thus round one went to the private over the public power interests. But still, a 100-mile stretch of the river south of Lewiston and north of the three new dams, little-traveled territory including the mouth of the Salmon River and some of the most breathtaking natural scenery, remained inviolate. There was still great hydroelectric and storage potential to be gained from building more dams in the canyon, and the Bureau of Reclamation, with the Army Corps of Engineers, worked out a plan for a dam to be called High Mountain Sheep, several miles downstream (north) from the three Idaho Power Company dams but just upstream from the confluence with the Salmon. This idea was so attractive to the private power interests that the Pacific Northwest Power Company of Portland, Oregon, asked the Federal Power Commission for permission to build the High Mountain Sheep dam without government aid. The Interior Department opposed this step, partly because of a then pending treaty with Canada on water rights and partly because of serious problems of how one can get salmon and other anadromous fish, who need to come upstream to spawn, over the hurdles of high dams or prevent them from becoming disoriented and then destroyed

* The three completed dams, about equidistant between Boise and Lewiston, are the Brownlee, Oxbow, and Hells Canyon—the latter, however, not to be confused with the massive storage dam favored by public power advocates in the 1940s and early 1950s.

by severe dam-created water fluctuations at places like the confluence of the Snake and the Salmon.

But the Federal Power Commission, notorious for its loyalty to the interests of the power industry, in 1964 went ahead and approved High Mountain Sheep anyway. By this time the Johnson administration was in office, and the Interior Department, headed by Stewart Udall, challenged the FPC order in court—creating an interesting case of two government agencies opposed in a court of law. Finally, in 1967, the Supreme Court ruled against the FPC approval of High Mountain Sheep in what must be considered one of the landmark conservation decisions of all time. Justice William O. Douglas (himself an avid conservationist) wrote the 7–2 decision of the court, reprimanding the FPC for failing to consider all the ramifications of the proposed dam and noting that the test of a hydroelectric project is "whether the project will be in the public interest." The public interest, wrote Douglas, would be determined by considering "future power demand and supply, alternate sources of power, the public interest in preserving reaches of wild rivers and wilderness areas, the preservation of anadromous fish for commercial and recreational purposes, and the protection of wildlife." A river, Douglas noted, "is more than an amenity; it is a treasure."

After the Supreme Court sent the matter back to the FPC for further consideration, the onetime enemies—Pacific Northwest Power Company, controlled by four private utilities, and the Washington Public Power Supply System, representing 17 public utility districts and one city system in Washington state—joined forces to make a single application to the FPC to build two dams in Hells Canyon—Mountain Sheep and Pleasant Valley. Thus the old argument about who should build dams on the Middle Snake was transformed into a dispute about whether any more should be built at all. In 1971 the chief examiner of the FPC recommended that a license be granted, stressing the need for additional hydroelectric potential and noting that "electricity is the lifeblood of our economy and technological civilization." But he recommended that the license be subject to a five-year delay so that environmentalists could try to include the Middle Snake in the National Wild and Scenic Rivers System—a protective step the Secretaries of the Interior and Agriculture had recommended a few months previously. Not long after the FPC announcement, Governor Andrus of Idaho drew up a statement, in which Governors Daniel J. Evans of Washington and Tom McCall of Oregon joined, opposing any new dams at all. "It is time that we recognize that Hells Canyon is a truly unique and magnificent national treasure," the governors said.

In Congress, the dispute suddenly became three-sided. On the development side were men like Idaho's Rep. James McClure. On the conservationist-preservationist side were men like Sen. Robert Packwood of Oregon, who were trying to stimulate "national passion" for a Hells Canyon-Snake National River, forever beyond the reach of the dam builders. And in the middle (in an interesting reversal of form) was Senator Church, who had joined with Jordan and others in recommending the compromise of a moratorium on further dam building in Hells Canyon until 1978. But Church's long-term stand was firmly anti-dam. As he told me in a 1970 interview:

The dam builders want a dam at Hells Canyon for power. My stand is that we can't begin to realize the future needs of the Northwest by developing the few available public power sites. We should begin to look now to substitute methods of power generation. . . .

Just to build a massive dam in that last remaining stretch of this glorious river and in the deepest gorge on the continent, a dam that makes no contribution other than producing electricity, is a very dubious proposition.

Conservationists Versus Users: A Vital Shift

With the possible exceptions of Colorado and Montana, Idaho has the most vigorous conservationist movement in the Mountain West today. Such a turn of events could scarcely have been predicted just a few years past. Idaho tore through the 19th century and burst into the 20th determined to "open up the wilderness" and "bring the people in." For decades, no one questioned the big users of public lands and resources—the logging companies, mines, and grazing interests. "Ten years ago," former governor Robert Smylie commented in 1970, "you could get no one's attention about air pollution except a fellow whose cattle were said to have suffered from the fumes from a phosphate plant. One person in several hundred would mention the greenish cast of the Coeur d'Alene River's estuary into the Lake. Nobody really objected to any kind of timber cutting." If more than half of Idaho had not been in the public domain—primarily National Forest holdings—the exploitation of the land might have gone much further than it did.

What Idaho still has, in an abundance unmatched in any state save Alaska, is high mountain wilderness. This is primeval land that has never been settled, never roaded or mined or logged, literally the last refuge of the continent where man himself is always visitor, never master. The only access is by foot or on horseback. Some 2.5 million acres remain in this untouched state. The land lies in central and northern Idaho in high terrain, much of it above the timber line, dotted with snow-capped peaks and glacial lakes.

Together with other wilderness areas of the nation, such territory accounts for 2 percent of the land surface of the U. S. A. today. A common complaint is that without roads or access, it is as good as useless to all but a hardy few long-distance hikers. Lumber and mining interests, of course, suggest that it is wasted, "locked up" land, that should be thrown open to "multiple use." Not so, reply the conservationists, who are concerned that a substantial portion of the primitive area of Idaho is still not sufficiently protected by federal legislation to prevent some logging or mine activity. Senator Church, who led the congressional fight for wilderness legislation, has declared that "without wilderness, the world is a cage." In Boise, I met

Ernest Day, one of the West's leading conservationists, who speaks of himself as "a wilderness activist." As Day puts the case: "I see the land not as locked up, but as preserved for future generations. If you let roads and lots of people in, you liquidate its wild character. We can stop 2 percent short without harming ourselves, to keep the land totally wild. More and more people can then enjoy it as a wild museum in future generations."

Camera in hand, Day has hiked into the most remote and rugged lands of Idaho, making a unique photographic record of the beauty and solitude of the wilderness. His pictures, ready ammunition in the fight to save natural areas, also dominate the state's handsome promotional folder for tourists.

Not all Idahoans share Day's enthusiasm for the great wilderness areas. The *Intermountain Observer* quotes an oldtimer's fiery contempt for conservationist thinking:

What the hell are all these outsiders doing here monkeying with Idaho business? Are they trying to make Idaho a rich man's playground? We got too much country bottled up now by the federal boys in wilderness and such rot—what we need is power for industry. We need roads, lots of them, so people can get out in the back country, not poor horse and foot trails that only youngsters can travel— which they won't do anyway.

Frank Church believes that the Wilderness Act of the early 1960s was a kind of watershed in Idaho politics and attitudes toward conservation. Predictably, the users of public lands—mining, grazing, and timber interests —condemned the legislation as a lockup of vital Idaho resources. Church even found most Democrats in the state separating themselves from him on the issue, and in his 1962 election campaign every important newspaper of the state (except the Lewiston *Tribune*, traditionally Idaho's only liberal-Democratic organ) opposed him. He likes to recall the remark made to him the weekend before the election by his father-in-law, a federal judge and former Idaho governor: "Look at the organized interests opposed to you— the newspapers, the cattlemen, the sheepmen, the mining association, the lumber companies, the doctors, the dentists, the chambers of commerce, are all against you. How do you think you're going to win this election?" Church said he hoped he would "luck out like Harry Truman did"—everybody against him but the people. He ended up winning by 24,528 votes.* "That demonstrated for the first time," Church believes, "that Idaho people cared a great deal about the outdoors. . . . From that point on, men in public life in Idaho began to recognize that times were changing, that the long dominant interests in Idaho politics could no longer . . . preserve their rights to the public domain as against the public interest."

Back in the Senate, Church then found widespread state support when he introduced legislation that would lead to the National Wild Rivers system. The prevailing Idaho attitude, to his surprise, was that the streams should be preserved in their natural free-flowing state, unobstructed and

---

* Church won again in 1968 by an even greater plurality of 59,088 votes—the same day that Idahoans merrily split their tickets to give Nixon a margin of 76,096 votes over Democrat Humphrey. Church won in every region, among all income groups, in all types of farm precincts, and by the biggest percentage of all in lumbering and mining territory.

unpolluted. "That didn't come easily," he adds, "to a state where irrigation is so essential and dams such a big part of the economy. It takes some sophistication to . . . see the need to keep some rivers undammed for their aesthetic and recreational value . . . to see a river as more than a potential irrigation ditch."

Neither wilderness areas nor wild rivers, however, would crystallize the conservation issue in Idaho to the extent of the dispute that broke out in the late 1960s over the proposal of the American Smelting and Refining Company (New York) to open a 740-acre open-pit mine to take molybdenum from the magnificent White Cloud mountains of central Idaho. If the multimillion-dollar ore find had been made on some low plateau or bush-covered butte, most Idahoans would doubtless have cheered a new economic development in their dollar-short state. But the White Cloud peaks, some 25 miles northwest of Sun Valley in one of the most beautiful Alpine regions of North America, are another story. Here majestic snow-covered mountains, dominated by 11,820-foot Castle Peak, thrust skyward, their granite peaks often veiled by a scarf of white clouds. Numerous crystalline lakes of azure blue, fed by the year-round snows of the high elevations, are tucked into the bases and hollows of the peaks, six or seven often linked by fresh-running streams. One local newspaper writer has depicted the lovely peaks and lakes, protected in the past by their very remoteness, as the "crown jewels of Idaho."

The open-pit molybdenum mine, projected to cover a 740-acre tract on the mountainsides only a mile and a half from Castle Peak, would doubtless inflict lasting scenic and ecological harm on the high, fragile White Peaks. Anyone who has seen other molybdenum mines, like the Climax Mine in the Colorado Rockies, knows that the mineral is recovered by literally eating away the side of a mountain. At peak production, the mine would produce 20,000 tons of ore each day, reducing it to metal at the site by crushing it, dumping it into a tailing pond, and then bubbling oil and a reagent through the water into a froth, a process by which the molybdenum floats to the top while the rest of the crushed ore sinks to the bottom. The broad meadows near the claim would soon be covered by tailings, because more than 99.5 percent of the raw ore becomes waste rock. But the damage would not be confined to the site itself. As one nature writer (John L. Mauk in *Seattle Magazine*) notes:

> Nature struck a delicate balance in the White Clouds. Bitter winters and rocky terrains allow only the hardiest of life to survive at the higher elevations. Farther down the sloping valleys, plants and animals are more abundant, but here too the life patterns have been stabilized only after long periods of trial and error. The introduction of even minor alterations in this wilderness will disrupt the equilibrium and completely alter the ecology of the immediate area and of regions many miles away.

As an example, bighorn sheep and mountain goats range along the narrow ledges and crags overlooking the mine site, while major populations of elk, mule deer, and smaller animals inhabit the lower meadows and forests. The continuous clamor of the mine operation—blasting, shoveling, trucking —would reverberate from cliff to cliff and drive many of the animals away. The streams, which are the headwaters of the Salmon River, would soon become silted and polluted, probably affecting the annual runs of salmon and steelhead trout in the Salmon and farther downstream in the Snake and Columbia Rivers. While American Smelting and Refining (ASARCO) claimed it would take all possible steps to protect the environment, the access road into the area would invite further intensive use of the area and draw less responsible mining operations. Within a year of ASARCO's first test site, other companies were searching for minerals in the shadow of Castle Peak, including one Denver firm which was found pumping bentonite slurry and tailings directly into the waters of one of the lakes. (When the Idaho Public Health Service threatened court action, the firm stopped the dumping, but one of its officials commented, "If ore is discovered, there won't be a lake there anymore anyway.")

Under an 1872 law which governs mining operations on public land, a prospector has open license to stake a claim on any "unreserved" territory and to work the land free of charge. Bound by that law, handed down from America's unfettered pioneer days when neither open-pit mining operations or a shortage of scenic areas were ever taken into account, the Forest Service instituted a series of delaying steps to hinder mining at White Clouds but appeared to lack final authority to stop the development. ASARCO promised big economic benefits for Idaho, and Don Samuelson, then governor, sprang to the defense of the mining company, declaring: "The raw materials are here and should be exploited to the fullest possible extent."

The conservationists, led by Ernest Day, saw the problem in a different light. "This is a classic confrontation," Day said, "between the old rape-and-run mining interests and the conservationists, defending a spectacular area of natural beauty." In the wake of Samuelson's defense of the mining project, Day angrily quit the position he had held (under appointment by Samelson's predecessor, Robert Smylie) as chairman of the State Parks Board. Senator Church quickly entered the controversy on the conservationists' side, as did practically all the newspapers of Idaho. In reply to ASARCO's promise of 350 jobs at the mine, with tax benefits to the state and county, opponents argued that the chief profits would go to New York —with Idaho left to clean up the mess. Economist John Merriam of Idaho State University pointed out that U. S. reserves of molybdenum (a metal used in the hardening of steel) are sufficient to last another 35 years or more. Most additional U. S. production at the present time would probably be sold overseas. "If the molybdenum in the White Clouds is preserved for the time being," Merriam said, "it could still be mined in the event of a shortage or a dire national emergency."

By summer 1970, with the aid of Republican Congressman Orval Hansen, Church had persuaded the other members of the Idaho congressional delegation—both conservative Republicans who in earlier times would almost certainly have sided with the mining interests—to join in sponsoring legislation to create a Sawtooth Recreation Area and National Park. The bill was modified the following year to omit, for the time being, the national park concept which would be more difficult to clear in Congress. But the legislation instructed the Interior Department to draw up a national park proposal. The recreation area would provide some immediate protection for the White Clouds area, though nothing Congress would do could completely negate valid mining claims already patented. However, legislation could give the Forest Service new tools to regulate surface-disturbing activities. And a national park, if finally approved, would provide Idaho with a powerful tourist magnet which it now lacks, enhancing the state's economy far more than mines in the White Clouds could ever be expected to do.

The mining interests, however, remain a potent force, providing, among other things, essential campaign funds for politicians of Samuelson's stripe. As Ernest Day sees it, "We're a user-oriented society in Idaho. And the users—the miners, loggers and grazers—all camp at the same campfire." All seek special government favors—the use of public land for private gain under preferential conditions. Cattle interests lobby for below-market-cost grazing fees, mining groups like ASARCO show few qualms about the location of their earth-scarring digs, lumber interests fight for more and more National Forest land to cut their timber. These tend to be the same user groups that fight tooth and nail against government regulation of the air and water pollution their activities produce. Despite its mountain solitudes, Idaho's air is imperiled by phosphate processing, smelter operations, lumber-waste burning, pulp mills, crop dusting, and a dozen other hazards. Pollution of the state's magnificent waterways is threatened by potato plant effluent, untreated municipal wastes, excrement and fluid run-off from feedlots, slaughter houses, farm chemicals, fertilizers and pesticides, and pulp mills—problems made all the more serious by dams which slow some fast-running rivers to near-stagnant ponds in the summer months.

But the conservationists are not without recourse, as they proved in 1970 when they caused Samuelson's defeat on the environmental issue and the White Cloud controversy in particular. Increasing numbers of their friends win state legislative seats, and the 1971 legislature passed landmark legislation to regulate strip mining. Senator Church's own reelection in 1968 was due in large measure to the fervor of outdoor-conservationist minded people who pitched in to help him in the face of opposition financed by the user interests. Wealthy converts to the conservationist cause, especially among professionals, have advanced it far beyond the old days when garden clubs and bird watchers were the most potent forces for preservation of the natural landscape. Compromises between users and conservationists will clearly have to be reached in future years, for all economic development involves some burden on the natural landscape. Not a few conservationists slip into a "preservationist" camp which would stop all mineral development, all new logging, all new power plants, regardless of the needs of the local residents or the nation at large. What the Idaho story of the last few years seems to say is that even in a capital-short and remote state, the battle will be fought on much more even terms than seemed remotely possible a few short years ago. In the terms of the relationship of the people to the land which gives them life and sustenance, there could not be a development of more momentous import.

NEVADA

GOMORRAH ON THE DESERT

THE GREAT Sierra Mountains block the moisture-laden clouds rolling in from the Pacific. Without water, the land of what is now called Nevada is a bleak, sun-scorched wilderness of mountain-rimmed basins and high plateau, a veritable desert. Even the bold Spaniards, first white explorers, recoiled from penetrating what their mapmakers called "the northern mystery." John C. Fremont, chief of the first U. S. Government exploration of Nevada, wrote: "The appearance of the country was so forbidding that I was afraid to enter it." This Great American Desert is not only essentially treeless—the ubiquitous sagebrush is the dominant form of plant life—but vast stretches of its territory are the salt and alkaline remnants of dead lakes, a soil that not even irrigation could redeem. A handful of lakes do remain, and in the softness of early evening the raw, harsh desert peaks may take on warm pastel hues, bringing a kind of haunting beauty to a hostile land. But man must struggle to sustain his life systems in this dryest of all the American states; in all the 109,889 square miles of Nevada (seventh largest in the Union) there are only two cities worthy of the name, Reno and Las Vegas. The rest are cow counties. In the words of the Western writer Neil Morgan, "There is very little but rock and sand, alkali-laden dry lakes, buttes and craggy mountains. The desolation of Nevada is awesome."

What then draws men? In the past century, it was the gold and silver in the hills. Cattle ranching has long eked out a bare existence. But today it is gambling. Fired by that spectacularly successful industry, catering ingeniously to Californian and transcontinental pleasure-seekers, Nevada for three decades has been growing by leaps and bounds. Its population—488,738 in the 1970 Census count—is more than 300 percent greater than the figure at the end of World War II. No other state's population has expanded at a comparable rate. Today there is hope for revival of the mining of precious metals, the cattlemen still ply their trade, and the chamber of commerce people talk of vast strides in shipping, industry, and outdoor recreation. But essentially Nevada remains a one-industry state. Some 60 percent of the people make their living off the gaming business. Take away gambling—legalized since 1931, the only American state to do so—and Nevada might well be one of the most desperately depressed regions of the hemisphere.

Chance and gamble have marked Nevada's history from the start. The first white men to try a permanent settlement were the Mormons, dispatched by Brigham Young in 1855 to "go to Las Vegas, build a fort there to protect immigrants and the United States mail from the Indians, and teach the latter how to raise corn, wheat, potatoes, squash, and melons." But the Paiute Indians raided the Mormon fields and planted none of their own, and while the Mormons did stay on, Nevada was not to be part of the great State of Deseret proclaimed by Young in 1859. For in the same year the Great Comstock Lode—the richest single treasure of gold and silver the world has ever seen—was discovered.

The little towns of Virginia City and Carson City became boom towns overnight. In poured the miners, speculators, gamblers, prostitutes, dance hall girls; not the least of the new residents was Mark Twain, who recorded that "there were banks, hotels, theaters, 'hurdy-gurdy houses,' wide open gambling palaces, political pow-wows, civic processions, street fights, murders, inquests, a whiskey-mill every 15 feet . . . and even some talk of building a church." Twain, after two years of writing truth and fiction for the *Territorial Enterprise,* was chased out of town in the wake of editorial insults that involved him in a law-breaking duel. But Virginia City has been a great grist mill for Western writers ever since; they like to recall figures like Julia Bulette, first white women to reach Virginia City in 1859. She came from New Orleans, masqueraded as a Frenchwoman, but had really been born in Liverpool. Julia's calling was prostitution; 17 years later a lover strangled her to death and took her furs and jewels. Virginia City saw to it that the perpetrator was promptly hanged, occasioning the closing of the mines for a day and one of the most riotous celebrations ever seen in the mining town.

More than a billion dollars worth of gold and silver came out of the hundreds of miles of shafts, tunnels, drifts, and inclines of the Comstock Lode, helping to finance the Civil War and creating many millionaires and multimillionaires, most of whom took their wealth to San Francisco or other more desirable places than the Nevada deserts. But by the turn of the century, the mines had been largely depleted, and Virginia City became the West's most illustrious ghost town. John Gunther would report in 1947:

Virginia City is a fragrant tomb. The population was 40,000 in its heyday, today, 2,000. Never have I seen such deadness. Not a cat walks. The shops are mostly boarded up, the windows black and cracked; the frame buildings are scalloped, bulging, splintered; C Street droops like a cripple and the sidewalks are still wooden planks; the telephone exchange, located in a stationery shop, is operated by a blind lady who had read my books in Braille. Further on is the rickety, worm-eaten shell of what was once a famous opera house.

Sadly, it must be reported that Virginia City today is more a tourist trap than a ghost town. I passed through during the early twilight of a clear summer day, that kindly hour when any place is at its best. There were the old Victorian mansions, the boardwalks, the sagging façades, the graveyard (where, Twain reported, the first 26 graves were occupied by murdered men). But the honky-tonk saloons—the Crystal Bar, the Old Comstock Saloon, the Red Garter, and the rest—were adorned with tourist-luring signs and a tacky commercialism pervaded the scene. A ghost town is a fragile thing, and in Virginia City, at least, the modern-day exploiters have found a way to spoil it.

But return a moment to the Virginia City of yore. Here, on October 26, 1864, a young man named Frank Bell, distant cousin of Alexander Graham Bell, sat down to tap out by telegraph the entire 16,000-word constitution of the new-born state of Nevada. Relayed over Chicago and Philadelphia, where the entire text had to be taken down by longhand and retransmitted, the telegram would be delivered in Washington two days later at a total cost of $3,416.77. Then (and one might say now) Nevada had few of the requisites of a viable state, but Lincoln needed more votes to push through the 13th Amendment abolishing slavery, and the speedy deed was done.

For decades after statehood, Nevada was exploited and controlled politically by outsiders, principally San Franciscans, who took the wealth from the Comstock Lode and controlled the Southern Pacific Railroad, which in turn ran Nevada politics. (Not until 1932 would a Nevada-born man be sent to the U. S. Senate; a measure of the shortness of the state's history is that the name of the man then chosen, Pat McCarran, still has a ring of current politics about it.) Free silver was the overriding preoccupation of Nevada's congressional delegation for many decades. Around the turn of the century, major gold and silver strikes at the isolated mining camps of Goldfield and Tonopah brought an upturn in the state's economy and a new complexion in ownership, since Nevadans held the controlling interest. The other power-wielders were the Cattle Barons, though they often battled among themselves over control of thousands of acres of bunch grass and wild hay to feed their herds. For many years, there were four times as many cattle and sheep in Nevada as people.

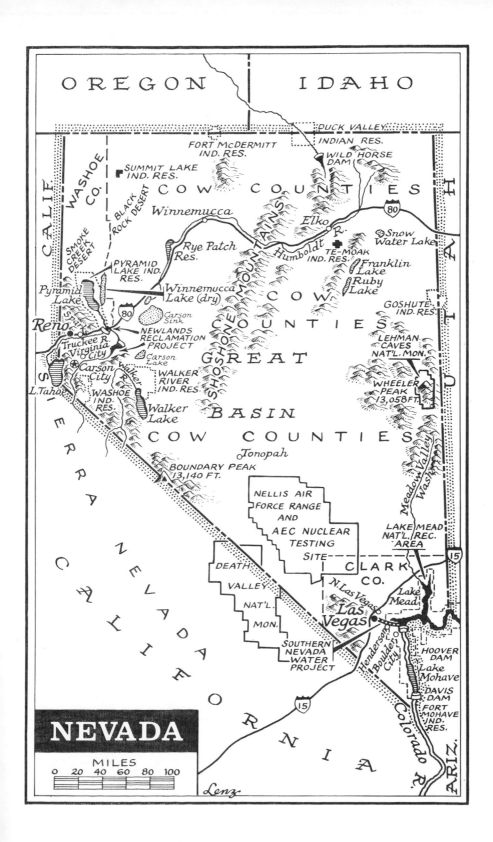

The great depression hit Nevada with unusual cruelty, and a desperate state government decided to legalize casino gambling. Thus begins the present-day story of Gomorrah on the desert.

The Gaming Business

A permissive, devil-may-care attitude about other people's morals goes hand in hand with the fast-buck atmosphere of a society born in mining camps. Nevada's legalized gambling, quickie marriage chapels (no waiting time required) and easy divorce laws (still six weeks' residency) are a great economic boon for hotels, guest ranches, justices of the peace, and lawyers. Open prostitution even flourishes in 15 of Nevada's 17 counties, the exceptions being Clark County (Las Vegas) and Washoe County (Reno), where local ordinances still forbid it. Nevada is the only state with a scheduled airline—Mustang Air Service—carrying customers from Las Vegas to lonely desert airstrips, each with its own bawdy house immediately adjacent. (One of these establishments, the "Cottontail Ranch" in Esmeralda County, is located on land leased by an unwitting office of the U. S. Interior Department's Bureau of Land Management.) In all, there are about 60 legal brothels in Nevada. The houses are a big business for the cow counties, just as gambling centered in Reno and Vegas sustains the economy of a state that lacks the industry or natural resources to be self-sustaining.

Casino gambling has been in and out of the door several times in Nevada. It sprouted naturally in the first mining camps, was illegal from 1864 to 1869, then legalized for 41 years, outlawed in 1910, then made legal again in 1931—in part as a device to draw in out-of-state money, in part to make legitimate an ancient trade that had proven totally unsuppressible in any event.* Mormons were deeply involved in the early fights over gambling, opposing it with all the resources at their command; with the population influx of the postwar decades, the Latter-day Saints no longer constitute a large enough population bloc to seriously threaten the gamblers' nirvana.

Prewar gambling was still reminiscent of the mining camp, operating in darkened halls, the dealers in shirtsleeves and green eyeshades. The larger

---

* Nevadans celebrated the official lifting of the gambling ban with a statewide carnival that lasted nearly a fortnight. But the man who introduced the gambling bill in the legislature —a bunkhouse cowboy named Phil M. Tobin—has never gambled in his life or seen the Las Vegas casinos. A Los Angeles *Times* reporter discovered Tobin in 1970 at a remote ranch on the edge of the remote Black Rock Desert near the Oregon line, doing what he has done his life long except for a few brief years in the legislature—"buckarooin' in this back country." Why did he introduce the gambling bill? "I don't like gambling. [But] I was just plumb sick and tired of seeing gamblin' going on all over the state, payoffs being made all over the place. The state was practically broke. But gambling wasn't contributing a cockeyed penny. . . . I took an awful dustin' from some of the groups, especially the preachers and the women. . . . But I've never been ashamed for what I done. Hell, it made the state. No doubt about it." What reward did Tobin get for introducing the gambling bill? Only three bottles of scotch that "some fella mixed up with the gambling crowd" put on his desk the night he proposed the bill. Since then, there has never been a testimonial dinner for Tobin, or any other kind of public recognition. As for the three bottles of scotch, he gave them away.

casinos begun in Las Vegas and Reno made a bid for elegance, but they were pale shadows of what is known today. In 1939, the WPA Writers' Project described Nevada gaming this way:

The most characteristic Nevada institution is the "club"—even the small community has one or two. But the gilded hot spots of the Reno and Las Vegas area are not typical. Basic equipment of the true Nevada club, which is usually a former store, consists of a bar, a few slot machines, and one or more big round poker tables with low-hanging, green-shaded lamps at their centers.

Today, of course, Nevada gambling operates out of plush palace-like casinos, built at a cost of millions, handling fantastic sums of dollars in each day of operation. Of the state's 1,000-odd gambling licenses, 80 percent are issued for just three areas: Las Vegas, Reno-Sparks, and along the rim of Lake Tahoe. "The days of 'Mom and Pop' casino ownership are nearing an end," comments Frank Johnson, chairman of the state's gaming control board. Seventy-five licensees develop more than 95 percent of the total gross win reported. Each year, ownership of the big operations gravitates increasingly into the hands of multimillionaire operators and big national corporations listed on the Wall Street boards. Gambling may be a sport for the player, but there is little gamble for smart ownership; for every dollar converted into chips, the averages say the house will win 22 cents. But enough people have to be persuaded to convert enough money; that requires intensive publicity costing millions of dollars, the kind of investment only the big operators can make. Nevada casinos spend more than $35 million a year for professional entertainers, by the estimate of the state's own gaming industry association—not to mention the uncounted millions invested in magazine and newspaper advertising, package tours, golf matches, drawings and contests for complimentary items from postcards to dinners (and still, on occasion, for girls for the high rollers).

The turn from the suspect old green-shade days to modern big business gambling began in the late 1930s when Harold Smith, later joined by his father, Raymond ("Pappy") Smith, an ex-carnival man, opened Harolds Club in Reno. The Smiths' formula for success and respectability rested on several pillars: conduct a scrupulously honest operation; run a well lit, well ventilated club, where everyone is made to feel at home; encourage gambling by the common man and, even more assiduously, the common woman; warn customers not to gamble more than they can afford to lose; be kind to losers (Harolds Club traditionally lets no one go home broke); foster a family spirit (even with baby-sitting); and advertise, advertise, advertise. A vigorous old gentleman with lots of moxie and ideas, Pappy Smith thought up the plan of blanketing the highways of the West with the ubiquitous "Harolds Club or Bust" billboards. I recall vividly seeing the Harolds Club signs over hundreds and hundreds of miles of an auto trip to the West Coast in the mid-1940s—and then being bitterly disappointed, on arrival in Reno, that I couldn't enter because I was a minor. Countless thousands of others were old enough, and did leave some of their money at Harolds. Smith succeeded fabulously in making gambling everyman's game, and scores of other casinos followed his formula. Except for a few hours when a minor fire struck, or on the occasion of the funerals of Presidents Roosevelt and Kennedy, the doors of Harolds Club have remained open 24 hours a day without interruption since opening day in 1937.

Harolds Club had a dozen or so successful direct imitations, all crowded close to Harolds in downtown Reno's gambling "Alley." The most successful of these was Harrah's Club, opened directly next door in 1946; since the owner's actual name was William Harrah, he could not be challenged for cashing in on the transcontinental advertising of his rival. Harrah's Club soon pulled ahead of Harolds in volume, and then began the march of casinos to the shore of Lake Tahoe. Significantly, neither Smith nor Harrah had been professional gamblers. But they put the old "pros" to shame and made Reno the gambling capital of the U.S.A.

It was not long, however, before brash little Las Vegas, a town of only 8,422 souls in 1940, began to overtake Reno as the gaming center—largely a phenomenon of its strategic location (much closer to population-heavy Southern California), and its warmer climate, not subject to Reno's midwinter slowdowns. The advent of air conditioning was another factor permitting Las Vegas, despite its desert location, to flourish. The Golden Nugget, downtown Las Vegas' first big casino, went up in 1946—and repaid its initial investment in nine months. But soon the Las Vegas downtown, a smaller version of Reno, was overshadowed by the Strip, glittering miles of deluxe casino hotels along U.S. 91. Up went Tommy Hull's El Rancho Vegas, the Flamingo Hotel (built by "Bugsy" Siegel, a notorious underworld figure), the Thunderbird, Wilbur Clark's Desert Inn, the Sands, Dunes, and many others.

Strip casino-hotels are designed for the big spenders, leaving the dollar-ante crowd for downtown or Reno. Opulent decor, wildly flashing signs, lavish floor shows, massive casino layouts—these are the hallmarks of the temples of hedonism along the free-spending Strip. "The Strip is three and a half miles of urgent incandescence, one long, glowing shout, a blaze of blandishments to witness Berle, Benny, Barbra, babes, even Bingo," a Los Angeles *Times* writer notes. Still a loss leader, Las Vegas' entertainment is the best of its kind at the cheapest prices in the U.S.A., drawing some 15 million people to the city each year. King of the Draw (until his 1971 retirement) was Frank Sinatra, but figures ranging in the hundreds of thousands also go to personalities like Sammy Davis, Jr., Jerry Lewis, Dinah Shore, Elvis Presley, Dean Martin, and Barbra Streisand. In 1969, Tony Bennett signed a lifetime contract with Caesar's Palace. The new International paid Barbra Streisand a cool million dollars in salary and stock for one month's stand when it opened. All of this is little more than a come-on for the cool casino interiors where the dice roll, the wheels turn, the cards are flipped day and night without cease. It is a clockless, windowless, encapsulated environment where somehow it always seems to be three o'clock in the morning. The scorched desert outside the door, where lizard, ground squirrel, and sagebrush once reigned supreme, might as well be a thousand miles away.

And the promotional hoopla for all this even seems to outdo the gaucheries of Miami Beach, as if that were possible. "In France, it's the Eiffel Tower. In India, it's the Taj Mahal. In Las Vegas, it's the Landmark," boasted TV spots for the 1969 opening of Howard Hughes' Landmark Hotel, claiming the world's largest swimming pool (240 feet) and the only high-altitude casino in town (on the 29th floor).

Nevada boosters may well have a valid point in saying that gambling is just a more open version of what all of life is—a gamble; that there is a touch of hypocrisy in the position of outsiders who feel it's quite proper to wager on the outcome of a horse race but find something less pious in the turn of a card. Gambling goes on in each of the 50 states; Nevada has simply been more honest in making it above-board and legal. Still, one can question *the style* in which Las Vegas does its thing. In the words of Neil Morgan:

The most insidious influence of Las Vegas is its destruction of wonder: the wonder of sex, the wonder of chance, and the wonder of oneself. Everything is settled fast in Las Vegas. Like the lava outcroppings of its desert, Nevada has become a molten overflow of the American passion for excess. It is a long way from Plymouth Rock.

Up to World War II, Nevada gambling, honest or not, had been primarily a home-grown affair. But the advent of Bugsy Siegel in Las Vegas was a sign of increasing out-of-state—and hoodlum—control. In 1947 the assassination of Siegel in his Los Angeles home in a classic gangland-style murder brought national attention to gangsterism in Nevada gambling, a phenomenon well documented by authors Ed Reid and Ovid Demaris in *The Green Felt Jungle* and Reid alone in the Las Vegas chapter of a subsequent book, *The Grim Reapers.** Mafia elements either owned or were partial backers of a high proportion of the Strip hotels. The state of Nevada did not even begin licensing of casino owners and operators until the 1945–49 period. In 1955 Governor Charles H. Russell acknowledged that the gaming industry had been infiltrated by elements of Murder, Inc., and Mafia types from New York, Chicago, Miami, Detroit, and St. Louis. A new state gaming commission began examining the backgrounds of casino operators and barring men with still-active associations with gangster elements or out-of-state gambling interests. Several licenses were suspended and potential owners barred, and in a highly publicized 1963 case the commission forced actor Frank Sinatra to give up his Nevada gambling license because he had entertained the blacklisted Chicago hoodlum king, Sam Giancana, at the Cal-Neva Lodge at Lake Tahoe.

* One of my Nevada newspaper friends, on reading the draft of this chapter, cautioned that Reid and Demaris had vastly exaggerated the hoodlum influence in Nevada gambling. One can hear a thousand assessments of the Mafia's role, depending on the source, and probably no one knows how much fire there is behind all the smoke—that is, how much the confirmed presence of hoodlums actually corrupts the gaming industry.

To hear gaming industry spokesmen and Nevada officials, one would conclude that gambling in the state is now as clean as a hound's tooth—or as close to that as it is possible to come. State licensing authorities see great peril if the Nevada gaming industry is infiltrated by organized crime, and they make a real effort to screen out undesirables. A highly regarded state newsman explained that "state control is so tight it's absolutely stupid for any major casino to try to cut corners through hidden financial interests or through hanky-panky in the mechanical department. The most valuable thing a casino operator has is his license. And with big corporate owners moving in, imagine what would happen at the Securities and Exchange Commission if skimming or other illegal activities were detected."

Yet the fact is that both illegal activities and ties to national syndicate figures are frequently turned up. In 1966, just before the opening of the incredibly gaudy Caesar's Palace on the Strip, Sandy Smith reported in the Chicago *Sun Times* that the casino-hotel, financed by an army of partners and $10 million from Jimmy Hoffa's Teamsters, had a number of known gangsters among its owners, including Giancana and his associate Tony Accardo from Chicago, plus New Jersey, Bronx, and New England hoodlums. Smith also asserted that the take on skimming—the hiding of part of the profits prior to the time they are counted for state and general taxes—totaled $6 million at six Las Vegas casinos in a single year. Late in 1968, Assistant Attorney General Fred M. Vinson told a congressional committee that Las Vegas "skim" money was being transferred by courier to numbered Swiss bank accounts "for the benefit of known racketeers." Late in 1970, federal agents arrested two executives of Caesar's Palace on the charge of using telephones in the aid of racketeering. The Justice Department charged that Las Vegas gambling houses were "in effect acting as illegal underwriters" of illegal bookmaking operations across the country. Early in 1971, six persons, including reputed underworld figures and race-track officials, were indicted on federal charges of concealing their control in 1966–67 of a Las Vegas casino, the Frontier Hotel. (The hotel was subsequently purchased by Howard Hughes.)

Las Vegas harbored high hopes in the late 1960s and early 1970s that the new generation of corporate owners—the Del E. Webb Corporation, Hughes Tool Company, International Leisure Corporation, the Hilton Hotel Corporation (which bought out most of financier Kirk Kerkorian's interest in Vegas casinos), Trans-Texas Airways, Continental Connector—would terminate all gangster influence in the once Mafia-controlled casinos they bought. Hughes, for instance, immediately ejected a hoard of unsavory managers from the Desert Inn when he took over in 1967.

But the new corporate management, less free-wheeling than its predecessors, made the apparent mistake of trying to redo the Las Vegas image, presenting the town as a family resort with golf courses and gourmet dining and deemphasizing attractions like the gaudy, bare-bosomed stage shows. Together with economic recession that made high rollers far more cautious, the new policy accompanied a distinct downturn in business that caused panic along the Strip. In 1970 the casino managements got together and agreed to go back to a hard-sell portrayal of Vegas an an uninhibited action town.

And concerns about Mafia influence remain. *The Wall Street Journal* in 1969 found that even at some Hughes casinos, men with long-time mobster connections were retained—because, the Hughes people said, they knew so much about the business that they were indispensable. And there was fear on the part of men like George Franklin, district attorney in Las Vegas, that "a maze of intricate corporate structures," representing interests difficult or impossible to trace, might serve only to hide the hoodlums rather than keep them out.

In the last analysis, total integrity may simply be incompatible with the type of business that gambling is. There is every reason to believe Nevada spokesmen when they say that the slots are honest (inspectors check to make sure they aren't plugged to prevent a jackpot), that a dealer second-carding or bottom-carding at a Twenty-one table will be caught, that roulette wheels aren't wired, that the dice aren't weighted. Enforcement in this area is vigorous; major establishments at Las Vegas, Reno, and Lake Tahoe have all been forced to close down until they got new ownerships after cheating was confirmed. The real problems come in the counting of the house's take (where skimming is a danger), in a hoodlum-type ownership, and in paralysis of regulatory machinery when an industry as wealthy and dominant as gaming in Nevada is involved. Politicians have little choice other than to be responsive to this monstrous income-producer on their own home ground. When the FBI began its investigation of skimming in the mid-1960s, Governor Grant Sawyer attacked Hoover's men for interfering in Nevada affairs and took his complaint all the way to the President of the United States.

With vast amounts of cash being handled, and the prospects for fast illicit profit so great, new and ingenious methods of cheating and manipulation sprout as naturally as sagebrush on the desert. Writer Omar Garrison observes aptly:

> There was not an experienced gambler in Las Vegas who did not believe, and privately proclaim, that gambling was a focal point for vice. The syllogism was simple, and as old as mankind: Gambling means easy money; easy money attracts criminals and prostitutes; criminals and prostitutes mean blackmail, thievery, narcotics, and all forms of carnality. The crime rate in Las Vegas was the highest of any city its size in the nation.

A small confirmation came from an even higher source, then-Governor Paul Laxalt, in 1968: "You're never going to eliminate the girls. It's a very old profession and a very lucrative one in Vegas." The same might be said of all the other vices that have accompanied gambling since time began.

The Invisible Mr. Hughes

In the predawn hours of Sunday, November 27, 1966, a special train halted at a Union Pacific grade crossing at a remote location north of Las Vegas, to be met by a small convoy of vehicles.* While curious train crews, who had been told to "stay the hell away," strained to see what was happening, a stretcher bearing an inert figure, the face covered, was lowered from the train and slipped into a station wagon. Not long after, the motor caravan was gliding through the never-never land of Las Vegas streets, down the Strip, up to the Desert Inn. The stretcher carried through the lobby attracted so much attention that no one bothered to look at the group of men walking behind it. But one of those men, it is now believed, was Howard Hughes, the billionaire figure so secretive that he has not made an appearance in public for nearly two decades. For four years, almost to the day, Hughes would remain in a clinically sealed ninth-floor penthouse, screened off from the world by heavy blackout draperies and a retinue of five male secretary-bodyguards (most of them, it later turned out, Mormons selected by Hughes because they do not drink or smoke or mix with stray women).

When he arrived in Vegas, Hughes had already made his mark on the world as designer and test pilot of airplanes, producer of movies (*Hell's Angels, The Outlaw*), airline mogul (he had just sold his millions of shares in TWA for $546,549,771), owner of Hughes Aircraft of California (annual sales of $500 million) and Hughes Tool Company of Texas, bon vivant in his youthful days, and possibly the wealthiest man in America.

A few weeks after Hughes' arrival, the Desert Inn told him he would have to leave to make room for a group of "high rollers" expected in town. Hughes' apparently instant decision was to buy the hotel—which he did, at a price of $13 million, taking over ownership from a syndicate headed by Moe Dalitz, formerly of the notorious Mayfield Road gang in Cleveland. It was the beginning of a fantastic Hughes buying spree which would include by 1970 close to a quarter of a billion dollars worth of Nevada properties: six Strip casinos—the Landmark, Sands, Frontier, Castaways, Silver Slipper, and Desert Inn (all save the Silver Slipper with their own hotels), McCarran Airport, almost every piece of raw land on both sides of the Strip for a four-mile stretch, the 500-acre Krupp Ranch, a television station (bought from publisher Hank Greenspun of the Las Vegas *Sun* for $3.65 million), a charter air service that handles 25,000 persons a month, and some 500 abandoned silver and gold mining claims throughout the state. He also purchased Air West, a major western region feeder line. After several unsuccessful tries, Hughes in 1970 even broke into the Reno scene by purchasing famous Harolds Club from the founding Smith family.

---

* For a major portion of this account, I am indebted to Omar Garrison's *Howard Hughes in Nevada* (New York: Lyle Stuart, 1970).

By 1970, the Hughes operations in Nevada had some 7,000 employees, with an annual payroll estimated at $50 million. Through his extensive holdings, and the fantastic wealth held in reserve, there was no question that Hughes was the most powerful man in Nevada. He ran his empire there through a Maine-born ex-FBI agent and promoter extraordinary, Robert A. Maheu—who, it later turned out, never met personally with Hughes during the entire period Hughes was in Las Vegas. The financial respectability Hughes brought to the state was almost universally welcomed, and the leading politicians leaned over backwards to accommodate him. "Howard Hughes," Governor Paul Laxalt announced in 1968, "is the greatest thing that has happened to Nevada since the Comstock Lode." (According to columnist Jack Anderson, Laxalt was deeply involved in helping Hughes acquire gambling casinos and was a central figure in arranging an ultimately unsuccessful deal to buy the Stardust in Las Vegas in 1968. At one point Hughes wrote a memorandum to Maheu suggesting "taking this opportunity to offer the Gov. a compromise which will place him in debt to us for a long time to come.")

On Thanksgiving eve, 1970, Hughes slipped out of Las Vegas as surreptitiously as he had come. His departure, in fact, was not revealed until several days later, and for more than 80 hours his own hotel security force did not know he was gone. Then ensued a fierce shootout in the Hughes corral as Maheu fought, unsuccessfully, to defend his job against his rivals, Hughes Tool Company chieftains Chester Davis and Frank (Bill) Gay. With a telephone call to Laxalt and later a handwritten letter, Hughes sealed Maheu's fate. (Maheu responded with a $50 million damage suit, saying an accord for life employment at $520,000 a year had been broken.) Later, it appeared that serious financial losses in the Hughes Nevada operations (reportedly $20 million in 1970, plus alleged kickbacks demanded by some of Maheu's men in purchase of dubious mining properties, and evidence of skimming in the casinos) may have played a role in Hughes' decision to oust Maheu.

Hughes' famous telephone call to Laxalt came from his new redoubt: a suite in the Britannia Beach Hotel on Paradise Island in the Bahamas. Hughes told Laxalt he was only vacationing in the Bahamas, but more than a year later he had yet to return to Las Vegas. Rumors about the state of his health, both physical and mental, inevitably multiplied with demands by the state gaming commission and the new governor Mike O'Callaghan that Hughes settle worries about who would be answerable for the Hughes gambling operations in the state. Lacking that assurance, the gaming commission said, it would issue no more licenses to Hughes Tool Company executives for gambling in the state. New handwriting and fingerprint samples from Hughes were then received, but by March 1972 it was still unclear whether the state would accept them and approve the casinos' relicensing. The casinos themselves ran a reported $10 million 1971 deficit, and Karl Fleming of *Newsweek* quoted critics in Las Vegas as saying that under Gay and Davis, "the Hughes casinos have all the joyous, bacchanalian atmosphere of a bank vault. They have staffed the operations with grim-visaged ex-FBI agents, Intertel security agents and stiff-necked amateur operators who apparently can't tell a natural seven from snake eyes." There was also no little bitterness in the state over the collapse of Hughes' grandiose plans for such projects as a monster airport for supersonic transports, a revival of silver mining, and whole new industries. But gradually Nevada was adjusting to life in the post-Hughes era. "Nevada," said Governor Mike O'Callaghan, "was here a long time before Howard Hughes, and it'll be here a long time after him."

Whether Hughes would ever return seemed increasingly doubtful in early 1972, when it was learned he had departed the Bahamas for Nicaragua, and later British Columbia. Hughes' newest peregrinations, like every rumor about the elusive multibillionaire, made page one of the newspapers. They coincided with the startling denouement of one of the most daring hoaxes ever attempted in American literary history: author Clifford Irving's purported *Autobiography of Howard Hughes*. Claiming he had interviewed Hughes on repeated occasions, Irving had presented the McGraw-Hill Publishing Company and the editors of *Life* with a remarkably intimate biography and forged notes and letters purportedly from Hughes. He also convinced McGraw-Hill to make an advance of $650,000, which his wife Edith, masquerading as "Helga R. Hughes," deposited in numbered Swiss bank accounts—the endorsements reading "H.R. Hughes." In fascination, Americans watched their daily papers for the latest revelation in the Irving affair. Eventually, Clifford and Edith Irving were indicted on federal conspiracy and mail fraud charges and, along with their researcher, Richard Suskind, by New York State for grand larceny and possession of forged instruments. All pleaded guilty, openly admitting the gigantic hoax. They had attempted it, court papers said, believing Hughes was either dead "or not of sufficient mental or physical capacity to denounce it." But they erred, drawing from Hughes a public denunciation—and, for themselves, likely prison sentences.

Another great mystery long surrounded the question of who would be heir to Hughes' $2 billion fortune when he dies. His former wife, onetime actress Jean Peters? Secret loves or an illegitimate child or grandchild? (Hughes once boasted he had deflowered 200 virgins in Hollywood, but there is no record of progeny.) Or perhaps his Mormon guards? Hughes himself cleared up the question to some degree in his January 1972 telephone interview with reporters, saying the bulk of his estate would go to medical research. But even with that bequest, a titanic battle for control of the vast Hughes empire, both within and without Nevada, seems inevitable upon his death.

Squaresville Too

The people who make their living in Nevada's big gambling cities divide into two quite distinct groups. There are those who make their living at the center of the action in the casinos, mixing drinks, running the tables, fixing the slots, counting the money, working with the professional entertainers. Some of these people live quite normal personal lives, but a high proportion belong to fast-moving, money-oriented, easy-divorcing crowds. Some gamble, but few to excess; as one gaming official told me, "You couldn't live in Nevada and have a gambling problem; it would be like an alcoholic tending bar."

The second—and numerically much larger—group of Nevadans are those who work from 9 to 5 in stores and offices, cling to the middle-class values of the rest of America, turn their lights out at 11, and understandably resent strangers who ask them how it is to work in a "sin city." These are the businessmen, construction workers, doctors, lawyers, teachers, accountants, hotel clerks, and maids. Against heavy odds, they seem to succeed in living rather conventional lives. In Las Vegas, they support 143 churches * and synagogues (not counting marriage chapels), as well as 129 Boy Scout troops.

But it is in Reno that one hears the stoutest defense of old-fashioned plain folks' values. Renoites point out that they had a viable community long before gambling, that they continue to view gaming with some suspicion. Reno casinos without large hotels, for instance, are restricted within a "red line" area including Harolds Club and the surrounding center-city blocks. To keep its image as a family town while gambling prospers in its midst, Reno goes to exceptional lengths to protect its young; excellent recreational facilities are offered (skiing, horseback riding, golf), and there are strict curfews in the downtown area. Las Vegas is less successful on this score; the restless society, without historical roots, produces a high rate of veneral diseases among its young, high crime rates, and many suicides.

Reno has always been a bit more staid and decorous than Las Vegas; a Reno civic leader told me: "Las Vegas is a one-horse town conceived, developed, promoted for gambling alone; our people simply don't want to go that way." Las Vegas, in turn, looks with some disdain on its northern neighbor, suggesting the moralism may sprout from pure jealousy about the fantastic economic strides Vegas has taken since World War II. The similarity to attitudes of San Franciscans and Southern Californians toward each other is striking, and of course it fits perfectly, since Reno draws its trade from the Bay area, Las Vegas from Los Angeles, San Diego, and their environs.

Non-Strip Las Vegas

Las Vegas was born by executive decision in 1905, as a railroad division point of the Union Pacific. For years, there was not much more to the town than a sleepy main drag and the rattlesnake-infested railway yard. Then in the early 1930s, just at the time that gambling became legal, the federal government began construction of the model town of Boulder City to house

* Including 26 congregations of the Church of Jesus Christ of Latter-day Saints alone.

the construction workers for the gargantuan Hoover Dam nearby. Boulder City never permitted gambling, and the workers began to frequent Las Vegas; today the old construction camp is a model town of green lawns and trim bungalows, in striking contrast to sprawling, dusty Vegas. The great dam, which took the lives of 98 men, remains one of the great man-made wonders of the world—in fact its foundation "pour" of seven million tons is the greatest weight ever placed on earth. With Lake Mead, a lovely 115-mile watersite created by the backup of the Colorado River, the dam remains an outstanding tourist attraction and makes its contribution to the Las Vegas economy.

Despite the abundance of cheap power from Hoover Dam, there has been little industrial expansion in the Las Vegas area except for chemical production at nearby Henderson, also site of a Titanium Metals of America plant. It is said that many casino owners oppose industrialization since it might weaken their power base. They do welcome the city's booming convention business, which will be all the bigger with scheduled expansion of the city's convention center so that it can easily handle 8,500 people at once. (Together with Los Angeles and San Francisco, Vegas will be one of the West's three principal convention centers). The big payrolls outside of the gaming and resort businesses are provided by the U. S. Government. Nellis Air Force Base, largest air base in the world, is eight miles out of town. Even more significant are the Atomic Energy Commission's Nevada Test Site, to which many Las Vegas workers actually commute 80 miles each way every day, and the AEC's Nuclear Rocket Development Station at nearby Jackass Flats. The joint military-civilian payrolls of the three installations total $140 million a year for 22,000 military and civilian employees.

Crowded into a dismal slum on Las Vegas' west side are 14,000 Negroes, some 12 percent of the city's population, many forced to struggle along on less money in a year than may be bet on a single roll of the dice in the Strip casinos. Up to 1964, Negroes were even barred from the hotels and casinos; that situation changed literally overnight when Bob Bailey, a one-time vocalist with Count Basie's orchestra, complained to federal authorities. Now blacks not only frequent the casinos but some have jobs there; the Los Angeles *Times* quotes Miss Deedee Cotton, an attractive young Negro cocktail waitress in one of the Strip casinos, as saying, "If you can't make it here you can't make it nowhere in the world, I don't care what your color is. This is a 24-hour city and more action flows than water through a faucet. If you got your thing together there ain't no reason you can't get a piece of the action." But there is a 20 percent unemployment rate among black males in Las Vegas, and in 1969 west side youths went on a three-day rampage of burning and looting that left two men killed and their community a shambles. Late in 1970, the U. S. Justice Department accused Las Vegas hotels, casinos, and trade unions of gross discrimination against blacks, saying that blacks were consigned to undesirable, dead-end jobs as porters, maids, and dishwashers but barred from high-paying and high-tipping positions such as bartending. Seventeen hotels and the locals of four unions of culinary workers, bartenders, teamsters, and theatrical and stage employees unions were required to come up with a plan to eliminate the effect of past discrimination and prevent future bias in employment.

Whether Republican or Democratic, most of Nevada's papers are dull and/or conservative. The glaring exception to this rule is the Las Vegas *Sun*, the property of flamboyant Hank Greenspun, who was once well described by the *New Yorker* as "an editor-publisher of the type popularly supposed to have gone out with derringer pistols and the Gold Rush." The Brooklyn-born son of a poor Zionist-minded family, Greenspun earned a law degree and passed the New York bar examination by sheer staying power, then distinguished himself in wartime Army service and arrived on the Vegas scene in 1946. With a breezy, winning manner, he was soon on a first-name basis with most of the gamblers and even managed to buy himself a 1 percent interest in the new Desert Inn. Greenspun's first climb to fame came in ˙1948 when an Israeli plane came into town to pick him up and it became known he was a major rustler of war matériel—planes, guns, ammunition—for the Haganah. This activity brought him a federal indictment for running guns to Israel in violation of the Neutrality Act, a charge to which he pleaded guilty and was fined $10,000. But no sooner had Greenspun made his name this way than he bought out a failing newspaper, named it the *Sun*, and began to pry openly into the hitherto-shrouded activities of the local gamblers and city and state officials.

Increasingly, Greenspun's journalistic attention turned to the unsavory business dealings of then-Senator Pat McCarran, most powerful man in the state, whose witch-hunting and anti-immigration activities Greenspun roundly detested. McCarran struck back by having the local gamblers and businessmen cut off their advertising in the *Sun*; Greenspun retaliated with a law suit, alleging a conspiracy to damage him, and eventually settled out of court for $80,500—and getting all his advertising back. The hold of the old-line McCarran machine on Nevada politics would never be the same afterward.

Greenspun is also remembered as the only man ever to get the better of Wisconsin's Senator Joe McCarthy in a public forum. This occurred in the 1952 Presidential campaign when McCarthy came to Las Vegas to address a big rally for the Republican ticket, broadcast statewide. For 17 minutes McCarthy laced into Greenspun and the Democratic Senate candidate of the year. Finally, McCarthy waved a copy of the *Sun*—possibly one containing a famous Greenspun editorial boasting of his conviction for aiding Israel—and howled: "This man, this confessed Communist, who confesses it here . . . !"

Knowing he had been slandered in the hearing of every voter in Nevada, Greenspun ran up to the platform, grabbed the microphone, and McCarthy jumped down. Greenspun yelled for the Senator to come back to the microphone and have it out, but McCarthy left the hall instead. Thereupon

Greenspun launched into an ad-lib denunciation of McCathy, lynch law, and fascism. And for years afterward, Greenspun continued to run unrestrained attacks on McCarthy, many of them libelous on their face. Greenspun, of course, had *de facto* immunity: quite correctly, he figured that if McCarthy sued him, he could sue McCarthy.

The *Sun* continues today as Nevada's most colorful and independent newspaper, even though Greenspun has made his peace with much of the local establishment and was a key figure in persuading Howard Hughes to come to Las Vegas in 1966. Day-to-day operation of the *Sun* is left to competent professionals, but the editorial page never fails to reflect Greenspun's hatred of extremists, his fervid defense of individual liberties. Personally a Republican, Greenspun was defeated in a run for the GOP gubernatorial nomination in 1962; he backed Eisenhower for President in the 1950s, Kennedy in 1960, Johnson in 1964, and Nixon in 1968. But then he became critical of the Nixon-Agnew regime in Washington and bitterly attacked the country's involvement in the Vietnam war. Few other small states in the U. S. A. could boast a comparably spunky and independent editorial voice.

Before we leave the Las Vegas scene, note must also be taken of Jimmy (the Greek) Snyder, the top sports and political oddsmaker of the nation today. "I was born in Steubenville, Ohio, the gambling town of gambling towns, and was 25 years old before I even learned that gambling was illegal," Snyder told me. During the 1950s he was in Colorado and Utah drilling for oil. Almost all his wells, he ruefully admits, turned out to be dry. Snyder heard about a well being drilled in Las Vegas, drifted into town, and before long was making odds, managing the sports books. He gave up odds-making as a livelihood several years ago, going into public relations instead. But asking Jimmy to forsake odds-making altogether would be like asking J. Paul Getty to ignore the stock market. So he does it principally for fun, feeding his results to the news media.

Jimmy the Greek's method for making incredibly accurate prognostications has little to do with hunch, but rather careful analysis and the use of a complex, nationwide intelligence system. He is reputed to know as much himself about professional football as anyone else in the U. S. A., and writes a column for Greenspun's papers which is syndicated to 50 or 60 other papers during the football season. At election time, Snyder subscribes to newspapers from all the states, gleans them for tidbits of information, and then does his own careful state-by-state surveys. First he makes an assessment of the likeliest percentage break between two candidates—if one contender seems headed for 51 percent and the other for 48 percent, with the remainder undecided, for example, Snyder will make the odds 6 to 5 for the leader. In 1968 his state-by-state investigations showed Nixon winning with 311 to 238 electoral votes (with 269 needed for election); thus he made Nixon a 4 to 1 or 5 to 1 favorite throughout the election campaign, even in the face of Humphrey's late rise in the polls. Snyder's only real mistake in 1968 was projecting the Presidential outcome in Texas; of 164 observers he contacted in the state, 162 thought Nixon would get a plurality. As it turned out, Humphrey squeaked to a narrow victory there. ("If I'd been a gambling man, that's one where I could have lost big," Snyder comments.) But the crafty Greek's predictions rarely miss the mark, either in Nevada or outside.

Reno—"Biggest Little City"—and the Imperiled Lakes

Feisty little Reno, the town that won its fame on gambling and divorce, was shocked to find its business taken from it in the postwar era by brash, cocky Las Vegas. Las Vegas not only proved that it could offer what Reno had, bigger and better, but had the advantage of a larger natural market in Southern California. Another problem was that in the promotional game, all-important to tourism, Reno's fiercely competitive casino owners and nearby attractions—Lake Tahoe, Virginia City, and Carson City—all fought with each other rather than pulling together.

Only in the late 1960s did a cooperative advertising and promotional effort, under the Greater Reno Chamber of Commerce, begin to develop. Taking a page from the successful Las Vegas effort, Reno began to offer low-price package tours—including three days and a night for little more than $20 a person, for instance. More important was the message to prospective visitors: that there are "two worlds of Reno"—downtown show business and gambling, but also all manner of outdoor recreational opportunities for a family vacation, ranging from fishing and horseback riding to rodeos, community concerts, and sightseeing at Lake Tahoe and Virginia City. "We expect it to have a great appeal, even if it's harder to sell than Las Vegas' simple 'Broadway of the West' pitch," according to chamber of commerce manager Jud Allen. As for the divorce trade, already undercut by Mexican one-day quickies and now threatened by a more liberal California law, Allen says: "We are just as happy that the divorce spotlight has been toned down. Divorce is not a happy image." Reno's 220 attorneys, half of whom have made a handsome living off divorces, may not be so pleased.

The truth is that except for Strip-like hotels, Reno has a lot more to offer than Las Vegas. It is far less desert-like; in fact, its situation in the high Truckee Meadows, fed by abundant water from the immediately adjacent Sierras, gives it a much softer, verdant feel. Some of the West's most handsome scenery, all with the backdrop of nearby snow-capped peaks, awaits the visitor who undertakes the short drives from Reno up to Lake Tahoe, across the hills to Virginia City, or down the valley to Carson City. To foster its image of respectability and family participation, Reno pushes tours that cover handsome residential districts, the campus of the University of Nevada, the museum and desert planetarium, and even a budding industrial park and view of nearby farmlands. The only green area of any consequence in all of Nevada lies in the few miles between Reno and Carson

City. To tide itself over the thin winter months, when snow often clogs the mountain passes from California, Reno is now billing itself as a major ski resort—easily reached from California by air.

Reno, of course, has no intention of giving up its gambling industry, and in fact the first Class-A casino-hotel in the city's history has just been built downtown by Harrah's. More hotel space will be a key to getting big tours and conventions, which the city has lacked. But the atmosphere seems sure to remain less frenetic than Las Vegas; with less casino overhead, for instance, Reno can be a bit more casual, tolerating the small player and the dear old grandmother in tennis shoes standing at a nickel slot hour after hour. Most of the dealers at the Reno tables are women, encouraging the newcomer to get his feet wet slowly. "If Las Vegas took the time to be so nice, they'd go broke," Allen told me.

Reno can also boast some diversification in its economy—a significant growth in light industry, the manufacturing plant of Lear Jet, Sea & Ski, and a lot of transshipment of goods to California utilizing the state's free-port law. And since 1968 it has been the home base of William Powell Lear, one of America's most remarkable inventor/promoters. Lear has some 150 patented inventions to his name, including the car radio, the automatic pilot, and eight-track stereo. In 1962, defying hoots of derison from aeronautical designers who said it couldn't be done, he designed, built, and certified the now-popular small private jet aircraft, the Lear jet. In 1967 an artery ruptured at the base of his skull, and he almost died. He was so depressed that he contemplated suicide by flying his plane into the Pacific; his wife dissuaded him at the last moment. A friend then suggested that Lear take on a new challenge, and when he asked what it should be, the friend glanced through the window at the Los Angeles smog and said, "Why not a pollution-free steam car?"

With that goal in mind, Lear moved to Reno in 1968, at the age of 65, bought 2,000 acres (which he called Leareno) where Stead Air Force Base was once located, hired 125 scientists, engineers, and draftsmen, and went to work designing a steam-turbine engine that could replace the internal-combustion engine. After he had spent $5.5 million, he almost gave up, but eleventh-hour laboratory breakthroughs and modifications kept the project successfully on the track. The heart of Lear's design is a 22-pound turbine that has only one moving part; he even believes the entire power plant might cost only $250 in full production. And the new engine would cut emissions of hydrocarbon, carbon monoxide, and oxides of nitrogen to practically nothing, an instant answer to the nation's worst air pollution problem. By 1971, Lear said that his vapor turbine engine was "at the point where success is imminent." Indeed, in early 1972 the first public demonstration of a successful Lear-designed steam vehicle was given.

Carson City (pop. 15,468) was the tiniest of America's state capitals until it shot past Juneau, Alaska and Pierre, South Dakota in the 1960s. It offers such attractions as a wedding chapel across the street from the State

Capitol with neon signs proclaiming: "Open 24 Hours. Bankamericard and Master Charge Welcome Here." "No other capital in America," Los Angeles *Times* writer Charles Hillinger notes, "boasts gambling casinos along both sides of its main street." There is also the Old Globe Saloon, across from the Capitol Building, in continuous operation since 1881, where the management will put a bottle of whiskey in front of you and let you pour your own for 50 cents a drink. Five miles out of town, just over the border of neighboring Lyon County, are some cat houses named Moonlight Ranch, Moms, Starlight, and, appropriately, Kit Kat. But Carson City itself has another character, of spacious lawns and stately lombardy trees and pleasing old white-framed homes. And the dignified State Capitol Building, built in 1870, is supplemented by a handsome $4 million legislative building dedicated exactly 100 years later.

Lake Tahoe, most beautiful of all those in the high Sierras, is the scenic jewel of the Reno area. Twenty-two miles long and up to ten in width, in spots as deep as 1,600 feet, it has evoked the praises of men like the naturalist John Muir, who wrote of "forested shores [that] go curving in and out among many an emerald bay and pine-crowded promontory," and of the "keenly pure" waters. Early in the 1860s, Mark Twain walked up from Carson City to Lake Tahoe to camp for several weeks, later reporting:

The forest above us was dense and cool, the sky above us was cloudless and brilliant with sunshine, the broad lake before us was glassy and clear, or rippled and breezy, or black and storm-tossed, according to Nature's mood. . . . So singularly clear was the water that where it was only 20 or 30 feet deep the bottom was so perfectly distinct that the boat seemed to be floating on air! Yes, where it was even 80 feet deep. Every little pebble was distinct, every speckled trout, every hair's breadth of sand. . . .

Why was such a national treasure not made into a national park? Gilman M. Ostrander, in his excellent book, *Nevada: The Great Rotten Borough*, poses just that question. Instead, he notes, it was left to the real estate developers, perhaps because early Nevada Senators, even those of a Progressive bent, thought more of Tahoe's potential for water power than as an irreplaceable scenic asset. What happened was that a well-to-do summer cottage crowd first built retreats along the lakeshore, followed by lodges, coffee shops, and bars with slot machines. But it was left for Reno casino mogul William Harrah, in the 1950s, to think of the fantastic profits to be gleaned from a large gambling casino directly at the lakeshore on the California border. His gaming hall at Stateline proved immensely profitable, the first of a group that now includes the towering Sahara Tahoe, Harvey's Wagon Wheel (yes, complete with glass elevator), the Cal-Neva, and many others. High on these once pristine, inviolate shores flash miles of gaudy neon beckoning the avaricious. It is all an obscene abomination, perhaps the most appalling assault on God-given natural beauty anywhere on the American continent.

Meanwhile, the massive land development in the Tahoe Basin releases vast amounts of minerals and fertilizers to flow into the lake. Combined with a daily burden of hundreds of thousands of gallons of daily effluvium from the resorts, an alarming threat is posed to the purity of Lake Tahoe. Under federal pressure, many Tahoe communities have made progress toward exporting their effluents up over the side of the basin, reducing nutrients in the lake; with a projected interceptor sewer system, the large number of potentially polluting septic tanks will be eliminated. But the problem of soil erosion from construction has yet to be solved.

Except for Tahoe, few lakes remain today in Nevada to break the monotony and bring life to the dry plateaus and mountains. One of these is blue-gray Pyramid Lake, the last vestige of a huge inland sea which once covered much of northern Nevada. Some 30 miles in length—actually larger than Tahoe—Pyramid broods in remote desert splendor among stark blue and purple mountains. The only water flow into Pyramid is from the Truckee River, a relatively small stream that flows over a course of some hundred miles from its origin at Lake Tahoe to the southwest. But the waters of the Truckee flowing into Pyramid Lake have been seriously diverted for irrigation under the Newland Irrigation Project, conceived by a grand 19th-century dreamer, Nevada's Senator Francis G. Newlands, some 70 years ago. The absolute level of the lake has sunk 80 feet, exposing to the air, as Lowell Smith and Pamela Deuel wrote in *Cry California*, "a bleached bathtub ring of calcium carbonate deposits and extensive sandflats." The salinity level of the lake has doubled, endangering the remaining fish.

Now Lake Pyramid stands in danger of ultimate extinction because of other water demands, in both California and Nevada. And it is not only conservationists who are concerned, but the impoverished Northern Paiute Indians, in whose reservation the lake, in its entirety, is situated. The 500 Paiutes living on the reservation, two-thirds of whom have an annual family income of less than $2,000, derive much of their scant livelihood from selling permits for boating and fishing on the lake, and would like to develop a resort there. The U. S. Reclamation Bureau's Derby Diversion Dam, built on the Truckee in 1905, has made it possible for the 1,000 farmers attracted to the Newland Project area to buy water at a ludicrously low price and produce crops valued at $4.5 million a year. The farmers, together with Nevada politicians sensitive to their demands, are adamantly opposed to Indian demands that more water be allowed to flow into Pyramid Lake. But the Indians, in contrast to past times when no one stood up for their interests, now have their own attorneys and assistance from the Native American Rights Fund, a Ford Foundation project. Among other things, the Indians claim that with an adequate water flow into Pyramid Lake, the recreational income would be three times that presently gained from irrigated agriculture from the river, and that the Reclamation Bureau has allowed "the waste of up to 200,000 acre-feet of water annually." Nearly all the irrigation ditches and canals are unlined, permitting tremendous loss of waste into the porous desert soils, and the city of Reno, which draws substantial amounts of water from the river, has not even installed water meters.

By the late 1960s, the issue of Pyramid Lake had become so acute that the governors of Nevada and California and the U. S. Secretary of the Interior felt obliged to come to Pyramid's shores for a conference on the problem. Yet despite the high-level attention and new court litigation, the Indians and their friends remain skeptical that by the time white man's law has finished its course, their interests will not again be sacrificed. That is the way it has always been for these invisible people in their tumbledown shacks, the first inhabitants of the land, so long ignored and progressively dispossessed.

As James Vidovich, chairman of the Pyramid Lake Paiute Indian Tribal Council, said before a 1969 California legislative hearing:

So long as there is a lake, a stream, a forest, a grassland, you [white men] must dam it, channel it, reforest it. . . . But, can you not leave one people alone? Can you not honor one promise? Can you not respect even one lake, and one stream, one nearly extinct breed of the fish and one natural pelican rookery, and one natural lake—the greatest of the lakes left from the days of the great glaciers? . . .

We have rights—rights to life that you did not bestow because it was not yours to give. Our lawyers tell us it is the right of aboriginal title. It was ours before it was yours to bestow. But you would take it from us.

State Government and Nevada Style Politics

In many ways, Nevada has the earmarks of a wealthy state today. Her per capita income of $4,562 ranks fifth among all the 50 states, and she has so ingeniously structured her tax system that the great burden falls on tourists, not resident Nevadans. It has not always been so. In the 19th century, the state failed to place significant taxes on mining, with the result that the incomparable treasure of the Comstock Lode was plundered from its hills with scarcely any compensation to the permanent settlers.* For years after the legalizing of gambling in 1931, that peculiarly extractive industry was also scarcely taxed. As John Gunther wrote, "Day by day, armored cars rolled and rollicked out of Las Vegas for Los Angeles, carrying cash away."

Finally, determining that it would not be a total economic colony of California, Nevada screwed up its courage to pass a gambling tax. Today gamblers pay a gross receipts tax on their winnings (3 to 5.5 percent, depending on the size of the establishment) so that more than a third of the state budget is financed directly from the gaming halls. (Respected legislative studies have suggested the gamblers could and should pay more.) Add in the state's 3 percent sales tax, its gasoline taxes and other user charges,

* The angriest debate of the constitutional convention of 1864 centered on taxing of the mining industry, with one delegate arguing for a substantial tax on mine property to "make those gentlemen who are rolling in wealth in San Francisco pay something for the support of our government, for the support of our common schools, and for the support of our courts." But his plea was rejected. The state has never placed a severance tax on mineral extraction. Today gold is being produced in growing quantities at Carlin and Battle Mountain, but the big boom in precious metals promised by the Hughes empire has yet to develop. Most mineral income comes from the big copper mines and smelters at Ely and Yerington, owned by Kennecott and Anaconda respectively.

and the 22 million-odd tourists who come to Nevada each year end up paying a major share of running state and local government. The state has no personal or corporate income tax, no estate or inheritance taxes, factors which have encouraged many a rich Californian to make his home in Nevada.

Up to the 1950s, Nevada had some of the most abominable school facilities in the nation. The sales tax, first enacted in 1955, plus local school bond issues, made possible the replacement of many squalid school buildings and elimination of a number of one-room rural schoolhouses. Teacher salaries, once among the lowest in the nation, now rank 13th among the states, with per pupil expenditures 22nd. No other state of the Union has a higher percentage of its school-age youngsters actually attending school, but overcrowding and inequitable school financing between rich urban and poor rural counties still pose serious problems. The University of Nevada, with branches both in Reno and (since 1951) in Las Vegas, has a rather docile student body but has been beset with internecine differences in many recent years. Nevada's per capita expenditures for higher education rank above the national average but below all other mountain and Pacific states except Idaho; little Wyoming, interestingly, spends twice as much. On other performance indexes, Nevada ranks sixth among the states in per capita expenditures for highways (an area in which she has traditionally excelled) and second in health and hospitals. But the state devotes only 2.5 percent of its budget to welfare payments, and their level is the lowest of any state outside the South (for a mother and three children, for example, $144 a month, a figure $160 below the government-estimated poverty level). Apparently the gambling society has little sympathy for the loser in society.

In 1971 the state's welfare director, George Miller, dropped 22 percent of the welfare recipients—some 3,000 men, women, and children—on the grounds that they had been cheating the state because they failed to report other income sources. The National Welfare Rights Organization, led by George Wiley, seized on the action as a *cause célèbre*, and with the help of the Rev. Ralph Abernathy of the Southern Christian Leadership Conference, staged a massive protest in Las Vegas. Some 1,000 protestors marched onto the grounds of Caesar's Palace on the Vegas Strip, past the entrance and a mall of fountains and a marble copy of "The Rape of the Sabine Women," right into the lobby and the casino, where about 200 astonished gamblers were obliged to stop their play at the crap and blackjack tables and the slot machines. No damage was done, but the welfare marchers had made their point in the most dramatic way imaginable. Not long afterward, a federal judge ruled that the state had "run roughshod over the constitutional rights of eligible and ineligible recipients alike" and ordered all 3,000 recipients restored to the rolls with back payments for their lost benefits. A report by the federal Department of Health, Education and Welfare said that only a tiny fraction of those struck from the rolls by the state were actually ineligible or cheating.

Nevada was strongly pro-Lincoln and pro-North at the time it was hurried into the Union, and remained generally Republican until an independent Free Silver party was formed in the 1890s, calling for free coinage of that metal, then so important to the state's economy. When free silverism failed, Nevada turned generally Democratic between 1900 and 1920, was strongly Republican in the 1920s, and then after 1932 turned solidly Democratic. Since World War II, Republicans have made occasional breakthroughs either capitalizing on Democratic dog fights or winning by virtue of especially attractive candidates. The Democrats enjoy a large registration edge —almost 2 to 1 in recent years—but this may be deceptive since many people register Democratic to participate in the primary, where the hot contests generally occur, but then feel free to vote as they please in the general election. Whether Democratic or Republican, Nevada politicians tend to be conservative—amazingly so for a state so liberal in the realm of private morals. Part of the reason is that the immigrant stream has contained a heavy component of "Arkies," "Okies," and other people from normally Democratic but conservative Southern and border South states. Also, the factors that led to a Republican era in neighboring Arizona—prosperous and technically minded working people in electronics industries, a wealthy retiree class, and a charismatic Republican leader like Barry Goldwater—have been absent in Nevada.

Typical of a small state, Nevadan politics have often been dominated by strong personalities over long periods of years. Key Pittman, United States Senator from 1913 to his death in 1940, has been described by Gilman Ostrander as "the one really wild man to emerge from Nevada into national and international politics" (he became chairman of the Senate Foreign Relations Committee in the 1930s). A Mississippi-born lawyer, Pittman participated in the great Alaskan gold rush, then came to Nevada, where he prospered as a mining lawyer and stockholder in many mining companies. He won election to the Senate as a champion of the state's poor against what he called "the money and corrupt influences" of the Republicans and the Southern Pacific Railroad. In Washington, Pittman was an unremitting champion of Nevadan interests, especially the cause of free silver. But he also became a confirmed drunkard with homicidal tendencies; he owned a six-shooter, which he usually carried with him, and in his last years he would go on drinking sprees in Washington; when refused service, Pittman would whip out his pistol and threaten to shoot the place up.

Pittman, however, would never exert the national power exercised by Patrick A. McCarran, his erstwhile political enemy and successor as Nevada's chief spokesman in Washington. A brilliant lawyer and politician who was hated and often rebuffed by leaders of his own Democratic party, McCarran first ran for the Senate in 1904 but had to wait for almost three decades before the right turn of events (a race on FDR's coattails) gave him a chance to win the long-coveted seat in 1932. Sporting his New Deal credentials, McCarran hurried to Washington to line up desirable committee assignments (Appropriations and Judiciary), a base of his future power. But within a few months time, McCarran had become an entrenched enemy of the Roosevelt regime. Ostrander describes McCarran as a pudgy little man with a great mane of flowing white hair, afflicted through his adult years by high blood pressure and ulcers (the latter forcing him to subsist on baby food). He reached his zenith in the late '40s and early '50s when his clarion call against the dangers of internal Communist subversion gave him power and influence perhaps second only to that of Joe McCarthy. As chairman of the Judiciary Committee, McCarran authored the Subversive Activities Control Act (later found unconstitutional in its major provisions by the Supreme Court), pushing it to approval over President Truman's veto. On foreign affairs, he championed the causes of Chiang Kai-shek's Nationalist China and Francisco Franco's Falangist Spain. His lasting legacy was the McCarran-Walter Immigration Act of 1952 (likewise passed over Truman's veto), which sought to confine almost all new immigration to the Anglo-Saxon, Teutonic, and, of course, Celtic. "McCarran was known locally," a Nevada newspaperman told me, "as a loyal and wonderful friend and a bitter, hateful enemy. You either loved him or hated his guts. A majority of Nevadans loved him."

The two Nevadans in the Senate today, Alan Bible and Howard W. Cannon, both Democrats, both moderately conservative, are fade-into-the-woodwork types in comparison to a Pittman or a McCarran. Bible got his start as a McCarran protegé and works quietly and effectively for Nevada interests on the Interior and Appropriations Committees. Cannon, a touch more sophisticated, sits on the Armed Services, Space, Commerce, and Rules Committees and got some bad publicity in the 1960s when it turned out that his administrative assistant (now deceased) had close ties to Bobby Baker. Cannon in 1964 won reelection over Paul Laxalt by an incredibly narrow margin of 84 votes on an official recount; in 1970 he defeated William Raggio, who had won a reputation as a tough district attorney in Reno, by a more generous margin of 24,349 votes. The Nixon Administration was gunning for Cannon, who had voted against the ABM and Nixon's disputed nominations of Clement Haynsworth and G. Harrold Carswell to the Supreme Court. Raggio entered the race on Nixon's urging, a message conveyed to him by Vice President Spiro Agnew. But his tough law-and-order stance, and even a personal appearance on his behalf by Agnew, failed to sway many voters.

Nevada's sole U. S. Representative, Walter S. Baring, has the distinction of voting the most conservative line of any Democratic Congressman outside the South. Several years ago he underwent an amazing transformation, from being a pro-labor New Deal Democrat in his first incarnation to the stance of a self-proclaimed "Jeffersonian States Rights Constitutional Democrat" in the second. Baring's constituents seem to approve the change, since he regularly beats his Republican oppositon by overwhelming margins; he has, however, had a couple of close calls in the primary when his own party leadership turned on him for his apostate ways. One secret to Baring's success, entirely aside from ideology, is the instant and effective reply he makes to every constituent's request. But Baring's appeal goes further; he is a genuinely charming man. "Walter can sell sympathy in a fantastic way," one of the local powers in Reno told me. "Whenever he flies in here, he's just lost his bags in Denver and he's sorry about that old crumpled shirt. Soon he has you so distracted that you're sidelined from what you wanted to talk to him about. We all call him 'poor Walter.'"

Old-style Nevada politics, marked by the machinations of personal political empires like McCarran's, received a major setback with the 1958 election of Grant Sawyer as governor. A young district attorney from Elko, Sawyer emerged from obscurity to win in a whirlwind campaign. He was an activist who tried to change things he thought needed improvement; he was aggressive, for instance, in boosting school aid, enlarging facilities at both university campuses, rebuilding a deteriorating orphans' home, and adding to the state hospital system. Penal reform was one of Sawyer's major interests; on taking office he discovered there were caves where prisoners until recently had been interned in the state prison at Carson City, built before statehood. Women prisoners were never permitted out for exercise, and there was not even a prison chapel. Sawyer was able to institute a number of reforms.* Most Nevadan observers I spoke with agreed with Neil Morgan's assessment: that while Sawyer was "no statesman," he did bring "verve and enthusiasm into Nevada government, where they were badly needed."

Sawyer won some measure of national attention as the first Nevadan to head the National Governors Conference. But trying for an unprecedented third term in 1966, he was upset by an attractive ex-trial attorney and self-made son of an immigrant Basque sheepherder, Republican Paul Laxalt. Laxalt had been an early supporter of Barry Goldwater for the Presidency and had barely lost a 1964 Senate campaign against Cannon, running on an ultraconservative platform. After that, Laxalt moved toward the center in his party, openly attacked Birchers in the GOP, called for some effort to get the Negro vote (which had gone against him monolithically in 1964), and beat Sawyer with ease. Laxalt's performance as governor turned out to be more custodial than innovative, but he retained great personal popularity and disappointed his party when he decided to retire in 1970, rather than running for reelection or taking on Senator Cannon again.

The salient political fact of life in Nevada today is that Clark County (Las Vegas and environs), staging a spectacular population growth from 48,289 in 1950 to 273, 288 in 1970, now represents more than half the state

---

* Prison reform in America has a way of being remarkably short-lived. In a 1971 review of the country's penal institutions, *Time* reported: "After a single night at the Nevada State Prison, 23 judges from all over the U. S. emerged 'appalled at the homosexuality,' shaken by the inmates' 'soul-shattering bitterness' and upset by 'men raving, screaming and pounding on the walls.' Kansas Judge E. Newton Vickers summed up: 'I felt like an animal in a cage. Ten years in there must be like 100 or maybe 200.' Vickers urged Nevada to 'send two bulldozers out there and tear the damn thing to the ground.'"

population—56 percent, to be exact. Once dominant Washoe County (Reno) trails with 121,068 people, 25 percent. Fast-growing Carson City, now a city independent of any county, grew 200 percent in the 1960s. The remainder of Nevada's 488,738 people are scattered through the cow counties, not one with a city even approaching 10,000 in population. Washoe County has been traditionally Republican, befitting its most settled character, and remains so today. Since 1920, Clark has been a Democratic bastion, and many thought that as it grew, Nevada would turn into a one-party Democratic state. Laxalt's strong run in 1964, and then his 1966 election when he almost won Clark County, seemed to upset all the old prognostications. But in 1970, some degree of normality was restored when Democratic gubernatorial candidate D. N. (Mike) O'Callaghan won election with a plurality of 6,297, virtually all his winning edge coming out of Clark County. O'Callaghan is a very independent soul who used a "common man" campaign technique to get elected, holding a 99-cent barbecue in a park while his Republican opponent invited wealthy backers to $1,000-a-plate affairs. Forty-one years old when he was elected, O'Callaghan is a one-legged ex-Marine. He said Laxalt's had been a "caretaker" regime and that Nevada needed an "activist" governor. Once installed in office, however, O'Callaghan made few waves. He emphasized economy in government and backed the state crackdown on alleged welfare abuses, stands which appealed more to conservative economic interests than the people who had elected him governor in the first instance.

With Clark County moving into control of both houses of the legislature as a result of the 1970 Census, the key question of Nevada politics will be how this dominant urban bloc in a vast, rural state exercises its power. Up to now, the real power of Nevada has still centered in the establishment in Reno—a combine of utilities, banks, mining, and livestock interests. Along with the gambling industry, insurance companies, and railroads, these have been the powerful lobbying forces at Carson City.* (Nevada lobbyists are not required to register, but in the small society of Nevada there is little mystery about who they are.) The overriding interest of most of the lobbies has been to minimize regulatory measures and hold down taxes. On the whole they have succeeded, giving Nevada government a cautious, still rural-oriented tone.

But what will happen as Clark County's urban voice becomes stronger in each succeeding election? Dr. Eleanore Bushnell, chairman of the political science department at the University of Nevada, speculates that "the conservative bias of the state may change and that welfare, roads, schools, and other population-created needs will be met with greater alacrity. . . . The very lopsidedness of Clark County's dominion may summon forth new political alliances."

* Organized labor is significantly missing from the list of Nevada powers and is renowned for its political impotency, despite some 48,000 members. Right-to-work proposals have five times been approved by the people of the state in general referenda.

Federal Dependency and Nuclear Blasts

Able congressional representation, with seniority and clout in Washington, is of cardinal importance to Nevada. Of the state's land area, 86.4 percent is owned by the federal government—second only to Alaska. Federal land management policies may make or break grazing or mining interests; water and reclamation policies can determine which areas of the state bloom, which remains desert. Las Vegas, for instance, now benefits from the federally financed Southern Nevada Water Project, which brings it water from Lake Mead; two major reservoirs, the key to future growth of the Reno-Carson City area, are included in the Washoe Project in northern Nevada. All this work is financed by Congressional appropriation. Federal investigations or legislation harmful to gambling could be crippling for Nevada; for this reason, to maintain the friendship of Southern Senators who might help them in a pinch, Nevada's Senators rarely vote to impose cloture. The Nevadans also stick together in support of mining interests, in opposing the reduction of silver in coins, and of course in fighting to keep a big federal defense payroll in the state. Overall, the federal government returns far more to Nevada in various expenditures each year than the state's citizens pay in taxes. It is an advantageous position, to be jealously defended.

Among the federal activities which Nevada's Senators have assiduously defended and fostered has been the program of nuclear detonations at the Nevada Test Site, covering 1,350 square miles of desert some 75 miles northwest of Las Vegas. More than 360 nuclear explosions have taken place in this Nevada wilderness since the program began in 1951 with a spectacular series of five above-ground tests that sent a flash of light over half a million square miles in four states, piercing the Los Angeles smog and causing radioactivity in snow that fell on Schenectady, New York, the next day. For a decade the cataclysmic flashes of light, the thunderous roars and jarring shock waves continued in atmospheric tests; then a world concerned about radioactivity in the atmosphere, leukemia and genetic harm to the race, forced the 1963 Test Ban Treaty with the Soviet Union. But the work at the Test Site has gone on, underground. Buried hundreds or thousands of feet below the surface, the blasts still shake buildings in Las Vegas, cause huge dust clouds, sometimes poison underground water, and occasionally release some radiation into the atmosphere. One test, in December 1970, blew a cloud of radioactive dust 8,000 feet into the air. The radiation was detectable over 13 states. The Atomic Energy Commission suspended operations for five months but then began again.

After some nervousness in the first years, Las Vegas gradually became accustomed to the big "thumpers" in the desert; in fact, few in the city were about to challenge the Atomic Energy Commission's assertion that the tests were an absolute necessity to maintain the country's deterrent nuclear capability. But as the megaton-stage detonations built up in the late 1960s, probing questions about their safety came from an unexpected source: Howard Hughes, onetime test pilot, known in earlier years as an outspoken patriot and anticommunist. The reasons for Hughes' concern—placing him in strange alliance with the ban-the-bomb protestors and the like—have never been completely clear, though some speculate he saw the possibility of water contamination and radiation leak as a kind of bacteria threat carried to grandiose proportions. (At the time of the first AEC test in the megaton range, two Pullman cars were noted on a siding at the Las Vegas station, possibly for a Hughes getaway if his nerves got the worst of him.) But Hughes failed to stop or delay the tests, and found no sympathy among the state's Congressmen. The reason seemed fairly simple: the Nuclear Test Site was employing 7,000 Nevadans at the Test Site, almost equal to the total private manufacturing payroll of the state and more, even, than the massive payroll of the Hughes Nevada operation.

In a July 1971 report to the President's Council on Environmental Quality, the AEC noted that 250 square miles of the Nevada desert were contaminated with plutonium 239. Buried deep beneath the desert are more than 300 pools of lethal radiation. All together, the *Christian Science Monitor's* John C. Waugh has noted, the crater-pocked Nevada Test Site is "a vast radioactive no-man's land bigger than Massachusetts." And it will stay that way for a long time, because the half-life of plutonium—the time required for it to decay sufficiently so that no radiation danger is present —is 24,000 years.

UTAH

THE STATE THE SAINTS BUILT

"WE BELIEVE . . . that Zion will be built upon this (the American) continent," wrote Founder Joseph Smith in the Articles of Faith for that most persecuted, enduring, and successful of the revivalistic-utopian religious movements of the early 19th century, the Church of Jesus Christ of Latter-day Saints.

Not many years later, on a July afternoon of 1847, Brigham Young, master colonizer and successor to the martyred Smith as prophet-president of the Mormons, would rise from his carriage sickbed at the mouth of a mountain canyon above the Salt Lake Valley and proclaim: "This is the place." Almost 1,400 miles across the trackless Great Plains from their last home at Nauvoo, in Illinois, Young had led an advance party of 143 men, three women, and two children in 72 covered wagons. Thousands of followers, pulling and pushing handcarts or riding in wagons, followed Young in one of the epic folk movements of American history; hundreds never made it, dying of disease, exposure, or starvation on the way.

But the Mormons persevered, and succeeded, for they were about the Lord's business. "Give me ten years, and I shall ask no odds of the United States," Young proclaimed that same summer of 1847 to the first settlers in the valley. Founder Smith had been murdered just three years before; the land upon which Zion was to be built lay arid and savage before the Mormons, the Great Salt Lake shimmering in the distance. But here, at last, the Saints hoped to escape the brutal persecution that had come down upon them in the East for their unique claims to divine authority, their clannishness and industry, and their practice of polygamy. This was the place to fulfill the dream of the murdered prophet—"to get up into the mountains, where the devil cannot dig us out, and live in a healthy climate, where we can live as old as we have a mind to." And even those bony mountains and the great saline lake would bear great resemblance to the low mountains and salty Dead Sea of Palestine, where the Israelites had hoped to build their Zion.

In truth, as the Old Testament had promised, the desert did bloom. For the first time since the early days of the Massachusetts Bay Colony, a pure theocracy—complete union of church and state—flourished in America. By the time Young died in 1877, there were 358 new communities in addition to Salt Lake City, with a combined population of about 140,000. Young had played his own role in the population explosion, taking unto him 27 wives and siring 56 children.

The Mormons were wrong, of course, in thinking that they could continue their pure theocracy, or be allowed to continue the practice of polygamy, without incurring the wrath of the Government of the United States. The great State of Deseret which Young proclaimed, to include all of what is now Utah and Nevada, most of Arizona, part of Idaho, Colorado, Oregon, New Mexico, and even a strip of coastal California, was eventually whittled down, by act of Congress, to what is now the state of Utah. With the Gold Rush came the first meaningful settlement of non-Mormons— "gentiles" in Utah—and the beginnings of bitter religious conflict within the state. Polygamy would be attacked as barbarous by the national political parties and would prevent Utah's admission as a state, despite at least five attempts, until 1896—and even then, her first men in Washington would be challenged on the issue of multiple marriage and some denied their seats.

Yet the Latter-day Saints Church and the people of Utah would survive all this and continue to prosper, and today Mormons still account for 70 percent of the population of Utah. It is still true, as John Gunther wrote 25 years ago, that "the particularity of Utah among American states is absolute, because its salient characteristics depend on the Mormon Church." Industrious beyond compare (the Beehive is fittingly the church and state symbol), public-spirited, supremely self-confident, the Mormons set the metes and bounds of Utah culture by their numbers. And they color each element of its life with the aggressiveness of their belief and life style. The pervasiveness of the influence is underscored by the all-encompassing nature of LDS Church affiliation for its members. "Ours is not an easy religion," a high official of the church has said. "We expect it to govern the individual's total life." Wallace Turner writes in his excellent book, *The Mormon Establishment*: "To be born a Mormon is to be born with a second nationality."

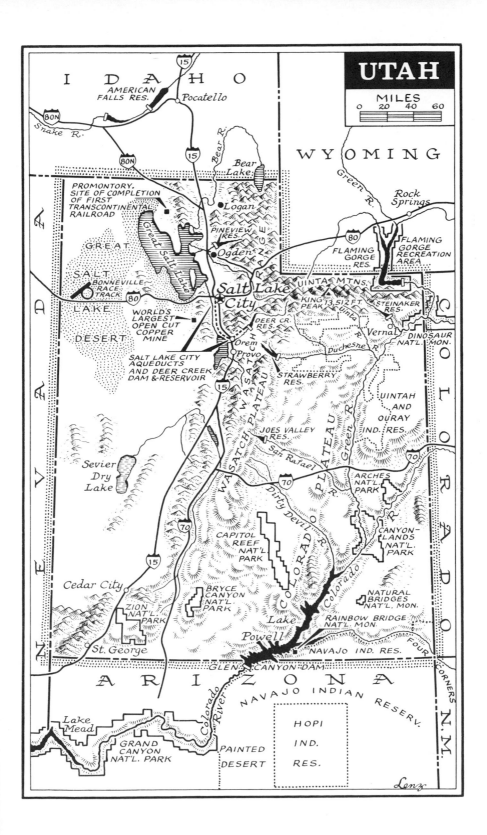

We will return to the Mormons and their unique civilization, but first a view of natural Utah.

Land and Water in Utah

The great land bulk of Utah is primitive, wild, high mountains, plateaus, canyonlands, and salt desert. It is as if a great physical wall had been erected to match the mental wall toward the outside world which the Saints often seem to have built for themselves. Populous Utah lies enclosed in a fertile strip of intensely settled land at the foot of the Wasatch Mountain rampart, stretching 150 miles north and south in the north central part of the state. This Wasatch Front area, in most places in the form of a valley 10 to 25 miles wide, holds about 82 percent of Utah's 1,059,273 people.* They live in settlements that range from metropolitan Salt Lake City down through cities like Ogden and Provo to humble little farm villages set along lines of Lombardy poplars, each with its own humble, sturdy Mormon meeting house. This remarkable concentration of population sets Utah apart from nearby states like Wyoming, Idaho, or Montana, where the larger cities and towns may be hundreds of miles apart. The closest model is the eastern front of the Rockies in Colorado.

The Wasatch peaks are adjoined on their east by the even higher Uinta Mountains (up to 13,500 feet), likewise 150 miles in length but unique in all the U.S.A. because they stretch east-west rather than north-south. Together these two snow-capped ranges furnish most of Utah's stream water and form the natural eastern boundary of Mormon country. In the mountains one will find some delightful ski resorts and, along the Wyoming border, the Green River's Flaming Gorge (so named by Major John Wesley Powell when he discovered it in 1869), a brilliant natural canyon where the Bureau of Reclamation completed a major dam and recreation area in 1963. The territory used to be so remote that it was used as a refuge by outlaws fleeing posses.

To the west lies the equally formidable barrier of the Great Salt Lake and the immense, hostile salt flats which western writer Samuel W. Taylor describes aptly as "The great and bitter barrier upon which for thousands of square miles there is no bush nor twig nor weed nor blade of grass nor living thing." The Great Salt Lake, largest body of water between the Great Lakes and the Pacific, used to be quite a tourist attraction with its buoyant waters (six times as salty as the ocean); then raw sewage from Salt Lake City and other towns, together with unfiltered industrial wastes, polluted it seriously. These conditions are now being corrected, at least in part, and Senator Frank Moss and others would like to create a national park at the lake. The ghostly vistas of gaunt, unvegetated mountains rimming these

* The state's population grew 29.3 percent, from 688,862 in 1950 to 890,627 in 1960; the 1960–70 growth rate was 18.9 percent, still well above the national average.

saline remnants of a great prehistoric freshwater sea (Lake Bonneville) are some of the most fascinating on the continent. Near the lake's northern tip is Promontory Point, where the golden spike was driven on May 10, 1869, the day the Central and Union Pacific lines joined to create the nation's first transcontinental railroad. To the west lies the Bonneville salt flats, legendary among sports enthusiasts who take an interest in racing automobiles against time. The desert land, interspersed with peaked mountains, stretches down the Nevada border in a band some 100 miles wide.

South of the high Uintas in eastern Utah one comes on the rugged uplands of the Colorado Plateau, a region which then broadens to cover practically the whole breadth of the state on the Arizona border to the south. It is a land of flat-topped mountains, deep-gouged canyons, and violent color; in all America there is no more brilliant sight than the crimson and buff pinnacles, spires, and walls of Bryce Canyon National Park, or any more breathtaking mountain and canyon grandeur than at nearby Zion, also a national park.

Bryce and Zion lie in southwestern Utah, not far from the little city of St. George, which was colonized in the state's earliest days by faithful Saints dispatched by Brigham Young. St. George has one of the world's 15 Mormon temples. With a low elevation and semitropical climate, the area is called Utah's "Dixie" and may develop into a new population center through its colleges, recreation facilities, and second homes owned by Californians. This would follow a grand old tradition, since Brigham Young had his winter home at St. George.

The dominant feature of the southeastern plateau region is the Colorado River itself, cutting a diagonal course from the Colorado to Arizona borders. This is also the area of the Four Corners, a portion of the Navajo Reservation, and the great new water playground called Lake Powell, which is the reservoir formed by the completion of Glen Canyon Dam in 1963. The Green River races down from the north to meet the Colorado in southeastern Utah. The *Deseret News* for September 11, 1861, had described the territory adjacent to the Green River as "measurably valueless, excepting for nomadic purposes, hunting grounds for the Indians, and to hold the world together." Today Americans view southeastern Utah differently; only after protracted debate about mining and grazing rights did Congress in 1964 approve creation of the Canyonlands National Park at the confluence of the Green and Colorado Rivers. The Senate report called the new park territory a "vast area of scenic wonders and recreational opportunities unduplicated anywhere else on the American continent or the world, . . . filled with mazes of canyons, gigantic standing rock formations, towering buttes, natural bridges or arches, balanced rock formations, and other evidences of mighty geologic forces and millions of years of erosions."

And still there are more wonders of the Colorado Plateau, as desolate as it may seem at first glance. Here one finds the unique dinosaur bones near Vernal, Rainbow Bridge—largest and most symmetrical natural arch in the world—the Capitol Reef and Arches National Parks, and Hovenweep National Monument, Dead Horse Point, and countless other sights of geologic wonder. Yet the remoteness lingers. Even today, there are only four crossings along the 400 miles of the Colorado and Green rivers in Utah.

Of all the 50 states, only Nevada exceeds Utah in dryness. The frantic effort to overcome this nature-given impediment has been underway since the first summer Brigham Young's Saints were in Salt Lake Valley. From the top of the new University Club office building in Salt Lake City, Jay Bingham, descendant of a pioneer Utah family and then director of the Western States Water Council, could show me the exact point where the first settlers, their wooden plows broken in the rough, dry soil, first dammed City Creek, a snow-fed stream running down from the Wasatch slopes, to irrigate their crops. It was the first irrigation project in the history of the American West. The site of those pioneer irrigated farms has since been engulfed by the Salt Lake City business district, but in the succeeding 12 decades, all up and down the front of the mountains, literally thousands of diversion dams, reservoirs, canals, and ditches have been built.

On several occasions, droughts have made it necessary to divert irrigation water for municipal supplies, making it impossible for Utahns to farm even the meager 5 percent of the state's land area which is considered arable. Thus agriculture, mainstay of life in the Mormon village of Young's day, has declined steadily in importance and now generates only a tiny fraction of the personal income realized in Utah. Most farm income derives from cattle, sheep, dairy products, and turkeys, but its total value ($213 million in 1969) ranks only 40th among the 50 states, in the Intermountain West surpassing only Nevada and Wyoming.

Keenly aware of the threat to Utah's future growth if more water were not made available, Utah's congressional delegation fought hard for approval of the 1956 Upper Colorado River Project including the two dams —Flaming Gorge and Glen Canyon—most important to the state. Neither provides water for irrigation or municipal use in Utah, but they control the flow of the Colorado by creating vast reservoirs that in turn enable Utah to draw more water from the Colorado's feeder streams for in-state agriculture and municipal supplies. Glen Canyon Dam is actually in Arizona, but its reservoir (Lake Powell) backs up a full 175 miles into Utah.

Since the 1950s, the principal goal of the congressional delegation has been to get funding for the so-called Central Utah Project, to bring the water flow from the high Uintas through a series of aqueducts over the mountains to the Wasatch Front. The biggest and most complex is the Bonneville unit, which delivers 300,000 acre-feet of water to the more heavily populated areas. Congressional funding for many parts of the Central Utah Project has been exceedingly slow, leading to partisan infighting and questions about the effectiveness of the state's delegation in Washington. Republicans and Democrats are both 100 percent for Washington building these projects to benefit Utah's farmers, industries, and cities; all qualms about the propriety of massive federal aid are quickly put aside, and the main argument is over which party gets the credit. Referring particularly to Utah, a former solicitor of the Interior Department told me: "The Bureau of Reclamation made the West. No question about it."

The LDS Church: Establishment and Belief

Four days after the Latter-day Saints arrived in the Great Salt Lake Valley in 1847, Brigham Young walked to a spot of ground between two forks of a small mountain stream, put his cane to the ground, and declared, "Here will be the temple of our God!" Today Temple Square occupies 10 acres in the heart of Salt Lake City, one of the most extraordinary religious shrines in the world, visisted each year by millions of the brethren and gentiles alike. The many-spired Temple, begun in 1853 and completed some 40 years later, soars above all else; no gentile may enter it, and indeed only those Mormons with "recommends" or permits from their ward bishops, indicating that they are "endowed" or are about to be, may go through its portals. Nearby is the great whale-shaped Tabernacle, built in the 1860s, a meeting hall open to all from which the Sunday morning concerts of the Mormon Tabernacle Choir have been broadcast from "the crossroads of the West" since 1929. Also on the Temple grounds stand an assembly hall, a gleaming new exhibition hall for visitors, statues of Joseph Smith and the Mormon pioneers pushing their handcarts across the plains, and the Sea Gull monument to honor the birds who swooped in from the west during the summer of 1848 to devour the crickets which had been laying waste the Mormons' first crops.

Even for the casual visitor to Temple Square, an instant briefing on the Mormon faith is available through exhibitions and lectures and explanations by the young volunteer missionaries on duty. The story is the now familiar one of Joseph Smith, who as a youngster in upstate New York disdained the Christian sects of the time for their quarrelsome bickering, withdrew to a grove of woods near his home, praying for guidance, and was visited by two Personages in a pillar of light, the Lord and his Son, who advised him indeed not to join the churches of the time. In the following years of contemplation, Smith would, by his account, be visited as well by John the Baptist and many of the Apostles, and by the angel Moroni, who led him to the golden plates from which he would translate the Book of Mormon, believed and revered by the Latter-day Saints on a level with the Bible. In 1830, Joseph Smith published the Book of Mormon and formally organized the LDS Church with himself as its Prophet and First President.

The Book of Mormon tells an extraordinary story—unsustained by other historical record—of how Israelites came to the New World in 600 B.C., were visited by Christ after His Resurrection, and later engaged in a great battle in which all save a young man named Moroni were killed. Moroni preserved the ancient records of the Book of Mormon on the golden plates and later returned as an angel to show them to Joseph Smith. The Mormon belief is that the Lord chose Joseph to restore the original Church of Christ in full detail—the Twelve Apostles, the First Council of the Seventies, and the other bodies.

In its own eyes, the LDS Church is no Protestant denomination, but rather the true and only "restored" Church of Jesus Christ. Rather naively, I asked a leading Mormon thinker in Salt Lake City if the waves of the ecumenical movement had washed up on Mormon shores. Absolutely not, was the reply, because the Saints believe that all the Catholic and Protestant churches long ago drifted into apostasy—the Catholics by infant baptism and the gaudiness of their religious practices, the Protestants by the doctrine of predestination. Thus the old denominations no longer have the authority to act in God's name. That power rests exclusively, the Saints believe, with their own church, for it was to Joseph Smith and his successors that Peter, James, and John restored the priesthood. This is a sort of monopoly-of-truth position that must be and is an offense to all others.

The Saints preach, for instance, that unless one is baptized into their "latter-day" faith, he cannot enter into the "celestial kingdom" after the day of resurrection, nor can a marriage be for "time and eternity" without a temple ceremony. The Mormons believe this so deeply that they spend $4 million a year to gather and store genealogical records that go back to the 14th century, so that they can trace their ancestors and arrange proxy baptisms and marriages for them. The priceless store of genealogical records is kept in Salt Lake City, with microfilm negatives kept in a great underground vault system built at the cost of $2.5 million within the granite cliffs of Little Cottonwood Canyon 20 miles southeast of the city. By the late 1960s, vicarious ceremonies had been performed for more than 30 million persons, including the ancestors of Mormons and many others, including all the dead Presidents of the United States and the entire royal families of Great Britain, France, and Germany. Critics of the Mormons question the fantastic investment of time and money by a church which, despite its many hospitals and schools, undertakes comparatively little to correct conditions of poverty and social injustice in the greater world outside its own ranks.

Even the outsider, though, is compelled to acknowledge and admire the vigor and optimism of the Mormon belief. It is not a dour faith. Marshall Sprague has well described Joseph Smith, in his youth, as "the sort of boy Mark Twain would have admired—merry, zestful, loving, mischievous, curious, precocious, gregarious, imaginative, and quite irresistible to men and women alike." Some measure of Joseph's loving spirit is reflected in every Saint. It is undergirded by the faith that he is one of the chosen people to build Zion on earth, and that the Saints are the finest people anywhere in any age, and that God's work is to be done here and now, not in a later age.

As in Joseph Smith's day, absolute authority lies with the upper hierarchy of the church, and especially the President-Prophet who alone is considered able to receive direct divine revelation. His administrative authority is shared with the First and Second Counselors whom he designates to serve with him in "The First Presidency," and with the Council of the Twelve Apostles, who choose the President—usually the man in their number senior in service. The Apostles remain in office until they are gathered to their eternal reward. The result of this self-perpetuating seniority system has been to put power in the hands of aged men to an even greater degree than one sees in the Roman Catholic Church. The "prophet, seer, and revelator" of the Saints at this writing is Joseph Fielding Smith, a stern authoritarian on matters of church doctrine despite warmness with his close associates. Smith was made an Apostle in 1906 and finally achieved his current exalted status in 1970—at the age of 93. He succeeded David O. McKay, who became President when he was 77 and served to the age of 96. President Heber J. Grant was 89 years old when he completed a 27-year rule in 1945. The average age of the Council of Apostles in the 1960s was almost 70 years. How different this is from Joseph Smith, who was 24 when he founded the LDS Church and only 38 the day he was murdered in Illinois.

But generations have passed since then, and one need only enter the quiet, sedate, and richly appointed central administration building of the church at Salt Lake City to sense the difference. The Mormon Church has become a settled establishment. The men who administer it are modest, clean-cut, courteous, gently commanding; the aura of integrity and efficiency is all-pervading. The upper leadership are virtually all men who have succeeded in some area of lay work before they were "called" to Salt Lake City; among them are former businessmen, farmers, ranchers, lawyers, physicians, and professors. The leadership of the LDS Church, then, is in the hands of men at once aged and successful. The caution and conservatism that emanates from such a group would seem all but inevitable.

In 1969 I talked with Hugh B. Brown, then First Counselor to President McKay. At 86 years of age he was still vigorous and alert, a man of dignity and presence and good humor, proud of his long service to the church, which began as a missionary to Great Britain in 1904. Born in Salt Lake City of pioneer parents, Brown had lived much of his life in Canada and served as an officer in the Canadian Army in World War I. He served as a stake president in Utah and Canada but practiced law all that time. For some years he taught religion at Brigham Young University. In the 1950s he organized an oil company in Canada, but "just when I was about to make a million, I was called back to Salt Lake City to serve in the Presidency," he recounts. Of course he came gladly; for a faithful Saint, there is no question of personal desire when the church expresses its will about his life. In the years that followed, Brown traveled more than half a million miles and visited every major country of the world save Russia and India on church business. A huge polar bear rug adored his office, doubtless gathered on one of those trips. Typical of many Mormon familes, Brown had been one of 14 children, married a granddaughter of Brigham Young, and had eight children, who in turn had brought 26 grandchildren and 29 great-grandchildren into the world by 1969.

In one sense, Brown is atypical: he is a Democrat and a liberal in politics. At the time of our interview, he was one of only two liberal Democrats among the top 30 leaders of the church; this unorthodox political thinking had already isolated him from much decision-making, despite his closeness to the then failing President McKay, and would lead to his demotion back to the ranks of the Apostles on McKay's death.

Let it not be thought that the advanced age of the church's leadership has in any way paralyzed its growth in our times. In 1945 there were 979,-454 Latter-day Saints, the great bulk concentrated in Utah and neighboring Arizona, Idaho, Nevada, and southern California. By 1970 the figure had soared to 2,926,473, an increase of 199 percent. By 1970, Utah had 777,633 Mormons—72 percent of the state's population. California had 367,615, Idaho 186,642, Arizona 94,092, Nevada 48,126, Colorado 36,381, Wyoming 28,219, Montana and New Mexico about 20,000 each. Where the most phenomenal growth had come, however, was overseas. From Great Britain to South America, from Finland to Rorotonga, from Japan to New Zealand, hundreds of thousands had been added in the greatest missionary era of the church's history. About the only areas untouched were the Iron Curtain countries and, for reasons we shall touch on later, Black Africa. The actual proselytizing was largely in the hands of the unsalaried young Mormon missionaries dispatched throughout the earth, some 13,000 at any given time by 1970. But the leadership came from the church's very unyouthful leader, David O. McKay, who became known as "the missionary president" and himself ranked as his greatest accomplishment "the making of the church a worldwide organization." A man known for his gentleness and good humor, McKay also radiated a confidence and natural-born authority that would inspire others—and do much, as one news magazine commented, to erase the previous image to the world of "Mormon leaders as dour, dark-suited figures."

McKay also met the church's growth by providing five new temples during the 19 years of his presidency—in Britain, Switzerland, New Zealand, Los Angeles, and Oakland. Previously there had been eight—four in Utah and one each in Arizona, Idaho, Canada, and Hawaii. The temples, which are not to be confused with the lower-ranking Mormon meeting houses, enabled overseas Mormons for the first time to perform the sacred Mormon ordinances such as endowment (a pledging of oneself to the church) and "sealing" of marriages "for time and eternity."

Yet while the church has been adding new temples and chapels and members in unprecedented numbers, hundreds of thousands have fallen away from the strict observance of the faith as prescribed by Joseph Smith and his successors. They still maintain their official membership, or at least take no concrete action to disaffiliate themselves, but the spark of complete dedication and obedience is gone. What are the reasons? Wallace Turner names several. First, there is refusal to follow the Mormon "Word of Wisdom," which the modern church has interpreted to forbid absolutely the use of tobacco, coffee, tea, and alcohol. (Actually, the "Word of Wisdom," given as a revelation to Joseph Smith in 1833, was only advice, and on the night before his murder he and his fellows sat in the jail at Carthage drinking wine which they had bought from one of the jailers.) Secondly, many Mormons refuse to offer up the full 10 percent of their income—*before* taxes—which the church demands of them, a sacrifice simply too great for many. Only one Mormon family in four, Turner reports, is estimated to tithe as the church would have them do. Third, many Mormons refuse at some point in their lives to meet the high demands on their time made by the church—for religious discussions, church social functions, youth work, production of goods under the church's unique welfare program, making calls as a priest, or a myriad of other church activities. The Saint who agrees to do all that is asked of him may easily use up four or five evenings of each week on church business, not to mention his Sundays. Some Mormons feel all the activity lacks deep social relevance on modern issues like the denial of jobs or housing to minority groups. The church's missions, for instance, have rarely enlarged their scope from old-style proselytizing to health and education projects. Few LDS activities are imbued with the outgoing selflessness of a program like the Mormons' temporary adoption of Indian children, under which they may spend their school years with a family of the Saints while returning to their families and reservations in the summers. Over 5,000 Indian children a year take part in the program, for which the foster Mormon parents are paid nothing.

Finally, "Jack Mormons" may be created by members' doubts about the closely circumscribed faith decreed by the church. To a large degree, Mormonism is a fundamentalist belief, highly intellectualistic and verbal in style, but not freely speculative. Yet by their emphasis on education, the Mormons are turning out thousands of college graduates with keen and inquiring minds; among these intellectuals the rate of falling away, in spirit if not in body, is significant. Many remain in the church only because their whole family history and life experience is so closely bound up with it; to request excommunication would simply be too wrenching an experience.

Mormon Dilemmas: Plural Marriage and the Priesthood for Blacks

For half a century, until church President Wilford Woodruff called for its cessation in 1890, polygamy was practiced by the Saints and was an integral part of their faith and way of life. Founder Joseph Smith was the man who turned his church into polygamous ways, and that by what he proclaimed was divine revelation. Writes Wallace Turner:

The LDS church became powerful and vigorous; this [Smith's] revelation almost destroyed it. This revelation was responsible for the creation of the Reorganized LDS church—as a haven for those, including the Prophet's widow, Emma—who denounced the plural marriage doctrine. It was responsible for bitter disputes with the United States government, for delaying Utah's admission as a state for many years, for imprisonment of the leadership of the Saints, for murders, for insurrection, for passage of federal laws which almost destroyed the LDS church financially.

Seven of the 10 presidents of the LDS Church have been polygamists, and the father of the current president, Joseph Fielding Smith, Jr., had six wives. But plural marriage is today outlawed by the Saints, and if any of their number is found "living in the doctrine," as they call it, he is promptly excommunicated.

Why did Joseph Smith—except for divine revelation—decree such a disastrous step for his church? Some say Smith felt it would be a way for widows to get husbands and for making good Mormon mothers out of women who would otherwise have been spinsters. Some, according to Marshall Sprague, "speak of the Prophet's good looks, great vitality and gentle ways, roll their eyes and murmur, 'Maybe Joseph just liked women.'" But raw sexuality was surely not a dominant motive; rather, in an Old Testament patriarchal way, the Mormon leaders were going about God's business of populating the world with the chosen people. Studies have indicated that even at its high-water mark, in the 1850s, polygamy was practiced by no more than 20 percent of the men in the church and that, of those, two-thirds had just one extra wife.

After President Woodruff's 1890 Manifesto, polygamy rapidly subsided in Utah, despite the painful adjustments required of many families. Statehood came six years later. With the oppressive burden of territorial laws and local federal law enforcement lifted from their backs, the Mormon authorities may have thought that a discreet degree of polygamy could then be tolerated. In 1898, however, they were rudely shocked when one of the Saints, a polygamist, was denied a seat in the U. S. House for that reason. Today, even if plural marriage were now suddenly made legal, polygamy would be rejected by the vast majority of the Saints because—if for no other reason—modern women would not tolerate it for a minute.

Yet surreptitiously, behind closed doors, often unknown to neighbors and associates, the practice of plural marriage continues among a small minority to this day. One of the major hideouts for polygamists is the lonely Strip Country of Northern Arizona, isolated from both the church authorities at Salt Lake City and the civil authorities in Phoenix. And in 1971, *Newsweek* estimated that there were "perhaps 20,000" members of polygamous families scattered across every county of Utah. One of them, 66-year-old Morris Q. Kunz, who has three wives living in adjacent houses in a Salt Lake City suburb and in 1945 spent two years in prison for polygamy, was willing to be quoted: "Persecution is a necessary prerequisite of salvation. . . . I have three wives, 30 children, eight stepchildren, more than 200 grandchildren, and six great-grandchildren, and I ain't dead yet." Another practicing polygamist said: "I believe in a God who is unchanging and the laws of the land do not change the laws of God. When the laws of the land restrict an individual, then the laws of God supersede."

The gravest theological problem of the LDS Church today, setting liberal against conservative within its ranks and jeopardizing its relations with the outside world, is its attitude toward Negroes. Negroes may join the church; there are said to be about 200 black members (out of close to 3 million). But a Negro may not join the priesthood orders which are absolute prerequisites for a man who hopes to enter a Mormon temple, or have his children and wives "sealed" to him for eternity, or gain full status in the celestial kingdom of eternity. This second-class citizenship is imposed on Negroes on the basis of several lines in the book of Abraham, part of the Mormon "Pearl of Great Price," which is Founder Joseph Smith's translation of hieroglyphics which were found on papyrus inside a mummy's wrappings. According to Smith's translation of what he claimed were writings of Abraham, African Negroes were "cursed . . . as pertaining to the priesthood" because they were descended from Ham (the son of Noah), whose black wife Egyptus was descended from Cain. Cain had been cursed by God for the murder of his brother Abel, the Bible reports.

Unlike the golden plates of the Book of Mormon, which Joseph Smith returned to the angel Moroni, the papyri of the Book of Abraham were preserved for examination by future generations, leading to highly embarrassing challenge of their authenticity by outside experts. Only reproductions were available for many years, the originals being thought to have been destroyed in the Chicago fire of 1871. But in 1958 they turned up in a storage room of the Metropolitan Museum in New York and were turned over to the Mormons. A panel of Egyptologists which examined the papyri said they were common burial documents and came nowhere close to being the account of Hebrew imprisonment in Egypt, as Smith and later church authorities have claimed them to be.

Many Mormons hoped that President McKay would have a revelation removing the priesthood curse from Negroes. But it was not to be, and in 1969 Brown signed, along with McKay and Second Counselor N. Eldon Tanner, a statement reaffirming the church's position on Negroes. The statement of the Authorities, together with the elevation of Joseph Fielding Smith to the presidency in 1970, came as a major disappointment to Mormon liberals who had hoped for a change in the doctrine on Negroes. As J. D. Williams of the University of Utah puts the case, there is not only great doubt as to the validity of the Book of Abraham as Scripture, but it represents events said to have taken place about 2100 to 1900 B.C. But, Williams points out, the much later Book of Mormon "makes it plain that God loves all mankind, all races, equally."

The church, however, appears adamant on the issue. The present President Smith, nonagenarian grand-nephew of the Founder, served for decades as the church historian and was a leading exponent of the exclusionary policy toward blacks, who he said were "an inferior race" because of the Mark of Cain, "their black covering emblematical of eternal darkness." In a 1964 interview with Wallace Turner, Smith said: "Young man, Joseph Smith did not decide that the Negro should not have the priesthood. Brigham Young did not decide it. David O. McKay did not decide it. I did not decide it. God decided it."

A radical shift in President Smith's attitudes is made all the more unlikely by his apparent isolation from the intellectual currents of his times; Mormon sources have told me that he rarely reads newspapers, magazines, or books from nonchurch sources. His First Counselor in the First Presidency is Harold B. Lee, a man now in his early seventies who is known as conservative, personally compassionate, and not as rigid in his attitudes as President Smith, but nonetheless not as broad or tolerant as the late President McKay.

Observers differ sharply on whether hostility to Negroes is an integral part of the Mormon world view. The General Authorities have emphasized that "each citizen must have equal opportunities and protection under the law with reference to civil rights," a view often expressed by George Romney. Shortly before President McKay's death, Negroes were, for the first time, admitted to the Mormon Tabernacle Choir. But Turner reports that "the overwhelming Mormon response to the current drive by Negroes to better their condition in American life has been indifference, inattention, irritation, and smug self-satisfaction that few Negroes live in the Mormon centers." For years, church leaders have insisted their church backs every civil right for Negroes, but when the issue of repeal of an open-housing law on the California ballot in 1964, the LDS Church in that state favored scrapping the legislation. The Utah Advisory Commission to the U. S. Commission on Civil Rights reported twice in the 1960s that Utah blacks were concentrated almost entirely in "ghettos or poor, overcrowded areas," and that Negroes were made to feel they were "generally unwanted and unaccepted." Yet the state of Utah has only a few thousand Negroes—a scant .6 percent of the population.

The tragedy in the Mormon-black division, at least in an outsider's eyes, is that it need not have been. Mormon doctrine notwithstanding, a Negro mortician named Elijah Abel became a friend of Joseph Smith and was admitted to the priesthood, to which he belonged for half a century and even became a high church official. And in the offshoot Reorganized LDS Church, Joseph Smith III, son of the first Prophet Joseph, in 1865 had a revelation which cleared the way for Negroes to become priests in that branch of Mormonism. Many blacks have joined the Reorganized church and risen to leadership positions within it.

The Mormons as Businessmen

The great theocratic corporation known as the Church of Jesus Christ of Latter-day Saints has on occasion been called the richest church in the world on a per capita basis. The assertion is not subject to proof or disproof, since the LDS Authorities have never agreed to make more than the sketchiest public accounting of the church's income and expenditures. The fetish for secrecy probably stems from the early days of persecution when church leaders had to fear the federal marshals swooping down on them to look for extra wives. The result has been to foster a ruling church oligarchy not responsible to its laity; this fits the patriarchal form of church government but can hide blunders or, as was discovered in 1969, an embezzlement of more than $600,000 by church bookkeepers.

Fortune, after a careful survey, estimated that the church's income in 1963 was about $110 million, more than 50 percent from tithing, the remainder from various business holdings. The rather unique—and commendable—practice of the Saints is to pay the full corporate tax rate on the earnings of the business corporations they own. Among church holdings are the Beneficial Life Insurance Company (life policies worth more than $700 million annually), Utah Hotel Company (owners of Hotel Utah, Salt Lake City's biggest and best), Utah Home Fire Insurance Company, Bonneville Broadcasting Company (television-radio in Salt Lake City, Seattle, Boise, Idaho Falls, and elsewhere), the Deseret News Publishing Company (which in turn owns 5 percent of the stock of the Los Angeles Times-Mirror Corporation), the Deseret Book Company, and a 30 percent but controlling interest in the quaint and ornate Zion Cooperative Mercantile Institution (ZCMI), the largest emporium of Salt Lake City, grossing over $35 million a year.

ZCMI is of more than passing interest, since it was begun in 1868 at the urging of Brigham Young, who called a group of merchants together and suggested that they pool their resources and take stock in a new company. So the hatter and the grocer and the pharmacist and the ladies' and mens' clothiers all got together and started the U. S. A.'s first department store. Among the Mormons' newest holdings is a big shopping mall being built to include ZCMI and other stores.

The church's Zions Securities Corporation owns about 30 acres in downtown Salt Lake City, including an $8.5 million, 19-story Kennecott Copper building constructed in the 1960s, the Beehive Bank Building, the Union Pacific Building, and many others. A purpose of the massive land holdings is said to be to protect Temple Square and its environs from undesirable intrusions. But oddly enough, the Church's own Hotel Utah has been criticized for overshadowing the Temple.

Finally, mention must be made of the Deseret Management Company, of which N. Eldon Tanner, Second Counselor in the LDS First Presidency, is president; it holds large blocs of securities and also controls major livestock holdings of the church in Utah and Wyoming.

Contrary to popular belief in the Mountain West, Wallace Turner observes, the men at the top of the church have *not* deliberately sought "to create a fat portfolio which gives the Saints control over a broad range of businesses." Compared to other financial empires in the U. S. A., the

Mormon holdings are quite modest in size. The church's wealth might be much greater if Brigham Young had not preached that mining was an unreligious way of life, thus opening the way for gentiles to come in and make millions from Utah's vast wealth in precious metals and copper, while the faithful Saints were instructed to stick to their irrigated farmlands.

Instead of plowing corporate profits back into business in the past several decades, the Mormons have been busy spending them to spread the Restored Gospel. In 1964 the missionary program of the church was reported to cost $17 million, and with inflation and increased numbers of missionaries in the field, the cost must be even higher today. The Saints believe deeply in education and reportedly spent about $25 million on universities, church schools, and seminars in 1964. By 1969, the total enrollment in LDS educational programs reached 215,600. Investment in new physical plant at Brigham Young University, the Mormon's leading institution of higher learning at Provo, Utah, has been estimated to run as high as $100 million since 1945—without a single mortgage. Not a penny of the BYU building fund, and only a modest number of research contracts, have come from Washington; former President Ernest Wilkinson insisted that federal aid would involve control. In return for this massive investment, the church seems to get a return of total academic orthodoxy. President Wilkinson, who favored instant expulsion for any student involved in disorders, ran a tight ship where hippies, miniskirts, and riots never made the scene. His young successor, Dallin Oaks, once chief clerk to Chief Justice Earl Warren, is a bright and more flexible man. Nevertheless, all prospective students must apply to their local Mormon bishop. Of BYU's 24,000 students in 1969, 200 were American Indian, 100 Polynesian, and only 10 Negro. Most of the Negroes came from Africa.

Huge church expenses have also been occasioned by the building of temples and hundreds of chapels and ward houses all over the world; the costs have ranged from a few thousand dollars for simpler places of worship to $7 million for the new temple at Oakland. Other financial drains are occasioned by the cost of running the Mormons' 16 hospitals and the massive and unique welfare program for its less fortunate members. But were it not for volunteer labor, the cost could be many times as high. Faithful Mormons are expected to give freely of their time to work in the LDS welfare program factories and farms, a huge business empire that ranges from canneries, spaghetti plants, and grain elevators to a cattle ranch in Canada, orange groves in California, and peanut farms in Texas.

There is good reason to believe that the church's financial practices, rather than stimulating the Utah economy, depress it. The church's power is so far-reaching that it is the silent third party to any business deal completed in the state, and its opposition to a project will probably be fatal. More importantly, the church drains a large portion of the potential risk and growth capital out of the economy. Plants, shops, stores, partnerships— all are held back in their growth because of the channeling of so much personal income to the church, often forcing individual Saints to go into debt. It is true that the church helps to relieve pressures on the state budget through its universities (in which some non-Mormons also enroll) and its welfare programs. But church policies are surely relevant in explaining two extraordinary facts about the state of Utah: that it ranks first in the United States in the average years of school and college completed by its adult citizens—but only 40th in per capita income.

Saints in Politics

Soon after their arrival in the Salt Lake Valley in 1847, the Mormons established their own pure theocracy. But gentile gold-seekers were soon criss-crossing the state, necessitating a separation of ecclesiastic and civic rule which came with establishment of the Mormons' State of Deseret in 1849. The word "deseret" means honeybee, reflecting the Saints' industriousness, but Congress in 1850 set up the Territory of Utah instead (named after an Indian tribe); this was to be the first of a long and painful set of reversals for the Saints until their state, pared down to a fraction of the State of Deseret that Brigham Young had envisaged, was finally admitted to the Union in 1896. The early Mormons attempted to show at least a *pro forma* respect for the division of church and state, and it is even recorded that Young, who served as governor of the territory until President Buchanan replaced him in 1857, used to sit on one side of his desk in the morning when he did state business, and then move his chair to the other side to do church work in the afternoon.

Between 1850 and 1896, J. D. Williams has written, "lay a wasteland of fear, ill-will and conflict" between the Saints and the federal government, delaying statehood for many years because "Congress was convinced that the Mormons had too many wives and too few political parties." Mining activity and construction of the transcontinental railroad brought thousands of gentiles to the territory and, in their wake, bitter conflict between the church-run People's party and the Liberal (antichurch) party. Federal laws not only outlawed polygamy but deprived convicted polygamists of the right to vote, and in 1887 Congress disincorporated the LDS Church and took from it all its property except places of worship and cemeteries. With many of its leaders in prison or forced underground to avoid imprisonment, and faced with bankruptcy, the church finally capitulated on the issue of plural marriage in 1890. A year later, the First Presidency said it wanted the existing parties scrapped and national parties instituted in their place. Many bishops at the ward level simply stood at the head of the chapel aisle and instructed all the people on one side to become Republicans, those on the other side to become Democrats. Soon both the People's and Liberal parties passed into history, and Utah has since had two viable parties with national affiliations.

Up to 1900, Utah was decidedly Democratic because the church leadership had collaborated with the Democrats in the Midwest before their great migration, and easily identified with the Southern Democrats when national party platforms condemned "the twin relics of barbarism—slavery and polygamy." But economic factors helped to break down the old Democratic loyalty, because the Republicans were for high tariffs. Utah was selling livestock, sugar beets, and metals and wanted no cheap imports. A personal factor was also decisive—the appointment to the U. S. Senate in 1902 of Republican Reed Smoot, an Apostle of the church, on instruction of the LDS Authorities. Smoot's church office, but even more importantly the false charges of polygamy leveled against him, cast a shadow over his right to his seat for some time, but he was eventually cleared and sat in the Senate for 30 years, becoming the most powerful Senator ever to represent Utah in Washington. Smoot became the great front fighter for a high tariff, and the tariff, in turn, would be the dominant issue of Utah politics until the advent of the New Deal in the early 1930s.

Smoot was a boastful man with a less than attractive political personality, but he gained great strength from the personal support of the LDS Presidents, one of whom let it be known he considered Smoot's remaining in office the "will of the Lord." According to political scientist Frank H. Jonas, a careful student of Mormon influence in politics, the leadership of the church held capitalistic and conservative views closely aligned with Smoot's. But gentile business support was also a mainstay of Smoot's strength, and rank-and-file Mormons are believed to have given him less than a majority of their vote in many of his races. Thus occurred a basic split in Utah politics which continues to this day. The church hierarchies from the parish level on up, peopled mostly with successful business and professional men, vote Republican. But the Mormons without positions—factory workers, small farmers, and others—are likely to support Democrats.

Even during the Smoot era, Democrats were frequently elected to high public office in Utah. The vital turning point, however, was 1932. Reed Smoot was seeking a sixth term in the Senate, and the then-LDS President, Heber J. Grant, let it be known he supported Smoot personally and unequivocally. But against all predictions, the hierarchy's prize Apostle-Senator was defeated by Elbert D. Thomas, a Democratic Mormon and political science professor at the University of Utah. Jonas records that "Smoot's crushing defeat marked the end of an era of Mormon influence in politics."

Senator Thomas, a soft-spoken and mild-mannered man, was Utah's leading Democrat for the next 18 years and rose to be chairman of the Senate Military Affairs and Labor and Public Welfare Committees, backing much liberal legislation. But according to Jonas' account, the LDS leadership never forgave him for unseating Smoot, and finally succeeded in ousting him in 1950. The man who opposed and defeated Thomas was Wallace F. Bennett, former president of the National Association of Manufacturers and a staunch Republican conservative who had extensive family and business ties with the LDS General Authorities. Bennett, a shy man with a manner that appears cool and aloof to many, was reelected to a fourth Senate term in 1968.

Heber J. Grant, LDS President throughout the New Deal years, was one of the most conservative leaders in LDS history, and an inveterate Roosevelt hater. He and other LDS leaders were so alarmed by Smoot's defeat, the repeal of prohibition, and the flocking of Mormons to federal relief and public works payrolls, that they issued an open statement endorsing Alf M. Landon for President in 1936. But Roosevelt carried Utah in a landslide. The nadir in church influence in Utah politics lasted until 1944, a period in which LDS backing, open or covert, went to Republican nominees, all of whom lost. The Utah legislature, despite frantic church opposition, passed legislation making it possible for the state to accept grants-in-aid under New Deal legislation.

After World War II, the LDS Church stepped up its interest in politics, scoring several successes and a few defeats. Successes included Bennett's election and, in 1948, the defeat of liberal Democratic Governor Herbert B..Maw, against whom the *Deseret News* carried on an incessant campaign on its editorial pages. But the legislature, despite its 90 percent-plus Mormon membership, occasionally defeated LDS-backed programs, and governors, both Mormon and non-Mormon, bucked the church on issues ranging from a Sunday closing law (which the church wanted to keep the Sabbath holy) to land disposition and acceptance of federal aid. In 1954, the church, in alliance with the Farm Bureau and other rural interests, tried to push through a reapportionment plan that would have reduced the power of the cities.* The people rejected the move. On a "moral" issue, however, the church is likely to win. In 1968, after the legislature had long refused to permit the sale of liquor by the drink in bars and restaurants, an initiative proposal was placed on the ballot. Proponents said liquor-by-the-drink was necessary to promote tourism and end the state's rather laughable "little brown bag" social practices. But President McKay urged "members of the church throughout the state, and all citizens interested in youth and avoiding the train of evils associated with alcohol, to take a stand against the proposal." It lost with support from only 34.7 percent of the voters. (Later, the legislature passed a law allowing miniature bottles to be sold in restaurants, as long as the customer did not have them served to him personally at his table. But a friend took me to a Salt Lake City bar where mixed drinks were openly served, in obvious violation of the law.)

The most nationally publicized episode of church involvement in recent politics came in 1960, when Presidential candidates John F. Kennedy and Richard M. Nixon both made stops in Salt Lake City to call upon the First Presidency of the church and speak from the podium of the Mormon Tabernacle. Kennedy, the Catholic, actually made the better speech for the occasion, sounding, as Jonas reports it, "better versed in Mormon history and doctrine than any 'Gentile' who had ever spoken in Salt Lake City." Nixon's later address was not as exceptional, but President McKay

---

* Church political pressure was so blatantly exerted in the reapportionment fight that the Internal Revenue Service felt obliged to warn it that its tax-exempt status might be in jeopardy.

told him—in words widely quoted by the state and national press: "I told your competitor that if he is successful in November, we would be behind him. I said today that I hope you are." McKay later insisted he was speaking for himself, not the church, but Utah went for Nixon.

In 1964 the Mormon Church leadership was courted as never before in national politics by President Johnson, who invited President McKay to visit with him at the White House, invited the Tabernacle Choir to sing at the White House, and came to visit twice himself. But no church endorsement, implied or otherwise, emerged in the election that year, and Johnson carried the state by a modest 37,843-vote margin. In 1968, again with no church endorsement, Nixon carried the state by a plurality more than twice as great. Later, Nixon appointed two Mormons—HUD Secretary George Romney and Treasury Secretary David Kennedy—to his cabinet. In all recent elections, the Republican Presidential vote in Utah has been several percentage points ahead of the national GOP average.

O. N. Malmquist, for many years political editor of the *Salt Lake Tribune*, insists that Utah may not be neatly classified as a Republican state. He points to the strong Democratic vote in New Deal days, an even split in gubernatorial control since World War II, frequent reversals in party control of the legislature, and a longtime practice of having a Senate delegation split between the parties. Utahns, one would have to say, differ from other Westerners in many things, but not in an inherent streak of political independence and a willingness to split election tickets. (Registration by party was once tried for a year but roused such protest that it was quickly dropped.) Nevertheless, when Utah does elect Democrats, they are likely to have some qualities that appeal to a conservative and/or Mormon temperament. Democratic Governor Calvin Rampton, a liberal on many issues, is conservative on fiscal matters and has built his record around industrial recruitment for the state. Democratic Senator Frank Moss has been a leading opponent of cigarette advertising and federal subsidies for tobacco growers.

One reason the church may be taking more of a back seat in Utah political campaigns is the unforeseen chain of events its intervention may trigger. In 1948, for instance, the church backed J. Bracken Lee, a Republican and non-Mormon, in order to get rid of Democratic Governor Maw, whose liberal policies were so unpalatable to the church. Lee was reelected four years later but became no small embarrassment for Utahns when he made statements highly critical of President Eisenhower and announced his intention not to pay his income tax because part of the money was going for foreign aid. In the next election, 1956, Lee was beaten for renomination as governor by George Dewey Clyde, a Mormon and more moderate conservative who had the support of Utah's then senior U. S. Senator, Arthur V. Watkins, a close ally of the Eisenhower Administration. Watkins will be remembered as the man who won national respect for the courageous role he played in the Senate censure of Joseph McCarthy. He was a Saint and worked closely with the church leadership, which surely was anxious to see him remain in the Senate.

But Bracken Lee was determined to have revenge, and he challenged Watkins for his Senate seat in 1958, losing the primary but then entering the general election as an independent. Lee split the Republican vote so deeply that Watkins was defeated by the Democratic contender, Frank Moss. A decade later, I asked Lee if he ever regretted causing the election of Moss, a liberal, to the Senate. "No," he snapped, "I had no use for Watkins; he was the one who dumped me as governor."

Once elected, Moss built up a broad base of support and won additional terms in 1964 and 1970, capitalizing on Utahns' preference to vote for the man rather than the party. And one might say that the net result of the church's intervention in 1948 was to bring about the defeat of Watkins, one of its most trusted representatives, and to cause the election for three terms of a U. S. Senator who, though he was one of the Brethren, viewed the world in a much more liberal way than the Authorities.

J. Bracken Lee offers a rather concise statement of the LDS Church's role in politics: "If the church wants to defeat you, I'm convinced it can defeat you. But it can't always elect. . . . You'll never get the church out of politics anywhere."

Malmquist, now retired from his post at the *Tribune*, recalls from a lifetime of reporting that there have been several Utah governors who were either non-Mormon or Mormons who failed to follow all the church's teachings. "But there have been few non-Mormons in the Senate or House in Washington," he adds. "That's sort of foreign relations, and there's a feeling that a Mormon state should be represented by a Mormon."

The Church and the Birchers

During the 1960s the threat arose that the even-keeled conservatism of the LDS Church leadership might be turned into the paths of right-wing extremism. The wedge for this movement appeared to be a man well known to most Americans, Ezra Taft Benson, a member of the Council of the Twelve Apostles. Benson is a grandson of an earlier Apostle of the same name who entered the Salt Lake Valley with Brigham Young on July 24, 1847. Benson was excused from his principal church duties during the eight years Eisenhower was President to serve as Secretary of Agriculture, fighting for a free marketplace farm economy policy that proved, if not economically unsound, at least politically hazardous in the extreme for his fellow Republicans. Returning to Salt Lake City in 1961, Benson became increasingly identified with the John Birch Society movement then gathering adherents in the state. Though not a member of the Society himself, Benson endorsed its goals, and his son, Reed Benson, became Utah coordinator and then national public relations director for the organization.

Like so many other LDS leaders, Benson is soft spoken and has an aura of sweet reasonableness about him; talking with him, it is hard to see the *bête noire* painted by farm and partisan opponents. The way the United States has been going is simply wrong, in Benson's view: "I think we've moved a long way down the soul-destroying road of socialism." He likes to think of Utah, and his church, as a conservative bastion because "we believe the Constitution was written by men whom God inspired and we see this country as God's base of operation in these later days." A "rather weak effort" was made to turn the country around in the Eisenhower days, Benson believes, but things have only gotten worse since. He believes there has been "Communist influence" behind many civil rights activities and some decisions of the Supreme Court too. His disenchantment was so complete that he voted for George Wallace for President in 1968.

Early in the 1960s Benson became so identified with the Birch Society that President McKay sent him, as a sort of exile, to Great Britain for two years. But not long after Apostle Benson's return from Europe, the Birch issue erupted again. Birch Society founder and head Robert Welch came to Salt Lake City for an April 1966 speech and publicly proclaimed that he found the LDS Church "a very good recruiting ground to go to. . . . If we are looking for conservative, patriotic Americans of good character, humane consciences, and religious ideals, where would you go looking for them more hopefully than among the Latter-day Saints?" Apparently Benson was pressured by other Apostles not to speak at the meeting at which Welch appeared, despite his previous plan to do so. Turner quotes a prominent Mormon, former U. S. Commissioner of Education Sterling McMurrin, as commenting on the seriousness of the incident and then explaining: "What is involved here is a typical Mormon abhorrence of extremism. The leadership of this church is politically conservative, but it is not extremist." But many of the rank-and-file were taking the Birch line seriously, and in the 1966 election John Birchers or others closely associated with them won 11 seats in the state house and one in the senate. That number, however, would be cut by more than half in succeeding elections.

By the late 1960s, the hard-core Birch element in Utah appeared, by reliable estimates, to be no more than 35,000 to 40,000. But no change of heart was apparent in Apostle Benson. "The John Birch Society is growing in influence, stature, respect, and power and doing a great job," he said. "I read their literature thoroughly. I've met their leaders and the members of their Council. Robert Welch has been smeared as probably no other American in my memory. . . . *American Opinion Magazine* [official Birch organ] is the best single source of reliable information I have regarding the problems currently facing our country." Benson advised me to get the latest copy of the magazine, with the Birchers' annual rundown of Communist penetration in the world, as a focus for my research on the U. S. A.

Did Benson agree with Welch that Eisenhower was an agent of the Communist conspiracy? No, he did not, "but I know he had some bad advisers around him. And I think that on the Communist conspiracy he was something of a dupe also." Did he think the men who sat around him in cabinet meetings were part of the Communist conspiracy? No, he did not, but some cabinet members "were clearly aiding and abetting the Communist objectives by some of their liberal and socialistic policies."

J. Bracken Lee, who was mayor of Salt Lake City until his retirement at the end of 1971, insists that the Birchers still have substantial influence in Utah, that a lot of state legislators are members, and that the Society, though a minority, influences Republican nominating conventions. Lee says he once visited a Birch meeting run by Welch but left after the leader had filibustered for a full day. "I liked Welch and what he was trying to do, but I didn't like the way he was doing it: to defeat the Communists you have to organize and work the way they do, by adopting their tactics. So I never did join up with him." Lee recalls there was a Salt Lake City police chief he was "sure was a member. He was talking Americanism and freedom and rights, but taking it away, running his department like a Gestapo. I fired him."

Economy: From Mining to Missiles to . . . ?

Utah has been a leading mining state ever since the 1870s, when the rails arrived to take out fortunes in copper and zinc and lead, adding to the glamorous early base in gold and silver. Lead and zinc have suffered some from foreign competition in recent years, despite the best efforts of Western Congressmen to keep the market alive through government programs. Copper is still a thriving industry, producing almost half of Utah's mineral wealth ($284 million out of $539 million in 1969, for instance). All sorts of world records have been set by Kennecott Copper's Bingham Canyon open-pit copper mine, located several miles southwest of Salt Lake City. It is the largest man-made excavation in the world—two and a half miles across and one-half mile down, a hole big enough to hold two Empire State Buildings. Gunther went and looked at the mine in 1944 and wrote of it as "an enormous declivity . . . which looks like the Great Pyramid of Egypt in reverse." But the intricately terraced hole has gotten a lot bigger since then, and is expected to last another 75 years. Already it has produced eight million tons of copper, more than any other mine in history. And just as a byproduct, it yields enough gold to make it second only to South Dakota's Homestake. There are about 7,000 miners at Bingham Canyon, a not insignificant segment of the 100,000 men in the state's basic labor pool. The unions are strong and add a liberal-Democratic ingredient to the Utah political mix. And when copper strikes, all of Utah suffers.

Kennecott used to be criticized as an unfair exploiter and indifferent Utah citizen. This criticism is much less frequent now. Unlike extractive industries in many states, it refines its product down to almost pure form before it ships it out of Utah; the result has been the growth of one of the world's largest concentrations of milling and smelting in Salt Lake and Tooele Counties, with handsome payrolls. Secondly, Kennecott must pay a state severance tax on the minerals it extracts. Finally, the firm has taken steps to improve its public image and contribute more to charity and other civic activities of Utah.

By 1960, oil and gas production had grown enough to rank second to copper in the value of mineral production in the state. Most oil wells are close to Vernal, not far from the Colorado border, and several big oil companies have Utah refineries. Coal ranks third in the state. Utah shares with Colorado and Wyoming the great oil shale fields along the Colorado River, promising a wealthy future. A vigorous uranium boom was touched off in 1952 when prospector Charles Steen discovered a $61 million deposit near the town of Moab. Moab promptly grew from 1,200 to 6,000 in population. Steen appeared to have "made it" for life, but by the late 1960s, living in a sumptuous home in Nevada, he faced bankruptcy over a tax dispute with the federal government. Uranium is just one of many minerals mined in Utah today; aside from those already mentioned, asphalt, molybdenum, iron ore, and potash are all important.

Perhaps the most startling mineral development in Utah is processing of the brines of the Great Salt Lake, once thought lethal and worthless, to produce magnesium chloride (used in electrolytic cells). National Lead and Gulf Western have invested some $90 million in chemical facilities at the lake, utilizing new technology similar to that carried on successfully in the Dead Sea. The lake is now estimated to hold $50 billion worth of recoverable minerals.

The catalyst of Utah's present-day industrial economy was the construction in World War II of the massive Geneva Steel Works in Utah County, south of Salt Lake City. Built by the government for war production at a cost of about $200 million, the plant was regarded as the most modern steel works in the world and later was sold to U. S. Steel at a bargain-basement rate of $47.5 million. Geneva's furnaces are still the only steel-producing unit between the Rockies and the Pacific Ocean and an oddity in the steel industry because no water transportation is at hand. The coal comes from mines in western Colorado and eastern Utah and the iron ore from Wyoming's Atlantic City and mines in southern Utah. A complete shutdown of the Geneva Works was threatened in the early 1960s because of the long distances from markets, high production costs, and Japanese competition. But the railways agreed to adjust freight rates, the Vietnam war stimulated steel orders, and the company decided to expand with new oxygen furnaces and other facilities. It hires 6,000 Utahns with an annual payroll of $35 million.

The arrival of Big Steel during World War II symbolized a shift of Utah from its exclusive dependence on farming and mining. The military played a role in wartime years by putting in air bases, proving grounds, and supply and ordnance depots, of which the largest—Hill Air Force Base, between Ogden and Salt Lake City—still employs over 14,000 civilians. Then came defense-related private industry, making Utah, from the mid-1950s onwards, a major center for research on and production of intercontinental ballistic missiles, rocket engines, aircraft navigational systems, and military computer components. Among them, firms like Sperry-Rand, Litton, Thiokol, Marquardt, Hercules, and Boeing employed tens of thousands in the heyday of the missile business. By the mid-1960s, defense-generated employment in Utah accounted for 8.8 percent of the labor force—the third highest percentage in the country. Federal civilian employment, ranging from air base workers to employees of the big IRS facility at Ogden, made up 10.8 percent of the civilian labor force—second highest in the U. S.

Not surprisingly, Utah has suffered from periodic traumas about possible military base closings and especially from the big letdown in the missile industry that began in the mid-1960s. Two groups went to work on finding and creating more stable industries—the Utah Industrial Promotion Board, created by the legislature at the urging of Democratic Governor Calvin Rampton in 1965, and a Republican-oriented business group, "Pro-Utah." Cause and effect are hard to prove, but the fact is that a number of civilian-oriented computer firms soon expanded or began work in Utah; most prominent among the group was Sperry-Rand, which put several thousand to work on manunfacturing Univac computers when its missile contracts ran out. This development, in turn, encouraged other research and development and electronic manufacturing firms to come in from the outside, and officials were hopeful that the state might be at a "takeoff" point in the competition for modern intelligence-type industries. Utah's ace in the hole—and likewise a serious problem—is its home-grown scientific intelligentsia. Huge sums are spent to educate thousands of young scientists in Utah universities, which is an excellent investment if they stay in Utah. If they leave the state, as thousands have in recent years, then the financial drain can be alarming. By the same token, many would remain in Utah, or return there, with the right job opportunities. Governor Rampton told me he had run a survey of expatriate Utahns, asking them if they would like to return to Utah if they had an opportunity to return with a good job. Eighty percent said they would. One can assume that the great bulk of these were Mormons anxious to return to the homeland of their faith.

As the 1970s opened, the not altogether happy economic report was that the state was creating only about 10,000 of the 15,000 new jobs a year needed to employ new Utah college graduates and prevent serious deficits in the state budget. Ranked in descending order of importance to Utah's economy were manufacturing, mining, defense, tourism, and agriculture. Utah was growing rapidly as a distribution center for West Coast markets, an activity stimulated by a freeport law enacted under Rampton in 1965. Tourism was on the upswing as a result of a major promotion effort. In the rural areas, a thriving needle trade was developing low but steady wages for many farm women. An effort to promote that rarest Utah commodity, in-state risk capital, was being made by a group of private businessmen organized into a new Utah Business Development Corporation and led by president Roy Simmons of the Zions First National Bank. Simmons is widely regarded as "the LDS banker" of Utah.

More such effort was clearly needed. Utahns, despite their exceptionally high worker productivity and sophisticated new electronic industries, have been earning substantially less than most Americans—and falling further behind, by measure of per capita income, each year. What makes Utah a low-wage state? For one thing, only 15 percent of its labor force has manufacturing jobs, which tend to be higher paid; the national average is 29 percent. Secondly, some 30 percent of the labor force works in federal, state, or local government jobs, with their lower-than-average wages; nationally, the figure is only 18 percent. As mentioned earlier, Mormon church tithing might restrict job-producing venture capital. Finally, there is Utah's "right-to-work" law, inhibiting the growth of unions. In the late 1960s, only 17 percent of the Utahn work force belonged to unions, a penetration ranking of only 37th among the 50 states. Industriousness, not self-interested militancy, is what the LDS Church and the entire Beehive State seem to expect of their people.

The Secular Government

An aura of caution and decorum, befitting the Latter-day Saints' view of the world, pervades the big, gray State Capitol at Salt Lake City. But one could not call it an ultraconservative or reactionary government; in fact the state has, for one thing, one of the best "mixes" in the country between property, sales, and income taxes, and, as we noted earlier, it places a meaningful severance tax on its extractive industries. The severance tax is 1 percent on metals and 2 percent on oil, and extractors also pay local property taxes based on the value of what they are actually mining. The tax burden carried by Utah citizens, as a percentage of income, ranks 15th among the 50 states, although it is lower than in most neighboring Mountain States. The government provided is fairly efficient and very honest, especially with a new state merit system. The federal government is a mainstay of Utah finances, not only through its huge payroll in the state ($608 million a year), but also by its direct grants, which are almost 50 percent higher than the national average.

The peculiar Mormon influences on Utah come into focus when one views the patterns of state spending. Geared to the Saints' principles of thrift, state outlays were for decades on a "pay as you go" basis, with no bonded indebtedness, until escalating university expenses forced the legislature to approve $67 million in building bonds in 1965. Education, in fact, is the one area in which Utah seems willing to spend unusual sums, a reflection of the Mormon belief that "the glory of God is intelligence." The state ranks, on a per capita basis, third among the 50 in state and local outlays for schools and colleges. The institutions of higher learning supported by the taxpayers include the University of Utah at Salt Lake City (23,600 students, especially strong in medicine, law, computer science, and ballet), Utah State University at Logan (8,500 students, used to be a farm institution), and junior colleges spread throughout the boondocks. The University of Utah is the center of liberal academic thought in the state, a fact which does not enhance its standing among conservative legislators, most of whom are Mormon and are already giving generous support to Brigham Young University through tithing.* In light of the political obstacles to university funding, it is amazing that the aid figure is as high as it is.

Utah has long been a leader in school consolidation and has only 40 school districts today (compared to several hundred or thousand in nearby states). High-school dropout rates are exceedingly low, and Utah leads the nation in college enrollment per 1,000 of population—nearly 20 percent ahead of the second-ranking state. An exceptionally high percentage of young Utahns pursue scientific careers, and the illiteracy rate is close to the lowest in the country.

There have been some colorful fights over school aid. When Bracken Lee became governor in 1949, he succeeded in curtailing revenue for education by insisting on big property tax cuts (saving Kennecott Copper alone, for instance, $800,000 a year). Educators soon developed a vivid distaste for Lee, matched by his own attacks on them for alleged greed, inefficiency, and harboring of incompetents within academic ranks. Various Utah teachers' groups engaged in running warfare with Lee and his successor, George Dewey Clyde, that culminated in a two-day "teachers' strike" in 1963 and imposition of sanctions on the state by the National Education Association. Increased school appropriations and teachers' salaries came during the gubernatorial term of Calvin Rampton, who was elected with the teachers' backing in 1964. By 1970–71, the average teacher's salary in Utah was $8,073, a figure 13 percent below the national average but high enough to work up some solid resentments in small towns where few citizens earn that much money, especially for a nine-month work year.

The munificence of Utah state government quickly vanishes outside the education field. The big counties (especially Salt Lake) feel they receive too little aid. State expenditures for health and hospitals rank 42nd among the states, on a per capita basis, and welfare expenditures are well below average with a ranking of 31st. One would expect the Mormons to take care of their own through their exceptional private welfare system, but other Utahns who need to go on relief get 19 percent less assistance than they would in the average state. Between 1953 and 1963, when national averages showed welfare expenses of state and local governments going up 40 per-

* In spring 1971, one of the University of Utah's 115 blacks was elected student body president.

cent, Utah reduced such spending by 25 percent. Neil Morgan has observed that despite the Mormons' own welfare system, "Utah would have blown away during the Depression if it had not been for federal aid; one in four Utahns was on direct relief." Only in the 1960s did the vestiges of visceral opposition to federal aid, whether for schools, welfare, or urban renewal, finally fade away.

Utah has frequently been criticized for an archaic criminal system, which has led in years past to serious prison disturbances. The state boasts of a low crime rate, but in fact it is murders and other violent crimes which are lower in number, while ordinary property crimes occur as frequently as in most states. Still on the law books of Utah in the late 1960s was the option of death by firing squad in capital punishment cases, a provision retained, some suggested, as a throwback to the doctrine of Blood Atonement preached by Brigham Young—that some sins are so grievous they can only be atoned by spilling the sinner's blood. On the lighter side, Mormons have encouraged the state to play moral guardian by enforcing the old laws that forbid selling liquor by the drink and even a statute which makes it illegal for youngsters to smoke or possess tobacco until they are 21. In most states, of course, the police have a lot more to worry about these days than plain old tobacco; I did hear that despite the docile Mormon student bodies for which Utah is known, there has been some experimentation with drugs on the campuses and in the high schools of the state, and Salt Lake City is now said to have hundreds of heroin users.

Reorganization of Utah state government, pressed by reformers who view it as atomized into too many boards and commissions and unresponsive to the governor, has had to proceed at a snail's pace since a major reversal in 1966. At the instigation of a reorganization committee, the legislature placed on that year's election ballot a number of constitutional changes, plus a call for a constitutional convention. "The Establishment in Utah and the entrenched wealthy interests," Jonas reports, opposed the convention idea; the people, in a negative and confused mood, voted down all the proposals. Among them had been such radical proposals as doubling the basic salary of state legislators from $500 to $1,000 a year!

Whether Republican or Democratic, the postwar legislatures of Utah have been conservative and 90 to 95 percent Mormon in membership. They have not, as one might have anticipated, been the scene of disputes between urban and rural or northern and southern areas. A traditional and still potent legislative alliance, according to Jonas, consists of "representatives of the property-minded farmers" working with spokesmen for "property-tax-minded big (and small) business and financial interests headquartered in the northern cities along the Wasatch Front." The leading postwar force in this alliance appears to have been the Utah Mining Association, backed up by such groups as the Utah Manufacturers Association, the Utah Industrial Council, the Utah Farm Bureau Federation, and the Salt Lake City Chamber of Commerce.

On the "liberal" side, the Utah Education Association has been most consistently active. Its natural allies include such groups as the Utah AFL-CIO, the Utah Farmers Union, and the League of Women Voters. Yet despite the teachers' success in raising their own salaries, the conservative alliance has rarely been dislodged from the saddle. Even Democratic Governor Rampton, who helped the teachers win some (but not all) of their demands, is a conservative on most fiscal matters. Rampton's political popularity has been based in no small measure on his success at state economic development, an issue popular with the business establishment. One dissenter from the prevailing politics in Utah told me the trouble with his state was that "we've never had a real brush with liberalism in state government—to learn from its glories and its mistakes."

Salt Lake City

The fascination of Salt Lake City's physical setting lies in the timeless mountains of the Wasatch Front, towering directly over the city. On a summer evening one will see them rising in a blue twilight with the flickering lights of the city below; snow-decked on a winter morning, they throw the Saints' Holy City into crystal-clear perspective. The setting is even more dramatic than Denver's, where the wall of the Rockies is really some 10 miles distant. At Salt Lake City, the mountains loom to their heights directly to the east. And on the sagebrush-covered clay and gravel hills just north of the State Capitol, modern houses of every architectural style seem to claw their way almost to the top of inhospitable peaks, each homesite offering a superb view of the Salt Lake Valley. Off to the northwest broods the Great Salt Lake; west and southwest lie the Great Salt Desert and occasional high snow-capped peaks; to the south there is the narrow fertile strip of the Wasatch Front. Within this setting, the high-set State Capitol, Temple Square, the downtown office structures, the broad streets (they are 132 feet wide, broad enough to turn a span of oxen as Brigham Young had commanded)—all suggest this is not just another provincial city. No distant board of directors makes the great decisions for Salt Lake City; this is no branch town. Its fate lies foremost in the hands of the General Authorities of the church, for whom it is Mecca.

The deliberate, decorous aura of establishment Mormonism lies heavy on the city. This is a place of quiet prosperity, of safe and solid progress, renewing its downtown at a stolid pace, distinctly not in a hurry. The people are well but not fashionably dressed; during the 1960s, as hemlines ascended across America, Salt Lake girls kept them a safe two to three inches lower. Few black or brown faces evidence themselves on Salt Lake City's streets, but there are a lot of handsome blond Scandinavians, Dutch, and Germans —converts from the areas where the church's missionaries have had the most success. The converts fail to make Salt Lake City cosmopolitan; they seem to share its middle-class atmosphere, just as the young Mormon missionaries that Salt Lake City sends out to proselytize the world rarely shed their cultural blinders.

There is vital interest in the arts in Salt Lake City. Its symphony is considered to be among the best dozen in the U. S. A., and there is the excellent Ballet West, associated with the university, whose repertory even includes some modern ballet frowned on by the church. But for casual night life, Salt Lake is a total bust. I have on my desk the reactions of two outsiders who passed through not long ago. One, from Atlanta, recorded that "a man without friends could easily die of boredom, there being few people on the streets after Woolworth's closes in late afternoon." Another, Dwight Jensen, from Idaho, wrote a column for the *Intermountain Observer* with the appropriate title, "Is There Life in Salt Lake City?" He noted that restaurants close at 10 P.M. on Saturday night and that the city has no place where a late-arriving stranger can go for a relaxing drink. Jensen suggested reworking the old jokes about Philadelphia—"I spent a year in Salt Lake City last week," or "I was in Salt Lake the other day, but it was closed."

Actually, the town is not all that closed. A few blocks from center city one can find—in striking contrast to the town's general well-scrubbed prosperity—a section of decay and litter, where streetwalkers parade before cheap private "clubs" at night. This eyesore was actually centered within a block of Temple Square a few years ago but has been pushed outward by construction which includes the new $19 million Salt Palace, an auditorium seating 14,000, which the city hopes will draw more convention business.

The city would have liked to build the Salt Palace under urban renewal, but Salt Lake voters turned that idea down after a referendum campaign in which John Birch Society members covered the county, house by house, starting each conversation with "Do you want to lose your home?"

Despite the modern-day economic growth along the Wasatch Front, many Salt Lake leaders think their city should be doing a lot better. "Why did Denver get the jump on us?" I heard one ask. Two reasons cited were Salt Lake's political ultraconservatism and the widespread feeling of outsiders that the Mormons really run a closed society. "What's more," my source said, "no Hoyts or Zeckendorfs were welcomed in Salt Lake City."

Salt Lake leaders are proud that their retail shopping core has not, like Phoenix's, rotted out. Despite satellite shopping centers, the downtown department stores—ZCMI, its competitor Auerbach's, Penney—have all invested several million in expansion in the last few years. The resilience of core business is all the more remarkable because Salt Lake City lost 13,569 people (down to 175,885) during the 1960s, while suburban Salt Lake County added almost 100,000 people, for a new total of 282,722. The fastest growing suburbs have been those east and southeast of the city, where the affluent and middle-income residents have migrated. This has left Salt Lake City with the slum areas, such as they are, on its west side, peopled by Spanish-Americans, a few blacks, and a few Indians. Salt Lake City also has a small Japanese colony, mostly a remnant of the World War II deportations from the coasts. The Japanese have prospered so much that the local banks consider them some of the best loan risks in the city.

Salt Lake City has two powerful newspapers, the morning *Tribune*, owned and managed by Catholic laymen, and the evening *Deseret News*, official mouthpiece of the LDS Church. The two get along quite well together, using the same business management firm, circulation, advertising, and production facilities. It was different in the early days, when the *Tribune* was violently anti-Mormon and the *Deseret News* practiced prejudiced, far right-wing journalism. Church news is still a priority for the *News*, but its journalistic partisanship has subsided markedly since World War II. Three of the LDS Apostles sit on the *News* board, but there have been a few policy issues on which the paper's executives have appealed past them directly to the First Presidency of the church. Both Salt Lake dailies, plus the state's other three dailies at Ogden, Provo, and Logan, are editorially Republican. Frank Jonas reports that practically without exception, the 50-odd weeklies covering Utah are "all conservative, all business-oriented, all Republican."

Utah's second-ranking cities—Ogden (population 69,478) and Provo (53,131)—lie 33 miles north and 42 miles south, respectively, of Salt Lake City, also on the Wasatch Front. Both are laid out in the typically Mormon geometrical plan of broad, straight streets, lined with stately trees, as Brigham Young had commanded the Brethren to build.

Ogden's history is not exclusively Mormon, since the transcontinental railroad arrived in 1869, bringing in whiskey-drinking, gambling gentiles who upset the Saints to no small degree. The city is still less responsive to church wishes than Salt Lake City. Hill Air Force Base is not far from town, and from the 1950s into the mid-1960s Ogden prospered through a great missile boom. Then that business began to phase out, and Ogden's population actually declined slightly between 1960 and 1970. A few miles north of Ogden is Logan (pop. 22,333), center of the Cache Valley farming area, a prototype of Utah's pleasant, typically Mormon and orthodox communities. The town has a progressive business climate and is the site of Utah State University.

Provo and neighboring Orem, site of the major metropolitan concentration of 137,776 people south of Salt Lake City, have grown rapidly in population. Economic mainstays are the big U. S. Steel Works, Brigham Young University, and, not far to the north, Kennecott Copper's Bingham Canyon mine. Mormonism is exceptionally strong here, both through BYU and the fact that steel and copper workers are largely recruited from the overwhelmingly LDS countryside.

And so we depart Utah, most stubbornly cross-grained and individualistic of all 50 states, prospering as the Mormon patriarchs decreed, their Zion on the American continent.

ARIZONA

OASIS CIVILIZATION

FOR 300 DAYS OF EACH YEAR, the sun beats down mercilessly on the shimmering desert. The landscape is interspersed with gaunt mountain peaks; the saguaro cacti hold up their useless arms; scattered mesquite strives for life. Along the desert floor the lizard, scorpion, tarantula, and Gila monster hold sway. Strange geological formations break the monotony of parched yellow sand; there are deep gorges, multicolored buttes and vista, and in the state's nothern reaches, cooler forests and the great Canyon of the Colorado. Repulsed by the harsh southern desert, where on summer days the temperature in the shade may soar to 120 degrees, a government surveyor reported to Congress in 1858: "The region is altogether valueless. After entering it there is nothing to do but leave."

Yet paradoxically, in this "land where time stands still," sixth in land area among the 50, yet so remote, a thriving oasis population has sprung into being. Today there are 1,770,900 people in Arizona—three times as many as there were at the end of World War II. Three-quarters of them now live in two great oases—Maricopa County (Phoenix), with 55 percent of the Arizona population, and Pima County (Tucson), with another 20 percent.

To approach Phoenix by air is to see in a glance both Arizona's growth and new life style. Suddenly, in the midst of the rugged, brown desert terrain, great splotches of green appear. All around the city there are verdant squares of irrigated farmland. And then one sees mile after mile of grassy suburban sprawl—many of the lawns harboring swimming pools that blink bluely into the sky. Finally, in unordered profusion along a single great palm-lined central "drag"—Central Avenue—are scores of sleek glass and concrete high-rise buildings, the commercial heart of what may be America's least planned great city.

Why have hundreds of thousands of Americans come to the oases on the desert? Chiefly, it would appear, for the sun or, more broadly defined, the good life of year-round golf, of the pool, the citrus tree, and perhaps one's own horse in the back yard, the life of studied relaxation and fun.

Yet how can the desert sustain such life? The answers, as we shall see, are two-fold: water (through one of the greatest diversion and storage projects on the continent), and air conditioning. Arriving on a mass basis in the early 1950s, air conditioning made the desert livable in the scorching summer months that used to send the wealthy scurrying for the mountains and the less fortunate stay-behinds to wrap themselves in wet sheets to survive the nights. "Without air conditioning," a Phoenix editor told me, "we might still be a winter resort with no more than 60,000 or 70,000 permanent residents."

A second attraction has been jobs. From a largely extractive economy—its big "C's" were cattle, copper, cotton, climate, and citrus—Arizona has been transformed into a progressive manufacturing state. The exuberance of the fast but honestly won dollar, of the economy where land and investments multiply in value in geometric progression, has pervaded postwar Arizona. In the most explosive growth period, between 1948 and 1963, Arizona led all the nation in seven important indexes of growth, from population to manufacturing employment to bank deposits.

The economic statistics leave out another vital figure. Between 1944 and 1968, the Republican vote for President soared 371 percent, the Democratic only 111 percent. What had once been a safely Democratic state was rapidly on its way to becoming a safe Republican state. The symbol and chief architect of this amazing transformation was Barry M. Goldwater, the man chiefly responsible for the summary one hears: "Sun, Goldwater, conservatism, and Arizona have become synonomous."

What then of the "old" Arizona, the Arizona of Mexican stoop labor, of Indians, cowboys, prospectors, and rip-snorting little mining camps? Some of this is still here—most certainly the Indians, who now outstrip all other Americans in the birth rate. But the Indians can no longer be called the essential Arizona story; as for the Mexicans, thousands live in abject poverty, but they are invisible people to the new Arizona. The overwhelmingly white, middle-to-upper class, well educated, high-income, confident Arizonan society has been too busy making money and relaxing to worry much about the unfortunate brother, be he Indian or Mexican or just plain poor white.

There are now the first signs of real concern from the conservative establishment about the Indians and Mexicans, who themselves are becoming increasingly vocal. But for the most part, postwar Arizonans, as one told me, have proven they "are simply not a concerned people."

Quick Early History and Boomtimes Economy

Arizona was admitted to the Union in 1912 as the last of the coterminous 48 states; unlike neighboring New Mexico, her terrain was so forbidding that little early Spanish civilization flourished within her borders, and the line of history up to recent times bears just the faintest relation to the civilization that exists there today. A quick and colorful review of the state's history appeared in the *Monitor*, magazine of the Mountain States Telephone Company. I will quote a key paragraph:

Arizona has been the home of hairy aborigines who stoned to death the giant sloth and the mammoth 20,000 years ago; of nomads who huddled in natural caves, hunting with spears and bows; of prehistoric Indians who engineered extensive irrigation systems and built canals, developing a civilization far beyond most of their contemporaries; of pastoral Indian tribes who ranged over Arizona, building pueblos, planting corn and cotton; of swashbuckling Spanish conquistadores who arrived to search for streets paved with gold, finding instead poverty, heat, drought and dust; of gentle missionary priests, some of whom died at the hands of the Indians they had come so far to save; and, of modern man who dammed the rivers to make the deserts bloom, leveled the mountains for their copper, built sprawling cities, mining towns, technological centers, industrial complexes.

Spain held the land until Mexico won its independence in 1822; Mexico in turn relinquished the land to the United States at the end of the Mexican War in 1848. A handful of gold and silver prospectors, fur traders, and brave early homesteaders (many of them Mormons from nearby Utah) then began to filter into the land, and territorial status was won in 1863. But the Indians, especially the Navajo and the fierce Apaches, resisted the white man's incursions with cruelty and cunning, and it was not until 1886, with the surrender of the Apaches' great chieftain, Geronimo, that orderly settlement could proceed. About the same time, the railroad came and Arizona's great copper deposits were discovered. Cattle and copper would dominate the thin economy for decades.

But it was water that Arizona needed the most if it was to grow, and in the Salt River Valley, where Phoenix began in the 1860s as a hay camp to supply forage for cavalry troops, the settlers began to utilize the canals constructed by the Hohokam Indians some 600 years before to bring the water onto the land. With adequate irrigation, they discovered, the desert can produce abundant crops. As a sort of prelude to statehood a year later, President Theodore Roosevelt in 1911 came to Arizona to dedicate the nation's first federal reclamation project—a great dam, on the Salt River, to provide better irrigation for Phoenix. With successive water pro-

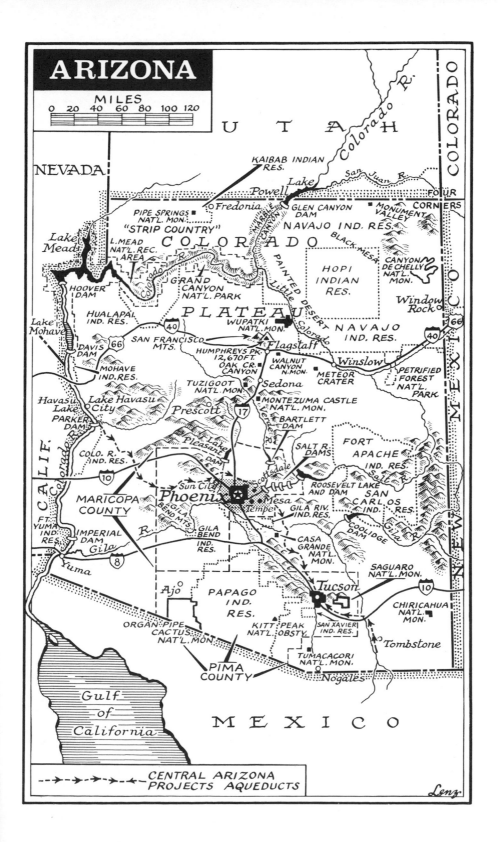

jects, this made possible the civilization on the desert we know today. ("Ever since," Andrew Kopkind remarked unkindly in the *New Republic* a few years ago, "Arizonans have been busy denying their parentage. According to the dominant myth, Phoenix rose from the desert by a mystical exercise of frontier spirit and Christian capitalism, unhindered by government.")

Arizona grew slowly in the years up to World War II, reaching a point of about half a million people by the time of Pearl Harbor. For wealthy Easterners, the dry, warm climate became an attraction, and many others came for relief from turberculosis, arthritis, and asthma. Farming gradually expanded as the federal reclamation projects multiplied. And from 1907 on, Arizona was the greatest copper mining state—a role she still fills today (95 percent of the country's copper reserves lie within 125 miles of Tucson, and the state accounts for 52 percent of the annual U. S. and 13 percent of world production. The industry employs more than 20,000 Arizonans and pays $177 million in wages each year.)

Arizona's growth in the early years of the century was precarious, and the Depression hit the state so hard that there was even talk of closing the University of Arizona. It was not until World War II that Arizona's earnest growth—first in military bases (the dry desert was especially suited for the training of fliers), then in research and industry—would begin.

Arizona's phenomenal postwar population increase, an average of some 50,000 a year, has been due primarily to immigration. Before the war, Southern states like Texas and Oklahoma had provided most of the new residents; since then the balance has swung to settlers from the Midwest and East with Illinois, New York, Michigan, and Ohio high on the list. But the influx has not been entirely jaded Northerners trying to escape ice and snow. Texas continues to supply many new Arizonans, and a high proportion, strangely enough, come from California; many of these are relatively new Californians who find the life on the coast too hectic or congested and take a step back to the quieter Arizonan milieu. Contrary to popular conception, Arizona has not become an old folks' haven; the state actually has one of the highest birth rates in the U. S. and a lower percentage of citizens over 65 than the national average. The population boom shows few signs of abating: between 1960 and 1970, there was a net migration gain of 228,000 persons and the overall population grew by 36 percent, a growth rate exceeded only by Nevada and Florida among all the 50 states.

Many of the first postwar immigrants were servicemen who had been stationed in the state during World War II, liked it, and returned with their families. In more recent years, a study by the Arizona Development Board has identified the chief motivations of new settlers as health, climate, transfer, and opportunity. The greatest opportunities have been in manufacturing, and within manufacturing, electronics has been the real boom industry. Companies like Motorola, Sperry-Rand, General Electric, and Hughes Aircraft (all with thousands of employees) found they could easily draw skilled workers to the Arizona environment. They also benefited from research work of the universities and cheap electric power from the nearby hydroelectric projects. Some of the electronic giants may have been attracted by the Army Signal Corps' electronic proving ground at Fort Huachua. The new products in the high-value-low-weight classification could easily be shipped out on completion. The state's biggest employer is Motorola, which at one point had over 30,000 employees and in 1970 still over 20,000. Just one of the spin-off firms from Motorola employed more than 1,000. The lion's share of this employment has gone to Phoenix, which now has 80 percent of Arizona's manufacturing employment, compared to only 9 percent for Tucson.

Some picture of the economic growth comes from federal figures which show the personal income of Arizonans rose in the 20-year span 1948–68 from $879 million to $5,034 million, an increase of 507 percent. Manufacturing led the parade with a 1,227 percent increase, followed by finance, insurance, and real estate (plus 850 percent), services, including tourism (plus 663 percent), government (plus 548 percent), wholesale and retail trade (plus 450 percent), and contract construction (plus 422 percent). Even taking account of inflation, these are impressive figures. But in the same time period, mining payrolls went up only 191 percent and farm income a scant 91 percent. Manufacturing moved ahead of farming in the 1950s and seems destined to stay ahead; as of the late 1960s, the annual manufacturing output was close to $1 billion annually, compared to $644 million for agriculture, $500 million for tourism, and $850 million for mining. Defense activity generates only 4.3 percent of the economic activity in the state, and there is less of a weapons emphasis in the industrial output than one finds in states like Washington and Utah. Nevertheless, the federal government played a major role in stimulating the start of all of this economic growth and in sustaining it through subsidized power rates from hydroelectric installations. Federal grants, per capita, are half again as large in Arizona as in the average state. Counting Indian reservations held in trust, Washington still owns 71 percent of Arizona; including the military, it pays out close to $500 million a year in salaries to its Arizona workers. Thus it still ill behooves Arizona to engage, as it does, in fits of federal-phobia.

King Copper, long dominant in the Arizona economy, slipped behind agriculture during World War II; the chief reason for this was the shift of old King Cotton from the Deep South to Arizona's and California's irrigated desert soils, where three crops a year can be grown. Arizona also became a veritable fruit and vegetable bowl, turning out vast crops of lettuce and cantaloupe, oranges and lemons. Feed grains also permitted Arizona to sustain a viable livestock feeding industry plus its range-land breeding stock activity. But now copper is outstripping agriculture and is likely to stay ahead because of the perennial water shortage and dropping water tables that inhibit farm growth; some irrigated lands, in fact, have already been abandoned because of water shortages.

The winter desert playgrounds around Phoenix and Tucson generate most of Arizona's growing tourist income and feed the economy doubly through the construction of huge lodges and motels; the go-go economic atmosphere, unhindered by tightly held old family wealth, has released the wellsprings of capital in a fashion unimaginable in the restrictive climate that pervaded Arizona a short generation ago.

Political Metamorphoses

Arizona politics is a story of metamorphoses. The state entered the Union during the heyday of the Progressive movement, with an advanced constitution which guaranteed women the right to vote, provided for workmen's compensation, and banned trusts and monopolies. With concern lest selfish interests dominate, the pioneer Arizonans gave their governor a short two-year term,* held state legislators to similar short terms, and subjected all state actions to referendum and initiative. President Taft actually refused to sign the first statehood bill because the proposed constitution provided for recall of judges; Arizona promptly submitted a new version with the offending section stricken. Taft signed the new statehood bill, and in the next election the voters merrily reinstated recall.

The constitution, however, proved to be no match for the copper interests, which proceeded to buy and control the legislatures with monotonous regularity. John Gunther reported that Phelps Dodge in particular extended itself in politics with a pervasive, autocratic control that made Arizona "the most corporation-ruled state in the Union." In much the same manner as Anaconda Copper in Montana, Phelps Dodge maintained an active lobby, "did favors" for those who cooperated with it, gave insurance contracts to "friends," kept its eye on judges and the like.† The copper companies, Gunther reported, "bribed anybody who got in their way, even governors, and the corporation commission of the state, designed to control such enterprises, became a commission actually of corporations; copper had such a grip on the whole community, in fact, that the Arizona term for conservative is still "copper collar.'" Among other things, the copper companies insisted on clearing all university regents and on one occasion imported a new university president from their other fiefdom—Montana.

* Not until the 1970 election did Arizona join the vast majority of states with four-year governor terms.

† An echo of Phelps Dodge's ancient paternalistic ways may still be found in the unincorporated town of Ajo (population 5,881), whose only reason for being is the New Cornelia openpit copper mine in the desert 100 miles from either Tucson or Phoenix. A *Newsweek* writer reported in 1971: "Ajo is owned lock, stock and rain barrel, by the Phelps Dodge Corp. The company provides the employment, housing, education, recreation, hospitalization and even the burial grounds for its employees and their families. What's more, Phelps Dodge pays 90 percent of the property taxes—and, in turn, controls virtually every aspect of life in Ajo." Among the advantages of life there are easy credit at the company stores, rentals as low as $26.50 a month for a three-bedroom house, and free medical care at the company hospital. For all this, Ajoites have to put up with such inconveniences as drinking water that arrives steaming hot after traveling six miles in pipes laid on the desert sands. The entertainment diet is limited to ten prosperous bars, high-school football games, and a rodeo that hits town once a year.

During the 1920s, Arizona seemed to have become a legitimate two-party state. But in the '30s and '40s it veered toward one-partyism of the Democratic variety, not dissimilar from the model of neighboring Texas; the difference was that while in Texas oil was the power behind the throne, in Arizona it was copper. With the Democratic nomination tantamount to election, the Democrats broke into bickering camps; a gubernatorial candidate would build a machine and go all over the state promising highway and state government jobs; if he won, he would clean out the state job rosters on a wholesale basis—even members of the state highway patrol. As in Texas, the conservative Democratic base was rural; this was where the copper barons controlled politics the most completely. With the legislature apportioned to favor rural areas, copper could rule too; this condition would extend into the postwar years, maintaining the rural-conservative-copper base even as the cities ballooned in population. When the Republicans finally came to power, the cities, not the countryside, would be their bastion, and in 1950 Howard Pyle, the first successful Republican gubernatorial candidate of modern times, attacked the Democratic party for being the vassal of Arizona's immense copper and other corporate interests.

"When we came out of the war," Goldwater recalls, "there was hardly any Republican party at all in Arizona. My uncle had formed the Democratic party in the Territory, but I felt the state needed a two-party system; a one-party system put up dogs for office, and if you want to see an example of the badness of one-party politics, take a look at George Wallace's Alabama today." Goldwater and his fellow Republicans made a start by taking over the Republican state convention in 1948, and the following year he teamed up with businessman Harry Rosenzweig and other would-be reformers in a bipartisan Phoenix Charter Government Committee. Goldwater was elected to the Council, and in 1950 he and his fellow Republican, radio commentator Pyle, decided the time had come to test the Democratic hold on Arizona. Goldwater ran Pyle's gubernatorial campaign, logging more than 50,000 miles in his private plane and carrying the candidate into the most isolated hamlets of Arizona. Pyle won by 3,000 votes in an historic reversal of Arizona's decades-old one-partyism; two years later Goldwater, preaching a conservative gospel and riding Eisenhower's coattails, was elected to the U. S. Senate and Republican John J. Rhodes broke the Democratic monopoly on seats in the U. S. House. Since the watershed elections of the early 1950s, the fortunes of the once mighty Democratic party have deteriorated steadily; in another key election—that of 1966—the Republicans swept every statewide office they contested and, for the first time in Arizona history, won control of both houses of the state legislature. In 1970 the Republicans continued their advance, not only retaining legislature control and all major offices they held but actually winning, for the first time, a majority of the supreme court and all three seats on the powerful Arizona Corporation Commission. They were able to write the new reapportionment plan, based on the 1970 Census, in a way that may ensure their control for years to come.

The early blueprint of Goldwater and his cohorts who planned the Republican growth from the late '40s on had been to make Arozona, a two-party state by 1970; in reality, Goldwater told me, "we went way ahead of schedule," and today he is concerned that the Democrats are so dormant that there is danger of a new kind of one-partyism in Arizona—Republican.

What turned Arizona to the GOP? First of all, it was the new population—heavily Midwestern, often Republican by heritage, an independent kind of people making a new start and repelled by the closed corporation of the fiefdom-ridden old Democratic party. Retirees tended almost by definition to be Republican; even more important, the new industries in which younger settlers found employment were highly technical and not of the mass production type with strong industrial unions. Motorola, the biggest employer, is the best example of this; it attracted technicians and engineers in large quantities and the unions never had a chance.

A second factor was the purchase in 1948 of the Phoenix *Republic* and *Gazette* by Eugene Pulliam, the ultraconservative publisher from Indianapolis. Pulliam was irked to see the Democrats running the state, and he determined to build a two-party system, using his papers in vicious fashion —especially in his first years in Arizona—to discredit any and all Democrats and promote the Republican cause. Interestingly, the Pulliam Arizona papers have become much more objective and statesmanlike since the early 1960s. Some close observers believe that Pulliam became upset when he himself became labeled by political opponents as an evil force, with "Stamp Out Pulliam" bumper strips sprouting around Phoenix. In 1964 a Republican county chieftain went into Pulliam's office and tried to dictate campaign coverage; this offended Pulliam greatly, and he threw the man out of his office. That same year, the paper switched to model election coverage, carefully balanced between the two parties, with editorializing restricted to the editorial page. Pulliam's shift in tactics may also be credited to his sincere interst in a real two-party system. Another major factor was doubtless Pulliam's decision to hire J. Edward Murray, a crackerjack professional journalist, as his managing editor; Murray was a key factor in having the papers' news coverage broadened to include the New York *Times* and Washington *Post*-Los Angeles *Times* news services, adding liberal columnists, devoting all of page two to foreign news, and improving local news coverage. The presence of a man of Murray's stature is the best reason I have heard for the vast improvement of the Phoenix papers while Pulliam's newspapers in Indianapolis continue unconscionable and gross distortion of the news for partisan political purpose.*

A final and essential factor in the Republican rise was the quality of its major candidates—men like Goldwater, Pyle, and Rhodes, men of integrity and ability who compared so favorably with the mediocre Democratic leaders on the state level. Since 1952, neither Goldwater nor Rhodes has ever lost an election in Arizona, though Goldwater squeaked through with

---

* Several attempts to launch competitive newspaper voices to Pulliam's have been attempted in Phoenix, and each has failed.

a meager 1-percentage point lead as the Republican Presidential nominee in 1964. Republicans have won seven of the 10 gubernatorial elections since 1950; since 1968, with the retirement of the redoubtable Carl Hayden (of whom we will have more to report later), they control both of Arizona's seats in the U. S. Senate. The "sunshine belt" tier of Republican growth, from Florida to California, has no firmer GOP bulwark. Registration, which stood almost 5 to 1 in favor of the Democrats in the late 1940s, seemed likely to show a Republican majority by early in the 1970s, eclipsing even the old tradition of conservative "pinto" Democrats registering in that party to participate in the active primary but then marking their ballots for a conservative Republican on election day.

Oddly enough, many of the Arizona Republicans' chief problems in recent years have come not from Democrats but from ideological right-wing zealots within their own ranks, members or at least spiritual brothers of the John Birch Society movement which erupted with special vehemence in Phoenix in the early 1960s. Goldwater, GOP state chairman Rosenzweig, and other "establishment" Republican leaders were obliged to take a leading role in repulsing the right-wingers in primary elections and battles for party control. Ironically, the right-wing reactionaries that caused the Arizona GOP such trouble were of the same stripe as the ultraconservatives which provided an early base for Goldwater in other states as he mounted his Presidential campaign in 1964. The Arizona right-wingers have been especially powerful in Phoenix, the banner city of GOP strength in the state, and in 1961 were part of the band that persuaded the state legislature to pass a loyalty oath for all state and local government employees—later declared unconstitutional by the U. S. Supreme Court. There is still a right-wing hard core in the state senate, which causes chaos and consternation for regular Republican leadership, and in recent years, under appointment by Republican Governor Jack Williams, the right wing has controlled the state department of public instruction. (Williams is a member of the Republican establishment but picks up some right-wing support and has himself some rather reactionary views on education.)

Today the major bases of Republican strength in Arizona are in Maricopa County in general, especially Phoenix's northern precincts, the suburbs of Scottsdale, Tempe, and Mesa, and the retirement community of Sun City, and high-income precincts in the eastern part of Tucson. The Democrats are generally stronger in the Tucson area in general, the black and Mexican-American precincts of the major cities, university communities, and in the rural counties where their old machines still hold on. Whether under Democratic or Republican rule, Arizona could never have been said—at least since the Progressive era—to have had a truly liberal state administration. Democrat Sam Goddard, governor for a single term during the 1960s, sought to liberalize the state but was hemmed in by a conservative legislature and proved so politically inept that the voters ousted him after two years in office.

Is there a possibility of a liberal reaction as the conservative establishment ignores minority group needs and scrimps on social welfare spending? The answer is probably no, because no appropriate political base is at hand. The Democratic party, especially in the legislature, is still heavily geared to rural conservatives who are unattuned to urban needs. The minority racial groups, aggregating about 27 percent of the population, tend to register and turn out to vote in extremely low numbers. (Less than a third of Arizona's eligible voters have even bothered to register, despite permanent registration laws.) The Republican party, given its special Arizona complexion, could hardly be expected to accommodate a liberal upswing, and several Democratic leaders candidly acknowledged in conversations I had with them that they have a hard enough time keeping the disparate parts of their party together, not to mention taking any controversial stands. About the best game the Democrats can play, they suggested, is to hope that the now dominant Republicans take to fighting and bickering among themselves, opening the way for Democrats to exploit the rivalries just as Republicans, in their rise to power, capitalized on the deep splits within Democratic ranks.

There is in fact a possibility that in 1974, when two leading Republican officeholders—Governor Williams and Senator Goldwater—are likely to retire from politics, that GOP infighting over the vacated offices may open the way for a Democratic breakthrough. This is especially likely in regard to the governorship, since the Democrats are again likely to nominate Raul Castro, a distinguished former judge and U. S. Ambassador to El Salvador and Bolivia who came within 7,303 votes of upsetting Williams in 1970. Castro, one of 14 children raised by immigrant parents, is the personification of the self-made man and an able campaigner who has broad appeal within and without his own party. He might well have won in 1970 if there had not been a drop-off in the normal Democratic vote in rural precincts, where some brass collar Anglo Democrats apparently cut him because of his Mexican ancestry. But Castro, if elected, would not bring a new era of liberalism to Arizona government, because his basic impulses are those of a conservative.

A chief characteristic of modern-day Arizona politics, making all predictions risky, is its open, rapidly shifting character, geared to the absence of old hierarchies and political machines. It is a society where, as one state legislator told me, "lots of people are moving into the state and everything is up for grabs." The legislator is David Kret, a state senator from Phoenix, whose own life story is illustrative. He was born in Philadelphia, lived in New Jersey, joined the Navy at 17, later became an engineer working for RCA, and was lured to Arizona in 1957 to take a job with Motorola. Three years later, without even having taken part in political activity, he was drafted for a local GOP legislature nomination and found himself elected. Eight years later, he had risen to be majority leader of the newly reapportioned state senate for a term. And by 1972, he felt confident enough of his standing in the state to run for Congress.

Arizonans are not likely, however, to accept a candidate who bids for one of the highest offices without solid background in the state. This was amply proven in 1970 when Sam Grossman, an ex-newscaster and real estate man from Beverly Hills, California, who had moved into Arizona only shortly before, sought to upset Senator Paul Fannin. Grossman was introduced by Pierre Salinger to one Richard Kline, operator of a Los Angeles political advertising firm, and Kline went to work to present Grossman, a tall, dashing figure, as the first perfect television personality to campaign on the Arizona scene. Extremely skillful television ads were produced by Robert Squier, a Washington, D.C., media expert who has worked for Humphrey, Muskie, and other top national Democrats. As a self-made millionaire, progressive but not liberal in his policy stands, and strong for anticrime and antidrug laws, Grossman looked like an ideal man to upset the rather colorless Paul Fannin. Polls actually showed him in the lead. But the Republicans—and Pulliam—were determined not to permit loss of a Senate seat to such an upstart. With the shots called by Republican campaign manager Stephen Shadegg, the Phoenix-based advertising man who had done much to launch Barry Goldwater in politics, a series of well orchestrated attacks on Grossman began to get prominent treatment in the Pulliam papers. One especially telling charge, made by state House Speaker John Haugh, was that Grossman had misrepresented his past history, especially by claiming six years residence in Arizona when legal records showed that as recently as a year before, he had sworn he was a resident of California. Grossman tried to retaliate with attacks on the Pulliam press, but the bubble had burst, his lack of depth support in his own party became clear, and he lost to Fannin by 48,772 votes (44.0 percent).

Arizona's Government, Education, Power Centers

The governor of Arizona for the past several years, Jack Williams, well mirrors the present-day Arizona mood by ruffling few feathers except to cut back, when he can, on state spending. Williams worked himself to the top of the radio business before becoming mayor of Phoenix and then governor; many Arizonans remember the line with which he opened his daily radio-talk show: "It's a beautiful day in Arizona. Leave us enjoy it."

A clue to the priorities and problems of Arizona state government may be seen in some of its per capita state spending figures in the late 1960s —seventh in education among the 50 states, 10th in highways, 42nd in health and hospitals, and 44th in public welfare. In 1965, Arizona voters by a 5 to 1 margin rejected a referendum to raise the state debt limitation from $350,000 to $100 million, leaving the state on a crippling pay-as-you-go basis for capital improvements to accommodate its burgeoning population. The Arizona State Hospital for the mentally ill (officially known until 1958 as "The Insane Asylum of Arizona") had until the very recent past scarcely any psychiatric staff and only in 1968 received accreditation—and that on a provisional basis. As for the prisons, Senator David Kret told me that the

Arizona system was "medieval," that the prevailing attitude was still to think of prisons as places for retribution, not rehabilitation. Despite some reform efforts, Arizona still runs the cheapest prison system in the U. S., with farm and manufacturing operations to make the prisons as self-sufficient as possible.

No state in the country spends less than Arizona to administer its aid for dependent children and old-age assistance welfare programs, and the state is only now recovering from its earlier fetish about accepting federal aid—a policy which, for instance, held up matching federal grants under the National Defense Education Act for several years. The legislature is woefully understaffed, slow-moving, and inefficient. Another state senator from Phoenix, Somers White, points out that among 90 legislators in both houses, only six are lawyers, and business heads are poorly represented; the roster shows instead many housewives, high school principals, a university coach, retirees, a gun store owner, a retired Navy officer, small retailers, realtors, liquor dealers, construction businessmen, farmers, and the like. Some of these have shown exceptional legislative skills but White is probably correct in suggesting that "as a group, it doesn't think enough about long-term planning—precisely when we should be thinking about controlling and channeling our growth so that on a problem like pollution, for instance, we avoid becoming another Los Angeles."

In 1971 the Arizona legislature ranked only 43rd among the 50 in a report of the Citizens Conference of State Legislatures. The report found Arizona 11th in its functional capabilities and 17th in its degree of independence from the executive but only 45th in accountability for its actions, 38th in information-gathering capability, and 50th in its degree of representativeness. Among other things, the Citizens Conference pointed out that legislators are not barred from practicing before state regulatory agencies, and that 70 percent of the rank and file in the house have no office space, private or shared, at all.

Even this state of affairs, however, would have to be called superior—in terms of the potentiality for representative government—to the condition before impatient courts took matters into their own hands and decreed a one-man, one-vote reapportionment plan for the legislature in 1966. Prior to that time, Arizona had one of the nation's most egregiously malapportioned legislatures. Conservative rural Democrats, responsive to copper and cattle interests, held an iron grip on the senate, and the house (since the early 1950s) had been controlled by a conservative coalition of "pinto Democrats" and conservative Republicans. By the single court decree, Maricopa County's share of state senate seats soared to 15 of 30 seats instead of the two seats out of 28 it had been accorded previously. The result of the reapportionment, in the succeeding 1966 elections, was to reduce the average age in the legislature about 20 years—and give the astonished Republicans complete control of both chambers for the first time in Arizona history. Ironically, Barry Goldwater opposed federally imposed reapportionment: "To hell with the party. I think each county is entitled to representation," he told me.

The first post-reapportionment legislature was able to break a long-standing legislative logjam on governmental reorganization and pass badly needed property tax reevaluation. "The lobbyists," Senator Kret recalls, "called us kindergarteners. We had a lot to learn. But we took on an impossible program and passed it." In effecting a massive tax assessment equalization plan, the legislature also revised Arizona's statewide tax system stem-to-stern, rewriting school finance laws and shifting more of the load for school support to the state. The reforms necessitated a doubling of the state income tax, but many homeowners' property taxes were reduced by as much as 50 percent. Few believe these reforms could have been accomplished without the break in rural control effected by reapportionment. The bold action apparently convinced Arizona voters that the GOP could deliver on its promises, and in the next election the Republicans scored another near sweep.

Since 1933, Arizona has had both a sales tax and a progressive income tax, creating the base for a sound fiscal system that many states with more "liberal" reputations might well envy. But Arizona has no severance tax on minerals, the result, one may surmise, of the successful efforts of copper lobbyists over the years. The copper lobbyists may soon be joined by oil lobbyists, since big oil companies have moved into the state in recent years to buy up leases on vast tracts of land.

Today Arizona's public schools continue to be among the best financed in the nation—a remarkable achievement in view of the fantastic enrollment growth from 100,000 in 1950 to 430,000 in 1970–71. Few states make a greater tax effort, related to personal income, for their schools. Educational requirements for teachers and their pay scales are well above national averages. But some observers believe more tax equalization is required to assure equally high educational standards in the state's 300-odd school districts—which are badly in need of consolidation.

Arizona also ranks high among the states in its support of higher education, with a 1970 enrollment of 56,600 (compared to 4,200 in 1941) at the three major degree-granting state institutions—the University of Arizona at Tucson, which was the original land-grant university, Arizona State University at Tempe outside Phoenix, and Northern Arizona University at Flagstaff. Lively and sometimes ferocious rivalry for state funds exists among these three schools and the rapidly expanding junior colleges; in the legislature, for instance, Tucson representatives, regardless of party or ideology, invariably stand as one in fighting for more U of A appropriations. For a state Arizona's size, the academic standing of the universities seems to be high. The University of Arizona, for instance, has taken advantage of its location to do outstanding work in anthropology related to ancient Indian cultures and experimental work in arid agriculture; it also has more astronomers than any other U.S. university. (There are two nationally renowned observatories in the state, taking advantage of the clear desert air.) Arizona State is strong in electronic research, rare earth chemistry, and as a center for Southwestern history.

Seventy percent of Arizona's high school graduates now attend college, resulting in a severe shortage of capital expansion and operating funds at the universities. Crowding has occasionally forced students to sleep in hallways. Richard Harvill, president of the University of Arizona until 1971, told me that his institution was the most heavily utilized of all land grant colleges, with the physical plant in use virtually every hour of the week including late afternoons, evenings, and Saturdays. One would expect the new urban legislators, many connected with the electronics firms in need of skilled manpower, to be strong for expanded facilities. But one university administrator told me: "We had an easier time lobbying the old cowboy senators than the newly reapportioned bunch. There was a sincerity and honesty and understanding that made it easy to work with the oldtimers. Today more partisan politics is involved, and keeping down taxes seems to be more important than it used to be." Most agree that the state will have to break its bonding bottleneck if the universities are to expand to meet enrollment demands. But there are some, like Senator Kret, who insist that Arizona should inaugurate state-supported kindergartens before additional university construction. (Initial kindergarten funding was not approved until the 1971 legislature session.)

Barry Goldwater, one hears again and again in Arizona, overshadows much of what happens in the state. Yet he rarely exercises his tremendous potential power. The universities provide an interesting example. The faculties include elements violently opposed to Goldwater; "if he were a Joe McCarthy, he could raise hell," according to Conrad Joyner of the department of government at Tucson. "But," says Joyner, "Goldwater stays away from us and protects us by not letting people say bad things about the universities." Actually, the Arizona universities are far from being hotbeds of radicalism; I even heard some criticism to the contrary, that the student bodies are quite muted and that the state could stand a few more courageous faculty willing to speak up on controversial issues. Acting as if campus-bred revolution were a real and present threat, the university regents often attempt to impose extremely restrictive codes of conduct. Such dictation was stoutly resisted by Harvill, and will probably also be resisted by his successor in the U of A presidency, John P. Schaefer, who like Harvill is likely to want to impose the tough regulations *himself*. Schaefer, a scientist in his mid-thirties, is an avid conservationist but also regarded as an uncompromising figure on law and order, which is believed to be the reason the regents selected him over more prestigious competitors for the presidency. (Jack Williams has been governor long enough to appoint men of his rigidly conservative philosophy to all but one of the 10 regent positions.)

Outside of Goldwater, with his great but largely unexercised power, and Pulliam, whose editorial voice is still exceedingly strong, it is difficult to pin down the true centers of power in Arizona today. "Since reapportionment," one legislator told me, "the major problem is that you can't identify a command position when you want to get something done. We're just over the reapportionment brink and the dust has yet to settle." The electronics industry could pack major clout if it wanted to but has taken little real interest in politics. The farm and copper interests still lobby effectively but lack the ultimate power of yesteryear. The Arizona Power Company flexes its muscles in politics from time to time, and land speculators are said to have important strength. Not to be discounted are the various education groups assembled in the "school lobby," as well as the universities, all after the legislature for more money. The new city legislators are urban in their outlook, but they have yet to unify in support of their respective municipal governments.

One group universally conceded *not* to be a major force in Arizona politics is organized labor. Arizona was one of the first states to adopt "right-to-work" legislation, and only 18 percent of its labor force is unionized—ranking 35th among the states. Almost forgotten now is the 1958 Senate campaign in which Goldwater focused his attack on the union bosses—an easy target, since they are so notoriously weak in his state.

One unusual forum in which Arizona issues are debated—and from which substantial public pressure can be generated—is the Arizona Academy, a group headed since its inception in 1962 by business consultant Lawrence Mehren, former vice president of the influential Valley National Bank in Phoenix. Inspired by the model of the American Assembly, the Academy began a series of biennial "town hall" meetings, usually at the Grand Canyon, discussing problems ranging from Arizona's tax structure to education, the water supply, crime, juvenile delinquency, and mental health. A typical panel might include a man from Mountain States Telephone, a Motorola vice president, a judge from Phoenix, a cattleman, and an AFL-CIO leader. In 1969 the Academy held a town hall on civil disturbances and then issued a report recognizing white racism, youthful doubts of adult values, and many other roots of modern societal discord. "It's one of the most amazing documents I've ever seen from the Arizona establishment," Professor Joyner commented.

Another noteworthy report came out of the 1970 Academy meeting, on the state's environment, which called for a halt to expenditure of public funds to attract more people and industry to Arizona and urged protection of the land instead of its continued exploitation. The town hall participants recommended that the state prohibit all billboards along its highways, ban all nonreturnable bottles and cans, create a water commission to research a total water plan, and set up an environmental council to collect information and advise the legislature. Establishment figures at the meeting, including U. S. Reps. Sam Steiger and John Rhodes, persuaded the town hall to vote down a plank that called for elimination of all industrial air pollution, but black and student participants scored on some major points, including the billboard ban. The 1971 town hall, on problems of drugs and alcohol, produced yet another surprise in a recommendation that marijuana possession be downgraded to a misdemeanor. At both the 1970 and 1971 meetings, Governor Williams appeared to make almost reactionary speeches—in one case blasting the ecology movement, and in the other urging revival of old vagrancy laws as a way to control youth on the drug and alcohol issue. But despite the heavy establishment role in the town halls, his advice was neatly disregarded in both instances.

Arizona's Remarkable Men in Washington

Arizona has dispatched a remarkable group of men to represent it in Washington. There was Carl Hayden, who served in Congress longer than any other man in American history, fighting doggedly for Arizona interests over most of this century. There was (and is) Barry Goldwater, who performed the miracle of becoming a Presidential candidate from one of America's most remote states by championing and embodying a conservative crusade which met immediate disaster at the polls but still echoes in the words and deeds of other national leaders. From the state came an able Congressman and then distinguished Secretary of the Interior, Stewart Udall, who proved to be a modern prophet in awakening the country to the dangers of despoiling its environment and God-given natural resources. Udall's skilled brother, Morris, is today one of the outstanding Democratic leaders in the House of Representatives and a possible future Speaker. In past years there was Senator Henry Fountain Ashurst, described by Arizona political scientist Ross R. Rice as "as literate and flowery an orator as the U. S. Senate has had in the present century." Less illustrious but likewise worthy of note are Ernest McFarland, who was Senate Democratic Leader until Goldwater defeated him for reelection in 1952, and John A. Rhodes, chairman of the Republican House Policy Committee.

"Seniority-encrusted Carl Hayden," Neal A. Maxwell of the University of Utah wrote in 1968 shortly before the senior Arizonan's retirement, "has been a kind of regional redwood who has defied time and the caprice of the ballot box; where some Western solons have elbowed their way briefly into senatorial history, Hayden is history." Born in 1877, 35 years before Arizona would even achieve statehood, Hayden was the first Anglo-American child to be born in Hayden's Ferry, Arizona—now the city of Tempe. In 1890, at the age of 13, he was taken to Washington to see the last parade of the Grand Army of the Republic. Six years later he went to Stanford to study economics and became a friend of fellow student Herbert Hoover. In 1906 he became the sheriff of Maricopa County. And in 1912, five days after Arizona gained statehood, Hayden took his seat as a member of the House of Representatives in Washington. Barry Goldwater was then only three years old, 80 percent of Arizona's people lived in rural areas, Indians wearing loincloths were still a common sight. Hayden would serve 15 years in the House, 42 in the Senate; then, a doddering old man of 93, shrunken three inches from his prime height of over six feet, Hayden returned to Tempe to await the end. His death came three years later, in January 1972.

What had Hayden wrought in Washington? An Arizona writer, Ray Thompson, answers the question: "Highways, dams and reservoirs, irrigation projects, a desert that bloomed beyond anyone's imagination; all these and more stand as monuments to his dedication, hard work, and love of Arizona." The crowning achievement, after decades of effort, was the passage in 1968 of the billion-dollar Colorado River-Central Arizona Project bill, the massive project (of which we will report more later) to ensure water to parched interior Arizona over decades to come.

Hayden also benefited Arizona untold times by the power he wielded as chairman of the Senate Appropriations Committee, overseeing billions of federal expenditures. As President Pro Tem of the Senate, he was third in line for the Presidency—although this came in later years of his Senate service when he would simply have lacked the physical strength and mental agility to handle the job.

Hayden did more, though, than stay quiet in Washington, build up unrivaled seniority, and enrich Arizona. He sponsored the 19th Amendment to the Constitution to guarantee women the right to vote, was father of the bill to establish the Grand Canyon National Park, and was coauthor of the legislation that led to the great interstate highway system. Hayden's total time in Congress, 57 years, was six more than his closest competitor, Congressman Carl Vinson of Georgia. Writer Nick Thimmesch was probably right when he said of Hayden: "Neither Arizona nor this impulsive nation will ever have another like him."

No Arizonan has won national prominence to compare with that of Barry Morris Goldwater, father of the Republican party in his state. His immigrant grandfather, Michel Goldwater, was an early Arizona settler who stemmed from a Jewish family of Russian background, though Goldwater himself was raised as an Episcopalian by his Protestant mother. "I'm proud of my Jewish father and grandfather," Goldwater has said, adding: "I've never been discriminated against because I am part Jewish"—a credit, one might add, to the openness of the Arizona frontier society.

Goldwater's political start, as a reform candidate attacking the then corrupt Phoenix city government, was nonpartisan and scarcely suggestive of his future role. "There's always been one and sometimes two Goldwaters damned fools enough to get into politics," he wrote. "It ain't for life and it may be fun." It was in his first Senate campaign, in 1952, that Goldwater's special brand of politics first surfaced. "What kind of a Republican are you, anyway?" he was asked at a rally. Goldwater's reply—just as accurate in describing his stand 12 years later when he ran for President, or today: "Well, I am not a me-too Republican. . . . I am a Republican opposed to the superstate and to gigantic, bureaucratic, centralized authority." Add to this Goldwater's belief in bold military action in the defense of American foreign ventures, and his moral crusade, proclaimed in 1964, against violence in the streets and the degeneration of traditional American values (Goldwater was the first national political figure to make this a major issue) and one has the philosophy of Goldwater the man fairly well encapsulated. As Theodore H. White said of Goldwater in *The Making of the President—1964,* "His world is the world of desert illumination, like his Arizona—black and white, blazing sun cut sharp by slanting dark shadows."

The Barry Goldwater of the early 1970s, grayed a bit but still the blunt, frank, athletic figure the nation came to know a decade before, shows few scars from his crushing 1964 Presidential defeat (when he ran 23 percentage points behind President Johnson and carried only five states, all in the Deep South, except for Arizona). Goldwater does take great pleasure in Vice President Spiro Agnew's onslaughts on the national press which treated him so unkindly in 1964. He would still unfetter the military to clean up the mess in Southeast Asia, and he points out, with great justification, that he was far more candid about the Vietnam situation in the 1964 campaign than was President Johnson, who made specious promises not to send American boys into a land war in Asia. Goldwater no longer talks of sawing off the northeastern seaboard and letting it float off to sea; in fact he would like to see a revival of Republicanism in the Northeast. But he is still caustically critical of Republican leaders who oppose war policies and new weapons systems—"Trojan Horse Republicans," he calls them, in words reminiscent of his 1964 defense of "extremism in the defense of liberty" which drove millions of moderate-to-liberal Republicans out of the party, some of them for good.

Goldwater's role in shifting the focus of American politics may be much greater than appeared when LBJ defeated him. He may have succeeded only in part in transforming the Republican party into the rigidly conservative vehicle which he envisaged in 1964. But Goldwater did skew the Republican course substantially to the right, expose the weakness of the once vaunted Eastern establishment in party ranks, and lay the groundwork for Agnewism and further Republican inroads in the South. Indirectly, he paved the way for a tough law-and-order Arizona Republican, Richard Kleindienst, to be nominated Attorney General, and for Arizonan William Rehnquist, who offended Arizona Negroes by his opposition to their rights protests when he lived in the state, to win appointment to the U. S. Supreme Court.

These political shifts and appointments will be Goldwater's legacy—not the legislative output of a man like Carl Hayden; in fact, Goldwater's name is attached to no major legislation, and in Arizona I even heard a prominent member of his party suggest that "Goldwater's not doing anything in Congress." * Goldwater is a symbol and a popularizer, not really a legislator by temperament. In his waning years (he celebrated his 63rd birthday in 1972), the softer sides of the Goldwater personality—travel through his beloved Arizona, photography of its native peoples and scenic wonders, and study and help for the Indians—may reemerge. Among the Indians with whom he has spent many days of his life, Goldwater is affectionately known as "Barry One Salt" or "Barry Sundust"; in sharp contrast to his raw disdain for laggards and others not wise enough to have inherited a department store or scratched their way to the top on their own, Goldwater has always taken a compassionate interest in the Indians and how their educational opportunities and economic lot might be improved. Not even among Indians themselves have I heard a more vigorous denunication than Goldwater's of the theory that Indians are more prone to alcoholism by virtue of their basic metabolism or psychology. (Goldwater only draws the line in defending Indians at militant "red powerism.") The Goldwater home on a hilltop above Paradise Valley near Phoenix is designed in the shape of an arrow and made of red sandstone which Goldwater discovered many years ago on the Navajo reservation. He treasures his collection of Indian memorabilia, including hundreds of colorful Kochina dolls, the masked religious figures of the Hopis whom he admires so much. One possible choice when he retires from the Senate, Goldwater says, is to return to a university position in Arizona working with Indian cultures.

Goldwater's political ally and fellow Senator from Arizona is Paul J. Fannin, a former three-term governor now in his mid-60s, business-oriented, a great upholder of the private enterprise system, conservative voting, and basically undistinguished. In 1970 former Interior Secretary Stewart Udall considered running for Fannin's seat and should have been considered to have all the necessary political attributes: member of an old Arizona family, the state's first cabinet member, a nationally prominent conservationist leader. It is a comment on how thoroughly Goldwater's politics have become Arizona's politics that a private poll taken by Udall showed he would lose to Fannin in Phoenix by a 2–1 margin. Udall decided not to run. His brother, Morris, holds onto the state's southern congressional district (including Tucson) only through long-term personal contacts, strong defense of district interests, and skilled campaigning. Even he admits that when he retires, the Democrats may lose their last Arizona seat in Congress. In 1971, Udall was the favored candidate of liberal House Democrats for the post of majority leader, losing to Louisiana's Hale Boggs, 140 to 88, on the second ballot.

* With the rest of the Arizona delegation, Goldwater has defended the vast federal appropriations required to fund the Central Arizona Project—a position which has led many to question the consistency of that position with his hostility to TVA. In 1970, Goldwater did take a major legislative initiative by cosponsoring an amendment to the Voting Rights Act to permit all Americans to vote at the age of 18. Goldwater said that television had given the public impression that young people were "an unclean, vile-tongued, rock-throwing, campus-storming, street-rioting bunch of hoodlums and misfits," but that he—Goldwater—knew from his own experience that this picture of the young "is distorted, stupid, and absolutely wrong."

Water Politics

Water has for decades been the overriding issue of Arizona politics, and with good reason. Central-southern Arizona, site of the great oasis cities, is true desert territory; the annual precipitation at Phoenix and Tucson usually comes to no more than a scant 10 inches, compared to 25 inches in most heavily populated areas of the United States. Starting with the pioneer Roosevelt Dam in 1911, virtually every river and stream of Arizona has been impounded behind stone, concrete, and earthen dams and carefully apportioned by use—the first priority to people and industries, second priority to agriculture. Were it not for heavy "mining" of underground waters, Arizona would have been able to mount and sustain only a small portion of the prosperous desert agriculture of the past several decades.

Without new sources of water, however, disaster would lurk around the corner, first for agriculture and perhaps eventually for people. Unfettered pumping of subsurface waters has already reduced the water table by hundreds of feet, and the depletion goes on at the rate of some 10 feet a year.* Arizona has already been obliged to place a moratorium on further wells for irrigation purposes, and a third of the lands once farmed have already been forced out of production, usually replaced by industries and homes which require substantially less water. Still, 90 percent of the state's water supply goes for agriculture, which accounts for only 10 percent of the economy. The beneficiaries are few: less than 900 farms, all of 2,000 acres or more, which account for 36.7 million of the state's total farm acreage of 38.2 million acres.

All too aware of its present and future water problems, central Arizona has long cast a covetous eye on the water flow of the great Colorado River that cuts through the northern reaches of the state and then along the border with California. For decades there was an abstruse but passionate struggle between Arizona and its Colorado River Basin neighbors over Arizona's share of the Colorado's waters. Arizona for more than 20 years refused to sign the Colorado River Compact allocating water between the upper and lower basin states; it also argued it had the right, under the doctrine of prior appropriation, to all the water flowing through its territory. In the 1930s, Arizona even went to the ludicrous extreme of sending out its national guard to try to stop by force of arms the construction of the great Boulder (now called Hoover) Dam, which would deflect precious water to California. But the dam was built anyway and Arizona finally joined the compact. Un-

* The present balance is as follows: annual use of water for municipal, industrial, and agricultural purposes 6.0 million acre-feet; supply from surface streams 1.5 million; natural replenishment of underground water 1.0 million; net overdraft of underground water 3.5 million acre-feet. Ironically, that overdraft is precisely equal, according to a 1966 study by University of Arizona economists, to the amount used each year in the state to irrigate land for feed grains and animal forage, both crops of low cash value that are easily grown in the more moist eastern sections of the U.S.

til 1963, the state was locked in protracted legal battle with California over division of the lower basin river flow (a case finally decided largely in Arizona's favor).

By edict of the Supreme Court, Arizona was finally guaranteed an annual 2.8 million acre-feet of Colorado River water; this was the signal for Senator Hayden and other members of the congressional delegation to revive in Congress their struggle for federal funding of the so-called Central Arizona Project (CAP). After five more years of wrangling on Capitol Hill, Congress in 1968 finally approved the project. It will consist of a 400-mile system of aqueducts and dams to divert a yearly 1.2 million acre-feet of Colorado's river allotment from Lake Havasu, behind the Parker Dam on the Colorado River, to the Phoenix and Tucson areas. (The Parker Dam lies some 150 miles northwest of Phoenix.) The cost of this gigantic system, together with power generation to pump the water, was authorized at $892 million; the remainder of the $1.3 billion authorized by the bill was for five reclamation projects on Colorado's Western Slope, the pound of flesh which Colorado's Wayne N. Aspinall, chairman of the House Interior Committee, exacted for his support of the bill.

By the early 1980s, it is estimated, the first Colorado River water will be flowing into central Arizona—the state's economy, incidentally, vastly enriched by the payrolls and materials supply for building the project. What will CAP then mean for the state? It will be an insurance policy for the future of the oasis cities, although there is reason to believe that with moderate population growth, the cities could take care of their reasonable needs for the foreseeable future (Phoenix from the Salt River project, Tucson from vast supplies of underground water which some experts believe may be enough for another 100 to 300 years). The real import of CAP is for agriculture. It gives the lush irrigated farmlands a reprieve from early extinction. But even CAP will supply only a third of the amount that would really be needed to correct Arizona's alarming depletion of its residual underground water. In not too many years, the last major underground sources will be exhausted. Unless still other sources of water are found—importation from the Northwest, desalinization of the Pacific, or another scheme not yet dreamed of—there will be a day of reckoning, probably early in the 21st century, when Arizona's booming agriculture will have shriveled to a fraction of its current proportions. Whether such a development would be a calamity in the eyes of the nation's taxpayers (who must put up the money to finance projects like CAP) is quite another question. Such is the power of the agricultural interests in Arizona that the state might well have come up with the financing for its own CAP, or at least some portion of it, if the federal government had not stepped in. The 1971 Nader report pleaded with Congress to stop CAP before the first actual construction money was appropriated. The report claimed that the project would not only "raid" the U. S. Treasury but force city dwellers in Tucson and Phoenix to underwrite water for agriculture. "While irrigators pay $10 to $20 per acre-foot of water," the report said, "the municipal and industrial users will have to pay $50 to $60 per acre-foot. Phoenix now pays only $3 per acre-foot for water obtained from the Salt River Project. Tucson pays only $9 per acre-foot for its water, which is pumped from underground."

CAP may work indirectly to stimulate industrial and population growth. But as one lifetime Arizonan put it to me: "We have a terribly arid state, so why bring more people here? The CAP water won't make any new development possible, but still the state and the chamber of commerce are working like the devil to get new industry here. I say, let the people go where the water is!"

The Culture of the Phoenicians

Phoenix is wrenched with change. In less than 10 years, 500 industrial plants move into town. Manufacturing now outsells the tourist trade 4–1. Now people come to Phoenix for jobs more than for the sun. They have built a city on wheels, built around more than 100 bustling, extravagant shopping centers, a city of near strangers where six out of 10 families moved into new homes in just six years.
   —John Barbour of the Associated Press, December 1968

Beyond the garish plastic signs hawking Kingburgers and Big Whoppers you can still see graceful palms, stark mountains, brilliant skies—and it does the soul good.
   —Steven V. Roberts in the New York Times, Feb. 24, 1970

In 1940, the Census found 65,414 people in Phoenix, in 1970 a total of 581,562, almost nine times as many. This is now America's 20th largest city. If Phoenix has any sacred value, it is growth. No American city today is more replete with the story of vibrant, ambitious young people who by pluck and luck and daring have come and made their fortunes in banking, building, real estate, insurance. Now corporate headquarters are being attracted, like the Greyhound Corporation, which moved its central office, including 500 executives of the parent corporation and subsidiaries like Armour & Company, from Chicago in 1971.

Most revered of the builders of modern Phoenix is Walter Bimson, who came in the late 1930s and by able management and endless promotion schemes built the Valley National Bank into such a powerful force that it became one of the West's largest banks and had an average of more than one depositor in every Arizona family. The rags-to-riches stories encompass such disparate figures as high-rise builder David H. Murdock, land speculator Lee Ackerman, gold-copper-uranium promoter Herb Miller, and Lavergne C. (Jake) Jacobson, who started in as a timekeeper for Del Webb at $25 a week and ended up some years later as vice president and general manager for Webb projects across the U. S., his personal worth set at several million dollars. This fabulously successful entrepreneurial generation, Goldwater told me, "has the same spirit of men like my grandfather. Now it's just a new set of pioneers."

One wonders. This same Phoenix has the highest divorce rate of all major U. S. cities save Las Vegas, an FBI crime index 55 percent above the national average, and a problem with its own youngsters blowing their minds on pot or speed or LSD that the city's own magazine says is "out of control." (The Maricopa County Medical Society reports that there are "20,000 documented cases of kids hooked on drugs" in the county, and the police chief asserts that 75 percent of all crimes in Phoenix are directly tied to drug abuse.) Few would maintain that Phoenix's rapid growth has brought grace or quality; instead a seemingly boundless "spread city" creeps out onto the desert and toward or onto the gaunt, forbidding Camelback and Superstition and Four Peaks which rim the center as grim reminders of the barren nothingness that preceded man's canals and hectic building. In many ways, Phoenix brings to mind the culture and attitudes of a Dallas—economically dynamic, fast-building, dedicated to wealth and free enterprise and right-to-work laws, sometimes tolerant of John Birchism and other forms of virulent right-wing activity. It should be reported, however, that Phoenix's ultrarightism has subsided since the early 1960s; as one Arizonan explained this to me, "If your President is Nixon and your governor is Jack Williams and your Senators are Goldwater and Fannin, it's hard to make anybody believe the Russians are about to take over."

Unlike rival Tucson, or Albuquerque in neighboring New Mexico, Phoenix has failed to retain any of the special Southwestern flavor of its birth. A prominent Tusconite with whom I spoke dismissed Phoenix as a "bland, commercial mercantile center—the Midwest with palms and a lot of the honky-tonk of Los Angeles." One sees some modern high-rise buildings of fair distinction (expecially along Central Avenue, the Fifth Avenue and Wilshire Boulevard of Phoenix all wrapped up into one), but the dominant image is of a rather monotonous, low-silhouetted city baking in its desert valley. City fathers, worshipping at the shrine of growth at any price, have repeatedly allowed zoning ordinances to be violated to please businesses. The developers, not the planners, have always been in the driver's seat. Virtually alone among major U. S. cities, Phoenix has no housing code and as a result is ineligible for federal urban renewal aid.

Early in the 1960s, as land prices escalated in the old downtown section, the developers jumped some 20 blocks northward on Central Avenue and started all over again with office buildings and shops. Five large department stores—including Goldwater's, sold out by the family in 1962—moved lock, stock, and barrel to the gleaming new uptown section. In the meantime, the old downtown went into a tailspin, held together by marginal businesses and the traffic in attorneys occasioned by the courthouse and nearby State Capitol Building. Crime spiraled in an especially decadent downtown section known as "The Deuce," where, according to *Phoenix* magazine, late evening visitors can expect to "be exposed to assault, rape, theft, and other crimes" and "there are frequent reports of Negro pimps who exploit poor, Indian prostitutes [who] solicit out of cheap bars and charge accordingly." (In safer areas, one quickly discovers that Phoenix has about the deadest night life of any major American city.)

In a determined effort to redeem its own downtown, Phoenix in 1971 opened a handsome new $21 million civic plaza and convention center there, complete with massive exhibition and assembly halls and a plush 2,500-seat concert hall for the Phoenix Symphony. But there were problems of parking space and adequate local hotel facilities for out-of-town conventions. Without urban renewal authority, the city could do little to clear out the surrounding blocks of dilapidated and unpainted shops, flophouses, nudie movie houses, and bottle-strewn alleys. That would have to be left to private initiative—and there were serious doubts whether local capital would have that much confidence in downtown's future.

Most of Phoenix, of course, consists of pleasant palm- and citrus-lined streets with the kind of decent housing one would expect from a population in which three-quarters of the household heads have finished high school and 40 percent have attended college. But there is an exception to this middle-class demiparadise—the huge "Southside" slum area, starting in the downtown and moving south, an area which visiting writer Andrew Kopkind aptly described a few years ago as "a cross between a Mississippi Black Belt Negro ghetto and a Mexican border town." Here live virtually all of Phoenix's blacks (about 5 percent of the population) and most of its Mexican-Americans (about 14 percent). There are many unpaved streets, unconnected sewers, and houses with outdoor toilets—conditions which many leading Phoenicians seem able to ignore completely and which, of course, might be substantially corrected by passage of a building code. But the people of the city turned down a code in a referendum a few years ago, and no one expects them to change their minds soon. (The Phoenix *Gazette*, ironically, supported the building code. But it had laid the seeds of the public action by its years of assault on urban renewal as a kind of sinister "federalized property management.")

The thing which brought many fugitives from the Northern states to Phoenix was its weather—the clean, dry air and blue skies and almost continual sunshine. But now this priceless asset is being threatened by air pollution—produced, apparently, both by the traffic flow of auto-happy Phoenix and the tons of sulphur dioxide spewed into the air from nearby copper industries. For 11 windless days in December 1969, Phoenix's famous mountain skyline disappeared behind a thick brown pall of polluted air, filling the city and the mountain canyons with smog and even forcing Williams Air Force Base to close its runways. Slowly, the state legislature has been responding with barely adequate air pollution legislation. (By 1971, the legislature had still refused to order an auto inspection system to control exhaust emissions. In 1970 rules were adopted to force copper companies to remove 90 percent of the noxious sulphur dioxide that spews forth from their smelters, but the companies seemed to be in a position to demand and get an extension of the 1973 deadline set for the new standards.)

Before the 1949 reform wave that carried City Councilman Barry Goldwater and his colleagues into office, Phoenix had had one of the most corrupt governments of the West, with widespread gambling, prostitution, and inadequate city services. The new charter nonpartisan government quickly cleaned house, installed an exceptionally competent city manager, and within two decades had annexed so much neighboring territory that its square mileage was up by more than 1,400 percent. Graft and corruption disappeared almost completely from city administration, and for 20 years there was no increase in property taxes. Some academicians have pointed to Phoenix, indeed, as one of the best examples of nonpartisan and business-dominated government in America.

The danger of such a government, of course, is that it may be insensitive to needs of the poor and minorities. Milton H. Graham, the mayor for several years during the 1960s, was a definite exception to this rule; though a Republican and self-proclaimed conservative, he worked effectively with the Mexican-Americans, started innovative local antipoverty programs and tried to get better housing for Phoenix's Negroes—many of whom still live in shacks. Graham quickly threw aside Phoenix's old bugaboo about accepting federal money and tried to get all the help he could from Washington. Some called him the most liberal mayor in the southern half of the country; this was probably an overstatement, but in 1969 the Phoenix establishment, including Barry Goldwater and the Pulliam papers, decreed Graham's defeat. He barely lost to the new Charter-backed candidate. The new mayor would be a financial executive not expected to stir up sparks.

Notwithstanding Phoenix's steady growth by annexation, the suburbs which surround it in the so-called "Valley of the Sun" now have almost as much population. The most illustrious of the group is Scottsdale, a dusty crossroads filling station at the end of World War II grown to 67,823 people by 1970 and now Arizona's third largest city, complete with a sprinkling of skyscrapers. The town started out as a subdivider's dream with exclusive residential sites and clever downtown decor that permitted Scottsdale to bill itself as "the West's most Western town." Actually all the false fronts, hitching posts, and peeled porticos are pseudo-West at best; as one observer noted, the place "resembles a Western movie set in which the director decides to replace horses with station wagons."

Scottsdale is also the location of many of the Phoenix area's leading winter resorts (especially at Camelback Mountain), the site of winter homes of a number of wealthy transcontinental commuters, and the post office address of many artists, writers, and craftsmen. The city imposes tough zoning, site, and design standards. Now under construction is a civic center, including City Hall, library, and other facilities, based on a design by Phoenix architect Bennie M. Gonzales that *Harper's Magazine* has hailed as "the most successful effort yet to combine the concepts of modern architecture with the Indian and Spanish traditions"—a welcome and long overdue innovation in the sterile architectural climate of Phoenix. The earlier exceptions, both worthy of special note, include Frank Lloyd Wright's ground-hugging Taliesin West, a school where architectural apprentices could come and work with him, constructed some 15 miles outside of Scottsdale, and Wright's delicately sculpted, circular auditorium on the Arizona State University campus at Mesa. Wright died in 1959 at the age of 90, but his widow, Olgivanna Lloyd Wright, described by *Life* as the "intense and restlessly energetic . . . principal guardian, teacher and evangelist of her husband's heritage of work and thought," personally directs the community of some 65 people, called the Taliesin Fellowship, at Taliesin West.

Mesa was up to 62,853 population in 1970 and has one of the seven major Mormon Temples of the world—a reminder that the Mormon influence, overwhelmingly conservative, is still a factor in Arizona life and politics.

On a lesser cultural note, the Phoenix suburbs also harbor the late Elizabeth Arden's very exclusive Maine Chance, where hundreds of well-heeled ladies from all states and abroad come for regimens of diet, exercise, and last-chance beautification.

. . . and the Tucsonians

Tucson is at once more traditional, more liberal, and more flavorful than Phoenix. It lies some 125 miles farther to the south (Mexico is just 66 miles down the road), but the city is cooler than Phoenix because it lies 1,500 feet higher.* Tucson's majestic Santa Catalina Mountains, set close-in to the north, provide an even more dramatic desert heights setting (and in their foothills, the poshest residential addresses of the city). With less water than Phoenix (it must depend chiefly on underground sources rather than diverted river water), Tucson lacks the great green splotches of irrigated land; here the cactus-dotted desert seems even more immediately at hand. The economy is expansive and progressive, but not at Phoenix's frenetic pace; in contrast to the we-arrived-yesterday rootlessness of the northern oasis, Tucson has a rich sense of history that stems from the many flags from Spanish and Mexican to Confederate to U. S., under which it has lived.

What strikes a visitor to Tucson most immediately and forcefully is the architecture; in place of Phoenix's bland modernity, Tucson has preserved the best of the old Spanish adobe style, the pale yellows blending marvel-

---

* Tucson even has more sunshine than Phoenix, as if that were possible. Meteorological records also show that it is less humid, a factor that can make all the difference in the hot Arizona summer; of all the travels for interviews for this book, I can recall no more miserable day than a semihumid 100-degree August day in Phoenix; Tucson the next day was hot, yes, but dry and livable.

ously into the desert sands. Many Tucson houses, in fact, are built of adobe brick brought up from south of the border. The Mexican flavor even makes the pace of life slower; it has not been many years, in fact, since Tucson businesses closed up tight for midday siestas. The societal roots go deeper here; the city is largely owned by a handful of old families, resistant to change, and one leading state officeholder (asking not to be quoted by name) told me that "what Tucson needs is about six high-priced funerals."

Western writer Neil Morgan has pointed to many of the remarkable similarities which Tucson bears to Albuquerque. Both were first Spanish settlements at the foot of picturesque mountains, both received veterans' hospitals after World War I, both are seats of state universities, and both saw their economies begin to expand with World War II-vintage Air Force bases. The University of Arizona unites and dominates Tucson; as Goldwater jokingly puts it, "Everyone in Tucson thinks a little more of the university than they do of the flag; say something against it and you're dead." (The lovely center-city tract for the university, historians variously record, was donated by public-spirited gamblers or some local madams, an interesting union of some of the world's oldest professions.)

Tucson's Air Force Base is named Davis-Monthan and is headquarters of a major missile installation. The other components of the city's military-industrial-scientific base include the Kitt Peak National Observatory some miles to the south, an Army electronic environmental test range to the west, a big Hughes Aircraft plant, Motorola and other electronic-age employers. Ups and downs in employment at Hughes have caused nervous fluctuations in the local economy. As noted earlier in this chapter, huge copper mines are located not many miles distant. The impact of all this has been to increase Tucson's population by a factor of more than five since 1945 (the 1970 Census total was 262,933). And a cosmopolitan mix it is—cattlemen and young radicals, professors and factory workers, a substantial complement of blacks and Mexicans, airmen and artists, convalescents fleeing Eastern winters, and Indians from the nearby Papago Reservation.

Tuscon has eschewed the Phoenix nonpartisan charter form of government for a straight partisan mayor-council form. The calibre of city leadership has not matched that of Phoenix; partisan control has switched back and forth between the parties, and the quality of winning candidates, in the view of some, has deteriorated rather badly in recent years, even though the government, as a whole, has remained fortuitously honest. The honesty factor is especially important in modern Tucson, for the city has been somewhat horrified to find itself selected as a retirement haven for Mafia leaders, including the notorious Joe Bonanno, the New York underworld kingpin labeled by *Time* as "one of the bloodiest killers in Cosa Nostra's history." Bonanno was followed to town by bigtime mobsters from Detroit and Chicago as well, and in the late 1960s the city was shaken by a series of dynamite bombings and shotgun blasts aimed at Bonanno and his cohorts.

Several Mafia figures also chose the city as a place to put their ill-gotten gains into restaurants, laundries, and real estate. In 1968 Congressman Morris Udall warned that the Mafia might soon move to what he called "Stage II, [in which] organized crime begins to actively operate narcotics distribution, bookmaking, organized pressures and extortions from businessmen in trouble, gambling and prostitution." But by the early 1970s, none of this had yet surfaced—a credit, Udall told me, to "alert newspapers and honest city officials." (In 1970 the Arizona *Republic* reported that Phoenix was also becoming a Mafia haven, with members of the underworld infiltrating numerous legitimate businesses, including not only such predictable enterprises as bars and restaurants but also ranches, beauty shops, car rentals, and legislative lobbying.)

Tucson has demonstrated none of Phoenix's scruples about accepting federal urban renewal aid, with the result that a handsome multimillion-dollar government and cultural center has risen adjacent to the major business center of the city. Both through the university and in the general community, Tucson ranks as one of the major cultural centers of the new Southwest.

For many years, Tucson enjoyed healthy newspaper competition between the Democratic morning *Arizona Daily Star* published by William R. Matthews and the Republican evening Tucson *Daily Citizen*, published by William A. Small. But in 1965, Matthews, seeing himself getting old, decided to sell out, and the *Citizen*, exercising a purchase option clause of a 20-year-old joint printing agreement, bought him out. Even though Small left Matthews in control of the *Star*'s editorial policy, the U. S. Justice Department blew the whistle on the deal, filing an antitrust lawsuit. The case went all the way to the Supreme Court, which declared the purchase illegal and forced *Citizen* publisher Small to divest himself of the *Star*—which he did in 1970, selling out to the St. Louis *Post-Dispatch*.* The P-D then did Tucson a great favor by dispatching Michael Pulitzer, grandson of the famous Joseph, to be publisher of the *Star*. Pulitzer, a charming and witty man, reorganized the paper, brought in a number of top-flight managers and reporters, and seemed well on his way to making the *Star* into the outstanding moderate liberal editorial voice of Arizona.

* This was the banner case that led to 1970 passage of the Failing Newspaper (later Newspaper Preservation) Act, which exempts from antitrust prosecution separately owned newspapers that share physical plants, pool profits, and fix joint advertising rates not necessarily based on costs. Udall stoutly defended the legislation, claiming that antitrust law as it was being applied "permitted the actual monopoly situation of Phoenix, but made illegal the situation in Tucson with the healthiest, most competitive newspapers in the Southwest." The bill slipped through Congress with minimal coverage in the nation's newspapers; nevertheless it has ample critics. Morton Mintz and Jerry S. Cohen wrote in *America Inc.* that the bill "tends to subvert the First Amendment by making it legal for established publishers to engage in monopolistic practices against which weekly newspapers and other potential rivals cannot compete." The *New Yorker* said the measure was "probably not so much a newspaper-preservation bill as a publisher-preservation bill" and added: "Any newspaper that has to be preserved this way might as well be preserved in formaldehyde." The act's passage legalized existing arrangements of 44 newspapers in 22 cities, including St. Louis, Pittsburgh, and San Francisco.

Natural Arizona and Assorted Folkways

Let us take leave of the people-packed oasis cities and turn our eyes to natural Arizona. Few men have known it as well as Josef Muench, one of the illustrious photographers for that most handsome of state pictorial magazines, *Arizona Highways*. (A cross-section of all America must have gotten a feel for the Arizona landscape from that magazine, which one discovers on newsstands thousands of miles from its state of origin.) Of natural Arizona, Muench has written: "It is because in Arizona the arresting framework, the very skeleton of the earth, is exposed, that the scenery is so compelling and meaningful. Its bone structure is superb."

On Arizona's northern roof lies the great expanse of the Colorado River Plateau, a high, rugged tableland gashed by huge canyons, the greatest that of the Colorado River itself. At the northeastern extremity lies the Four Corners juncture, the only point in the Union where so many states touch each other. This is the land of the Navajos and the Hopi, of the Painted Desert, Petrified Forest, mysterious and remote Monument Valley, the gigantic Hoover and Glen Canyon Dams, and of course Grand Canyon National Park, that most breathtaking and spectacular natural phenomenon of the North American continent. Just to stand on the canyon's rim and look into its depths is an experience even the most jaded child of the neon generation will never forget; sadly, all too few tourists take the time or expend the energy to hike down to the canyon floor, passing by foot the grand tableau of two billion years of exposed geologic history which the virile Colorado has laid bare. (The trip into the canyon, of course, can also be made by muleback; this seemingly dangerous jaunt is great fun, but months-ahead reservations are required, and the assault to a city-dweller's posterior can be as physically debilitating as the hike. Now several thousand people a year also see the canyon from rapids-shooting big rubber rafts; at the other extreme, there are millions more who have only viewed the canyon from the window of a transcontinental jetliner.)

The Grand Canyon in the 1960s found itself in the vortex of a political battle between conservationists and the dam builders who wanted to construct hydroelectric dams both up- and downstream from the national park territory as part of the monumental Central Arizona Project.* Against the combined congressional forces of the seven Colorado River Basin states, the increasingly potent conservationist groups of the nation—led by the California-based Sierra Club—defeated the proposed dams, which they

---

* The dams would not have supplied more CAP water but simply provided power generation income to pay for pumping water along the aqueducts in central Arizona. Interior Secretary Udall suggested thermal power generation, at another location, to fill the same role, and Congress finally accepted his suggestion. The power will be supplied by the new Navajo Power Plant near Page, Arizona.

claimed would ruin the scenic beauty of the free-flowing Colorado and the canyon itself. The canyonlands which were saved from flooding are so inaccessible that only a few thousand hardy souls actually see them in any given year, but the conservationist victory there was to lay the groundwork for ensuing battles over natural wonders from the California redwoods to the Florida Everglades, battles in which the utilizers and exploiters of the land would find the tables of national opinion suddenly turned against them.

Few regions of the continental U. S. A. are as remote from civilization as the Strip Country of Arizona, a northwestern triangle of some 8,500 square miles bounded by the Colorado River and the Utah and Nevada borders. The scale of the harsh plateau, peaks, and gorges is so immense that man seems dwarfed here; in fact there are less than 1,800 souls in the entire region (a population density less than .004 percent that of the country as a whole). The few souls are mostly in little hamlets like Fredonia, Moccasin, and Colorado City. The latter settlement, known until a few years ago as Short Creek, harbors a substantial community of Mormons still actively practicing polygamy in violation of all their church ordinances and civil statutes. Governor Pyle in 1953 sent in a raiding party that arrested members of many polygamous families at Short Creek. But Wallace Turner has reported in *The Mormon Establishment* that plural marriage still flourishes at Colorado City and that missionaries go out to recruit girls, widows, and even single men and whole families to join their colony.

Separating northern Arizona from the southern desert area is a fairly narrow belt of high mountains, many heavily timbered in soft ponderosa pine. Transversing the state diagonally, from northwest to southeast, this belt escapes the extreme aridity of most of Arizona, its meadows and high forests showing a more fertile face to the world. Set at the foot of the lofty San Francisco Peaks is Flagstaff (26,117), the principal town north of Phoenix and trading center for the cattle and sheep ranchers, lumbermen, and Indians in a region that extends 60 miles southward and 200 to the north. Flagstaff is also host to Northern Arizona University and the Lowell Observatory, where the planet Pluto was discovered some 40 years ago.

Flagstaff will be remembered by almost any tourist who has passed through northern Arizona as the chief jumping off point for the Grand Canyon and the other scenic wonders of the region; millions more may recall it as the principal Arizona city on fabled old U. S. Route 66, a road which surely deserves an epitaph before the prosaic new interstate engulfs it for all time. The Los Angeles *Times West Magazine* dispatched a writer, Zora Reshovsky, to do just that in 1969; I trust many will share with me the flood of reminiscences evoked by these quotations from her article:

Route 66 . . . silver thread, looping together a giant patchwork of Americana. Concrete artery that tilted a nation of nomads Westward. Route 66—Grand Inspirer—more than any other highway in the history of the world. John Steinbeck called it the "Glory Road" in *Grapes of Wrath* and spun vivid characters around its background. A TV series bore its name. Half of Bobby Troup's hit song, capturing the rhythm of miles clicked off, was composed as he motored West. Those that remember—"*Get Your Kicks on Route 66*"—still sing his song as they ride out in search of America.

Out of 1,388 miles from Oklahoma City to California—the route of the dust-bowlers in flight—230 have not yet been converted into the super-highway great zooming white Interstate. As we click off this mileage we say our goodbyes to sights and a style of touring you won't find on the new road. . . . A pink stucco deserted "Modern Motel" where the weeds are as high as a buffalo's eye. . . . Concrete shells of former gas stations. . . . LIVE BOAS. FIERCE RATTLERS. OVER 100 SPECIES. NOTHING LIKE IT! There used to be a dozen carny snake villages on Route 66. . . . Saddest of all, so long to the tiny squat white cafe. . . . Route 66—*So long!*

So much could be said of the fascinating sights, natural and man-made, in the Flagstaff orbit: spectacular Oak Creek Canyon with its red-rock formations; Walnut Canyon with its prehistoric cliff dwellings; ghostly Meteor Crater; picturesque Sedona (2,022) with its artists, writers, movie sets, and a superfluity of tourists; the ghost mining town of Jerome; and, along the way to Phoenix, the first territorial capital of Prescott (13,030), where Barry Goldwater has begun each of his campaigns for public office, even the Presidency.

The great desert, commencing where the mountain belt ends and marching southward into Mexico, beckons us. But should we really dismiss it as "desert"? True, writes Steinbeck in *Travels with Charley*, it is a "mysterious wasteland, a sun-punished place." But he quickly adds: "It is a mystery, something concealed and waiting." There is a breed of desert men, their habitations huddled in protected places at the end of tracks in the sand and rock, "not hiding exactly but gone to sanctuary from the sins of confusion." And at night, Steinbeck reminds one, "in this waterless air the stars come down just out of reach of your fingers. In such a place lived the hermits of the early church piercing to infinity with unlittered minds. The great concepts of oneness and majestic order seem always to be born in the desert." Of the natural order he writes, too, for "in the war of sun and dryness against living things, life has its secrets of survival"—the oily armor of the dusty sage, protecting its inward small moistness, the hard dry outer skins of animals, defying desiccation, the secret burrows and shaded sides of outcroppings where rodents and reptiles go to escape the sun's unremitting glare.

Walk through the desert under the noonday sun, and it appears dead. "But when the sun goes and the night gives consent," writes Steinbeck, "a world of creatures awakens and takes up its intricate pattern. Then the hunted come out and the hunters, and hunters of the hunters. The night awakes to buzzing and to cries and barks." So often as he reads here and elsewhere of the western "desert," the reader would do well to bear this other world in mind.

One would think of the desert as indestructible, but even here the ecological battle is mounting. Along the rivers, for instance, grow water-consuming plants like mesquite shrubs and salt cedar trees; their greenness is not only balm to the eye but protection and nest sites for doves and waterfowl and song birds, rabbits and the wild swine called javelina. But now huge swatches of river plant life are being removed by the Bureau of Reclamation and Army Corps of Engineers. The reason? Partially, the government men say, to control floods; more importantly, they figure the plants soak up too much water, and with their removal, there will be more water for people and irrigation. Conservationists dispute the allegation, saying destruction of the plants will simply increase evaporation; the great fear, in the words of an official in the Arizona Game and Fish Department, is that Arizona will be turned into "a sterilized, paved, channelized, neatly drained state."

Another conservation issue, common to all the West but most vividly disputed in Arizona, surrounds the millions of mining claims staked by private citizens on public land. The federal mining law of 1872, a relic of pick-and-burro prospecting days, declares that "All valuable mineral deposits in lands belonging to the United States, both surveyed and unsurveyed, are hereby declared to be free and open to exploration and purchase, and the lands in which they are found to occupation and purchase, by citizens of the United States." A claimant need only file his claim in the local county courthouse, and federal officials have difficulty knowing where the claims have been made and when the law is being abused. Mining claims, according to a report by William K. Wyant in the St. Louis *Post-Dispatch*, "have been used for real estate developments, fishing cabins, even brothels." And if a prospector actually removes minerals, he need pay scarcely any money to the owners, the people of the U. S. Before leaving office as Interior Secretary in 1969, Stewart Udall called the 1872 mining law "an outright giveaway of vital national resources." The conservation issue arises when bulldozers penetrate and scar the back country, following federal law which says claimants must scar the surface—even if the minerals they seek lie thousands of feet down. In Arizona alone, there are some 1,000,000 outstanding mineral claims on public land.

Across the desert, wonders abound to draw weekenders from Phoenix and Tucson and tourists from afar. There are the great stands of saguaro and organ pipe cactus, the colorful Salt River Canyon, charming old Spanish missions, the notorious old Tombstone, the town they said was "too tough to die." Driest and lowest place on all the desert is Yuma, in far southwestern Arizona; by virtue of its summertime temperatures—120-degree days are common—Yuma is the hottest city of the U. S. A. But the Colorado River goes right by its doorstep, and by irrigation Yuma has fostered a prosperous agriculture in citrus, pecans, dates, and cotton. Amazingly, Yuma supports a population of 29,007 people and has been growing at a rapid clip. Increasing salinity of the Colorado's waters poses a future threat to the area, however.

All along the Colorado River, as it divides Arizona from California, dams have produced lakes richly stocked with fish and popular with speed-boats and water skiers. More than 35,000 boats are registered in Arizona, mostly owned by residents of Phoenix and Tucson and trailered over huge distances (sometimes as far as Lake Mead and Lake Powell in the north) for weekend and vacation fun. According to Ben Avery, the engaging out-doors writer for the Phoenix *Republic,* "nearly everybody has a housetrailer or a boat, and when they get off from work they head for the nearest mountain or lake. . . . We've become a state of year-round nomads." Fish-ing is the most popular sport of all, but almost every kind of outdoor sport seems to flourish: year-round hunting for coyotes, jack rabbits, cottontails, and mountain lions; mountain climbing; winter golf; archery; pistol and skeet shooting (Arizona has the only running deer and boar ranges in the U. S.); four-wheel drive clubs; and that modern abomination, the mountain motor bike. The state has at least three active sky-jumper groups, and an active glider club.

"Our people have become the damndest explorers you ever saw," Avery relates. Not only do they visit the Grand Canyon and the many national monuments (there are 17 monuments, more than any other state), but they love to poke around Indian ruins and isolated scenic places. "I've been here for 60 years and not seen all the spots yet," Avery says. Many Ari-zonans, he points out, have become rock hounds; the greatest prize is the agate from petrified wood, which can be found even outside the national forest. For the very adventuresome, some of this exploring is not without dangers. As Avery points out, "There are thousands of acres of isolated desert where if you get lost, you stay lost." Arizona is the location of the old Spanish Camino del Muerto—the highway of death, lined by graves.

Even the Arizonans who stick closer to home seem to spend great chunks of their time outdoors. The house without a backyard pool is some-thing of a rarity, and in hot weather city kids seem to spend more of their time under water than on top. Winter golf is one of Arizona's most popular sports. Many people have built a backyard corral and bought a horse or two for their children to ride, but even this can yield to a temptation to join the weekend exodus from the cities, since it is easy enough to buy or rent a horse trailer and head up to the mountains for camping.

If all of this is not enough to keep one amused, it is easy to take off for Mexico for the weekend. Many Phoenix and Tucson families do just that. Or for a touch of the off-beat, they can visit the London Bridge. Oil and real estate man Robert P. McCulloch spent $10 million to buy the bridge, have it shipped by ocean freight seven thousand miles across the Atlantic, through the Panama Canal, up to the West Coast, and then by truck across the mountains to his remote new development called Lake Havasu City on the Arizona-California border. There, like a great jigsaw puzzle, the old granite chunks were reapplied to a concrete shell to create a perfect restoration of the bridge London decided had to go when it began to sink into the mud of the Thames. When the deal was announced, it all sounded like a bit of a joke—but then Lake Havasu City itself was a little hard to believe when McCulloch early in the 1960s announced this entirely new, self-sustaining city (projected to have a population of 100,000 and eventual invested worth of $7 billion) on the edge of the lonely 100-square-mile lake formed by Parker Dam on the Colorado. McCulloch expects the bridge to pay off handsomely in promotion and to be a great tourist attraction—drawing, of course, more land investors to his already fast-growing city of 8,000 permanent inhabitants. With a few more Bob McCullochs on the scene, one has to feel, the nation's population redistribution problems would begin to solve themselves. (But then again, there is only one London Bridge.)

Lake Havasu City is not to be confused with the old folks' retirement communities springing up on the southwestern deserts. The McCulloch development has attracted several viable industries to provide permanent payrolls and already has a healthy school system in operation.

Arizona does harbor prominent developments exclusively for retirees—foremost in the group Del Webb's Sun City of 13,670 inhabitants 20 miles outside Phoenix. Opened in the early 1960s, Sun City consists of thousands of low, white-roofed, pastel-tinted houses built around a continuous golf course and a 33-acre artificial lake. There are three big shopping malls, a hotel, countless hobby shops, shuffleboard and other light sports facilities—but, of course, no schools. As fast as Del Webb can finish new houses (about seven a day are completed), new customers (minimum age 50) are there to fill them. Sun Citians seem delighted with their new environment, not the least sentimental about severing ties with their old communities and living away from children and grandchildren; they have exchanged all that, in the words of one observer, for "security, congenial company, and what elderly people really want most—independence." Which is not to say that all are happy (or could be anywhere); that universal bogeyman of old age, boredom, always threatens, and one hears that there is not a little quiet, desperate drinking in the kitchens.

The "Other" Arizona: The Indians

Seven out of every 100 Arizonans today are Indian, the highest percentage of any state in the Union; in raw numbers, only one state—Oklahoma—has more Indians than the 95,812 counted in Arizona by the 1970 Census. The Arizona Indian is land-rich and dollar-poor. Some 20 million acres—more than a quarter of the entire state—are set aside for his reservations; among these is the great Navajo Reservation which spills over into New Mexico and is the largest in the U.S.A. (Of the special world of the Navajos we will have more to report at the end of the New Mexico chapter.) In Arizona, it is worth noting that all privately owned, taxable land accounts for only 10.2 million acres, only half the Indian total.

The importance of Arizona to national Indian policy is reflected in the fact that some 40 percent of the Bureau of Indian Affairs' annual budget is spent in the state. Among all federal departments, more than $300 million is pumped into the Arizona Indian community in a year, covering every kind of program from education to housing to establishment of modern job-providing industries on the reservations. In one year in the late 1960s, I calculated, the federal government was spending more than $2,500 for every man, woman, and child on Arizona reservations. Yet the vast bulk of the Indians continue to live in what white America would consider desperate poverty; the failure of federal policies must be laid both to governmental bureaucracy (especially the BIA) and to the stoic resistance of the Indian to imposition of the white man's ways.

This is not to say that the educational attainments of the Indians have not been vastly improved in recent years; the young Indians of today, in the opinion of their friend Barry Goldwater, will insist on a standard of living far superior to their parents' at the same time that they learn to esteem and understand their own peculiar culture with a depth unknown since the first incursions of white "civilization."

Thirteen tribes of Indians live in Arizona, each with a distinct culture. Among the most fascinating are the Hopi, who practice communal farming and live on high mesas in the midst of the Navajo Reservation near Four Corners; unlike the nomadic Navajo, the Hopi are a stationary people, many living in homes built centuries ago. The Hopi are thought to be the oldest extant tribe in the U. S.—literally the first "Americans," and their village of Oraibi is the oldest continuously inhabited town in the country. "The wisdom and reasoning" of the Hopi, Goldwater relates, "is scarcely to be believed"; the IQ of their children is often superior to that of whites, and the young people are sought assiduously by electronics firms for complex wiring tasks.

The Hopi are deeply split between those who control the tribal council and a group of so-called traditional leaders who reject proposals for working more closely with white men. It was the tribal council which made a controversial contract with the Peabody Coal Company of St. Louis (a subsidiary of Kennecott Copper) to strip-mine a small portion of Black Mesa for coal to feed electric generating plants which are part of the huge new Western power grid, supplying current to the West Coast. The project will eventually provide employment for 375 Indians at a pay of $10,000 a year, a munificent wage on the reservation. The coal, a low-sulphur anthracite, is ground into powder, mixed with water, and sluiced through a 275-mile pipeline to a power generating plant in southern Nevada. Peabody Coal has obligated itself to undertake a model reclamation plan, refilling each strip, covering it with topsoil, and then seeding with alfalfa, sweet clover, Russian wild rye, and sand dropseed—a process which should make the land, long ravaged by erosion, better in appearance and more fertile for grazing than it had been before. But the traditional Hopi in 1971 filed a court suit to stop the strip-mining, claiming that "the process known as strip-mining is a desecration, a sacrilege, contrary to the instructions of the Great Spirit and to the essential relationship to the land that is embodied in the Hopi culture."

The Apache, descendants of the fiercest warriors of yesterday, are depicted in a state tourist booklet as "prosperous cattlemen living mostly in the rolling hills of the east central portion of the state." But Robert F. Cooley, an Apache Indian and acting superintendent of the San Carlos Reservation, reports somewhat differently: The average income of his people is about $2,000 a year for an average family of 4.4 persons, and the reservation labor force of some 1,700 able-bodied males is usually unemployed except for about 420 on permanent jobs near the reservation. "The Apaches," Cooley told reporter Robert Fenwick of the Denver *Post*, "are a segregated group—economically, socially, educationally, politically, and geographically segregated. . . . The Apache male is affected psychologically by the fact that his role as a male has been destroyed. He's a hunter and a warrior. There's nothing about holding a job that fulfills the part he feels he should play."

Some of the best and the worst conditions among Indians are to be found in Arizona, I heard from Robert L. Bennett, former Indian Commissioner (the first Indian ever to have held that post). Among the most fortunate, Bennett named the Pima Indians outside Phoenix, who have worked extensively on joint business ventures with nearby communities and established a sound economic base for themselves. At the other end of the scale, he said, are the Cocopah Indians, neglected and impoverished on their hot desert reservation near the California and Mexican borders. The Papagos, near Tucson, are another tribe in desperate straits; the life expectancy of these hard-pressed people averages only 17 years! Tiny in numbers (only 200) and living in a separate world of grim privation are the Havasupai Indians, whose reservation is set deep in the Grand Canyon of the Colorado, accessible only by helicopter or a narrow trail traversed by pack mules. Don Dedera, a columnist for the *Arizona Republic*, reported in 1968 that the average income of the Havasupai was only $25 a month and that the five "richest" Indians made no more than $1,500 a year. He told of Indian women in the throes of childbirth, struggling on foot up the miles-long canyon trail and eventually collapsing in an agonizing attempt to reach a doctor or hospital 129 miles away. Housing is of mud and cardboard—six people to a room—with dirt floors; there is no running water or sanitary facilities and "no privacy other than the dark of night." The Havasupai, Dedera insisted, are actually not happy, just stunned: "Generations of isolation, poverty and futility (and ignorance) can freeze a group into immobility."

Arizona's Indians have never been a potent political force; until 1948, indeed, they were legally barred from voting because of their "guardianship" status. After that and until the passage of the federal Civil Rights Act, literacy requirements barred many from the polls, and in any event there was lack of motivation among the inhabitants of the isolated reservations. Those Arizona Indians who have voted have generally cast Republican ballots; recently two Navajos ran, albeit unsuccessfully, for the state legislature on the Republican ticket. Apache County, in the far northeast, is two-thirds Indian, and the Indians could take control of the county government if they cared to turn out their vote. "They don't participate in our politics because they don't think much of it," Goldwater notes wryly. But he suggests that the better-educated Indians are beginning to take as much interest in state government as in their tribal government; clearly Indian political influence can only increase in the coming years.

... and the Mexicans

Arizona has the most docile and acquiescent contingent of Mexican-Americans in the Southwest, though an impatient younger generation may soon change all that. Few are of pure Castilian descent, but rather they are a fusion of Spanish and Indian blood and have for generations been the chore boys of Arizona, performing grueling stoop labor in the fields and manning the copper mines; today many are enclosed in the barrios of Phoenix and Tucson. Of Arizona's large migrant farm worker population, which is heavily Mexican, a minister for the Arizona Migrant Ministry has said: "They live out on the fringes of life, as well as the fringes of the communities. People seldom see them, and if they do, they sort of hope that somehow they're going to go away." The average Mexican or Mexican-American farm worker in Arizona was earning $48 to $90 a week in 1968, depending on the season and work available; the average factory worker in the state earned $124.

Yet responsible Anglo leaders of Arizona will blithely tell one that there is no discrimination against Mexican-Americans, that many have risen to positions of economic prominence and can freely marry whites. (To which a Southwestern newspaperwoman I know remarks, "How do you pass into a white society if your name is Joe Gonzales? Your daughter might; you never will. That's why there are so few influential male Spanish-Americans, for discrimination hits them hardest.")

Some 330,000 Arizonans, or about 19 percent of the population, are of Spanish-speaking origin, but their political influence has never been great. "Get two Mexicans in a room and you have two political parties," one hears. So instead, the Mexican-American is likely to be dependent on the Anglo political culture; from the ancient *patron* system, there is a feeling that if some small favor is done—from paving a local street to arranging a welfare check—then a special political debt is owed. Of the 90 members of the Arizona legislature, only five have Spanish surnames; by a proportionate standard, there should be at least three times as many.

The greatest barrier to Mexican-Americans in improving their lot is doubtless language; Spanish is still the native tongue in a vast proportion of their homes, and as with the French-Canadians of New England, the constant immigration and interchange with the nearby homeland tends to underscore rather than mitigate the cultural-language gap. Some 20 percent of adult Arizonans with Spanish surnames have not completed five years of schooling, and the English-speaking capacity of this group is minimal.

In Tucson I met with two Redemptionist priests, Padres Ucente Jose Soriano and Alberto Carrillo, working in a short-term intercity apostolate to try to improve the lot of the Mexican-Americans in the barrios. Education, they insisted, is the gut problem of their people, whose educational attainment is one year below that of Negroes in the region. The young Mexican-American, they said, is thrown into a school system where authorities may even put him, if he has a language problem, into a class for the retarded. On Tucson's west side, 44 percent of the children don't know English when they start school. "Talk of violence?" the priests say. "A Mexican child at six or seven is asked to speak a language he doesn't understand, and when he fails to comprehend, the 'bully Anglo culture' tells him he's dumb. No wonder he becomes hostile and hates the educational system." A new state English-training program for young Mexicans was instituted in the late 1960s, but at an annual expenditure of $25 per pupil, there was some doubt as to what would be achieved; many Mexicans would prefer instead a classroom pattern shifting gradually from Spanish to English in the first three grades, with the teachers—especially the often inflexible Southern whites on school staffs—instructed to show respect for the children's peculiar Mexican culture. Without such changes, it is argued, there will be little improvement from the current 50 percent dropout rate of Mexican youngsters from high school, or their strikingly low college attendance rate.*

Yet an amazing political sophistication, according to Padres Soriano and Carillo, is being demonstrated by the young Mexican-Americans in high school. "They are learning pride in their own Mexican culture, how to press through the verbiage of the Anglo politicians, and are determined that if there's to be law and order, the establishment must observe it too. They see how many Mexican politicians have been bought out in one way or another, and they are determined it will not happen to them. These kids will be the councilmen, mayors, and legislators of the next 20 years."

It may be so, but great obstacles—in education, political sophistication, in learning to deal with the white establishment—still remain. Some middle-class Mexicans sympathize with their young, but many more tend to withdraw in horror at the sight of the new militancy. This is especially true in Tucson, where older Mexicans can remember when their group constituted a majority of the city. Phoenix Mexicans are more likely to be immigrants themselves, and form less of a cohesive neighborhood. A measure of the

---

* Not surprisingly, the percentage of young Mexican boys drafted in Arizona is four times as high as the rate among Anglos, and they accounted for a high degree of the state's Vietnam casualties.

chasm separating the young Mexicans and the existing order is that they now like to call themselves "Chicanos." But to Barry Goldwater, "Chicano" is just "a dirty word."

Now the time has come to press on to Arizona's sister sunstate of New Mexico, which preceded her into the Union by but a few months, is so alike in geography, but so totally variant in character.

NEW MEXICO

THE GENTLE CULTURE

BEFORE JAMESTOWN OR PLYMOUTH ROCK, while most of what is today the United States slumbered through its last age of innocence, Spanish conquistadores pushed deep into New Mexico and mingled their blood with the native Indian to form what is romantically called La Raza, the New Breed, the Cosmic Race. And they began a line of governors which runs continuously—under four flags—from 1595 to the present day.

Nowhere on the American continent does history seem so deep or so immediate. Santa Fe became New Mexico's capital in 1609 or 1610 (the history books differ); its Palace of the Governors is the oldest public building in the United States. In the early 17th century, the ravages of the Inquisition were felt here. The Pueblos, whose own history goes back thousands of years before the Spanish, drove their European masters out in 1680, a situation corrected by a bloodless Hispanic reconquest a dozen years later. With Mexico's independence in 1821, New Mexico became one of her provinces; by warfare, the United States won the territory as its own in 1846. During the Civil War, the Confederate flag even flew briefly over Santa Fe. Finally, in 1912, New Mexico achieved statehood, a young 47th among the 50 we now have.

New Mexico's population was almost entirely Indian and Hispanic until the 1880s, when Anglo-Saxon ranchers and merchants began to move in. Religiously, this was to prove no great problem, since New Mexico could simply copy the Catholic-Protestant accommodations made elsewhere in Western culture. Politically, the Anglo incursion would lead to remarkable cooperation between the races. Economically, though, the Hispanos suffered through loss of many land rights at the hands of what has been well described as "a new, fast-talking, hell-for-leather culture which sought big money, lots of land, and plenty of income." As we shall note later, the land issue would be a spark for wider Hispanic revolt in recent times.

Starting around the turn of the century, the native ethnic base was further diluted by the arrival of large numbers of Texans in eastern New Mexico; the next decades also brought many migrants attracted by the dry, clean air as a way to solve their tubercular and other health problems.

Up to World War II, however, the dominant image New Mexico offered the world was still that of a sleepy land of *mañana* and *poco tiempo*. Then at first secretly, came the great change. From the laboratories at Los Alamos emerged the first atomic bomb, to be detonated in the early morning hours of July 16, 1945, on the desert north of Alamagordo. Perfecting, building, and storing nuclear weapons and working on other atomic research, a whole civilization of scientists and technicians has been transplanted onto New Mexican soil. At Los Alamos they *are* the town; at Albuquerque they have populated the fast-growing Eastern Heights section, adding a substantial new kind of population which is transforming the state's politics. But the new settlers have not come, like the swarms of migrants to Arizona and California, to obliterate the old culture. The humor, the charm of the Spanish-American, the dignity of the Indian culture, has been too strong to permit that. In some of the pueblos, life has been going on continuously for more than 30,000 years. As Neil Morgan has observed,

> The sense of timelessness overwhelms; it is so obviously bigger than the invasion of any single wave of culture that it is a cohesive force. . . . The New Mexico in-migrant does not think for a moment that he will change the land; there is too much evidence all around him that others have tried for thousands of years, without effect.

In such a civilization, men are expected to live in peace and mutual respect with their brothers, and while this is not universally the case in New Mexico, it is most often so. David Boroff has written that the word "ethnic" is "something of a cult word in New Mexico," meaning "respect—even reverence—for other cultures in the area. It means liberalism, sophistication, and charms of the primitive." Even if the native Indian or Hispano finds himself at the bottom of the economic totem pole, it is still fair to speak of New Mexico, as Boroff does, as "a decent state and a humane one." New Mexicans see themselves as less self-aggrandizing than their Texan or Arizonan neighbors, and they have a strong tradition of civil liberties written into their state constitution, adopted in 1910, which declares:

The right of any citizen of the state to vote, hold office or sit upon juries, shall never be restricted, abridged or impaired on account of religion, race, language or color, or inability to speak, read or write the English or Spanish languages. . . .

The McCarthyism of the 1950s, for instance, found scarcely any support in New Mexico.

Six population groups appear significant in New Mexico: Spanish-American, Pueblo Indian, Navajo Indian, Mormon, Texan, and Anglo. For the most part, however, New Mexicans use "Anglo" as a catch-all encompassing real Anglo-Saxons, Jews, Chinese, or anybody else without some native New Mexican blood (Indian or Spanish) in his veins. Regarding the Spanish term, an early word of caution is required: it is *not* synonymous with the term Mexican-American used throughout the rest of the Southwest. Some of the state's more militant young Hispanos have taken to calling themselves Chicanos, or identifying with Mexican stock elsewhere, but the great bulk of Spanish-speaking peoples in New Mexico have no more association with the nation south of the border than the fact that their ancestors passed through there many generations ago. Of actual first- and second-generation Mexicans in New Mexico, there are relatively few (26,770 in 1970)—only a fraction, the Census figures show, of the number in California or Texas.

Since the start of World War II, the population balance has veered so sharply toward the Anglos that the count of New Mexicans with Spanish surnames is now just 26 percent in a total population of 1,016,000—down from 45 percent in a population of 531,818 in 1940. As the Anglos have poured into New Mexico, many young people of Spanish stock have migrated outward, mostly to California. Today, the Indians represent 7 percent of the New Mexico population, so that together with the Hispanic, they account for a 33 percent native population, compared to 65 percent Anglo and 2 percent Negro. Thus New Mexico necessarily takes on many of the political and cultural characteristics of other Western states. But still, there is that vital and unique legacy of the Spanish civilization that lived here, isolated and an island to itself, for so many generations.

Land of Enchantment

Few state nicknames are more aptly chosen than New Mexico's "Land of Enchantment." True, much of the landscape is harsh, unredeemed desert, and across the eastern reaches there are endless miles where the wind sweeps unchecked across the bunch grass. But by the same token, there are deep, picturesque canyons and vividly hued mesas, buttes, and rock terraces. Their reds and yellows, when the sun strikes them in favorable perspectives, are as otherworldly and hauntingly beautiful as any scene on the North American continent. And at night, in John Gunther's words, there is "the purple desert flowing endlessly under lonely stars."

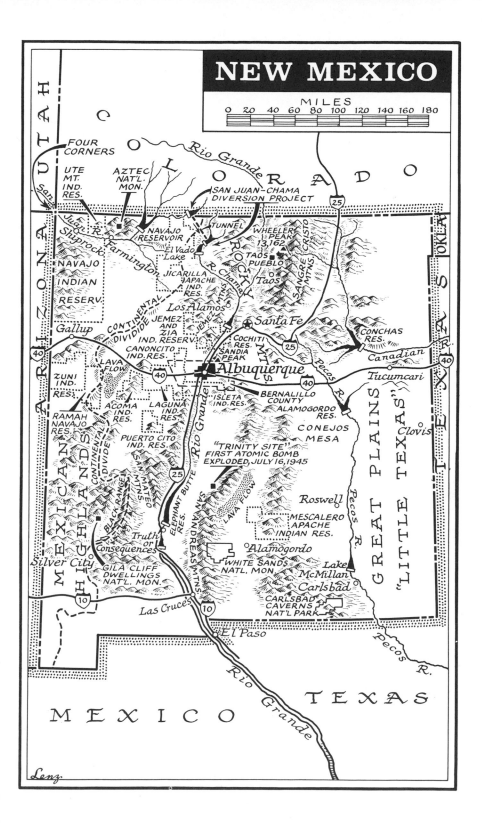

NEW MEXICO

MILES
0 20 40 60 80 100 120 140 160 180

UTAH

ARIZONA

COLORADO

OKLA.

TEXAS

FOUR CORNERS
UTE MT. IND. RES.
AZTEC NAT'L. MON.
Rio Grande
SAN JUAN-CHAMA DIVERSION PROJECT
San Juan R.
Shiprock
Farmington
NAVAJO RESERVOIR
TUNNEL
El Vado Lake
R. Chama
WHEELER PEAK 13,162
TAOS PUEBLO
SANGRE CRISTO MTNS.
Taos
JICARILLA APACHE IND. RES.
NAVAJO INDIAN RESERV.
ROCKY
CONTINENTAL DIVIDIDE
Los Alamos
JEMEZ AND ZIA IND. RESERV.
Gallup
CANONCITO IND. RES.
COCHITI RES.
SANDIA PEAK
CONCHAS RES.
Santa Fe
MTS.
Pecos R.
Canadian R.
LAVA FLOW
ZUNI IND. RES.
Albuquerque
Tucumcari
ACOMA IND. RES.
LAGUNA IND. RES.
ISLETA IND. RES.
BERNALILLO COUNTY
ALAMOGORDO RES.
RAMAH NAVAJO RES.
CONTINENTAL DIVIDE
PUERTO CITO IND. RES.
CONEJOS MESA
Clovis
Rio Grande
"TRINITY SITE" FIRST ATOMIC BOMB EXPLODED, JULY 16, 1945
SAN MATEO MTS.
Black Range
Roswell
GREAT PLAINS "LITTLE TEXAS"
MESCALERO APACHE INDIAN RES.
Pecos R.
Truth or Consequences
ELEPHANT BUTTE RES.
SAN ANDREAS MTNS.
LAVA FLOW
MEXICAN HIGHLANDS
Alamogordo
Silver City
GILA CLIFF DWELLINGS NAT'L. MON.
WHITE SANDS NAT'L. MON.
Lake McMillan
Carlsbad
Las Cruces
CARLSBAD CAVERNS NAT'L PARK
El Paso
Pecos R.

MEXICO

Rio Grande

TEXAS

Lenz

Geologic ages have subjected the land of New Mexico to great uplifts and displacements of the earth's crust. At one extreme, in the southeast, where the land dips to less than 3,000 feet over sea level, the summers are intolerably hot, and where there is sufficient moisture there may even be subtropical flora and fauna.

In the north, the mountains ascend to heights of more than 13,000 feet, yet few pass timberline or reach the level of eternal snow. These are the southernmost of the Rockies, somehow softer and mellower than their younger, more jagged neighbors to the north. Among these mountains, the coolest life zone of New Mexico, lie fabled Santa Fe, Los Alamos, characterful Taos, and dozens of little hardscrabble Spanish villages and Indian pueblos where life continues much as it did centuries ago. This is Rio Grande Valley country, named in honor of that sparse but famous river, so thoroughly dammed up and diverted for agriculture that its flow is no more than waist-high most of the year. The Rio Grande runs centrally on a north-south course from the Colorado border in the north to Mexico in the south. The Rio Grande area most celebrated and most visited stretches from Taos down to Albuquerque in center state, a valley floor some 40 miles wide and 160 miles long guarded by the Sangre de Cristo Mountains on the east, the Jemez on the west, and the Sandia Peaks near Albuquerque on the south. Writer Oliver La Farge refers to this as a valley of "special magic" where "for thousands of years people have been drawn and stayed in the slow, sunlit peace between the mountains."

South of Albuquerque, one speaks of the Lower Valley of the Rio Grande, or Rio Abajo; here the river courses into hotter and lower territory, near the region the Spanish called Jornada del Muerto (Journey of Death), where, fittingly, the first atomic bomb was detonated. This is also the territory of New Mexico's famed White Sands. Little Spanish farm villages and Indian Pueblos recur along the valley, and more and more irrigation farming has been attempted. Finishing its course through New Mexico, the Rio Grande passes Las Cruces and exits past El Paso to veer eastward and form the Texas border with Mexico.

While most of New Mexico's people, life, and history have always been along the central north-south strip of the Rio Grande, there are other and distinct regions both to the east and west. In northwestern New Mexico one discovers the bleak Four Corners territory left to the Navajos on their reservation atop the Colorado Plateau, shared with Arizona; of this land the New Mexican authors George Fitzpatrick and John Sinclair have written:

Nowhere is the drama of geology, mythology and romance so strikingly entwined. . . . Here the mountains meet the deserts; the remnant-blisters of tortured ages of volcanic violence—knobs and plugs and bulges—mark the land.

Shiprock . . . is the most dramatic and best known landmark of this broad terrain. Towering nearly 2,000 feet above the surrounding mesa, . . . early white settlers likened it to a ship under full sail. But to the Navajos, on whose reservation it stands, it is the Rock With Wings. It was this great bird that brought them from faraway lands over wide waters to this new country, where now it stands guard over them for all time.

Also tucked into northwestern New Mexico is the fertile valley of the San Juan, flowing down from the Rockies, an area long celebrated for its apples and peaches and other products of the irrigated soil, in more recent years an important oil-producing area. Farmington is the chief city. In the lands south of the Navajo Reservation and west of the Rio Grande, bordered on the west by Arizona, lie the gaunt Mexican Highlands with their desert plains and forbidding mountains. It is a land of few people, except in Gallup, Silver City, and smaller towns along the occasional river valleys; this is Continental Divide country, the locale of many ghost mining towns but also most of New Mexico's modern-day uranium, copper, and zinc production.

Finally, there is the spacious, level country of "Little Texas" that occupies most of eastern New Mexico. This is essentially a Great Plains area like neighboring Texas and Oklahoma, with irrigation farming along the Pecos River. Texas ranchers and farmers began to pour into this territory around the turn of the century; their input has been Baptist, Democratic, conservative, sometimes even "Birchist." They began to challenge the dominance of New Mexico's native peoples and also brought the first serious ethnic prejudices to the state. A lively animosity between the Texas-born and other New Mexicans infected the state's life for several decades, with traces of bitterness to this day. Aside from wheat, Little Texas is heavy with oil rigs, an industry centered in towns like Roswell and Hobbs. At Carlsbad, vast quantities of potash are mined. But even here New Mexico offers some enchantment; one finds it principally underground in the limestone cave formations at Carlsbad, so spectacular they were declared a national park.

A postscript to this geographic tour: when one thinks of the Land of Enchantment, one should remember its immensity and its aridity. Only four other states have more land area or a more lightly scattered population. In California there are 15 times as many people in each square mile, in New Jersey 113 times as many. And of all 50 states, none has as small a portion of its land surface in lakes and rivers as New Mexico—a minuscule .002 percent.

Life Styles and Politics: The Hispanic Ingredient

New Mexico politics tend to be intense and personal, stemming from the state's small population and unique ethnic combinations. As one observer put it some years ago, "Politics here can be viewed as the illegitimate product of the worst of the Anglo tradition as exemplified in the Tweed Ring and the worst of the Spanish tradition as practiced by the decayed *patron* system." Spoils politics was long rampant, and for many years state employees were regularly assessed about 2 percent of their salaries for the party in power. Enactment of state personnel acts in the early 1960s, however, has reduced the possibilities for spoils.

New Mexico never had powerful statewide political organizations, but rather a complex of family and political alliances that dictated choices at the polls. The late Will Harrison, a distinguished state newsman, wrote a syndicated column so immersed in the web of personal loyalties and rivalries that no outsider could comprehend it. Harrison delighted, though, in telling the story of the night when the Associated Press, trying to smoke out the returns from the Spanish-American precincts in the mountainous north, set up special election wires. "How many votes you got up there?" an AP reporter asked at one point during the evening. Back came the reply, in a native voice: "How many you need?"

Old-fashioned vote stealing seems to be on the decline, helped along by the advent of voting machines. The last great rhubarb over the outcome of an election was in 1952, when Democrat Dennis Chávez defeated Republican Patrick A. Hurley by an announced margin of some 5,000 votes. Hurley contested the election, and, as Morgan reports the incident:

Before the fun was over, a United States Senate committee had probed and condemned New Mexico election procedures. Registration books had turned up in unexpected crannies, some with torn, burned and water-smeared pages, and ballots had been burned. One ballot box, its keys locked inside, was opened in front of a bevy of witnesses; inside, observers found only the keys and a *ristra*, the string of red chili peppers used so widely in New Mexico both as food and decoration.

Even a decade later, there were 13 New Mexico counties with more registered voters than adults in the Census count, and one county, Guadalupe, even managed to cast more votes in 1960 than it had inhabitants 21 or over.

The anthropologists and sociologists have had a field day in analyzing the life style of the rural Spanish communities which gave New Mexico politics, especially in earlier days, so much of its special flavor. According to one account *

Villages were not only isolated from centers of civilization in Spain and Mexico, but from each other. . . . The village economy was semicommunal. Land was cultivated by large family groups incorporating several generations. . . . The economic unit was the community, not the individual. Within the semicommunal village, family and church were the dominant institutions. Family and village often tended to be almost synonomous, while religion—a devout Catholicism—was the center, the core of all institutional activity. The third institution was the *patron* system. A large landowner, a person of wealth, an influential politician—anyone with prestige, power, resources, and a sense of obligation toward a given community might become a *patron*. . . . Margaret Mead sees the *patron* as the link between the village and the larger community. . . . A picture emerges of . . . local one-party dominance maintained by the *patron* in his role of father figure and conservator of village solidarity.

* By Jack E. Holmes, in *Politics in New Mexico*, summarizing the analyses of others.

Political scientist Jack E. Holmes takes some exception to this standard interpretation, pointing out that rather viable two-party competition, rather than *patron* dictation, has long been the pattern in areas where Hispanos constituted a substantial majority of the population. The more important factor, he suggests, is that in New Mexico—as opposed to Texas, Arizona, or Colorado—the Spanish-Americans, where they have the numerical power, confidently take over the local government and run it, rather than meekly deferring to the local Anglo power structure. This indeed is the distinguishing factor of Hispanic politics in New Mexico. One will hear a lot of jocularity, as I did from one newspaper publisher, about the Spanish-American being the result of "a conquistador and an Indian girl who couldn't run fast enough." But that was a long time ago, and the state has its large class of prominent Hispanic families who have never borne the cross of minority discrimination or developed any kind of inferiority complex in regard to others. They are a proud people, accustomed to roles of leadership. Spanish-speaking New Mexicans, in fact, have often emigrated to other states to become prominent Hispanic leaders there, carrying with them a political poise and self-confidence so notably lacking among large portions of Mexican-Americans. For instance, California's first Hispanic Congressman, Ed Roybal, is a native of New Mexico, as is Dolores Huerta, César Chávez's right-hand aide in the farm labor movement. (In the same way, West Indian blacks, possessed of similar cultural advantages, have rapidly risen to the top ranks of American Negro leadership.) When the son or daughter of a prominent New Mexico Hispanic family marries outside native ranks, the Spanish family may well have the attitude that it is doing the others a favor.

Still, there is no denying that the *patron* system often led to a unique brand of rural machine politics. No less an authority than Ruby A. Ortiz, Democratic chairman of Bernalillo County, told me of continuing situations in northern New Mexico where one *patron* will have 40 to 50 votes controlled in his "family." Nor is there much denying that a lot of cash passes hands in New Mexico elections. As a factor in state politics, however, this may be declining; civil service reduces the incentive for payoffs, and especially among younger Hispanos, there is a recognition that if the politicians can "buy" the vote of a family or town, they will have no obligation to do anything to help it until the time comes for another payoff in another election. Now there are a number of attractive Hispanic political leaders who can draw a strong vote in the small villages, regardless of how the *patron* may feel about them.

Early in this century, the rural Spanish vote averaged around 60 percent Republican; with the coming of the New Deal and the passage of time, it turned more toward the Democrats, although it will still switch freely back to the Republicans, especially if the Republican candidate is Hispanic himself or makes a special bid for Spanish support. Where Spanish-Americans migrate to the cities or other areas with an Anglo majority, they tend to register and vote heavily Democratic, reflecting their underdog status. But urban Hispanos have not become politically quiescent; generally they turn out in far greater numbers in city primaries than do the Anglos. The bulk of major Spanish-American officeholders in recent years have been Democrats, but in 1968 and again in 1970, an attractive Hispano, Manuel Lujan, was elected to Congress on the Republican ticket from the northern New Mexico district. New Mexico has not had a Spanish-American governor since 1921, but the Hispanic contingent in the state legislature is substantial, ranging generally between 20 and 30 percent of the seats. No other state legislature has a comparable percentage of minority group members. Usually, one of the two U. S. Senators and one of the two Congressmen from the state will be Spanish-American, likewise a record of minority group representation which no other state can match.

Yet while Spanish-Americans have at the upper echelons moved so far in New Mexico politics, the festering sores of old injustices produced in the 1960s a strange and revolutionary folk movement in the very same rugged uplands of northern New Mexico where settled village *patron* politics so long flourished. For decades, the Spanish-speaking townspeople of this region have nursed bitter resentments about the fashion in which the old "Santa Fe Ring" of Anglo and upper-class Hispano politicians succeeded in taking from them, by taxation, fraud, theft, and in some cases legal purchase, the vast land grants made by the Spanish crown in colonial times and guaranteed by the Treaty of Guadalupe Hidalgo at the end of the Mexican-American War. Now the best farm and ranchland is in the hands of blue-eyed Anglos; as for larger grazing lands, most of them are controlled by the National Forest Service, which in drought times may cut back severely on grazing rights in its territory, thus eliminating virtually the only source of income for the Hispanic townspeople. In huge, rural Rio Arriba County, ranging northwesterly from a few miles north of Santa Fe to the Colorado border, the descendants of the proud Andalusian pioneers find themselves living in squalid adobe shacks, many with raw tarpaper walls and tin roofs. The scenery of red-tinged mountains, mesas, and buttes may be spectacular, but in 1970 34 percent of the people had incomes below the federally established poverty level, compared to 19 percent in the state as a whole. Of the county's 25,170 people (20,691 of them Spanish-American), less than a third aged 25 or more had finished high school. Fifty-eight percent of the dwelling units lacked some or all plumbing facilities.

Yet the Hispanic people are traditionally placid and long-suffering, and the situation might never have come to the attention of the outside world had it not been for a single individual of rare charisma—Reies Lopez Tijerina, a Texan native of Mexican extraction and onetime Pentecostal minister, who came to Rio Arriba County early in the 1960s, seized upon the land issue, and began his revolutionary *Alianza Federal los Pueblos Libres*— Federal Alliance of Free City-States. For the poor Hispanic peasants, Tijerina painted a glowing picture of ancestral lands returned to them; the movement, Joseph L. Love wrote, included "such diverse phenomena as peasant anarchism, banditry, and millennarianism (the belief that divine justice and retribution is on the side of the rebels and that the millennium is at hand.)"

Guns in hand, Tijerina and his followers in 1966 laid physical claim to part of the Carson National Forest in northern New Mexico; then, a year later, came the violent "courthouse raid" at the town of Tierra Amarilla, where armed men attacked the Rio Arriba courthouse, shot and wounded two officers, and took two hostages. The New Mexico establishment, which had previously ignored Tijerina's demands for return of the ancestral lands, reacted with a widespread manhunt using National Guard armored vehicles; the civil rights of many Hispanic villagers were allegedly abused, but Tijerina could not be found. Eventually, he and several *Alianzans* were arrested and tried. Tijerina, who had been known as *abogado sin libros* (lawyer without books) in his youth, dismissed his attorney and conducted a flamboyant, arm-swinging defense in his own behalf—and won a stunning acquittal. Later, however, he was tried on related charges and served two years (1969 to 1971) in federal prison.

By that time, however, the *Alianza* had gone far beyond Tijerina. A number of his followers were involved in a 1969 Chicano Youth Liberation Conference in Denver organized by militant Denver Hispano leader Rudolph ("Corky") Gonzales; out of the conference came a petition to President Nixon demanding that all of New Mexico and Colorado, plus vast areas of California and Arizona, be returned to the Chicano people. Tijerina angrily divorced himself from this demand and resigned as head of the *Alianza,* writing from his jail cell: "My motto is Justice, not Independence or Revolution." Yet it was indisputable that Tijerina's less cosmic land demands had inspired the militant young Hispanos of New Mexico (who now dismissed Tijerina as unstable) to radical new courses of action with unforeseeable consequences. The task of confronting the establishment fell to new groups like the Black Berets in Albuquerque and La Gente in Santa Fe. Any establishment Anglo or Spanish-American politician in New Mexico will say that Tijerina's movements and its offshoots have negligible support, and in terms of numbers they are doubtless correct. But at the same time, it seems likely that Hispano-Anglo relations in New Mexico will never be quite the same again.

Tripartite Politics and Senatorial Patrons

Let the reader be warned: the real power of modern New Mexico lies not with the Hispanic peoples, however unique and romantic their story may be, but rather with the more prosaic Anglos who outnumber them so conclusively. Politically, the state may be regarded as tripartite—Spanish-American, Texan, and post-World-War-II Anglo.

As the bulk of the Spanish votes drifts into the Democratic column, a traditional Democratic base—Little Texas along the state's eastern border —moves toward the Republicans, much in the style of nearby Oklahoma and Texas, and apparently for many of the same economic and racial reasons discernible in those states. The Republicans began serious Little Texas breakthroughs with Presidential victories in the 1950s, and in 1968 followed up by casting the crucial vote to send a conservative Republican, Ed Foreman, to the U. S. House. Foreman, in fact, had actually represented a Texas district in Washington a few years previously. During his first congressional incarnation, Foreman was not only a zealous, pugnacious right-winger, but engaged in a fist fight with a Democrat on the House floor; representing New Mexico, he managed to hold his conservative temper in check but was narrowly defeated for reelection in 1970. Republican victories in local races in Little Texas appear increasingly likely in the next few years. The city of Roswell in Little Texas is the home base of New Mexico's wealthiest man, oilman Robert O. Anderson, who built a $1 million inheritance from his Chicago banker father into a present-day fortune of some $150 million. He is reputed to own more land than any other man in America. Senator Clinton Anderson told me that Robert Anderson (no relation) is "a smart, nice person," but added ruefully that "most of his political money goes to the Republicans."

The third great vote block, the postwar influx of technocratic emigrés centered on the East Heights of Albuquerque, is moderately Republican and moderately conservative in its voting habits. This is the most dynamic area of New Mexico in population growth, making long-term Republican prospects in the state bright indeed. Notwithstanding its substantial Hispanic minority, Albuquerque and surrounding Bernalillo County in 1968 cast a 55 percent vote for Nixon for President—well above the statewide vote of 51 percent cast for the Republican ticket. A similar 55 percent for Nixon was cast at Los Alamos, home of the nuclear elite, and in Little Texas. Thus New Mexico, despite its unusual ethnic history and mix, appears to move toward a realignment of voters familiar elsewhere. The poor, Hispanic, and Catholic areas, or those with large numbers of miners and other laborers, become Democratic; the wealthier, technologically oriented areas, along with prosperous oil and farm territory, move Republican. But communities like the Albuquerque Heights and Los Alamos, while Republican by inclination, also love to split their tickets; New Mexico seems likely to reproduce little of the Republican monotony that has developed in neighboring Arizona.

Since it joined the Union, New Mexico has never failed to support the winner in a Presidential election. Its small number of electoral votes. excludes it from major attention in Presidential campaigns, though the new Presidential primary, a preference poll held for the first time in 1972, began to increase its importance in national politics. In state elections, the state started out in the Republican camp, moved toward two-partyism in the 1920s, and then went solidly Democratic for years following the advent of the New Deal. In that long Democratic era, only one Republican—Edwin Mechem—won more than a single statewide victory. A staunch conservative and competent administrator, Mechem was elected four times as governor but only once for a consecutive term; apparently New Mexican voters viewed him as a handy instrument to effect an occasional cleansing of the Augean stables at Santa Fe. Concluding his last gubernatorial term in the early 1960s, Mechem arranged to have himself appointed to a vacant U. S. Senate seat, but the voters promptly ousted him in the next election. The state legislature, except for a one-vote Republican House margin in 1952, has been solidly Democratic since early New Deal days. And from the mid-1930s to 1968, New Mexico sent solid Democratic delegations to Congress.

A shift to real two-partyism seemed to be heralded by the 1966 elections, when the Republicans not only elected David F. Cargo, a liberal young attorney, to the governorship but also captured several other statewide posts. In 1968 they continued their winning streak by ousting the two veteran Democratic U. S. House members from the state. Cargo, a maverick and erratic figure especially detested by the right wing of his own party, won another term as governor in 1968 but two years later was defeated by a conservative primary opponent when he sought to become U. S. Senator. The 1970 election saw a Democratic sweep of all major offices at stake, except for the massive plurality Manuel Lujan achieved in winning reelection to Congress from the northern district. The new Democratic governor elected in 1970, Bruce King, was a former speaker of the state house of representatives and member of an old ranching family in Santa Fe County.

Extensive discussion of New Mexico's governors would be beside the point, for their powers are strictly limited, and none in recent years could be considered a "great" leader. The central power in New Mexico politics lies with its congressional delegation, and especially the two U. S. Senators; they are the real *patrons* of the state today, and have been for many decades. The reason for this rather unusual state of affairs is deceptively simple: New Mexico, on its own, lacks many of the attributes of a viable economy. Its independent industrial base is almost negligible. Without federal aid, from reclamation projects to the gigantic infusions of dollars for atomic and space contracts, New Mexico would lose population at an alarming rate, descending to the status of a kind of Afghanistan of North America. All eyes are on the Washington delegation, to keep the federal dollars flowing.

Fortuitously, the state has had exceptionally qualified Senators over many decades, distinguished not only by their ability to obtain federal appropriations but by their sympathy for the underprivileged and skill at manipulating the jungle-like factions of New Mexico politics. Republican-Progressive Bronson Cutting, described by John Gunther as "one of the ablest Senators the country has had in this century," controlled major segments of the New Mexico press, had his own influential faction operating in the state legislature, and worked effectively to obtain a significant share of political nominations for Spanish-Americans. Democrat Carl A. Hatch, a reformer of the old school, sponsored the landmark Hatch Act for the regulation of political activity by government employees.

New Mexicans consider the late Senator Dennis Chávez as the man principally responsible for the outpouring of federal projects into the state in the postwar period and hold him in such reverence that they had his statue erected in Statuary Hall at the U. S. Capitol. Much of Chávez's power came from his chairmanship of the Defense Appropriations Subcommittee. A diminutive figure of uncanny political skills, Chávez was born into a poor family at Los Chavez, worked his way through college and law school, won a term in the U. S. House in the early 1930s, and then in 1935 was appointed to the Senate seat vacated by Cutting's death, surviving through five subsequent elections until his death in 1963. An accomplished speaker in both English and Spanish, he was popular not only in the Hispanic north (where he helped clean up some of the less savory political conditions) but also on the Texan east side counties for which he helped obtain a number of military installations. "Chávez's tactics were not always open and above board, but he was very effective for New Mexico," one of his admirers told me, adding: "When he died, his estate was only about $150,000, indicating that he'd done a lot more for the state than for himself." Former Repulican Governor Tom Bolack credits Democrat Chávez as being "a man truly for the poor folks" who also got federal loans and grants to save Farmington (Bolack's home town) at a crucial point. In each election, Chávez had a handpicked man for governor; if his candidate lost the Democratic primary, he would give sub rosa support to the Republican—the major reason, it is widely believed, for many of Mechem's gubernatorial victories.

Clinton P. Anderson must be accounted one of the most creative legislators ever to serve in Congress. A native of South Dakota, he arrived in New Mexico at the age of 22, ill and weak from tuberculosis. He was soon cured, and as a reporter for one of the Albuquerque papers, played an important role in uncovering the Teapot Dome scandal of the 1920s. Anderson also became a successful businessman, served in prominent state and federal jobs in New Mexico in the 1930s, and then went to the U. S. House in 1941, where he served for two terms. In 1945 President Truman appointed him Secretary of Agriculture, and in 1949 he went to the U. S. Senate, where he was to remain for more than two decades, rising to heights of power and influence equaled by few in his time. Anderson is a kindly man of impeccable honor but also—as his longtime antagonist, Lewis Strauss, would learn to his sorrow in the late 1950s—a wily and tough opponent, and one who keeps grudges.*

Anderson played old-style politics in New Mexico, working just through

* Anderson had tangled repeatedly with Strauss when the latter was chairman of the Atomic Energy Commission, especially over the controversial Dixon-Yates contract, and Anderson led the Senate battle to reject Strauss's nomination as Secretary of Commerce, the first Senate rejection of a Presidential cabinet appointment since 1925.

the people at the top and getting his man elected governor in election after election by withholding his endorsement in the Democratic primary until a crucial point and then throwing the extra needed support to the candidate he liked—and thought could win. Anderson's greater contribution to the state, however, was to take up where Chávez had left off the fight for atomic, space, and military installations in New Mexico. In a 1970 interview, Anderson told me he had been able to block the removal of many projects from New Mexico "on a personal basis." A review of Anderson's committee assignments—chairman of the Senate Space Committee, chairman in several Congresses of the Joint Atomic Energy Committee, and second-ranking Democrat on Interior and Finance—is testimony of his power.

But it is in the water and conservation field, not scientific-military establishments, in which Anderson takes the most pride and feels he has made the most lasting contribution to his state. He was floor manager of many successful reclamation bills, including the Upper Colorado River storage project enacted in 1956 and the Navajo-San Juan projects for New Mexico, approved in 1962, providing irrigation for Navajo lands and transmountain diversion of Colorado River water into the Rio Grande Valley. Colorado River water is expected to start flowing toward Albuquerque in the mid-1970s and will, in Anderson's words, "assure us a lifetime supply of water" and the potentiality of continued growth in the state. "It will be more important than all the Sandia [nuclear] plants," Anderson told me; "once the water supply is guaranteed, you're home safe."

Anderson's other notable achievements—most of as much importance to America as a whole as to New Mexico in particular—have ranged from authorship of Medicare legislation (including the creative concept of placing it under Social Security to avoid a vast new administrative bureaucracy) to creation of water research centers in all the states, each tied, at Anderson's suggestion, to the state land grant college in order to neutralize conservative opposition. To these could be added his fight for flexible rather than rigid farm price supports, battles for wilderness legislation and Indian rights, a successful effort to modify the Senate filibuster rule, and of course guidance of the entire U. S. space program through his Space Committee chairmanship.

Aging and in ill health, Anderson decided not to seek reelection in 1972. His slot as senior Senator will then be filled by Democratic Senator Joseph Montoya, possessor of sterling Hispanic-liberal credentials and practitioner of an old favors-for-friends politics frowned on by many of the emerging new forces in New Mexico politics. In 1968, Montoya tried to dictate selection of a Humphrey-pledged delegation to the Democratic National Convention. But a group of younger McCarthy-Kennedy oriented "peace" Democrats, centered in Albuquerque, Santa Fe, and Las Cruces, fought him to a near draw; within a year Montoya had been transformed from "hawk" to "dove" on the Vietnam war. After a campaign in which he stressed his classic liberalism and long list of legislative proposals, Montoya won his 1970 reelection campaign with 52.3 percent of the vote.* He holds key Appropriations and Public Works Committee assignments of no little importance to New Mexico.

Government: Lobby-Ridden and Inefficient

Politics used to be a closed business in New Mexico, and the state was run by what was called "the Third House," a group of lobbyists who met in the old De Vargas Hotel. But the old gangs have been broken up.
        —*John Gunther,* Inside U. S. A.

Just how thoroughly politics and government have been reconstructed in New Mexico, traditionally a high-tax and high-corruption state, is open to question. Progress has certainly been made through institution of civil service, excising the worst of the old spoils system. But even though taxes per capita are among the highest in the country, the actual delivery of services to the people is jeopardized by a creaky form of broad- and special commission-laden government that requires extraordinary numbers of state employees for its administration. The legislature appears to be one of the most professionally staffed in the country, especially for a lightly populated state, but powerful new lobbies—ranging from schoolteachers to liquor dealers to banks and truckers—have arisen to take the place of the corrupt old railroad lobbies and the cattle barons. Nor should an obituary yet be written for the cattlemen; while reapportionment has diluted their power (cattle growers held 38 percent of the legislative seats as recently as 1957), they are still able to get through an amazing number of bills favorable to their special interests.

In a perceptive account of New Mexico politics today, Harry P. Stumpf and T. Phillip Wolf have reported that assorted business groups have assured themselves, through manipulation of the legislature, such a favored position that a substantial portion of business in the state is noncompetitive. Not only do fair trade laws maintain liquor prices at an artificially high level (encouraging many New Mexicans to buy their spirits in adjoining states) "but transportation and a host of other enterprises also use the states many commissions and boards to fix prices." The *New Mexico Bluebook* of 1965–66 listed 136 state agencies which regulate trades or professions normally in the private sector. Examples were the Liquified Petroleum Gas Commission, the Peanut Commission, the Dry Cleaning Board, and the Plumbing Administrative Board.

Wayne Scott of the Albuquerque *Journal* reported from Santa Fe in

---

* The *National Observer*'s James M. Perry, who watched Montoya on the stump, noted that "Little Joe" has a flamboyant, arm-waving speaking style. Like Dennis Chávez, he speaks two languages. "When he speaks in English, Montoya is pompous and bombastic. When he speaks in Spanish, he is earthy and ebullient."

1965: "Youngsters who sell newspapers and rake leaves . . . may have to secure state licenses if the current trend of legislation continues." He noted that the legislature had just approved two more licensing boards (for psychologists and photographers), had a third vetoed by the governor (to license septic-tank cleaners), and was then considering licensing of TV repairmen, piano players, marriage counselors, and pesticide applicators. Stumpf and Wolf commented:

> When activities which are protected from direct price competition are added to those actually undertaken and financed by government, perhaps only one-fourth to one-third of New Mexico's economy operates in terms of traditional free enterprise. The question may properly be asked if New Mexico does not have a kind of economic socialism for private gain.

Bearing in mind the dubious cost effectiveness of New Mexico state government, it may be reported that the state ranks ninth in the U. S. A. in the relative tax effort of its people related to personal income, and in terms of spending, also related to income; second among all the states in education; sixth in public welfare; 11th in highways, and 25th in health and hospitals. But the welfare load is so heavy that the average monthly payment for a family with dependent children is $37 below the national average, or 34th among the states. Sales, luxury, minerals severance, and income taxes all add substantially to the state treasury, the income tax having been increased several-fold in the late 1960s. Few states, however, have such serious problems in actually getting the people to pay income taxes; the rate of evasion in the mid-1960s was said to run about 15 percent. The minerals severance tax is an important source of income, and the Albuquerque *Journal* has long urged it should be increased, a step successfully resisted by the powerful oil and gas lobby. Finally, it should be mentioned that the state's financial picture is substantially sweetened by the input of federal grant dollars, which is 90 percent higher than the per capita average in the rest of the country.

A major effort to revamp the rather outmoded state constitution was made by a constitutional convention in 1969. The delegates recommended switching to a short ballot with four- instead of two-year terms for the governor, consolidation of 300 administrative boards and units into a 20-agency cabinet, and to permit municipal home rule charter. Albuquerque voted overwhelmingly in favor of the new constitution, but the rest of the state went against it so strongly that it lost narrowly. Thus it may be years before the government in Santa Fe is finally able to put its house in order.

Among the interesting lobby victories of recent years has been the success of the truckers in getting approval of a "big truck bill" permitting twin-trailers and high weights; a toy model of one of the big "double bottoms," I discovered, adorns Senator Anderson's office in Washington. New Mexico also has highly militant teachers' unions—the National Education Association and American Federation of Teachers, sometimes quarreling bitterly between themselves. A teachers' strike was staged in Albuquerque in

1968, and the education lobby has persuaded the state, though personal income ranks only 43rd among the states, to finance its local schools at one of the highest per capita rates in the country. Yet the quality purchased has not been uniformly high, as evidenced by continued double sessions, the absence of kindergartens, and the fact that over 60 percent of the state's high schools have not been regionally accredited. New Mexico youngsters do not have special difficulty in gaining acceptance to good universities, however.

The state's several public universities and junior colleges are also accorded generous state financing. The largest of them are the University of New Mexico at Albuquerque and New Mexico State University at Las Cruces; of the former I heard from some longtime state observers that it was "a good B-minus university" with outstanding departments in anthropology and Latin American studies but weaknesses in some of the basic sciences. New Mexico State is considered by many superior in agriculture and technical fields; it pioneered, for instance, in a master's degree course in pure computer techniques. Thomas Popejoy, who did a creditable job as president of the University of New Mexico for 20 years up to the late 1960s, was rated locally as an "excellent politician who had the good sense to let the faculty take care of the academic field while he concentrated on the business end and lobbying the legislature for funds." Under Popejoy, the university grew dramatically in enrollment and gained a fairly good reputation in the Southwest. Popejoy would have been an unlikely choice as university president in a more populous state; he rose to fame in 1929 by kicking a field goal for the university in a game with its arch rival, the University of Arizona and, after getting his bachelor's degree, worked in the university business department and then up to the presidency. No sooner had Popejoy retired than charges began to ricochet about the state to the effect that pornographic poems were being introduced in some English classes at the university, prompting the legislature to set up a special investigating committee. Such issues frequently balloon to the proportions of *causes célèbres* in small, personal states.

Among power groups in New Mexico, organized labor has fared especially poorly; union membership is only 43,000, or 16 percent of the labor force, a rate of organization 40th in rank among the states. The unions have had a fair degree of success in mining communities; the potash workers at Carlsbad are said to be the highest paid miners in the United States. But organized labor has been held back by the resistance of defense- and research-related industries to unionization, and the fact that so much of the state economy is split up into small establishments hard to organize. Oddly enough, the Catholic Church is reported to have defended labor interests with even more eloquence than labor leaders themselves. The Catholics, for instance, spoke up against proposals for banning the closed shop. (New Mexico is one of the few mountain states without a right-to-work law). The Archdiocese of Santa Fe appears to be one of the most liberal in the U. S.

today, willing to take such steps as picketing the state legislature on race issues. The Archdiocese also led New Mexico Catholics into a precedent-shattering affiliation with the New Mexico Council of Churches. Strong liberal trends have also been noted among Protestant denominations in New Mexico, but the local Episcopal bishop reacted angrily in 1969 when the executive committee of his national church approved a grant of $41,000 for Tijerina's *Alianza*.

A final note about New Mexico's state government, with special relation to the Spanish-Americans. In most areas of New Mexico life, the average Hispano has ended up with the least attractive jobs; as Senator Chávez once commented: "If they're going to war they're Americans; if they run for office, they're Spanish-Americans; if they're looking for a job, they're damned Mexicans." But not so in state government bureaucracy. Will Harrison reported in 1964 that the Hispanos occupied 70 percent of the positions in the state highway department, 70 percent of those of the bureau of revenue staff, 72 percent in the motor vehicle division, 92 percent of the penitentiary's jobs, 86 percent in the state mental hospital, and lesser but still large percentages in nearly every other agency of the state. Commenting on these figures, Jack E. Holmes wrote:

Many of these workers are now well enough trained and educated to have an even chance in the competitive examinations by which many are admitted, but before the days of a merit system, the bureaucracy was an instrument incidentally useful in training and acculturating at a relatively small cost a large and oftentimes seriously disadvantaged sector of the population. It is a matter which some other states might do well to ponder.

From the Atomic Economy to "HELP"

As World War II began, the mesa called Los Alamos (The Poplars), a pine-covered shelf of the Jemez Mountains some 35 miles northwest of Santa Fe, held only a ranch school for boys and a few ranch homesteads. But Dr. Robert Oppenheimer had visited the ranch school frequently on pack trips from his nearby mountain home, and when the need rose to select a totally remote location for secret atomic weapons research, it was Oppenheimer who recalled and recommended the Los Alamos school site. The fantastic secrecy of the early years, before Hiroshima and public disclosure of what had been wrought on the mesa, is legendary. Scientists went about under assumed names: Enrico Fermi was known as "Henry Farmer" and Niels Bohr as "Nicholas Baker," the word "physicist" was banned (everyone was known as an "engineer"), personnel were not allowed to travel more than 100 miles away and even forbidden to have personal contact with relatives. All mail came to "P.O. Box 1663, Santa Fe, New Mexico," and the children born to Los Alamos families had "P.O. Box 1663" entered on their birth certificates as "place of residence."

Since 1957, the gates of New Mexico's secret city have been open to the world, and Los Alamos has lost the raw construction-camp aura of its first years. The scientists have escaped from bleak governmental rental housing to build handsome homes of modern style, surrounded by Russian olives and pines, arranged in view of the brooding Sangre de Cristo (Blood of Christ) Mountains. Some 11,310 people now live at Los Alamos, and in their number are no less (by a count in the late 1960s) than 615 Ph.D's, 368 holders of Master of Science degrees, and another 695 with Bachelor of Science degrees.

Predictably, the level of income at Los Alamos far exceeds that of the rest of New Mexico, though almost all of it is gained from immediately earned income, not ancient familial wealth. Community organizations abound, the children excel in statewide merit scholarship competitions, library loans exceed every other New Mexico town save Albuquerque, newspaper readership of local, state, and even Denver and New York newspapers is high, and the highly educated wives of the scientists help stimulate avid cultural interests, ranging from study of Indian art to the Santa Fe Opera. Politically, Los Alamos splits its tickets and votes a highly independent line; its state legislators have been sponsors of quality, innovative legislation of statewide as well as local importance. One hears that there is no town in New Mexico where concern about modern environmental problems is higher or ethnic prejudices less. Writing of "La Dolce Vita, R and D style," Jack E. Holmes has pointed to the remarkable similarities between Los Alamos and Oak Ridge, Tennessee, that other city sustained almost in entirety by the Atomic Energy Commission. Though the two are 1,400 miles apart, Holmes suggests, they are doubtless far more similar to each other than to their in-state neighbors.

Dr. Oppenheimer left Los Alamos in 1945, to be succeeded by his collaborator, Dr. Norris E. Bradbury, who would serve until 1970, gaining an illustrious reputation for work he fostered, both in advancing nuclear weaponry and in the peaceful uses of atomic energy. Among the interesting new pursuits have been controlled uses of thermonuclear energy, space physics, research and design in nuclear rocket propulsion, health research, and meson physics. (The meson facility was approved in 1968 by President Johnson, overriding Bureau of the Budget objections as an apparent favor to Senator Anderson for having remained quiet about his opposition to the Vietnam war).

Since the days of Oppenheimer at Los Alamos, New Mexico has become dotted with atomic laboratories, test sites, manufacturing and storage facilities which account directly for about 16 percent of the persons employed in the state—a figure which does not even consider the payroll from the hundreds of millions of dollars worth of defense and space projects built there. In 1970, as an example, the federal government spent $1.5 billion in New Mexico; of this, Defense Department outlays were $362 million, those of the Atomic Energy Commission $374 million. Federal expenditures in the state are twice as high as the federal taxes paid from it.

The initial spin-off from Los Alamos was the wartime atom bomb test site at White Sands, north of Alamagordo, where extensive rocket and missile testing has since taken place. The largest nuclear related installation is the Sandia Laboratories at Albuquerque, a branch of Los Alamos until 1969, which takes the nuclear explosive device developed at Los Alamos and proceeds with design engineering and prototype production of the actual weapons, including fusing and firing systems and guidance and control mechanisms. "Our main job is weapons design—you might say we are basically traders in technology and applied research," J. A. Hornbeck, president of Sandia, said in an interview. Sandia also operates New Mexico testing facilities, including rocket sleds, lasers, nuclear reactors and centrifuges, and a test site in Nevada. With the Department of Defense, it has cradle-to-grave responsibility for maintenance of the nuclear arms stockpile and bears a portion of the readiness activity to see that the country can resume atmospheric nuclear weapons tests on short notice. Sandia's payroll has been a fairly constant 7,000—largest in the state of New Mexico—since 1956.

The complexity of interrelationships in the country's military-industrial complex is illustrated by Sandia's many roles. It is a laboratory of the Atomic Energy Commission and headquarters of AEC Albuquerque operations; at the same time, in terms of ownership, it is a subsidiary of Western Electric, which in turn is a subsidiary of American Telephone & Telegraph. But the actual AEC contracts, and the responsibility for their performance, lie with the University of California, which also operates Los Alamos and the sister nuclear weapons laboratories at Livermore, California. Yet the final consumer of what Sandia and the other laboratories produce is the Department of Defense—operating in turn the three branches of the armed services, each of which is a consumer of certain types of nuclear weapons.

Nor is Sandia the only atomic support agency in Albuquerque. During World War II, Albuquerque sold airport land to the Army for $1; this was the beginning of Kirtland Air Force Base, which in the postwar years became the base where nuclear weapons were actually married to aircraft. Eventually, as rockets came in, the Air Force gave the land back to the city, vastly improved; a handsome new Albuquerque Airport terminal, built in a Spanish theme, now occupies part of the site. The Air Force still operates at Kirtland with a special weapons section and laboratories, but on a reduced basis. Another Albuquerque weapons facility, ACF Industries, for several years produced the castings for weapons but was phased out in the 1960s. A progression of cutbacks of this type is reason for alarm in the congressional delegation, and Senator Anderson fears that more will come in future years as competition for facilities, especially with Texas and the Deep South, intensifies. What Albuquerque hopes is that the abandoned nuclear and missile facilities may be snapped up by private industry, bringing some much needed diversification; at the urging of the congressional delegation, for instance, General Electric took over the ACF plant and now employs about 1,100 there. The nuclear complex has also spun off four or five private electronic firms, which could contribute to building a more rounded economy and save the day for Albuquerque if, by some unlikely turn of events, peace were to break out in the world and nuclear research was downgraded. Early in the 1970s, a number of well known national corporations announced the opening of new industrial plants to employ several thousand in Albuquerque—the best economic news that atom-dependent city had heard in many years.

New Mexico will need many powerful new economic inputs in order to raise its lagging standard of living and hold in place the 7,000 engineers it has on location. The state ranked 45th among the 50 in new jobs added during most of the 1960s, and Albuquerque workers earn about $2,000 less than their counterparts in other Western cities. Except for Alaska, there is no other state in which government workers represent such a huge percentage of the whole—over 30 percent in the late 1960s. And except for Nevada, no state of the Mountain West has such a low percentage of its workers in manufacturing. The problem, in essence, is that except for federal contracts and expanding tourism, New Mexico has done little to add to the old base of cattle and mining it had before World War II.

There are only a few bright spots in the private sector. One of the most interesting has been a successful promotion, begun under Governor Cargo in 1967, to make New Mexico a location for filmmakers. The natural landscape of mountains, mesas, and deserts provides a uniquely photogenic backdrop, and a state Commission on Filmed Entertainment has gone all-out to attract the film industry to the Land of Enchantment. A movie leaves 40 to 50 percent of its budget in the community where it is filmed, and by the end of 1970, 54 movies had left $35 million in the state. Now New Mexico is experiencing a development of more dubious value: sale of gigantic tracts of its desert land for recreational communities. *Time* reported in February 1972 that about 100 companies controlled more than one million acres in New Mexico and had plotted out enough lots to triple the state population to three million. Some of the developers are reputable, but Horizon Corporation, the largest subdivider in the state, is supplying the future residents of its Rio communities, covering 150,000 acres, with neither water nor sewage systems.

In order of magnitude, the mineral industry is of immense importance to New Mexico, one of the chief oil and gas, uranium, potash, and copper producers of the Union. The value of minerals produced has been pushing toward the $1 billion mark and ranks seventh among the states. The importance of mining for most New Mexicans, however, may not be great. Most of the oil and gas, for instance, is sent outside the state for refining, and the total number of mining employees is only 16,600—less than a fifth the number employed by government. The state's crude oil and natural gas reserves are being fast depleted.

Agriculture ranks after government and mining on the list of important New Mexico industries, though it has faded rapidly in terms of employment. The state's ranches and farms generate products sold for about $350 million a year—two-thirds of that figure from cattle and sheep, the rest from cotton, dairy products, and vegetables. The average income of New Mexicans engaged in agriculture rose from an incredibly low $2,297 in 1957 to $6,300 in 1968, testifying not only to the increasingly good living earned by the big cattle growers but to the rapidity with which marginal producers are being forced off the land.

In fact, it could be said that inequality of income, rather than overall lack of it, is New Mexico's most pressing problem. In 1970, for instance, per capita income in rural Sandoval County, heavily Hispanic and Indian in complexion, average $1,557, while the figure in Los Alamos was $4,809. The figure in Bernalillo County (Albuquerque) was $2,872, but in the mountain county of San Miguel, east of Santa Fe, only $1,508.

No easy and rapid solution can be found for the poor people of rural New Mexico, so devoid of their own economic leverage, frequently shortcut in state educational aid, deprived of the lucrative farm irrigation benefits or the defense jobs which have brought good times to many other New Mexicans. This is not to say, however, that important efforts are not underway to correct the situation. In 1962 the U. S. Agriculture Department was authorized to provide local groups with technical and financial assistance in developing their natural resources. Through Senator Anderson's office, working with the people in north central New Mexico, government agencies, and local civic organizations, a proposal was developed for what became the Northern Rio Grande Resource, Conservation and Development project (RC&D). The program was put under the direction of a steering committee made up of a good cross-section of public officials and local people. By 1970, approximately 450 new permanent jobs had been created in the district. Some 155 projects had been completed or were under construction, costing $16 million in all. Among these were flood control projects, farm improvement, construction of new irrigation systems (some of the old systems were antiquated and were wasting 50 percent of the water), roads and recreational facilities, opening of new outdoor recreational areas, and establishment of a new lumber mill. Claude Wood, Senator Anderson's administrative assistant, points out that this was a pilot project of its kind in the country, since duplicated in dozens of other locations.

The RC&D project, in turn, triggered one of the most imaginative poverty programs in the U. S., supported chiefly by the federal Office of Economic Opportunity with significant help from the Ford Foundation. Formidably titled the Home Education Livelihood Program for Underemployed Seasonal Agricultural Workers, a name charitably shorted to HELP in normal parlance, it is directed by Alex R. Mercure, a native Hispano of unusual business and organizational skills.

As Mercure sees it, the basic problem of the New Mexico economy, and in turn of the state's poor rural people, is the export, unprocessed, of virtually all raw products—not only oil and gas, of which we have spoken previously, but also coal, wool, livestock, animal hides, and apples. As a result, he says, the Spanish-Americans of the northern counties, though proud of their culture and language, find themselves forced to depend on subsistence farms, construction jobs which are only seasonal because of the snowy winters, a few maintenance jobs at Los Alamos, summer tourism, and migratory farm work. In towns like Roswell, Las Cruces, and Clovis in south and eastern New Mexico, most Spanish-speaking people—especially the more recent Mexican immigrants—tend to be a voiceless people, suffering from a range of economic problems not unlike those of their brothers in the north.

HELP's two-step program starts with adult community education centers, run by local poor people who will decide what skills need to be taught, followed by rural economic development as an outgrowth of the adult education. The aim of the education programs, focused on literacy, citizenship, and some specific skills, is to give people maximum alternatives, permitting them either to make a decent living as farmers in their local setting or equipping them for the city if that is their choice. Mercure's thesis is that "you don't have to move the un- and underemployed off the land—you can make jobs for them where they are." In order to accomplish that, both farm and small industrial cooperatives are being formed, all aimed at increasing the overall dollar income of the rural areas. The income from an apple crop, for instance, can virtually be doubled if the harvest is graded, sorted, packed, and stored—which is precisely what one of HELP's co-ops is doing in a $400,000 plant at Chama, New Mexico. Affiliated farm co-op members in northern New Mexico are feeding cattle on local grain until they reach full slaughter weight instead of following the prevalent practice there of shipping out steers at one-third weight. Other HELP co-ops have built their own homes, increasing their own real income at least 30 percent in the process. Some have begun manufacturing a range of products from crates to woven goods, using local raw materials.

The HELP program has discovered, according to Mercure, that when local people are given the responsibility for planning their own programs, they will not only perform creditably but will show phenomenal ingenuity in creating new facilities at low cost. "The very poor," Mercure points out, "have a number of strong positive values taught by necessity—tremendous frugality and creativity among them." In one area, the people built a 6,000-square-foot storage shed for $1,200, even though the economic experts (including HELP headquarters) told them it couldn't be done; in some areas new houses were built at an investment of only $5,000 each. "If my calculations are right," Mercure says, "investment by the state in creation of jobs in meaningful, profitable enterprises, without profiteering by anyone, can yield four times as much back to the state, through taxes and reduced welfare, as the original investment. And then there's the other kind of yield yet to be measured: human development. By making people self-sufficient, independent, and self-determining individuals, they start making a contribution that reverses the whole poverty-welfare cycle." A long-term solution may take time to achieve, he says, but "if we keep putting bandaids on the sores and not curing the source of the problem, we'll spend a helluva lot of money on bandaids."

For the most part, HELP steers clear of local political establishments, although it has ruffled feathers in a few communities by telling farm workers that there is a $1.30 an hour state minimum wage law that covers them. And HELP has refused dollar grants which would have involved it directly in services, emergency food, or medical supplies, insisting that those fields be left to the local welfare and public health authorities. Mercure's program, instead, sticks to something closer to old-fashioned capitalism,* takes ingenious advantage of the cooperative and self-help traditions of rural areas, and appears to be succeeding more than most U. S. poverty programs in the process.

Santa Fe, Taos, Pueblos, Hippies, and Penitentes

The first name applied to New Mexico's capital city was *La Villa Real de la Santa Fe de San Francisco de Assisi,* which may be translated as The Royal City of the Holy Faith of Saint Francis of Assisi. Happily for Anglo-Saxon tongues, only Santa Fe would remain of the first name; still, there is a kind of surrealistic timelessness that hangs over this delightfully unplanned city of narrow, winding streets, high walls shielding Hispanic gardens, and ancient adobe buildings of a terra cotta tone that seems part and parcel of the natural landscape. The plaza in front of the Palace of the Governors might be called America's oldest shopping center, since the Indians have been coming there since 1610 to display jewelry and pottery on the blankets they spread on the sidewalk. The architectural integrity of Santa Fe is jealously guarded by a group known as the Old Santa Fe Association, which started in 1926. It was the moving force behind an Historic Zoning Ordinance, written by author Oliver La Farge and passed by the city in 1957, which specifies that within the historic zone—the boundaries of Santa Fe in 1776—any new buildings must be constructed in either Spanish Pueblo or Territorial style. In 1971 construction began on a 50-store shopping center in the old Pueblo style, seven blocks from the old Plaza; some believe that Santa Fe may become the fashion shopping center of the Southwest, just as San Francisco is on the coast.

Santa Fe's physical setting is one for which the early Spanish are to be congratulated: within the valley of the Rio Grande, but high, northern, on a 6,947-foot plateau much cooler and less arid than the valley's lower reaches. Neil Morgan has written well that "there is no town in the West which more immediately whets the inquiring mind, soothes the jaded eye, or solaces the downhearted." I imagine even the early Anglo settlers, arriving at the end of the 1,100-mile-long Santa Fe Trail from Independence, Missouri, must have felt much the same way.

* By late 1970, almost $1 million in private mortgage money had been attracted for HELP projects.

Santa Fe is a fusion of Spanish and Indian cultures where the Anglo incursion—from businessman to the now-omnipresent hippie in the central square—seems to do little to change the mold cast by history. The culture, the air, the brooding mountains all seem to have been part of drawing an exceptionally cosmopolitan assemblage of artists and writers to Santa Fe. Just touching the surface, one might mention the writers Oliver La Farge and Winfield Scott, the architect John Gaw Meem; Georgia O'Keeffe, *grande doyenne* of American painting *; or the Indian, Maria the Potter, who has been a primary figure in the revival of ancient pottery making. Each summer, under the portals of the Palace of Governors, Indians from throughout the Southwest stage a remarkable market of their crafts, and a perpetual art show seems to thrive along with artists' studios on Canyon Road. The museums of Santa Fe, especially strong in native and Indian art, are considered among the finest of the West.

The true cultural gem of this city, though, is its opera, set in dramatic mountain terrain five miles north of the city. The Santa Fe Opera Company is virtually the single-handed creation of one man, general director John Crosby, a transplanted New Yorker. Crosby was determined in the early 1950s to conduct, preferably opera, and picked Santa Fe, for its cultural tradition and weather (ideal for outdoor summer theater), to start a completely new opera. With his own money and that of a few wealthy, prominent Santa Fe citizens, Crosby built his opera "house" and started performances in 1953, soon drawing some of the nation's most talented up-and-coming operatic singers. The repertory was a mix of the traditional and premieres of outstanding new operatic works, some American, some from abroad.

During a July night of 1967, Crosby's first opera house burned to the ground, apparently the work of an arsonist. Yet in the face of awesome odds, Crosby was able—with the help of insurance money and many new contributions—to build a new house ready for the opener in summer 1968. Like the first house, the new lacks side walls and leaves a swatch of exposed sky above; its redwood and adobe sculptured structure has been described as "a bold cross between an open-air arena and a Pueblo fortress." Critical acclaim, both for the opera house and for the richness of its performances, has been almost universal.

The opera's contribution to Santa Fe is not negligible. In the words of Mike Valentine, head of the city's chamber of commerce: "The opera

* Miss O'Keeffe is actually seen quite rarely in Santa Fe; she lives instead a quite hermetic existence in an adobe house on a high bluff overlooking the Chama River Valley at Abiquiu, where all of her neighbors are Indian or Hispanic. She has been spending her summers in the New Mexico desert since 1929 and has lived there year-round since the late 1940s, producing paintings that reflect a kind of mystic communion with the harsh desert landscape. In 1971 she celebrated her 84th birthday. When one of her rare exhibits opened at the Whitney Museum of Modern Art in New York in 1970, critic Robert Hughes wrote in *Time:* "To call her 'provincial' because her images are mainly from New Mexico is like calling Gauguin provincial because he worked in Tahiti. . . . Every work in this show . . . stands to the art of painting as Shaker barns do to architecture—plain, the forms reduced to their simplest and most mysterious denominators, not an ounce of fat left. She works on a level of strenuous responsibility that other American figurative artists never reach, or attain only in brief spurts."

people are our best tourists. They have contributed to raising our standards of restaurants and hotels.* They go to our museums and our theater. They are our second biggest business during July and August. Government is first, of course, since Santa Fe is the state capital."

And that state government has itself been doing some new building, most notably a capitol building completed in 1966 on the design of a Santa Fe architectural firm; its low, circular form is a direct adaptation of the Pueblo Indian kiva—the round, half-below-ground ceremonial chamber known for many centuries. Also incorporated in the design is the colorful Zia Pueblo Sun symbol, which also appears in the state flag and has been made familiar to many Americans by its inclusion on the state license plate. The new capitol includes offices for legislators, a convenience still absent in many states. The building's color, of course, is terra cotta.

Culture, tourism, and government so dominate Santa Fe that it is easy to forget there is also a continuing population growth (41,167 in 1970) and a city government with its own peculiar problems, not the least of which is whether it should bother to repair its unpaved and decayed roads. (It had finally decided on some long overdue repairs in the late 1960s, causing hard-to-imagine traffic jams.) Morgan reports that startling poverty exists among some of Santa Fe's natives, "though in the Latin tradition, the city does not worry much about such matters."

Several miles farther up the valley from Santa Fe lies the town of Taos (population 2,475), an art colony since the turn of the century; D. H. Lawrence, who spent many years writing in northern New Mexico, called Taos' valley view the most beautiful in the world. The multistoried Taos Pueblo, surviving from the gold age of Pueblo culture some 800 to 1,000 years ago, is world renowned. It is the northernmost of 19 Indian pueblos (villages) spread down the length of the Rio Grande Valley, their ancestral settlements and way of life as close to the primitive as one will find among any American Indians today.

Set in the Sangre de Cristo Mountains some 25 miles east of Taos is Blue Lake, part of a 48,000-acre watershed where the Taos Pueblo Indians have been in residence since the 14th century and which they consider the source of all life. In 1906 the federal government appropriated the land, without compensation to the Taos, to be part of the Carson National Forest. The federal takeover was a profound offense to the Taos. Their religion prohibits interference with the natural condition of these sacred lands, and despite their desire to keep it as an untouched wilderness area, the Forest Service constructed trails and facilities for tourists. The Taos believe that the entire watershed "is permeated with holy places and shrines used regularly by the Indian people; there is no place that does not have religious significance to us."

For years, the Taos sought return of the lands. They finally succeeded

* Santa Fe has a number of excellent gourmet restaurants, serving delicate Spanish and spicy Mexican foods—the kind of gastronomic delight all too rare outside of a few major American cities today.

in 1970 when Congress approved a bill to return the watershed to them in perpetuity, to be held in trust by the Secretary of the Interior. Senator Anderson, as well as Senate Interior Committee Chairman Henry Jackson of Washington State, opposed the legislation because it would set a "bad precedent" in permitting Indians across the country to obtain recovery of their ancestral lands. But a strange coalition backed the Taos' demand— President Nixon, Vice President Agnew, Interior Secretary Walter Hickel, and liberal Democratic Senators Fred Harris, George McGovern, and Edward M. Kennedy. When the crucial Senate vote was taken, Juan De Jesus Romero, 90-year-old spiritual leader of the Taos, was in Washington and thanked Congress through an interpreter for "restoring our Indian religion and our Indian lives." Back home, the bells pealed at the tiny adobe Roman Catholic Church, built by the early Spanish missionaries, and the people ran to it tearfully to give thanks. Strangely to outsiders, the Taos see no conflict between their Catholic religion and belief in their own ancient native religion, which is filled with secret ceremonies no outsider has ever been allowed to witness.

Most of the Pueblos live on in grinding poverty, though some groups have collective wealth from uranium or other minerals. Television is reported to have erased some of the ancient innocence. And now there is growing danger that the communal spirit, always so strong among the Pueblos, may be jeopardized by the new concepts of law and adversary justice being introduced from the outside. Traditionally in Indian culture, a young offender who has robbed or stolen is brought before an Indian judge and asked if he did it; almost always, he pleads guilty, feeling he has brought shame on his community and wants to be punished so that he can hold his head up again proudly thereafter. But the alien legal aid concepts being introduced—that "you're wrong only if you are convicted"—is causing many to be acquitted on technicalities, seriously undermining the Indians' concepts of right and wrong. Among the Pueblos, the impact is double, because their government is a theocracy, with the governmental functions carried out by the priest. If "civil rights" become more important than the community, it may become hard for the community to exist.*

Nevertheless, the Pueblos have to date remained so conservative that they have even refused to participate in the white man's elections; as Jack Holmes has pointed out, the ancient theocracies are "systems in which majoritarian voting would be highly out of place." In Sandoval County, north of Albuquerque, only 1 percent of the Indians voted until recently, although they make up about half of the population. But there are now

* Congress has passed legislation requiring that Indian governments provide their people with the same rights other citizens are entitled to under the Bill of Rights. The Indian Pueblos of New Mexico, for the most part, are opposed to granting these rights, and in 1971 legislation was pending giving them an extension of time so that they might develop constitutions and necessary machinery to provide for right of counsel, trial by jury and other features of Anglo-Saxon jurisprudence. They are being assisted in that task by the American Indian Law Center at the University of New Mexico, which is headed by Robert L. Bennett, who was Commissioner of Indian Affairs under President Johnson.

signs that even the ingrown Pueblos will start to vote in increasing numbers, perhaps fulfilling the prediction of decades ago that if the Indians got
the right to vote (finally assured them by a court decision of 1948), they
could represent the balance of power in New Mexico politics.

Taos today is not only distinguished by its arts, the Pueblo, and the
best ski area of New Mexico, but as a center for a new breed of rural
hippies. Peter Nabokov reported in *The Nation* in 1970 that Taos especially,
but also Santa Fe and Espanola, became targets of settlement in the wake
of the summer of 1967, when "the paradises of Haight-Ashbury, the East
Village and Sunset Strip turned into nightmares for white middle-class dropouts, castoffs and runaways." The hippies assert that they have a natural
tie to the land, growing out of a universal, "natural" link between man and
planet. They have consequently begun to purchase huge chunks of land for
their settlements; some of the local Hispanos and Indians have been less
than cordial to the new culture communes and "free" life style intruding
into their remote lands. Townspeople of Taos and the other nearby communities have shown predictable concern that the dirt and drugs would
rub off on their own children, leading to signs making the young people
unwelcome in shops and a Molotov cocktail thrown into one of their coffee-
houses. But the repression cannot be too severe; as I write I have a postcard
on my desk from a close friend, reporting: "I'm staying at a commune in
Santa Fe and grooving on the wide open spaces. It's a totally new scene;
you'd better believe it."

Yet in these same mountains, a fantastic old scene continues: the
special religious and political life of *Los Hermanos Penitentes*, that unique
Catholic lay order which has even been outlawed at times by Mother Church
for its practice of flagellation, which is said to have included, in times past,
the actual crucifixion of a "chosen" member on Good Friday. At one time
there were so many *Penitentes* that their vote was a special prize sought
by politicians and considered key in some elections; today it appears that
only two or three thousand remain.

Urban Centers of a Still Rural State

Albuquerque, New Mexico's only really metropolitan city, was founded
in 1706 by a group of families who decided to name it after the Duke of
Albuquerque, Viceroy of New Spain. In the first 234 years of its history, the
city grew to 35,449 souls; in the next 30 years (from 1940 to 1970), it added
six times that amount to reach a new total of 243,751, with another 72,023
in the surrounding county. Still unclear is whether this growth, most spectacular under the stimulus of mounting federal nuclear and space contracts
in the 1950s, will continue. The rate of growth slackened substantially in
the 1960s. But there does seem to be room for growth on Albuquerque's
spacious plateau; in land size, the city ranks fifty in the country. And of

course it has a physical setting of unusual interest, with the spectacular, rough wall of the Sandia Peaks close by in the northeast and the shapes of extinct volcanic cones on the northwestern horizon. There is sunshine 76 percent of the time and, because of the high altitude, extremely low humidity. The average maximum temperature is a quite comfortable 46.4 degrees in January and 91.2 degrees in July.

Much of the old Spanish style has been retained. Beside the Rio Grande, there is quaint "Old Town" with its flat-roofed colonial buildings and plaza ringed by shops and restaurants, where the San Felipe de Neri Church has been holding services each Sunday since 1706. The campus of the University of New Mexico has scored great success in retaining the old architectural flavor in its new buildings, as have many homes and, pleasingly, the new Sunport airport. Yet, depressingly, much of Albuquerque lacks any architectural distinction. One feels that with foresight and planning, the town might have come close to the quality of Santa Fe—but that the effort was simply not made. Perhaps the worst eyesore is the main drag of Central Avenue with its flashy neon signs advertising the expensive new motels at one end, the flaking, stucco "motor courts" of yesteryear at the other. The newer, more expensive housing on the East Heights, peopled by so many atom-age technocrats in the past 20 years, contains some pleasing ranch and adobe styles, but as David Boroff has pointed out, Albuquerque also has its "mean, cramped little stucco houses and dusty bungalows with dead lawns—the homes of the lower middle class."

West of the Santa Fe railroad tracks, which cut a raw north-south swatch through the center of the town, lies "The Valley" and an area of depressed housing, occupied mostly by Hispanos and Negroes, which was appropriately selected as a target for the federal model cities program. High levels of unemployment, drug addiction, and crime have afflicted the poor communities, and there have been frequent charges of brutality against a police department known for its "quasi" military operations and low levels of morale. The situation has been exacerbated by thousands of hippies who have filtered into Albuquerque, where they laze around in the parks and seek occasional work for food and marijuana. In June 1971, the city suffered its first major riot when some members of a crowd of almost naked hippies and teenagers from the barrios, gathered for a rock concert, set upon police. "Peace" was finally restored by the National Guard, which made 300 arrests after tear-gassing a large section of the city. The total damage included $3 million in damage from fire bombings and injury of 15 persons by gunshot. But city officials, according to reports of outside newsmen, showed great reluctance to confer with the leading local militant group, the Black Berets, a "brown power" organization with some black membership that had been complaining loudly about unemployment and alleged abuse by the police. (A continuation of such tensions, one sadly concludes, may soon make it necessary to reevaluate the general view of New Mexico as a state of tolerance and good will).

Albuquerque's old downtown area, lying close to the Santa Fe tracks, was moving toward a condition of serious decay in the late 1950s when the city fathers, egged on by the Albuquerque *Journal,* decided to seek urban renewal. Led by the Bank of New Mexico, a substantial amount of new high-rise office building was undertaken, but many splotches of unsightly cleared land remained vacant year after year. In the meantime, the heart of the retailing activity moved to locations like the excellent Winrock (for Winthrop Rockefeller) and Coronado Shopping Centers on the East Heights.

Sandia Laboratories and the atom-age economy of Albuquerque remain highly dependent on federal government spending. The fight for contracts and projects is never-ending, and one of the chief disappointments in recent years has been the inability of the city's Lovelace Clinic and Foundation to become a major federal contractor after the tragic airplane crash of its guiding force, W. R. (Randy) Lovelace II, in the 1960s. The clinic did pioneer work on the medical effects of space environments on men, as well as the biological effects of blast and radiation. The officials at Sandia Laboratories assure a visitor that their work will have to go on even if international tensions subside, but one has to believe the real hope of Albuquerque lies in encouraging more and more private industry.

Albuquerque has a city manager charter form of government which has been effectively free of partisan control since the mid-1940s. An effort to combine the city government with that of Bernallilo County was attempted in the 1960s but rejected by the voters. On the newspaper front, the traditionally conservative Albuquerque *Journal,* with the largest circulation in the state, has recently been moving toward moderate liberalism under editor Robert Brown. The *Journal* consistently fights big-interest domination of the state government. The Albuquerque *Tribune* (Scripps-Howard) and Santa Fe *New Mexican* are inclined to be liberal and Democratic in state politics, though the *Tribune* is more conservative and chamber-of-commerce-oriented on local issues. None of the papers seems comparable to the Denver *Post,* from nearby Colorado, in overall quality. Albuquerque apparently has no aspirations to be a really cosmopolitan city; its distinguishing marks might be said to include scenery, air, and an all-enveloping friendliness for the visitor.

Once one departs the Albuquerque and Santa Fe scenes, few cities worthy of the name show up in New Mexico. With fluctuations in military spending and oil finds, some rise in population, others decline. A growing center in the last few years has been Las Cruces (pop. 37,857), low in the Rio Grande Valley, where there is a big payroll from the Hollomon Air Force Base (which includes a missile development center) and from the White Sands Missile Range. Las Cruces lies in the heavily irrigated, fertile Mesilla Valley, where cotton is the big crop; agriculture is a major interest at New Mexico State University, located in the town.

Roswell (33,908) received a rude shock in 1967 when the Walker Air Force Base, a Strategic Air Command bomber center that had enriched the local economy ever since World War II, suddenly departed, causing a population drop of 7,000 and throwing thousands of homes on the market. Slow recovery with new industries has since been effected, but there may be a limit to how many firms or people want to come to the semidesert flatlands of rock and sagebrush where Roswell sits, baking in the sun, some 200 miles southeast of Albuquerque. Principal income these days comes from oil and irrigated farming.

Another Little Texas town, Hobbs (26,205), is New Mexico's biggest oil city now. Clovis (28,495) is a big cattle town, while Alamagordo (23,035) calls itself "Rocket City" and lives off federal contracts in large part. Farmington (21,979) is running out of oil and losing population in the process; the cities-in-decline list also includes Carlsbad (21,297), which lost more than 4,000 souls in the last decade. But now we are down to Gallup (14,596), which is primarily an Indian trading center, and it is time to be off to the Navajo Reservation before we take our final leave of the Land of Enchantment.

Land of the Navajo

It was just over a century ago that the federal government finally despaired of making everyday frugal farmers out of the wild and adventurous Navajo Indians whom it had corralled during Civil War years and marched to detention in eastern New Mexico. These were the Dineh, the People, the Navajo; the archeologists tell us they are descended directly from nomads who migrated to North America across the Bering Strait when it was a land bridge. Their language group is called Athabascan, like the Indians of Alaska. Probably not too long before the Spaniards arrived, the People had migrated southward to the starkly beautiful desert land of what is now known as the Southwest's Four Corners area. From the Spanish they quickly learned the use of horses and how to raise sheep and goats. And so, for centuries, they lived in relative peace in isolated mud huts (called hogans), many miles from the next neighbor, each family carving out a large stretch of the high, arid land to graze his sheep.

This life the government sought to change when it became tired of the Navajos' freewheeling raids, their slave business, and theft of horses by the hundreds. An 1864 military expedition under the command of Kit Carson slaughtered all the Navajo sheep, destroyed their fields, and herded the Navajo families on a bitterly remembered "Long Walk" to Bosque Redondo in eastern New Mexico, where a four-year experiment in "civilizing" would fail so miserably. The captivity did, however, force the Navajos to form a central tribal council and sign a peace treaty that they have never broken. Under the pact, several thousand were allowed to return, with a few sheep and goats, to the high desert country of the Four Corners region, a land so gaunt and inhospitable that no white man could then dream of its being put to productive use.

The story of what then happened is not without irony. Instead of dying off, as many in Washington privately hoped they would, the Navajo multiplied and multiplied from the band of a few thousand that returned to Four Corners in 1868; today they number 120,000 and continue to grow in population at a rate exceeded by no other group in these United States. As a result of this fecundity, there will probably be, in a generation, twice as many Navajo as there are today. The 1970 Census found about 55 percent of the Navajo Reservation population was in Arizona, slightly over 40 percent in New Mexico, and the remainder in Utah.

As for the land no one wanted, it contains today some of the world's most scenic attractions and a fabulous concentration of national parks and monuments, either entirely enclosed or on its borders—Lake Powell and the Grand Canyon of the Colorado, Monument Valley, Mesa Verde National Park, the Petrified Forest, and many others. It also appeared that the stern red-rock land was not as worthless as men thought, for in recent years discoveries in gas and oil, coal and uranium have produced operating mines that pay millions of dollars in royalties to the Navajo. In sheer land bulk holding, the Navajo are as fortunate as one could hope for: their reservation, some 23,500 square miles in area, is as large as the states of Massachusetts, Connecticut, and New Hampshire combined.

This is not to say that the Navajo do not suffer from poverty and neglect on their remote reservation, for as any visitor to the land of the Navajo can see, the life conditions are as appalling as any on the continent. According to the U.S. Public Health Service director on the reservation, Dr. George E. Bock, the infant mortality rate is 42.3 per 1,000 births, twice the national average, and the occurrence of tuberculosis and hepatitis is 10 times the average in the country as a whole. Deaths from diseases associated with unsanitary conditions are 11 times the national average. (Only a fourth of the homes on the reservation have sanitary facilities.) Surplus food and food stamp distribution has been notoriously poor. At least two-thirds of the Indians on the reservation live below the nationally established poverty line, and average schooling—especially among adults—is less than a third that of other Americans. Many Navajo speak only the most faltering English or none at all.

Until the last two decades, the Navajos' plight was little known because of their complete isolation, like a separate country within the United States. With bitter memories of the "Long Walk" of 1864, the Navajos were leery of any contact. Moreover, they gathered into seminomadic family groupings for their shepherding life, with no real tribal organization. Finally, the rugged landscape—high plateau sliced by high ridges and deep canyons, with scarcely any roads—made travel difficult always and impossible in many seasons of the year.

Earnest change began with World War II, when so many Navajo youth went off to war. By 1950, reservation population was increasing so rapidly that available grazing land was not enough to support the Navajo. Congress responded that year by passing a 19-year program for schools, hospitals, roads, and irrigation facilities, followed up eight years later by another $20 million for all-weather roads across the reservation. Now many once inaccessible areas, including the picturesque Navajo capital of Window Rock, have been opened up, both for the Navajo and outsiders. (Much remains to be done, however. There are only 800 miles of paved roads, compared to 25,991 miles of paved road in West Virginia, a territory of smaller size.) The Navajo Tribal Council, set up in 1938 by the Bureau of Indian Affairs, has assumed great importance in determining the use of royalties from oil and gas and other minerals and in directing general economic policy.* But the democratically elected 74-member council is quite unwieldly, and the inefficient, rather bloated tribal government uses up $8 million, half the annual tribal budget, in salaries alone.

By now, only a small proportion of the Navajo make a living from sheepgrazing; they have turned, instead, to service jobs, manufacturing, irrigated farming, tourist support, or—in the case of a *majority* of the population—to the jobless rolls. Some startling economic breakthroughs have been staged however. At Shiprock, nearly 1,200 Navajo now assemble transistors and integrated circuits for the Fairchild Camera & Instrument Corporation. The dexterous and patient Indian women hired for this job, Fairchild has found, have learned through years of rug-weaving to visualize complicated patterns not yet completed and thus can memorize complex integrated circuit designs and make subjective decisions in sorting and quality control. After some initial problems with communication and work hours, the plant became most profitable. Also on the reservation, General Dynamics has a factory for assembling components of guidance systems, computers, and test and calibration systems; several other plants are either in production or planning to come. Commenting on all this activity in 1970, *Business Week* wrote: "The Navajo, after 100 years of near-starvation, has change jingling in his Levis and a pickup truck at the hogan door." A less happy result, one might add, is that fewer and fewer Navajo want to invest the countless hours it takes to weave a rug or fashion silver jewelry, so that the output of these ancient handicrafts declines even as the national demand for true, indigenous native art increases.

The Tribal Council has shown no little acumen in fostering economic activity. Fairchild, for instance, moved into a building built for it by the council, and in perhaps its most daring venture, the council in 1958 appropriated $7.5 million to start a huge sawmill in the ponderosa hills near Window Rock, thus launching the highly successful Navajo Forest Products Industries. Tourism is another source of income, and the Navajo have not only been promoting reservation tours of several days' duration but have

* The Navajo received $100 million in bonus money from oil firms in the early 1950s, and there have been royalty payments of about $10 million a year, accounting for almost all tribal revenues. Those royalties are now declining, however, and the oil firms show no interest in further drilling in the area. The tribal government is obliged each year to use up more of the oil bonus money, and the economic future is most uncertain.

also invested $880,000 in a modern new 56-room motor inn at Window Rock.

Sometimes the old and the new blend in disquieting ways. Standing on a plateau not far from Farmington in the northeast part of the reservation, I could see the ghostly form of Shiprock in the distance and feel the time-lessness of the Four Corners territory. Yet closer by, there was a gaping open-pit coal mine, surrounded by huge heaps of slag marching toward the skyline. And next to the mine, using its output, was a modern power plant, its stacks pumping heavy black smoke banks into the pristine air. This is the Four Corners Power Plant, first of the series of gigantic Southwestern power plants operated by the combine of private power companies, WEST (Western Energy Supply Transmission Associates), which were discussed in the opening chapter of this book. The dense black plume from this plant's smokestacks has been tracked by plane for 215 miles and was easily visible to astronauts in the Gemini 12 spacecraft from 170 miles altitude. According to a lawsuit filed by five Navajo in 1971, the plant pumps out 351 tons of particulate matter and 373 tons of sulphur dioxide each day, more than all the power stations of New York City. They have challenged the two leases that the government signed with the Navajo Tribal Council for the use of reservation land, alleging that adequate environmental safeguards were not made. They claim that the pollution causes irritation to human beings and animals, damage to the vegetation of the Navajo grazing lands, and impairment to the "esthetic and cultural enjoyment of the Navajo Reservation." The power companies are trying to perfect electrostatic precipitators and wet scrubbers that would remove 99 percent of the pollutant load, in contrast to the initial equipment that removed only 78 percent of the fly ash. But even then, the air pollution from burning of the low-grade coal will be substantial, and questions will remain about the wisdom of polluting reservation skies and tearing up reservation earth for coal in return for a few hundred jobs and a few millions of dollars a year in income—to satisfy the seemingly insatiable demand for power of distant Southern California and cities like Phoenix, Albuquerque, and El Paso.

Sheep have been the traditional symbol of wealth for the Navajo, but that value may have to be shifted as irrigated crop farming grows in importance. Work is underway on a major irrigation system for the Navajos' benefit, tied in with the Navajo Dam project on the San Juan River near Farmington. According to the planners' projections, the project will make 110,000 acres of land arable and create 8,800 farm jobs for the Indians; the total economic impact ought to be $86 million a year. Water experts doubt the cost effectiveness of the $175 million project, but the argument has been convincingly made that the Indians, after being cheated out of so many millions of acres of land and water rights, deserve a bit of the agricultural subsidization the white man has dealt himself so freely. Typically, Congress and the executive branch dragged their feet for several years in actually funding the Navajo project, even after its authorization in 1962. At the same time, related projects to divert water from the San Juan basin to Albuquerque proceeded at full steam. Since they had given up some of their rights to San Juan water in return for the irrigation system, the Navajo understandably saw this as a typical piece of the white man's treachery.

One man intensely interested in how the Navajo can take advantage of their newly irrigated land is one-time Governor Tom Bolack, a gruff, self-made oil millionaire who has built his Square B Ranch at Farmington into a showcase of successful irrigated farming techniques. The cornucopia of fruits and vegetables and grains pouring out from Bolack's ranch is a sight to behold, and he has simultaneously created a delightful refuge for deer, rabbits, hens, ducks, geese, and other wildlife. Providing wildlife food and wetlands cover for game, in Bolack's opinion, could greatly increase the benefits to the Navajo from their newly irrigated land, not to mention the obvious benefits of diversified crops in addition to the more obvious corn and alfafa production.

Not all Navajo are enamored of the new manufacturing and agricultural approaches. There are many oldtimers who prefer to eke out a bare existence tending a few sheep and goats and living in primitive mud-covered hogans or tarpaper shacks without windows, water, or lighting. The Navajo, Marshall Sprague has written, "are generally sturdy, stubborn, temperamental, artistic, humorous, patient, conservative, and uncomplaining." Change comes slowly, and acculturation is a difficult and painful process.

Indeed, the adjustment to a new age often poses the most poignant problems for the young, for whom there should be the most hope. Lack of educational opportunity is no longer the problem; today virtually all Navajo children attend school, and the first substantial numbers are going on to college. This represents a change of monumental proportions from just two decades ago, when only one Navajo child in 10 attended school. Up to 1946, in fact, the Navajo totally rejected the validity of the white man's education and had to be practically coerced to go to the schools run by the Bureau of Indian Affairs. But, as the Indians have learned, acquisition of an education may create as many problems as it solves. All too often, the teaching, whether at BIA or public schools located near reservations, has shown little sensitivity to or understanding of the Indians' particular culture and values. Not until the late 1960s were the first steps taken to set up schools which the Indians would actually run for themselves, representing a new approach in which many saw great hope. The Navajo culture and tradition is also taught, along with modern skills, at the new Navajo Community College at Tsaile Lake, Arizona, the first college ever created on a reservation. Such innovations represent a sharp break with past educational theory, which sought to force the young Navajo into the white man's mold. The result of that was often disastrous; as the Rev. Benjamin P. Ford, vicar of the San Juan Episcopal Mission to the Navajo, states the problem: "To a degree, you dehumanize a person when you change his culture."

At the old BIA boarding schools, for instance, Indian youngsters were once punished for speaking their native tongue. Still today, they learn about the white man's values of making money and using time for material gain. Then, when they return home, there is the cultural shock: the real goal of the old folks is simply to live in harmony with nature. For the Indian youngster with a view of the wider world, a placid summer keeping sheep may test his patience to the limit. He will tell one that he loves his parents and wants to visit home—but that he doesn't want to stay here. Yet the same youngster will face frightful obstacles in the outside white world, for he simply lacks its drives. In Ford's words, he is an "in-between guy," in the most difficult of all social roles.

Perhaps the worst situations arise when a Navajo divides his time, half on and half off the reservation. Alcoholism, broken families, and lives of violence are all too often the result. Confused, frustrated, and afraid, the Indians sometimes turn to alcohol as a form of semisuicide; the parents of teenagers with problems also drink frequently and sleep around.

On the reservation near Farmington, I saw a not untypical wretched hovel of a home occupied by a Navajo family, located beside an unsightly drainage ditch, an abandoned and gutted automobile hulk in front. The son of this family, Ford told me, had been a bright and sensitive youngster, active with the mission, whom Ford hoped might one day become one of the first Navajo priests of the church. Then the young man went off to Vietnam, where he served with courage and distinction as a helicopter pilot, surviving the downing of his aircraft on three occasions. His military service completed, the young man returned home, met with some of his young friends, had a few beers, and then with his friends along for the fun, ran a stop sign, gunned his automobile to 70 miles an hour, and collided with another automobile. Instantly, he was dead—less than three hours after his return home.

One could blame the Navajos' problems on peripheral towns like Farmington, where the trading posts and bars are all white-owned and the alcohol made available which the reservation wisely forbids. Much more exploitive than Farmington, in fact, is the dusty, unkempt town of Gallup, with its dreary bars and pawnshops. Gallup gladly takes in the Indians' cash but, when they misbehave, confronts them with tough old-style Spanish police who will knock an Indian on the head at the slightest provocation. As Calvin Trillin, author of *U. S. Journal*, reported in 1971 in *The New Yorker* magazine:

Gallup is noted for its drunken Indians. People who are interested in alcoholism—psychiatrists, government health officials, church people, foundation field workers—usually come to Gallup sooner or later to take a tour of the wreckage.
For those who can't believe their eyes, statistics are available. Watching inert Indians being picked off the sidewalk and hauled to jail, the visitor can learn that Gallup—the most active trading town on the border of the Navajo reservation—has almost 800 drink-arrests a month, almost all of them involving Navajos. . . .
The road from Gallup to the reservation line—a road so littered with tossed-out

wine bottles and beer cans that its shoulders glisten in the sunlight—is said to be the most dangerous stretch of highway in New Mexico, or maybe anywhere. The single greatest cause of death among Navajos is auto accidents.

Yet the same Gallup town fathers who aid and abet all this have for years earned a small fortune from the splendid Inter-Tribal Indian Ceremonial held at their town each summer.

Still another problem for the Navajo is the decline of their ancestral religion, an intricate structure, as one writer has noted, of "walking in harmony" with nature and the spirits that inhabit the land. The old medicine men are dying off, and few young men are willing to undergo the years of training required. An effort to incorporate traditional Navajo mysticism with Christianity is made by the semisecret Native American Church.

Despite every problem of continued poverty and painstaking acculturation, the visitor to the land of the Navajo must come away with hope. One could surely have predicted that the process of bringing an isolated, nomadic people out of their historical cocoon, putting them into the mainstream of American life, and at the same time preserving the best of their culture, would bring trial and tribulation. Slowly but surely the dependence on the white man and his paternalistic, bureaucratic Bureau of Indian Affairs is reduced. The Indians gain increasing political self-confidence and even elect two of their number to the New Mexico state legislature. (In Arizona, the Navajo tend to be Republican; in New Mexico, Democratic.)

Finally, one must take account of the able and sometimes visionary Navajo leaders of the last several decades: Chee Dodge, late chief and Tribal Council chairman, who made the speech which persuaded his people to accept education; Paul Jones, former leader who insisted on using mineral royalties to build facilities and draw tourists, rather than doling it out on an expedient per capita basis; Mrs. Annie Dodge Wauneka, Chee Dodge's daughter and a foremost leader in the struggle for education; Raymond Nakai, the council chairman from 1963 to 1971, who spearheaded the effort to draw industry to the reservation and make the Navajo an economically self-sufficient people; and finally the present council chairman, Peter MacDonald, a 43-year-old World War II veteran and the first college graduate ever to head the Navajo, who defeated Nakai by a margin of 18,000 to 12,000 votes to win his position. MacDonald was born near Four Corners, dropped out of school to enlist in the Marine Corps, and later completed his education at the University of Oklahoma, becoming the first (and until now, the only) Navajo electrical engineer. MacDonald had a high position with Hughes Aircraft in California but left it to return to the reservation in 1963, becoming head of the Navajo Office of Economic Opportunity, which for five years operated with an annual $8 million budget. An engaging and outgoing man, he developed his political base in that position.

On the day of MacDonald's inauguration in January 1971, the temperature was 10 below zero for the outdoor ceremonies—dropping to 40 below by the time of the inaugural ball, a reminder of the harshness of the reservation environment. MacDonald is a great believer in economic self-determination for his people, but he believes the federal government must help with projects like roadbuilding, bringing electric power into all areas of the reservation, and making ample water available for manufacturing. Without federal aid to restructure the Navajo economy, MacDonald insists, his people will be doomed to "poverty of the soul" just as most of them have, until the very recent past, seemed doomed to remaining miserably poor.

An interested observer at MacDonald's inauguration was Louis Bruce, the Indian who presently heads the Bureau of Indian Affairs and is spearheading the Nixon administration's policy to make the BIA more Indian-controlled and oriented. (More than 55 percent of BIA's national staff is now made up of Indians, and Indians presently hold most of the important administrative posts on the Navajo reservation, including the directorship—positions previously held by whites.)

Late in the 1960s, Howard Gorman, a perennial Tribal Council member, was interviewed by writer Marshall Sprague for Time-Life's book on the region. With enthusiasm, Gorman spoke of the new economic projects on the reservation. But he wondered how long it would take, the long walk to salvation of the Navajo People and all the Indians of the mountain states:

> We have to do it all ourselves, the way we built the lumber mill, or it's no good. Your [the white man's] way is one way—material wealth and success, progress. The old way is the Navajo way, the way we love—the way of the sheep, the hogan, our land and sky and all our little rituals to keep well, to keep happy, to keep evil away. We can't go your way too fast, and we can't go *all* the way your way. Only far enough to stand still, as we say. How much longer? Who knows?

ACKNOWLEDGMENTS

THESE BOOKS HAD TO BE, by their very character, a personal odyssey and personal task. But they would never have been possible without the kind assistance of hundreds of people. First there were those who encouraged me to go forward when the idea was first conceived: my wife Barbara (little imagining the long curtailments of family life that would ensue, and whose encouragement was vital throughout); my parents and other relatives; my editor, Evan W. Thomas, vice president and editor of W. W. Norton & Co.; John Gunther; my agent, Sterling Lord, and his assistant at that time, Jonathan Walton; Richard Kluger, editor of my first book, *The People's President;* writer Roan Conrad; editor Joseph Foote (who would later help with many other aspects of the book); William B. Dickinson, editor of *Editorial Research Reports;* Thomas Schroth, then the editor, and Nelson Poynter, publisher of *Congressional Quarterly;* author Michael Amrine and his wife Rene; Richard M. Scammon, director of the Elections Research Center and coauthor of *The Real Majority;* and D. B. Hardeman, professor of political science and biographer of the late House Speaker Sam Rayburn. Later on, those who encouraged or helped me to keep the project moving included F. Randall Smith and Anthony C. Stout of the Center for Political Research; author David Wise; columnist-reporters Bruce Biossat and David S. Broder; and Bernard Haldane. A year's fellowship at the Woodrow Wilson International Center for Scholars provided intellectual and physical sustenance toward the end of the project.

My very warmest thanks go to those who read the draft manuscript in its entirety: Evan W. Thomas; Russell L. Bradley; Jean Allaway; Frederick H. Sontag, public relations consultant of Montclair, N.J.; Kay Gauss Jackson, former critic for *Harper's Magazine;* Donald Kummerfeld; Western newsman M. DeMar Teuscher; and copy editor Calvin Towle at W. W. Norton & Company. In addition, each of the state chapters was submitted to several persons living in, and having extensive knowledge of, the state in question. The returning corrections and amendments were immensely helpful. The names of those readers appear in the longer list of names below; I choose not to list them here lest someone hold them responsible for something said or unsaid in one of the chapters, and of course the full responsibility for that lies with me.

Various friends and associates helped with many of the details of research, and for that I am especially indebted to Oliver Cromwell, Ursula Lang, Monica and Jason Benderly, Barbara Hurlbutt, Richard Baker, Nancy Nelsen, James Allaway, David B. H. Martin, John Gibson, and Claudia Teuscher. And without the cheery and efficient services of my typist, Merciel Dixon, the manuscript would never have seen the light of day at all. Rose Franco of W. W. Norton helped in innumerable ways; I am indebted to designer Marjorie Flock of the Norton organization; and credit goes to Russell Lenz, chief cartographer of the *Christian Science Monitor,* for what I feel is the superb job he did on the state maps.

Across the country, people gave generously of their time to brief me on the developments of the past several years in their states and cities. I am listing those from the eight mountain states below, together with many people who helped with national and interstate themes. The names of some officials are included whom I had interviewed in the year or two prior to beginning work on this project, when the background from those interviews proved helpful with this book. To all, my sincerest thanks.

PERSONS INTERVIEWED

Affiliations of interviewees are as of time of author's interview with them.

ALLEN, Jud, General Manager, Greater Reno Chamber of Commerce, Reno, Nev.

ALLOTT, Gordon, U. S. Senator from Colorado

ANDERSON, Clinton P., U. S. Senator from New Mexico

ANDERSON, John, Former Governor of Kansas and Chairman, Citizens Conference on State Legislatures, Kansas City, Mo.

ARMSTRONG, Bryn, Executive Editor, Las Vegas *Sun,* Las Vegas, Nev.

AVERY, Ben, Outdoor Writer, *The Republic,* Phoenix, Ariz.

BARNARD, Dr. Robert, Mayor, Aspen, Colo.

BARNES, Mrs. Verda, Administrative Assistant, Office of Sen. Frank Church (Idaho)

BENNETT, Gordon R., Chairman–Executive Director, Unemployment Compensation Commission of Montana, Helena, Mont.

BENNETT, Robert L., Director, American Indian Law Center, University of New Mexico, Albuquerque, N.M.

BENSON, Ezra Taft, Elder, The Church of Jesus Christ of Latter-day Saints, Salt Lake City, Utah

BINGHAM, Jay R., Director, Western States Water Council, Salt Lake City, Utah

BOLACK, Tom, Former Governor, Oilman and Rancher, Farmington, N.M.

BOYD, William J. D., Assistant Director, National Municipal League, New York City

BRODER, David S., Correspondent and Columnist, Washington *Post,* Washington, D.C.

BROWN, George L., Jr., State Senator, Denver, Colo.

BROWN, Hugh B., The First Presidency, The Church of Jesus Christ of Latter-day Saints, Salt Lake City, Utah

BROWN, Robert, Editor, Albuquerque *Journal,* Albuquerque, N.M.

BURKE, Carl, Attorney and Democratic Campaign Manager, Boise, Idaho

CAHILL, Robbins E., Managing Director, Nevada Resort Association, Las Vegas, Nev.

CAMPBELL, Don, Business Editor, *The Republic,* Phoenix, Ariz.

CAMPBELL, Duncan R., Publisher, *Montana Standard,* Butte, Mont.

CARILLO, Padre Alberto, All Saints Rectory, Tucson, Ariz.

CASSELLA, William N., Jr., Executive Director, National Municipal League, New York City

CERVI, Gene, Publisher, *Cervi's Rocky Mountain Journal,* Denver, Colo. (Deceased)

CHURCH, Frank, U. S. Senator from Idaho

CLARK, Ramsey, Attorney General of the U. S., Washington, D.C.

CLARKE, W. A., President, Bank of New Mexico, Albuquerque, N.M.

CONWAY, Jack, Director, Center for Community Change, Washington, D.C.

CORLETT, Cleve, Press Secretary, Office of Sen. Frank Church (Idaho)

CORLETT, John, Political Editor, *The Statesman,* Boise, Idaho

COYLE, Ed, Editor, *The Missoulian,* Missoula, Mont.

CROWELL, Charles M., Chairman, Wyoming Game & Fish Commission, Casper, Wyo.

DAY, Ernest, Conservationist, Boise, Idaho

DAY, Samuel H., Jr., Editor, *Intermountain Observer,* Boise, Idaho

DECK, Art, Executive Editor, Salt Lake *Tribune,* Salt Lake City, Utah

DeMICHELE, Mrs. Peggy, Administrative Assistant, Office of Sen. Mike Mansfield (Mont.)

DIGLES, Joe, Nevada Resort Association, Las Vegas, Nev.

DOCKSTADER, Raymond, Legislative Assistant, Office of Sen. Mike Mansfield (Mont.)

DUFFIELD, Richard, Democratic State Chairman, Tucson, Ariz.

DYER, Dwight, Press Secretary, Office of Sen. Alan Bible (Nevada)

DUNAWAY, William, Editor, Aspen *Times,* Aspen, Colo.

ENGLUND, Merrill, Administrative Assistant, Office of Sen. Lee Metcalf (Mont.)

ERLANDSON, Ed, Executive Director, *The Missoulian,* Missoula, Mont.

FINCH, Bill, Radio Station KVOR, Colorado Springs, Colo.

FLANIGAN, Robert M., Republican State Chairman, Denver, Colo.

FLINCHUM, James M., Editor, *Wyoming State Tribune,* Cheyenne, Wyo.

FOOTE, Joseph, Author, Washington, D.C.

FORD, The Rev. Benjamin P., Vicar, San Juan Mission to the Navajos, Farmington, N.M.

FOX, Francis, Director of Aviation, Hughes Nevada Operation, Las Vegas, Nev.

FOX, Morley, Washington Representative, Central Arizona Project, Washington, D.C.

FRANKLIN, Ben, Correspondent, New York *Times,* Washington, D.C.

FREEMAN, Orville, Secretary of Agriculture, Washington, D.C.

GAVIN, Tom, Columnist, Denver *Post,* Denver, Colorado

GOLDWATER, Barry, U. S. Senator from Arizona

GRAY, Harold, Assistant Director, Adult Education, University of Montana, Missoula, Mont.

GUNTHER, John, Author, New York City (Deceased)

GUNTHER, John, U. S. Conference of Mayors, Washington, D.C.

HANSBERGER, Robert V., President, Boise-Cascade Corporation, Boise, Idaho

HANSEN, Orval, U. S. Representative from Idaho

HANSEN, Clifford, U. S. Senator from Wyoming

HARDEN, Kenneth, Executive Director, House Democratic Congressional Committee, Washington, D.C.

HARVILL, Richard, President, University of Arizona, Tucson, Ariz.

HAURY, EMIL, Professor of Anthropology, University of Arizona, Tucson, Ariz.

HEATH, Grant W., LDS Church Information Service, Salt Lake City, Utah

HORNBECK, J. A., President, Sandia Laboratories, Albuquerque, N.M.

HOYT, Palmer, Editor & Publisher, Denver *Post,* Denver, Colo.

IKARD, Frank, President, American Petroleum Institute, Washington, D.C.

JOYNER, Mrs. Ann, Tucson, Ariz.

JOYNER, Conrad, Professor of Government, University of Arizona and Vice-Mayor of Tucson, Ariz.

KING, Verl, Assistant Director for Development, Idaho Water Resources Board, Boise, Idaho

KRET, David, State Senator, Scottsdale, Ariz.

KIRKLAND, Lane, Secretary-Treasurer, AFL-CIO, Washington, D.C.

KUGLIN, John, Capital Correspondent, Great Falls *Tribune,* Helena, Mont.

KUMMERFELD, Donald D., Director of Research, Center for Political Research, Washington, D.C.

LARSEN, Leonard, Washington Correspondent, Denver *Post,* Washington, D.C.

LASHMAN, L. Edward, Jr., General Manager, Urban Housing Associates, Ltd., Denver, Colo.

LEE, J. Bracken, Mayor, Salt Lake City, Utah

LEERIGHT, Bob, Associated Press Correspondent, Cheyenne, Wyo., and Boise, Idaho

LEHMAN, Amer, Farmer, Idalia, Colo.

LEONARD, Paul, Editor, *Nevada State Journal,* Reno, Nev.

MACFARLANE, Robert, President, Idaho State AFL-CIO, Boise, Idaho

MALMQUIST, O. N., Former Political Editor, Salt Lake *Tribune,* Salt Lake City, Utah

MARTIN, Robert H. (Terry), Wyoming Manager, Rocky Mountain Oil & Gas Assn., Casper, Wyo.

MAXWELL, Neal A., Executive Vice President, University of Utah, Salt Lake City, Utah

McMAHON, Donald F., Former President, Federation of Rocky Mountain States, New York, N.Y.

McMANIS, Robert M., Vice President for Marketing, Husky Oil Co., Denver, Colo.

McMILLION, John, Newspaper Correspondent, Albuquerque, N.M.

McPHERSON, Harry C., Jr., Special Counsel to the President (Lyndon B. Johnson), Washington, D.C.

MERCURE, Alex P., State Program Director, HELP (Home Education Livelihood Program for Underemployed Seasonal Agricultural Workers), Albuquerque, N.M.

METCALF, Lee, U. S. Senator from Montana

MILLER, Bill, Executive Officer, Office of the Mayor, Denver, Colo.

MONBERG, Helene C., Correspondent for Colorado Newspapers, Washington, D.C.

MONDERER, Mike, KRCC-FM, Colorado Springs, Colo.

MONTOYA, Joseph M., U. S. Senator from New Mexico

MOORE, Dale G., Chairman of the Board, Western Broadcasting Co., Missoula, Mont.

MOORE, The Rev. Peter and Mrs. Mary, Albuquerque, N.M.

MUNSON, Charles G., Director, Gaming Industry Assn. of Nevada, Reno, Nev.

MURRAY, Ed., Managing Editor, *The Republic,* Phoenix, Ariz.

NEUMANN, Peter, Correspondent, Colorado Springs *Free Press,* Colorado Springs, Colo.

O'BRIEN, Lincoln, Publisher, Farmington *Daily Times,* Farmington, N.M.

O'CONNELL, Ken, Executive Vice Pres., Las Vegas Chamber of Commerce, Las Vegas, Nev.

ORCUTT, John P., Commissioner, Colorado Department of Agriculture, Denver, Colo.

ORLICH, Dan, Casino Manager, Harold's Club, Reno, Nev.

ORTIZ, Rudy A., Bernalillo County Democratic Chairman, Albuquerque, N.M.

PEARSON, Henry, Director, The Utah Foundation, Salt Lake City, Utah

PEIRCE, Everett and Frederica, Aspen, Colo.

PETERSON, Sandra, Office of Sen. Frank Moss (Utah)

POTTER, Todd, Director, Bureau of Employment Security, Department of Labor, Washington, D.C.

RAMPTON, Calvin L., Governor of Utah

RICH, Gen. Maxwell E., Executive Director, Salt Lake Area Chamber of Commerce, Salt Lake City, Utah

RIPLEY, Anthony, Correspondent, New York *Times,* Boulder, Colo.

RONCALIO, Teno, U. S. Representative from Wyoming

ROONEY, John, Democratic State Chairman, Cheyenne, Wyo.

ROSENTHAL, Jack, Vice President & General Manager, KTWO Radio and Television, Casper, Wyo.

ROTH, Herrick S., President, Colorado Labor Council, AFL-CIO, Denver, Colo.

SAMUELSON, Don, Governor of Idaho

SCAMMON, Richard M., Director, Elections Research Institute, and former Director of the Census, Washington, D.C.

SCOTT, Wayne, Capital Correspondent, Albuquerque *Journal,* Santa Fe, N.M.

SHADDUCK, Louise, Administrative Assistant, Office of Rep. Orval Hansen (Idaho)

SHAFFER, Dale, Legislative Assistant, Office of Sen. Gordon Allott (Colo.)

SHELDON, B. T. Burt, Wyoming Natural Resource Board, Cheyenne, Wyo.

SIMMONS, Roy, President, Zions First National Bank, Salt Lake City, Utah

SIMPLOT, J. R., President, J. R. Simplot Company, Boise, Idaho

SMITH, Tony, Press Secretary, Office of Sen. Barry Goldwater (Ariz.)

SMITH, Walter, Director, Utah Industrial Promotion Division, Salt Lake City, Utah

SNYDER, Jimmy (The Greek), Las Vegas, Nev.

SOBSEY, Chester B., Administrative Assistant, Office of Sen. Howard W. Cannon (Nevada)

SONTAG, Frederick H., Public Relations Consultant, Montclair, N.J.

SORIANA, Padre Ucente Jose, All Saints Rectory, Tucson, Ariz.

STERN, Mort, Assistant to the Publisher, Denver *Post,* Denver, Colo.

SWISHER, Perry, Columnist and Former State Senator, Pocatello, Idaho

TEUSCHER, M. DeMar, Political Editor, *Deseret News,* Salt Lake City, Utah

TOOLE, K. Ross, Professor of History, University of Montana, Missoula, Mont.

THOMSON, Thyra, Secretary of State, State Capitol, Cheyenne, Wyo.

TOOLEY, R. Dale, Former Denver Democratic Chairman, Denver, Colo.

TRAVIS, Terry, Hughes Nevada Operation, Las Vegas, Nev.

UDALL, Morris K., U. S. Representative from Arizona

VINSON, Fred, Jr., Assistant Attorney General, Criminal Division, Department of Justice, Washington, D.C.

WARDEN, Scott, State Advertising Director, Helena, Mont.

WARREN, Wallie, Political Public Relations, Reno, Nev.

WEINBERG, Edward, Attorney and former Deputy Solicitor, Department of the Interior, Washington, D.C.

WELLES, Chris, Author, Dumont, N.J.

WHITE, Somers H., State Senator, Phoenix, Ariz.

WIECK, Paul R., Correspondent, Albuquerque *Journal,* Washington, D.C.

WILKERSON, Ernest, Attorney and Former Gubernatorial Candidate, Casper, Wyo.

WILKINSON, Al, Former Anaconda Company Lobbyist, Butte, Mont.

WILLIAMS, J. D., Director, Hinckley Institute of Politics, University of Utah, Salt Lake City, Utah

WOOD, Claude E., Administrative Assistant, Office of Sen. Clinton P. Anderson (N.M.)

WOODWARD, Don, Business Editor, *Deseret News,* Salt Lake City, Utah

WYNN, Bernie, Political Writer, *The Republic,* Phoenix, Ariz.

ZUCKERT, Eugene, Former Secretary of the Air Force, Washington, D.C.

BIBLIOGRAPHY

DESPITE THE MANY INTERVIEWS for these books, extensive reference was also made to books and articles on the individual states and cities, their history and present-day condition. To the authors whose work I have drawn upon, my sincerest thanks.

NATIONAL BOOKS

Book of the States, 1968–69. The Council of State Governments, Chicago, 1968.

Brownson, Charles B. *Congressional Staff Directory.* Published annually, Washington, D.C.

1969 Census of Agriculture, Bureau of the Census, Washington, D.C.

1970 Census of Population. Bureau of the Census, Washington, D.C.

Citizens Conference on State Legislatures. Various studies including "Recommendations for the States," by Larry Margolis. Kansas City, Mo., 1971, 1972.

Congress and the Nation, 1945–64, and Vol. II, *1965–68.* Congressional Quarterly Service, Washington, D.C., 1967 and 1969.

Dixon, Robert G., Jr. *Democratic Representation —Reapportionment in Law and Politics.* New York: Oxford University Press, 1968.

Editor and Publisher International Year Book— 1971. Editor and Publisher, New York, 1971.

Employment and Earnings—States and Areas, 1939–69. U. S. Department of Labor, Bureau of Labor Statistics, Washington, D.C., 1970.

Encyclopedia Americana, 1969 Edition. New York: Americana Corporation. (Includes excellent state and city review articles.)

Farb, Peter. *Face of North America—The Natural History of a Continent.* New York: Harper & Row, 1963.

Fodor-Shell Travel Guides U. S. A. Fodor's Modern Guides, Inc., Litchfield, Conn., 1966, 1967. (In several regional editions, the best of the travel guides.)

From Sea to Shining Sea—A Report on the American Environment—Our Natural Heritage. President's Council on Recreation and Natural Beauty, Washington, D.C., 1968.

Gunther, John. *Inside U. S. A.* New York: Harper & Row, 1947 and 1951.

Hess, Stephen, and Broder, David S. *The Republican Establishment—The Present and Future of the G.O.P.* New York: Harper & Row, 1967.

Life Pictorial Atlas of the World. Editors of *Life* and Rand McNally. New York: Time, Inc., 1961.

Man . . . An Endangered Species? U. S. Department of the Interior Conservation Yearbook, Washington, D.C., 1968.

Marine, Gene. *America the Raped—The Engineering Mentality and Devastation of a Continent.* New York: Simon & Schuster, 1969.

The National Atlas of the United States of America. Geological Survey, U. S. Department of the Interior, Washington, D.C., 1970.

Pearson, Drew, and Anderson, Jack. *The Case Against Congress.* New York: Simon & Schuster, 1968.

Rankings of the States, 1971. Research Division, National Education Assn., Washington, D.C., 1971.

Reid, Ed. *The Grim Reapers—The Anatomy of Organized Crime in America.* Chicago: Henry Regnery, 1969.

Sanford, Terry. *Storm Over the States.* New York: McGraw-Hill, 1967.

Scammon, Richard M., ed. *America Votes—A Handbook of Contemporary American Election Statistics.* Published biennially by the Governmental Affairs Institute, through Congressional Quarterly, Washington, D.C.

State and Local Finances and Suggested Legislation, 1971 Edition. Advisory Commission on Intergovernmental Relations, Washington, D.C.

State Government Finances in 1969. U. S. Department of Commerce, Bureau of the Census, Washington, D.C., June 1970.

Statistical Abstract of the United States, 1970. U. S. Department of Commerce, Bureau of the Census, Washington, D.C., 1970.

Steinbeck, John. *Travels With Charley—In Search of America.* New York: Viking, 1961.

Steiner, Stan. *La Raza—The Mexican-Americans.* New York: Harper & Row, 1969.

Survey of Current Business. U. S. Department of Commerce, Office of Business Economics, Washington, D.C., monthly. August editions contain full reports on geographic trends in personal income and per capita income.

Thayer, George. *The Farther Shores of Politics.* New York: Simon & Schuster, 1967.

These United States—Our Nation's Geography, History and People. Reader's Digest Assn., Pleasantville, N.Y., 1968.

Tour Books, 1970–71. American Automobile Assn., Washington, D.C., 1970.

Uniform Crime Reports for the United States, *1969.* U. S. Department of Justice, Federal Bureau of Investigation, Washington, D.C., 1970.

Whyte, William H. *The Last Landscape.* Garden City, N.Y.: Doubleday, 1968.

Williams, Joe B. *U. S. Statistical Atlas.* Elmwood, Neb., 1969.

The World Almanac and Book of Facts. Published annually by Newspaper Enterprise Assn., Inc., New York and Cleveland.

REGIONAL BOOKS

The most comprehensive books covering the region are *Politics in the American West,* ed. Frank H. Jonas, which has individual chapters on each of the states and excellent summary chapters by Jonas and Neal A. Maxwell (Salt Lake City: University of Utah Press, 1969); *The Mountain States,* by Marshall Sprague with introduction by A. B. Guthrie, Jr. (New York: Time-Life Library of America, 1967); and *Westward Tilt—The American West Today,* by Neil Morgan (New York: Random House, 1961).

Other sources consulted for the regional introduction included: "The American West—Perpetual Mirage," by Walter Prescott Webb, *Harper's Magazine,* May 1957; "Commentary," by Wallace Stegner, *American West Review,* March 15, 1967; "The 1968 Elections in the West," ed. Conrad Joyner, *Western Political Quarterly,* September 1969; "This Land Is No Man's," by John Barbour, AP dispatch in the St. Petersburg *Times,* Sept. 29, 1968; "Montana Lists Woes of Mountain States," AP dispatch in *Idaho Statesman,* March 11, 1970; "It's Mountain Standard Time," *Fortune,* September 1970; "The Rocky Mountain States Organize for Growth," by D. W. Galvin, *State Government,* Winter 1969; "Change in Policy on Federal Land Urged in Report," by Gladwin Hill, and "Persuasive Land Use Counselor—Wayne Norviel Aspinall," by Marjorie Hunter, New York *Times,* June 24, 1970; "Cattlemen Use Taxpayers' Range," by Jack Anderson, Washington *Post,* Feb. 15, 1970; "A Windfall for the Livestock Barons," editorial by Sam Day in the *Intermountain Observer,* Dec. 6, 1969.

"Mike Mansfield: Straight Shooter in the Senate," by Julius Duscha, *Washingtonian,* September 1970; *Man . . . an Endangered Species?* (Washington: U. S. Department of the Interior, 1968); *A Review of Inter-Regional and International Water Transfer Proposals* (Salt Lake City: Western States Water Council, June 1969); *Travel in the West—1968 Profile of the Travel Industry* (Annual Report of the Western Governors Travel Council, 1968); "Smog Over the Great Plains," by Jack Waugh, *The Nation,* June 14, 1971; "Coal Rush Is on as Strip Mining Spreads into West," by Ben A. Franklin, New York *Times,* Aug. 22, 1971; "Nader Report Blasts Reclamation Projects," by William Greider, Washington *Post,* Nov. 7, 1971.

COLORADO

Chief sources of published background on modern Colorado included: "Colorado: The Colorful State," by Rudolph Gomez in *Politics in the American West* (Salt Lake City: University of Utah Press, 1969); *Colorado Government and Politics,* by Curtis Martin and Rudolph Gomez (Boulder, Colo.: Pruett Press, 1964); the Colorado chapter of Neil Morgan's *Westward Tilt—The American West Today* (New York: Random House, 1961); "The Rockies' Pot of Gold—Colorado," by Edward J. Linehan, *National Geographic,* August 1969; *Democratic Representation—Reapportionment in Law and Politics,* by Robert G. Dixon, Jr. (New York: Oxford University Press, 1968).

Regular news and feature coverage of the Denver *Post* provided substantial background material. Articles especially helpful in preparing the chapter are noted below.

DENVER   "Denver Chamber of Commerce Puts City Problems High on Its Agenda," Denver *Post,* Sept. 15, 1969; "Mile High Observations," guest column by James D. Braman, Jr., *Cervi's Rocky Mountain Journal,* Sept. 3, 1969; "Denver," by Anthony Ripley, *City,* January–February 1971; *Preservation News* (special issue on Denver), published by National Trust for Historic Preservation in the United States, August 1969; "Denver Faces Decision on Auto Problems," by Dick Johnston, Denver *Post,* June 1969; "Denver," by George Sessions Perry, *Saturday Evening Post,* Aug. 24, 1946; "Front Range Warning Given," by Dick Johnston, Denver *Post,* Jan. 7, 1970; "City Government Entering New Era," by John Morehead, Denver *Post,* June 20, 1971; "The Sign Busters," *Newsweek,* June 7, 1971; "Denver's Papers Lose Three Leaders," by Anthony Ripley, New York *Times,* Jan. 17, 1971; "Eugene Cervi, Crusading Denver Editor, Dies," by Ellen Hoffman, Washington *Post,* Dec. 17, 1970; "Death of a Democrat," by D. Lynch, *Colorado Democrat,* Dec. 19, 1970; "Blasts in Denver Destroy 24 Buses," by Anthony Ripley, New York *Times,* Feb. 7, 1970; "'Progressive' Denver Seeks to Bar Busing," by Lawrence Feinberg, Washington *Post,* Sept. 15, 1969; "Denver High Schools' Radical New Program," *Life,* May 29, 1970; "Denver—Old Roaring Capital of the Mountain West," by Vincent McHugh, *Holiday,* May 1970; "Personalities: Big John," *Time,* May 25, 1970; "John M. King—The Tycoon at Work and Play," by Olga Curtis, Denver *Post Empire Magazine,* March 15, 1970; "A Kingdom Besieged," *Time,* Aug. 3, 1970; "King Denies SEC Loan Charges," by Jack Phinney, Denver *Post,* Jan. 26, 1971; "Oilman King Loses His Spread," *Business Week,* April 3, 1971; "Bitter Lessons" (about William M. White), *Forbes,* Nov. 15, 1971.

OTHER PLACES   "Boulder," by Jan Weir, *Guestguide,* Winter/Spring 1969; "Battle on Heroin Uniting Boulder," by Anthony Ripley, New York

Times, Nov. 29, 1970; "Dug in for Doomsday," by Roger Rapoport, Los Angeles *Times West Magazine,* May 17, 1970; "A Colorado 'Museum' Contains the Seeds of American History," by David Brand, *Wall Street Journal,* Aug. 23, 1971; "Southern Colorado Comes Out of the Shadow," by Cal Queal, Denver *Post Empire Magazine,* Dec. 7, 1969; "Report to Erase Hint of Mafia in Colorado," Denver *Post,* Jan. 21, 1970; "Skiers Standing in Line to Escape Urban Crowds," by Martin Arnold, New York *Times,* April 8, 1969; "Golden Triangle Enjoys Top Growth," by Louis Newell, Denver *Post,* April 13, 1969; "Colorado Ski Country U. S. A.," by Lillian Miller, *Guestguide,* Winter/Spring 1969; "Oil Shale Development," by Hoyt Gimlin, *Editorial Research Reports,* Dec. 11, 1969; "U. S. Opening Shale Deposits to Oil Drillers," by Shirley Elder, Washington *Evening Star,* June 29, 1971; "Hippies May Elect Sheriff," by Leroy F. Aarons, Washington *Post,* Oct. 18, 1970; "Culture for Executives," *U. S. News & World Report,* Sept. 7, 1970.

ENVIRONMENT "Colorado Assembly Roundup—Environment Issue Will Continue," by Fred Brown, Denver *Post,* March 15, 1970; "Country Awakes to the Peril of Pollution," by Gladwin Hill, New York *Times,* Dec. 30, 1969; "Industry of Mass Death Seen as Threat to Great Outdoors," by Marquis Childs, Washington *Post,* Aug. 13, 1969; "In the Nation: Taking on a Nuclear Giant," by Tom Wicker, New York *Times,* March 1, 1970; "Atomic Power Abuse: The AEC in Colorado," by Anthony Ripley, *Washington Monthly,* July 1970; "Power Plants Resented in Colorado," by Gladwin Hill, New York *Times,* May 28, 1971; "Saving the Slopes," *Time,* Jan. 10, 1972.

GOVERNMENT AND POLITICS "The Public Record of John A. Love," *Candidates 1968* (Washington: Congressional Quarterly Service, 1968); "Third-Term Race Set in Colorado," by Anthony Ripley, New York *Times,* April 4, 1970; "Big Ed Was Political Workhorse with Mustang Streak," by Leonard Larsen, Denver *Post,* May 31, 1970; "Prisons: Crusading Cons," *Time,* Oct. 4, 1968; "Black and Proud Behind Bars," by Donald Bogle, *Ebony,* August 1968; "New Lobby's Impact Growing in Call for Social Legislation," Denver *Post,* Jan. 20, 1970; "Veteran Legislator Pans 'Good Old Days,' " by Tom Gavin, Denver *Post,* Jan. 7, 1969; *Fourth Annual Colorado Business/ Economic Outlook Forum—1969* (University of Colorado, Graduate School of Business Administration and Colorado Division of Commerce and Development, December 1968).

WYOMING

Unsophisticated Wyoming has one of the best histories of any state, written by T. A. Larson of the University of Wyoming—*History of Wyoming* (Lincoln: University of Nebraska Press, 1965). Substantial background fact and quotation were also drawn from: Mae Urbanek's *Wyoming Wonderland* (Denver: Sage Books, 1964); the Wyoming references in Neil Morgan's *Westward Tilt* (New York: Random House, 1961); "Wyoming: The Frontier State," by Ralph M. Wade, in *Politics in the American West,* ed. Frank H. Jonas (Salt Lake City: University of Utah Press, 1969); and "Wyoming" by Hamilton Basso, in *American Panorama,* a Holiday Magazine book (Garden City, N.Y.: Doubleday, 1947).

Other articles of special use included: "The Lonesome Land—Wyoming Emptier and Its Economy Lags as People Move Away," by Dennis Farney, *Wall Street Journal,* Oct. 3, 1969 (an article from which I borrowed the heading for the chapter); "The Wyoming Mentality," by Dwight Wm. Jensen, *Intermountain Observer,* March 15, 1969; "Who Wants Equality?" by Suzanne Hunsucker, *The Nation,* Nov. 9, 1970; "Mineral Future Bright for Wyoming," by Irving Garbutt, Casper *Star-Tribune,* March 15, 1970; "The Disgrace of It: The Hearing on Proposed 1 Percent Minerals Tax," editorial in Casper *Star-Tribune,* Feb. 9, 1969; "They'd Better Lose This One," editorial in *Wyoming State Tribune,* Feb. 10, 1969; "He's a Sucker for the Balance of Power" (regarding Sen. Gale McGee), by Bryne Nelson, Washington *Post,* May 8, 1966; "Hansen Anticipates Economic Growth," Denver *Post,* Jan. 1, 1970; "Wyoming: As Feudalism Crumbles, a Progressive Broad-based Republicanism Emerges," *Ripon Forum,* August 1969; "The High Cost of Democracy," *Time,* Nov. 23, 1970; "Black, White and BYU," by Dwight Wm. Jensen, and "Wyoming's 'Black 14' Issue Deserved More Serious Study," letter to the editor from Ernest H. Linford, *Intermountain Observer,* Nov. 15, 1969, and Jan. 10, 1970; "Wyoming Divided over Eagle Deaths," New York *Times,* July 4, 1971; "Ill Wind in Casper," by David Shaw (of the Los Angeles *Times*) in the Washington *Post,* July 18, 1971.

MONTANA

Outstanding books on Montanan culture have included Joseph Kinsey Howard's *Montana—High, Wide and Handsome* (New Haven: Yale University Press, 1943), and K. Ross Toole's *Montana— An Uncommon land* (Norman: University of Oklahoma Press, 1959, 1970). My chapter title consists of the Howard title with the word "remote" added by Toole. One of the better entries in the Federal Writers' Project American Guide Series was *Montana—A State Guide Book* (New York: Viking, 1939). The romance of the Copper Kings' era is well captured in the book *Copper Camp,* by writers of the Works Project Administration (New York: Hastings House, 1934). In preparing this chapter, I was especially helped by the chapter by A. B. Guthrie, Jr., "Montana," in *American Panorama* (Garden City, N.Y.: Doubleday, 1947); the "Mountain North" chapter of Neil Morgan's *Westward Tilt—The American West Today* (New York: Random House, 1961); "Montana: Politics Under the Copper Dome," by Thomas Payne, in *Politics in the American West,* ed. Frank H. Jonas (Salt Lake City: University of Utah Press, 1969); and the subchapter, "Mike Mansfield: Painful Exercise of Power," in *The Case Against Congress,* by Drew Pearson and Jack Anderson (New York: Simon & Schuster, 1968).

Perhaps the best general article on Montana in recent years was Margaret Sherf's "One Cow, One Vote—A Strenuous Session in the Montana Legislature," in *Harper's Magazine,* April 1966. In addition to regular coverage of state activities in the Great Falls *Tribune* and the *Missoulian,* the following articles provided background for this chapter:

ECONOMY AND CITIES "Faces Behind the Figures" (regarding Anaconda), *Forbes,* Aug. 1, 1970; "A Mandatory Cleanup Investment," *Fortune,* April 1971; "In Path of Mine, a Whole Town May Move," by Ed Christopherson, New York *Times,* Aug. 15, 1970; " 'Butte's Downhill Run Ending,' Says City's Reform Mayor," by John Kuglin, Great Falls *Tribune,* April 30, 1969; "Butte Madam Tells of Payoffs, Spurs Crusade Against Corruption," "Butte Madam Describes Love Affair with Politician, 'Dimple Knees,'" and "Mayor, Police Chief Differ over Mining City Vice Activity," by John Kuglin, Great Falls *Tribune,* Oct. 13, 15, and 18, 1968; 'The Great Western Bus Ride," by Jack Kerouac, *Esquire,* March 1970; "Montana Power's Double Coup," by Gretchen Billings, *Intermountain Observer,* March 8, 1969; "IRS' Take in Montana Less Than U. S. Spends," by Paula Wilmot, Great Falls *Tribune,* Dec. 26, 1969; "Eastern Montana Bracing for 'Monster Coal Rush,'" by John Kuglin, Great Falls *Tribune,* May 13, 1969, and succeeding parts of 13-part series through May 25, 1969; "Strip Coal on Way in Montana," *Christian Science Monitor,* Sept. 23, 1971; "A House that Divides Town May Not Stand" (regarding Great Falls), by Anthony Ripley, New York *Times,* May 11, 1970; " 'Progress' Fouls Montana Sky With Smell and Smoke," by Haynes Johnson, Washington *Post,* Feb. 14, 1970; "Montana Upholds Deal on Pollution," New York *Times,* June 7, 1970; "Copper: A Bitter Aftermath," *Newsweek,* April 15, 1968; "EPA Denies Smelter Charge," by Elsie Carper, Washington *Post,* Feb. 19, 1972; "The Passing of the People's Voice," by Gretchen Billings, *Intermountain Observer,* Nov. 29, 1969.

ENVIRONMENT, INDIANS "Return of the Buffalo," AP dispatch by Steve Moore, Washington *Post,* Nov. 27, 1969; "Autos Conquer the Heights and Some of the Spirit of Glacier Park," by Douglas E. Kneeland, New York *Times,* July 28, 1970; "Home, Home on the Road for a Nation of Nomads," *Life,* Aug. 14, 1970; "Huntley's Resort Meets Protest," by Anthony Ripley, New York *Times,* April 25, 1970; "Senator Mansfield Praises Huntley's Resort Plans," by William D. James, Great Falls *Tribune,* March 30, 1970; "Chet Heads for the Hills," by Thomas Thompson, *Life,* July 17, 1970; "For Chet Huntley, Few Worries over a Herd of Elk," *Life,* Oct. 15, 1970; "The Crisis of Our National Forests," by James Nathan Miller, *Reader's Digest,* December 1971; "Hope Has Little Meaning for Blackfoot Indians," by Steven V. Roberts, New York *Times,* May 6, 1969.

GOVERNMENT "Gov. Anderson's Legislative 'Pluses' Outweigh 'Minuses,'" by Jerry Madden, Great Falls *Tribune,* March 27, 1969; "Montana Fish and Game Director Arouses Governor's Ire with Strict Stand on the State's Ecology," New York *Times,* July 27, 1970; "Lawmakers Make Over-all Poor Showing," editorial in *The People's Voice,* March 28, 1969; "Tolerant Reaction Asked to Babcock's U.N. Stand," AP dispatch in Great Falls *Tribune,* Sept. 16, 1962; "Forty-Second Legislature Adjourns in Montana," by Wayne P. Merkelson, *National Civic Review,* September 1971.

CONGRESSIONAL DELEGATION "Original Dove of Peace" (regarding Jeanette Rankin), by Margaret Crimmins, Washington *Post,* June 12, 1970; "Power-company Adversary—Metcalf Probes 'Whys' behind Electric Bills," by Lucia Mouat, *Christian Science Monitor,* Aug. 20, 1970; "Mansfield Shuns the Credit," by Dana Bullen, Washington *Evening Star,* March 13, 1970; "Mansfield Voice of Democrat Ranks," by Harry Kelly, Seattle *Post-Intelligencer,* Dec. 26, 1969; "Mansfield Questions Wisdom of Expanding ABM," by Shirley Elder, Washington *Evening Star,* Feb. 1, 1970; "Nixon, Mansfield Cooperate Quietly," by Jack Anderson, Washington *Post,* Feb. 7, 1970.

Also consulted in preparation of the chapter were several publications of the Montana Employment Security Commission, the Montana Highway Commission, the Anaconda Company, and editions of *Montana Business Quarterly,* published by the Bureau of Business and Economic Research, University of Montana, Missoula.

IDAHO

Valuable historic, geographic, and economic background is included in *The Idaho Almanac—Territorial Centennial Edition 1863–1963,* published by the Idaho Department of Commerce and Development under the direction of the department's executive secretary, Louise Shadduck (Boise, 1963). Other important sources included "Idaho: The Sectional State," by Boyd A. Martin, in *Politics in the American West,* ed. Frank Jonas (Salt Lake City: University of Utah Press, 1969); "Idaho," by A. B. Guthrie, Jr., in *American Panorama* (New York: Doubleday, 1947); the chapter of Neil Morgan's *Westward Tilt* on the Mountain North (New York: Random House, 1961); *Sunset Travel Guide to Idaho* (Calif.: Lane Books, Menlo Park, 1969); and *Idaho Industrial Opportunity* (Boise: Idaho Department of Commerce and Development, 1969).

Substantial background was gleaned from ongoing press coverage of the *Idaho Statesman* of Boise and the *Intermountain Observer.* Especially important articles from those publications, plus other articles which provided helpful information:

GENERAL: "The State that Never Should Have Been," by John Corlett, *Idaho Statesman,* June 21, 1970; "Idaho—A Land for Living, a Land for Growing," *Monitor,* magazine of Mountain States Telephone, Denver, issue No. 3, 1969; "Newspapers: Independence in Idaho," *Time,* May 23, 1969; "The Indians: A Fight to Preserve Identity," by Dwight Wm. Jensen, *Intermountain Observer,* Nov. 29, 1969; "The legacy of the Golden Spike," by Sam Day, *Intermountain Observer,* May 10, 1969.

ECONOMY, FARMING "The Idaho Economy: The First Years Were the Best Ones," by Sam Day, *Intermountain Observer,* Aug. 23, 1969; "Mining and the Idaho Economy: Is the Tail Wagging the Dog?" by John H. Merriam, *Intermountain Observer,* April 26, 1969; "Growers Burn Potatoes in Idaho War of Prices," by B. Drummond Ayres, Jr., New York *Times,* March 12, 1970; "Desperate Farmers Take Fiery Gamble," *National Observer,* March 16, 1970; "Their Backs to the Wall," by Sam Day, *Intermountain Observer,* May 9, 1970; "A State that Sits on a Hot Seat—Which Way Idaho? A Recreation Mecca or a Semi-industrialized Society?" by Ferris Weddle, *Intermountain Observer,* July 19, 1969.

POLITICS AND GOVERNMENT "The 1968

Elections in Idaho," by Herbert S. Duncombe and Boyd A. Martin, *Western Political Quarterly,* September 1969; "Conservatives Rule Republican Roost," by Robert E. Smylie, and "Demos Make the Most of the Issues," by Sam Day, *Intermountain Observer,* June 20, 1970; "He Never Stopped Learning," (about Len Jordan), by Perry Swisher, *Intermountain Observer,* Sept. 4, 1971; "Oregon Native Cecil Andrus Serves as First Idaho Democratic Governor in Years," by Harry Bodine, *Sunday Oregonian,* July 25, 1971; "Glen Taylor: A Man Ahead of his Time," by F. Ross Peterson, *Intermountain Observer,* Jan. 1, 1972.

BOISE AND ITS CORPORATIONS "Bob Hansberger Shows How to Grow Without Becoming a Conglomerate," by John McDonald, *Fortune,* October 1969; "Will Quality Tell?—Is Boise Cascade Just Another Conglomerate? . . . ," *Forbes,* July 15, 1970; "Boise Cascade—'The Biggest Risk Would Be to Slow Down,' " by Dwight Wm. Jensen, *Intermountain Observer,* July 19, 1969; "The Battle to Save Lake Tahoe's Beauty," by Dwight Wm. Jensen, *Intermountain Observer,* Dec. 13, 1969; "Boise Cascade, Onetime Wonder Company, Loses Wonder, Investors and Profitability," by A. Richard Immel, *Wall Street Journal,* Dec. 29, 1971; "Jack Simplot and His Private Conglomerate," by Charles J. V. Murphy, *Fortune,* August 1968; "The Slipping Image of Jack Simplot," by S. Chambers, *Intermountain Observer,* May 23, 1970; "Boys of Boise Revisited," by Alice Dieter, *Intermountain Observer,* Jan. 16, 1971; "Corporations: Lessons from the Land," *Time,* April 12, 1971; "Recreational Land Developer Bullish about Future," by Charles E. Dole, *Christian Science Monitor,* Jan. 15, 1971.

CONSERVATION "Showdown at Castle Peak," by John L. Mauk, *Seattle Magazine,* August 1970; "Silent Mountain Peak Presided over Idaho's Biggest Battle of 1969," by Alice Dieter, *Intermountain Observer,* Dec. 27, 1969; "Ernest Day: There Are More Nuts like Him Every Day," by Alice Dieter, *Intermountain Observer,* June 21, 1969; "The Shifting Battles of Hells Canyon," by James Weatherby, *Intermountain Observer,* Aug. 18, 1970; "Battle of the River," by Sam Day, *Intermountain Observer,* Aug. 23, 1969; "Now I've Said It," by Gene Shumate, *Idaho Statesman,* Jan. 19, 1969; "Exporting Water: Not Whether, but How," by Perry Swisher, *Intermountain Observer,* April 12, 1969; "What Good Is the Wilderness?" by James Calvert, *Intermountain Observer,* April 18, 1970; "The Making of a Political Issue," by Robert E. Smylie, *Intermountain Observer,* April 11, 1970; "Three Governors Try to Bar Dams," by Wallace Turner, New York *Times,* Aug. 1, 1971; "Is Church Soft on Conservation?" by Sam Day, *Intermountain Observer,* June 5, 1971; " 'Rent-a-dam' Plan for Southwest Idaho," by Sam Day, *Intermountain Observer,* Jan. 23, 1971; "Wilderness Outpost: The Embattled Sawtooths," by Ferris Weddle, *Intermountain Observer,* June 5, 1971.

NEVADA

For a small state, Nevada has been remarkably well analyzed and documented. All excellent sources, most helpful in writing the Nevada chapter, included: Gilman M. Ostrander, *Nevada: The Great Rotten Borough, 1895–1964* (New York: Alfred A. Knopf, 1966); Omar Garrison, *Howard Hughes in Las Vegas* (New York: Lyle Stuart, 1970); Eleanore Bushnell, "Nevada: The Tourist State," in *Politics in the American West* (Salt Lake City: University of Utah Press, 1969); and the Nevada chapter of Neil Morgan, *Westward Tilt—The American West Today* (New York: Random House, 1961). A chilling view of Mafia influence, challenged as an exaggeration by local partisans, appears in the Las Vegas chapter of Ed Reid's *The Grim Reapers* (Chicago: Henry Regnery, 1969).

Other sources consulted, in addition to regular coverage of state affairs in the *Nevada State Journal* and Las Vegas *Sun,* included:

"Respectability Gamble at Vegas May Pay Off," by William Greider, Washington *Post,* Dec. 15, 1968; "Mathematics of Gaming Assures Casino Businessmen of Profits," by Philip Greer, Washington *Post,* May 18, 1969; "Las Vegas—Making the World Safe for Frivolity," by Charles Champlin, *Los Angeles Times West Magazine,* Oct. 19, 1969; "Another Las Vegas," *Fortune,* November 1969; "Las Vegas: The Game is Illusion," *Time,* July 11, 1969; " 'Cleanup' of Las Vegas Fails to Oust Hoodlums Who Run the Gambling," by Steven M. Lovelady, *Wall Street Journal,* May 23, 1969; "Performing Arts," by Margot Hentoff, *Harper's Magazine,* November 1969; "Our Far-Flung Correspondents: Out Among the Lamisters," by A. J. Liebling, *The New Yorker,* March 26, 1954; "Of Gamblers, a Senator, and a *Sun* that Wouldn't Set," by Richard Donovan and Douglas Cater, *The Reporter,* June 9, 1953; "Forgotten Cowboy Put Nevada in the Chips," by Charles Hillinger, *Los Angeles Times,* Aug. 9, 1970.

"Las Vegas Sheds 'Good Old Days' Almost Overnight," by Jack Waugh, *Christian Science Monitor,* Nov. 28, 1970; "Las Vegas Held Best U. S. City for Black Progress," by Ray Rogers, *Los Angeles Times,* July 1969; "Vegas Protest Draws 1,000" and "High Rollers Don't Know Vegas' Poor Are There," by Leroy F. Aarons, Washington *Post,* March 7 and 14, 1971; "U. S. Accuses Las Vegas Hotels, Casinos and Unions of Bias," by Ken W. Clawson, Washington *Post,* Dec. 21, 1970; " 'The Other' Las Vegas Shows Its Head," by Steven V. Roberts, New York *Times,* Oct. 11, 1969; "The 'Golden Crescent' of the Southwest," Associated Press dispatch by John Barbour, *Arkansas Gazette,* Dec. 15, 1968.

"Smart Money Is Betting Hughes' Las Vegas Venture Will Pay Off," by Arelo Sederberg and John F. Lawrence, Washington *Post,* Jan. 5, 1969; "Hughes Las Vegas Purchases Climbing Past $230 Million," by Arelo Sederberg, Denver *Post,* Aug. 31, 1969; "Laxalt Praises Hughes as Great Boon to Nevada," by Richard Rodda, Sacramento *Bee,* Jan. 27, 1968; "Hughes Holdings Span Nevada," by John C. Waugh, *Christian Science Monitor,* Sept. 30, 1970; "Shootout at the Hughes Corral," *Time,* Dec. 21, 1970; "Howard Hughes and His Hired Hands," by Jack Anderson, Washington *Post,* Aug. 7, 1971; "Hughes Empire—from Casinos to Satellites," by Al Delugach, *Los Angeles Times,* Dec. 17, 1970; "Billionaires: Waiting for Hughes," *Newsweek,* Sept. 13, 1971; "Las Vegas Deal—Hard Sell to Gain Gamblers," by David Lamb, *Los Angeles Times,* Oct. 20, 1970; "Nevada: Life Without Hughes," by Karl Fleming, *Newsweek,* Nov. 8, 1971; "The Fabulous Hoax of Clifford Irving," *Time,* Feb. 21, 1972.

"Nevada Capital Keeps Flavor of Wild West," by Charles Hillinger, *Los Angeles Times,* Aug. 25, 1970; "Bill Lear: Inventor of the 'Impossible,' " by Ronald Schiller, *Reader's Digest,* August 1971;

"Father of Executive Jet Stemcleans Auto Fumes," by Leroy F. Aarons, Washington *Post,* March 28, 1971; "Autos: Lear Steams Back," *Newsweek,* Sept. 21, 1970; "A Piece of Work for Now and Doomsday" (Hoover Dam), by Joan Didion, *Life,* March 13, 1970; "Nevada Indians Fight for Lake," by Steven V. Roberts, New York *Times,* Feb. 25, 1969; "Nevada's 'Gem in the Mountains' Dispute," by Kimmis Henrick, *Christian Science Monitor,* Sept. 3, 1970; "The California-Nevada Interstate Water Compact: A Great Betrayal," by Lowell Smith and Pamela Deuel, *Cry California,* Winter 1971–72.

"About 355 of 'THOSE THINGS' Have Exploded in Nevada," by Gladwin Hill, New York *Times Magazine,* July 27, 1969; "250 miles of Desert Polluted," by John C. Waugh, *Christian Science Monitor,* Sept. 26, 1970.

"Agnew's Nevada Success Offers a Glimpse of Fall's High Stakes," by Haynes Johnson, Washington *Post,* Sept. 20, 1970; "D. N. O'Callaghan" (biographical sketch of new governor), Washington *Evening Star,* Nov. 4, 1970; "The Shame of the Prisons," *Time,* Jan. 18, 1971.

"A 'House' Is Not a Home in Rural Nevada," by Charles Hillinger, Los Angeles *Times,* June 16, 1969; "Legal Prostitution Spreads in Nevada," by Gerald Astor, *Look,* June 29, 1971; "U. S. Is Landlord to Nevada Brothel," by Charles Hillinger of the Los Angeles *Times,* Atlanta *Journal and Constitution,* May 9, 1971.

Special publications of use included *Gaming in Nevada,* a booklet published by the Gaming Industry Association of Nevada, Inc., and various editions of *Nevada Highways and Parks,* publication of the Nevada State Highway Department, Carson City, Nev.

UTAH

A fine and sensitive account of the Latter-day Saints and their role in Utah life is incorporated in Wallace Turner's *The Mormon Establishment* (Boston: Houghton Mifflin, 1966). Frank H. Jonas' chapter, "Utah: The Different State," in his *Politics in the American West* (Salt Lake City: University of Utah Press, 1969) is a treasure trove of facts and insights on modern Utah government and politics. Other books especially helpful in preparing the chapter included *Utah: A Guide to the State* (New York: Hastings House, American Guide Series, 1941); "Utah," by Samuel W. Taylor, in *American Panorama* (Garden City, N.Y.: Doubleday, 1947); the Utah chapter of Neil Morgan's *Westward Tilt* (New York: Random House, 1961); and Ward J. Roylance, *Utah: The Incredible Land* (Salt Lake City: Utah Trails Co., 1965).

Press articles and periodicals consulted, in addition to regular coverage of the *Deseret News* and Salt Lake *Tribune,* included:

LDS CHURCH "Mormonism: Rich, Vital, and Unique," by Seymour Freedgood, *Fortune,* April 1964; "A Church in the News: Story of Mormon Success," and "A University Without Trouble," *U. S. News and World Report,* Sept. 26, 1966, and Jan. 20, 1969; " 'This Is the Place'— And It Became Utah," by Fawn M. Brodie, New York *Times Magazine,* July 20, 1947; "Mormon Church Helps Indians up the Ladder," by Sandra Lundquist, *Intermountain Observer,* Jan. 3, 1970; "Mormons: Bringing in the Ancestors," *Time,* Aug. 22, 1969; "Joseph Smith and His Southern Strategy," by Roger O. Porter, *Intermountain Observer,* May 16, 1970; "Mormons Reaffirm Curb on Ne- groes," by Wallace Turner, New York *Times,* Jan. 9, 1970; "David O. McKay . . . 'Missionary President,' " by Alden Whitman, New York *Times,* Jan. 19, 1970; "Prophet, Seer and Innovator" (regarding David O. McKay), *Time,* Feb. 2, 1970; "Sturdy Leader of the Mormons: Joseph Fielding Smith Jr., New York *Times,* Jan. 24, 1970; "A New Prophet," *Newsweek,* Feb. 2, 1970; "Mormon Liberals Expect No Change," by Wallace Turner, New York *Times,* Jan. 25, 1970; "The Whispered Faith," *Time,* Oct. 11, 1971; *Discrimination in Housing in Utah,* by the Utah Advisory Committee to the United States Commission on Civil Rights (Salt Lake City, August 1966); various publicity releases and fact books issued by the Church of Jesus Christ of Latter-day Saints.

OTHER "The 1968 Election in Utah," by JeDon A. Emenhiser, *Western Political Quarterly,* September 1969; *The Utah Story,* folder by the Utah Travel Council, 1969; "Utah Governor Won't Pay Taxes; Rebels at Aiding Other Nations," New York *Times,* Jan. 7, 1956; "Is There Life in Salt Lake City?" by Dwight William Jensen, *Intermountain Observer,* Aug. 2, 1969; "Great Salt Lake," by Samuel G. Houghton, *Nevada Highways and Parks,* Summer 1969; "Uranium King's 'Mi Vida' Sours Toward Bankruptcy," by Richard P. Spratling, AP dispatch in Houston *Chronicle,* April 13, 1969; "Garment Trade Develops as Big Employer in Utah," New York *Times,* July 6, 1969; "Urban Shadows Fall on Sunny Salt Lake City," *Newsweek,* March 15, 1971; various publications of the Utah Committee on Industrial and Employment Planning.

ARIZONA

Excellent reviews of modern Arizona appear in the following books: "Arizona: Politics in Transition," by Ross R. Rice, in *Politics in the American West,* ed. Frank Jonas (Salt Lake City: University of Utah Press, 1969); Arizona chapter of Neil Morgan's *Westward Tilt* (New York: Random House, 1961); "Arizona," by Debs Myers in *American Panorama* (New York: Doubleday, 1947). *Arizona—A State Guide,* in the American Guide Series (New York: Hastings House, 1941), provides fine background on the older Arizona. Poverty conditions in Arizona and other Southwestern states are examined in the *Summary Report—National Conference on Poverty in the Southwest,* a report on the conference at Tucson in January 1965, published by the Choate Foundation, Phoenix.

Other articles and news stories of special use, in addition to ongoing coverage in the *Arizona Republic* and *Gazette,* and *Phoenix,* the city magazine, included: "A Kaleidoscopic Look at Amazing Arizona," by Lindsay Smith, in *Monitor* (published by Mountain States Telephone, Denver, undated); "Arizona," an advertising insertion in *Fortune,* November 1969; "Town Hall—Open Forum at the

Grand Canyon," *Phoenix,* December 1969; "Let the Grass Grow Long" (regarding Arizona State Hospital), by Ray Thompson, *Phoenix,* November 1969; "The CAP and Arizona's Economy," by Lawrence Mehren, *Phoenix,* April 1969; "Arizona Celebrates Gains in Water Drive," *Christian Science Monitor,* Nov. 24, 1970; "West's Thirst for Water is Questioned," by Anthony Ripley, *New York Times,* Jan. 17, 1972; *Arizona Revisited,* unpublished manuscript by Conrad Joyner, University of Arizona, about 1965; "State Spotlight: Arizona," *Ripon Forum,* January 1969; "State Must End Land's Plunder, Town Hall Says," by Bob Thomas, *Arizona Republic,* Oct. 22, 1970; "Williams-Castro Contest Viewed as State's Closest in Many Years," by Walter W. Meek, *Arizona Republic,* Oct. 18, 1970; "Castro Loss Laid to Slim Rural Margins," by Bernie Wynn, *Arizona Republic,* Nov. 5, 1970.

CONGRESSIONAL DELEGATION "Carl Hayden," by Nick Thimmesch, *Los Angeles Times West Magazine,* Jan. 5, 1969; "The Honorable Carl Hayden," by Ray Thompson, *Phoenix,* June 1970; "The Public Record of Barry M. Goldwater," *Congressional Quarterly Special Report,* July 31, 1964; "Pure Goldwater—Same As Ever," by James M. Perry, *National Observer,* June 22, 1970; "Goldwater Stand a Phoenix Issue," *New York Times,* Nov. 9, 1969; "Young Vote" (regarding Goldwater position), United Press International dispatch, March 9, 1970; "Goldwater Blasts 'Trojan Horse' Republicans," by Dennis Fisher, *Chicago Sun-Times,* May 16, 1969; "Campaigning by 'Media': A Bubble Bursts in Arizona," by Leroy F. Aarons, *Washington Post,* Oct. 29, 1970.

PHOENIX "Phoenix Conflict: Rapid Growth of City vs. Good Life," by Steven V. Roberts, *New York Times,* Feb. 24, 1970; "Headaches Chase Mayor of Phoenix," by Robert McGruder, *Cleveland Plain-Dealer,* Jan. 29, 1969; "Modern Times in Phoenix—A City at the Mercy of Its Myths," by Andrew Kopkind, *The New Republic,* Nov. 6, 1965; "Desert Cities Grow Rapidly but Affluence Brings Problems," by John Barbour of the Associated Press, *Richmond Times-Dispatch,* Dec. 15, 1968; "Many Areas in West, Once Famed for the Air, Befouled by Pollution," by Earl C. Gottschalk, Jr., *Wall Street Journal,* April 21, 1970; "Phoenix," by V. Warner Leipprandt, Jr., *Moun-*

tain Bell, 1970; "Divorce—Crippler within the County," by Carol Crown, *Phoenix,* August 1969; "Phoenix's Handsome, New Civic Plaza," by Peter C. Boulay, *Phoenix,* June 1970; "Retreat on the Desert" (regarding Elizabeth Arden's Maine Chance), *Phoenix,* January 1970; "Phoenix Rapidly Becoming Mafia Haven," by Don Bolles, *Arizona Republic,* Nov. 11, 1970; "His Greyhound Goes to Phoenix" (regarding Gerald Trautman), *Business Week,* July 3, 1971; "A Thriving, Growing Place" (Scottsdale), by Leo Moore, *Phoenix,* January 1971; "Guardian of a Great Legacy" (about Mrs. Frank Lloyd Wright), by Loudon Wainwright, *Life,* June 11, 1971.

TUCSON "Tucson: Our Sister City to the South," by Mary Ann Abosketes, and "Tucson: The Growing-Up Years," by John Riddick, *Phoenix,* January 1970; "Crossed Gunsights—Wyatt Earp vs. Joe Bonanno," by David Snell, *Life,* December 1968; "Udall Warns of Mafia Threat," by Bob Thomas, *Arizona Republic,* Oct. 17, 1968; "Portrait of an Obsolete Mobster" (Joe Bonanno), *Time,* Aug. 22, 1969. "A License to Fix Prices," *Time,* July 20, 1970.

GEOGRAPHY AND CULTURE "For the Retired, a World of Their Own," by Paul O'Neil, *Life,* April 15, 1970; "So Long, Old 66," by Zora Reshovsky, *Los Angeles Times West Magazine,* Nov. 2, 1969; "The Lake People—Who Wants to Live in Lake Havasu City?" by Carol Brown, *Phoenix,* December 1969; "How to Build a River in the Arizona Desert to Flow under the London Bridge," by William Robbins, *Esquire,* February 1969; "The Arizona Strip—Remote America," by James E. Cook, in *Arizona* (Sunday magazine of *The Arizona Republic*), Jan. 12, 1969; "Golden Anniversary of Grand Canyon of the Colorado as a National Park," by John V. Young, *New York Times,* Feb. 2, 1969; "Life with Big Daddy" (about Ajo, Ariz.), *Newsweek,* Aug. 23, 1971; "Environment: Big Dig at Black Mesa," *Newsweek,* Feb. 8, 1971; "Arizona Strip Mining Project Leaving Navajo Land Unscarred," by Gladwin Hill, *New York Times,* Jan. 24, 1971; "Mesa Mines: Hopis Profit at a Price," by Leroy F. Aarons, *Washington Post,* June 7, 1971; "Change In U. S. Mining Law Being Fought in Arizona," by William K. Wyant, Jr., *St. Louis Post-Dispatch,* Dec. 13, 1971.

NEW MEXICO

Much fascinating detail on modern New Mexico politics (from statehood up to the mid-1960s) appears in Jack E. Holmes' *Politics in New Mexico* (Albuquerque: University of New Mexico Press, 1967). Substantial material for the chapter was also drawn from three excellent chapters in regional books: "New Mexico: The Political State," by Harry P. Stumpf and T. Phillip Wolf, in *Politics in the American West,* ed. Frank H. Jonas (Salt Lake City: University of Utah Press, 1969); the New Mexico chapter of Neil Morgan's *Westward Tilt* (New York: Random House, 1961); and "New Mexico," by Oliver La Farge, in *American Panorama* (New York: Doubleday, 1947). State "color" may be found in two in-state books—*This is New Mexico,* ed. George Fitzpatrick, and *Profile of a State—New Mexico,* by Fitzpatrick and John L. Sinclair (Albuquerque: Horn and Wallace, 1962 and 1965 respectively).

In addition to regular coverage in the Albuquerque *Journal* and *Tribune,* the following articles provided valuable background:

"A New Yorker's Report on New Mexico," by

David Boroff, *Harper's Magazine,* February 1965; "GOP Grips New Mexico," by Carroll W. Cagle, *Christian Science Monitor,* Nov. 15, 1968; "The Great Land Grab Game," by Carroll Cagle, *The Black Politician,* Spring 1970; "New Mexico: The Agony of Tierra Amarilla," *Time,* Nov. 29, 1968; "La Raza, the Land and the Hippies," by Peter Nabokov, *The Nation,* April 20, 1970; "La Raza: Mexican Americans in Rebellion," by Joseph L. Love, *Trans-action,* February 1969; "Freed Chicano Gets Hero's Welcome," by Leroy Aarons, *Washington Post,* July 27, 1971; "Communicating in Los Alamos—Don't Call Him Doctor!" by Walter B. Kerr, *Saturday Review,* April 11, 1970; "New Mexico: Dollars in the Desert," *Newsweek,* Oct. 26, 1970; "New American Land Rush," *Newsweek,* Feb. 28, 1972; "Clinton P. Anderson," in *Elections of 1966* (Washington, D.C.: Congressional Quarterly Service, July 22, 1966); "Mr. Montoya: Pushing the Old Politics," by James M. Perry, *National Observer,* Oct. 5, 1970.

Also "Santa Fe: Our Last Unspoiled City?" by Chandler Brossard, *Holiday,* May 1969; "Santa

Fe's Attractions Spill over the City Line," by W. Thetford LeViness, New York *Times,* Dec. 14, 1969; "Santa Fe Capitalizes on Its Atmosphere," *Business Week,* April 10, 1971; "Banning Topsy: The Story of Santa Fe," *Mountain Bell,* 1970; "Opera in the Wilderness," by Margaret Carson Sherrod, *Holiday,* June 1970; "Festivals: Out of the Ashes," *Times,* Aug. 23, 1968; "Georgia O'Keeffe's World: She Re-creates an Awesome Nature," by Bill Marvel, *National Observer,* Oct. 19, 1970; "Loner in the Desert," by Robert Hughes, *Time,* Oct. 12, 1970; "Albuquerque Divided over Cause of First Major Riot," by Martin Waldron, New York *Times,* June 20, 1971; "In Roswell, N.M., Closing of Air Base Wasn't the End," by Martin Waldron, New York *Times,* July 9, 1970; "Unusual Coalition Backs Indians' Sacred-Land Claim" by Robert Hornig, Washington *Evening Star,* Sept. 28, 1970.

SPECIAL PUBLICATIONS *Seventh Annual Summary Study of the Economy of the State of New Mexico* (Albuquerque: Bank of New Mexico, April 1969); *Los Alamos Scientific Laboratory of the University of California* (publication of the Laboratory, October 1968).

THE NAVAJOS   "New Horizons for the Navajo," by Marshall Sprague, chapter of *The Mountain States* (Time-Life Library of America, 1969);

"Navajoland," by Jack Schaefer, *Holiday,* February 1968; "Industry Invades the Reservation," *Business Week,* April 4, 1970; "New Hope for the Navajo," by William Greider, Washington *Post,* May 30, 1970; "Navajo Woman in Government? Why Not!" by Frank Daugherty, *Christian Science Monitor,* July 25, 1970; "Navajos Establishing Own School So Far-Flung Children Can Return," by William Greider, Washington *Post,* April 1970; "Food for First Citizens," by William Payne, *Civil Rights Digest,* Fall 1969; "A Salute to the Navajos, a Nation Within a Nation," by John V. Young, New York *Times,* June 23, 1968; "Indians and Friends on Warpath Against Sooty Power Plant," by Barry Kalb, Washington *Evening Star,* May 12, 1971; "The Dilemmas of Power," *Time,* June 1971; "U. S. Journal: Gallup, N.M.—Drunken Indians," by Calvin Trillin, *The New Yorker,* Sept. 25, 1971; Ex-Marine Is Picked to Head Navajos," New York *Times,* Nov. 15, 1970; "Navajo Seeks Reform," United Press International dispatch in Washington *Post,* Feb. 14, 1971; "Navajos Create First College on Reservation," by Ruth Ann Ragland of the Associated Press, Boston *Globe,* Aug. 29, 1971; "Problems of the Navajo Reflect the Dilemma of American Indians," by Hal Lancaster, *Wall Street Journal,* Oct. 13, 1971.

INDEX

Page references in **boldface** type indicate inclusive or major entries.

THE AUTHOR

NEAL R. PEIRCE began political writing in Washington in 1959 and is author
of the definitive work on the electoral college system, *The People's President*,
published in 1968. He was political editor of *Congressional Quarterly* for nine
years and became a consultant on network election coverage, initially for NBC
News and after 1966 for CBS News. In 1969 he became a founding partner
of the Center for Political Research and subsequently politics consultant for
its weekly publication, the *National Journal*. In 1971, he became a Fellow of
the Woodrow Wilson International Center for Scholars.

A native of Philadelphia, Mr. Peirce graduated from Princeton University,
Phi Beta Kappa, in 1954. He lives in Washington with his wife and their two
daughters and a son.